INFELICITIES

INFELICITIES

REPRESENTATIONS OF THE EXOTIC

Peter Mason

THE JOHNS HOPKINS UNIVERSITY PRESS
Baltimore and London

Printed in the United States of America on acid-free paper
Color insert printed in Chile
9 8 7 6 5 4 3 2 1

The Johns Hopkins University Press
2715 North Charles Street
Baltimore, Maryland 21218-4319
The Johns Hopkins Press Ltd., London
www.press.jhu.edu

Library of Congress Cataloging-in-Publication Data will be found at the end of this book.

A catalog record for this book is available from the British Library.

ISBN 0-8018-5880-1

Para Marisol Palma, mi hermana en Santiago

Niemand wandelt ungestraft unter Palmen.
[You cannot walk among palm trees with impunity.]

Inscribed on the back of a tiger in the colored drawing *The Zulus,* sketchbook by Adolf von Menzel, 1885

CONTENTS

ILLUSTRATIONS

*Color illustrations follow p. 112.

ACKNOWLEDGMENTS

The present volume is intended as a modest contribution to a discussion which involves all those interested in the problems raised by the question of representations, irrespective of the limits drawn by academic boundaries and their enforcers. Since the issue is obviously an interdisciplinary one, I am especially grateful to all those from different disciplines who were prepared to discuss or comment on part or all of the manuscript: Mary Bouquet, Elizabeth Edwards, Elizabeth Honig, Debora Meijers, Joanna Overing, and Claudia Swan.

Like *Deconstructing America,* this work was written without the support of any academic or other institution in the country in which I reside. I am therefore all the more grateful to those colleagues in various countries who kindly supplied me with articles and other materials to which I would otherwise have had no access: Margarita Alvarado Pérez, Fernando António Baptista Pereira, Klaus Barthelmess, Ernst van den Boogaart, Mary Bouquet, Dietrich Briesemeister, Mario Caro, Raymond Corbey, Sarah Deleporte, Elizabeth Edwards, Manuel Gutiérrez Estévez, Christian Feest, Michael Harbsmeier, Maarten Jansen, Adam Jones, Joep Leerssen, Allan Lund, Arthur MacGregor, Edmundo Magaña, Debora Meijers, Annerose Menninger, Alessandro Minelli, Frank Müller, Giuseppe Olmi, José Pardo Tomás, Richard and Sally Price, Claudio Rolle, Ben Schmidt, Rudolf-Alexander Schütte, José da Silva Horta, William Sturtevant, Claudia Swan, and Thomas Theye.

On the editorial side, Linda Forlifer did a wonderful job in ironing out some unintended infelicities. Once again, it has been a pleasure to work with Henry Tom and his team at the Johns Hopkins University Press. Particular thanks are due to the Fundación América, Santiago de Chile, for assisting with the color work, and to Jorma Puranen for permission to use *Imaginary Homecomings.* My debt to Roberto Edwards extends beyond his generous collaboration on this project.

The support I have received from Florike Egmond is in a class of its own.

INFELICITIES

1 INFELICITIES, OR THE EXOTIC IS NEVER AT HOME

Exoticism and the Exotic

You cannot walk among palm trees with impunity, and your sentiments must surely alter in a land where elephants and tigers are at home.

Goethe, *Elective Affinities*

Never has it been so difficult to delineate the exotic as it is today. Perhaps there was once a time when names like Samarkand or Nepal had an exotic ring for the West, before the voyages of exploration had seriously diminished the capacity for wonder.[1] But today, with the presence of immigrants from virtually all over the world in Europe, with the opening up of the Third World to Western tourism and in particular to its sexual and other kinds of voyeurism, and with the global dissemination of a metropolitan technology, the banality and repetitiveness of travel brochures only show how hard it has become to imagine what is exotic. The exotic has acquired a *déjà vu* quality. Traveling has become tourism.

However, this *déjà vu* aspect is not a particularly recent phenomenon. Colonial reification was already turning the picaresque Bedouin and the harem *odalisque* of North Africa into exotic and glamorous objects in the nineteenth century, as part of an attempt by European art to appropriate the visual culture of the whole planet into its own self-conceived mainstream. Flaubert's attempt to escape from what he experienced as the crushing banality of his own society by seeking new material—and therefore producing new texts—in Egypt was doomed to failure from the start, as the sights by which he had hoped to inject an alternative note into his own works proved to be only a painful recollection of an Orient which had already been appropriated by Europe (Terdiman 1985). The same overpowering and numbing mustiness of the preexisting Orientalist archive had similar effects on Vigny, Nerval, Kinglake, Disraeli, Burton, and others (Said 1978; Hentsch 1988; Mitchell 1989). This domestication of the exotic deprives it of its very exotic quality.

But if we resist this domestication of the exotic, do we not err in the other direction in postulating a "wild" exotic? Is the exotic wild or domesticated at all?

The exotic, it will be argued, is not something that exists prior to its "discovery." It is the very act of discovery which *produces* the exotic as such, and it produces it in varying degrees of wildness or domestication. In other words, the exotic is the product of the process of exoticization. In this sense, the present project has affinities with studies like *Imagining India* (Inden 1990), *Reinventing Africa* (Coombes 1994), or *Deconstructing America* (Mason 1990), to name but a few. What such titles stress is that their object of study is a representational effect, produced and reproduced in a process which has not stopped at the transition from colonialism to postcolonialism. As a construct, the exotic is always up for renegotiation; as an invention, it is always open to reinvention; as a field of forces in which Self and Other constitute one another in a lopsided relation, it is always open to contestation.

To say that the exotic is a representational effect is not to deny that it can be *presented* as well as *represented.* This distinction can be made clear by way of an example. When the North American collector Charles Willson Peale heard that gigantic bones had been discovered near New York, he proceeded to excavate them and transfer them to his museum in Philadelphia, where they were reassembled beside the skeleton of a mouse. Peale also completed an oil painting, *Exhuming the First American Mastodon,* which he displayed in the same room as the mastodon. Moreover, his son Rembrandt wrote a *Historical Disquisition on the Mammoth, or Great American Incognitum, an Extinct, Immense, Carnivorous Animal, Whose Fossil Bones Have Been Found in America.* This book was also exhibited in the Mammoth Room, each of its ninety-two pages being hung in a gilt frame.[2]

The painting is a visual or graphic *representation* of the exhumation (and of a good deal more); as an artifact, it is *presented* in the museum. The disquisition is a textual *representation* of the mastodon; it, too, is *presented* as an artifact in the museum. As for the restored skeleton, this is a case of *presentation,* for the actual bones which were exhumed are transferred to the museum, where they are themselves *present;* unlike a replica, they actually *are* (a part of) the mastodon. At the same time, the reconstruction of the mastodon is an act of *representation,* as is clear from the disputes which arose on the various ways in which the creature could be reconstructed; the reconstruction makes imaginative use of what is *present* (the partially recovered bones) to *represent* the creature which no longer exists (the extinct mastodon).

In all of the representations of the exotic considered in the following chapters, some element is always present—like a mastodon bone—which guarantees a metonymic link between the representation and what it represents: the exotic peoples and objects on display which came from exotic lands, the exotic paraphernalia in the ethnographic portrait which were painted from direct observation, and so on.

The exotic is produced by a process of decontextualization: taken from a setting elsewhere (it is this "elsewhere" which renders it exotic), it is transferred to a different setting, or recontextualized. It is not the "original" geographic or cultural contexts which are valued, but the suitability of the objects in question to assume new meanings in a new context. In this respect, exoticist representation can be seen as the opposite of Edward Said's "Orientalism"; although the latter fetishizes authoritative knowledge and geographic specificity, often with a view to actual domination, exoticist representation is indifferent to ethnographic or geographic precision and tends to serve imaginative rather than concretely political ends. "Exoticised subjects," as Guest puts it, "are characterized as sports, marked as singular tokens lacking any significance beyond that of a fragmentary and unrepresentative (perhaps unrepresentable) insularity" (1992, 102).

In stressing that the exotic is the product of the work of exoticization, we shift the emphasis from the geographic or cultural provenance of the exotic to the modalities by which the exotic is produced in the West. After all, the term *exotic* did not enter the English language via *The Tempest,* despite the exotic setting of Shakespeare's last play; one of its earliest occurrences is at the very end of the sixteenth century, when Ben Jonson used it in a context of magic and witchcraft. This centripetal move toward rather than away from Europe follows Parkin's injunction to cultivate a different sense of the exotic: "we excavate the bizarre, unfamiliar and irreducibly different in us all as we continually reformulate our various relationships to and understandings of the material world, a process that is always emergent and never finished" (1993, 97). A good example of the recognition of the continually transformable stranger within us all is provided by Remak in his citation of the following passage: "The natives were wilder than the place. Our near neighbours . . . were more like savages than any people I ever before lived among. Many a night they passed on the beach, singing, or rather howling; the women dancing about among the waves that broke at their feet; the men leaning against the rocks and joining in their loud wild chorus" (1978, 59). Polynesia? South America? No—Mary Shelley on her house in the Bay of Spezia, between Genoa and Leghorn. And this passage provides us with the working definition of the exotic that will be explored in this book: the exotic is that quality evoked by dancing women and carousing men in the Bay of Spezia.

Although the notion of the "continually transformable stranger within us all" might suggest some vague appeal to universal values and a lack of attention to historical specificity, the cases dealt with in this work all fall between 1500 and 1920. This time span corresponds exactly to that covered by Sweetman in *The Oriental Obsession: Islamic Inspiration in British and*

American Art and Architecture 1500–1920 (1988). It includes the wave of interest in Orientalist representations, particularly of Turks, during the sixteenth century (when the ethnographic accuracy of these representations was generally higher than that of their nineteenth-century counterparts). It also includes the influence of the discovery of the Americas, which soon left its mark, not just on what we might anachronistically refer to as European ethnographic descriptions of the New World, but also on a much wider range of visual representations, including themes such as the Adoration of the Magi or diabolical images of hell (Honour 1975).

This time span also includes the emergence of exoticism as a fashion in the nineteenth century, when the term itself was first coined as a substantive in the French language (Pucci 1989). An early-twentieth-century interest in exoticism can be seen, for example, in Gilbert Chinard's *L'exotisme américain dans la littérature française au 16ᵉ siècle* (1911), while Victor Segalen, author of *Essai sur l'exotisme* and many other works before his death in 1919, was rejecting established exoticisms in a quest for more radical encounters with the Other (Clifford 1988, 152–64; Baudrillard and Guillaume 1994).

It would no doubt be possible to write a conventional history of exoticism, of the times and places in which exoticism as a fashion loomed large or faded into the background. Indeed, focusing on a period roughly a century ago suggests a link between these fashions or movements and the age of empire. After all, this is the epoch with which colonialism is most associated in a conventional sense. However, just as the anthropologist Nicholas Thomas has called into question "the assumption that colonialism in general is typified by this period" (1994a, 9), we may also query the extent to which exoticism in particular can be conceived within such narrow confines. It is in an attempt to overstep them that the present project is conceived not about exoticism but about representations of the exotic. Without losing sight of the historically situated nature of forms of exotic expression, it seems worth investigating the ways in which the exotic was given shape over a longer historical period—for present purposes, the last five hundred years.

The present volume shares the same self-imposed limitations as *Deconstructing America* with regard to a possible contextualization within colonial history. Given the stress on the provisionality of the context in the present work, it would hardly be possible to sustain the thesis that the analysis was made possible by colonial history in the first place. As we shall see, there are good arguments against assigning priority to the context of colonial history or to any other context.[3] Such a limited view can hardly be seen as an adequate response to persistently difficult political or other questions.

Instead, I have attempted in some cases to show how the refractions of a particular work may well reflect areas which one could label as, say, political. The discussion of ethnographic realism in the Dutch colony in Brazil provides a case in point: the functions of representation serve economic, political, and sexual political ends. The specificity of the case, however—and of all the other cases discussed here—should serve as a warning against attempts to draw general conclusions of any kind. The reader will search in vain for some overarching principle of interpretation (cf. Mason 1995). Moreover, once the question is raised of whose representations are under discussion, it will be obvious that the history of European representations contained in this volume is a limited view. This is caused partly by my own limitations and partly by the nature of the medium in which my argument is expressed. Fortunately, there are forums for expression by voices from the Third and Fourth Worlds, and there are events where Native Americans can present their own photographs or videos. They may do so within a traditionalist mode or in the hybrid mode that academic postcolonialism narcissistically welcomes (Thomas 1996). But the story told here, for better or for worse, is a European one.

In *Deconstructing America,* very little textual analysis was presented in the writer's own voice and there was a deliberate reduction of authorial reflexivity to a minimum. This seemed appropriate—and unavoidable—if a text about the Other was also to be receptive to the voice of the Other and marked by the presence of the Other, however fleetingly. In proceeding to write about representations of the Exotic, it seems equally fitting and inevitable that the text itself will be marked by the Exotic (cf. Mason 1993b) or will even become a party to the activity of exoticization. And since one of the features of the exotic that will repeatedly crop up in the following pages is that the exotic is never at home, subject as it is to an ongoing process of decontextualization and recontextualization, the form of the account given will also be marked by displacement. The effects of the exotic on texts about the exotic, so aptly summed up in the quotation from Goethe's *Elective Affinities* cited at the beginning of this introduction, is one of the subthemes of the present work. This explains why some of the discussions in the following pages may seem to lack a clear focus to some readers, for at times a subject is dealt with while it is in transit from one context to another, with a degree of blurring as the unavoidable result. Moreover, just as exoticization produces its own object, so the object of the present study—the exotic—is produced within and by that very study. There is no preexisting corpus of material which can be classified as exotic and then described in detail. We only have the workings of the exotic imagination, throwing up the exotic in the course of its wanderings.

Like *Deconstructing America,* the bias in the selection of the illustrative material for the present volume is on the Americas. This time, instead of treating the effects of considering America as the Other, it is the effects of considering America as the Exotic which are under scrutiny. One of the main conclusions is that, while the Other has a voice of its own (though not everyone is prepared to listen to it), the Exotic is dumb. Hence the strategy of effacing the voice of Self in favor of the voice of the Other, which governed the structure of the previous volume, is impossible here. An explanation for why this is the case is advanced in the final chapter: the Exotic is dumb because it is the Pseudo-Exotic.

From Original Context to Family Resemblance

> The first rule for putting a jigsaw together is that all the pieces must join up with no gaps in between. The second is that the completed jigsaw must make sense—for example, even if a piece of sky fits perfectly in the middle of a field we must obviously look for a different place for it. And if, when the jigsaw is near completion, we see that the scene is of a "pirate ship," we will infer that a further group of pieces showing "Snow White and the Seven Dwarfs" belongs to a different puzzle altogether.
>
> Settis, *Giorgione's Tempest*

Thus far it has been suggested that the exotic is produced by a process of decontextualization and recontextualization. This raises the question of the appropriateness of the fit between the detached object and its new surroundings. To the extent that this fit is infelicitous, the exotic is never at home. But was it ever at home to begin with?

The question of the proper context will be discussed drawing on the work of the philosopher John Austin and on the important critique of it by Jacques Derrida. However, we will need more than their primarily linguistic arguments to deal with the preponderantly visual representations considered in this book. The present chapter, therefore, extends their insights to the field of visual images as it concludes with a "deconstructive" reading of Erwin Panofsky's fundamental writings on iconography. The reader's patience may be tried by this rather technical discussion, but it is necessary for an understanding of the subsequent chapters.

In his theory of speech acts, J. L. Austin proposed a distinction between utterances that are constative or informative and those that are performative. An example of the latter are the words "I do (sc. take this woman to be my lawful wedded wife)" as uttered in the marriage ceremony. The words have no meaning apart from the act that they themselves constitute, though before that act is brought to a successful conclusion a good many other things will have to be right and go right. Naturally, things can go wrong on the occasion of such utterances, too. To quote one of Austin's examples, if the person who names a ship by smashing a bottle hung at the stem and proclaiming "I name this ship the *Mr. Stalin*" was not the person designated to name it, then something has gone wrong. When an utterance is made in a situation which can be judged to be out of context, Austin claims (1962, 22), such language is being used in ways which are parasitic upon its normal use and which fall under the doctrine of the etiolations of language. A large part of Austin's analysis of performative utterances ("performatives," for short) is taken up with examples of misunderstanding through failure to grasp the implicit context. Take the following discussion of the sign "Bull": "if we just stick up 'Bull' it would not be quite clear that it is a warning; it might be there just for interest or information, like 'Wallaby' on the cage at the zoo, or 'Ancient Monument.' No doubt we should know from the nature of the case that it was a warning, but it would not be explicit" (1979, 243). In this example of a minimal sign—the word *Bull*—we are presented with an utterance which is not normally thought of as just saying something, but of performing an action of some kind—in this case, warning of the presence of a dangerous animal. The very possibility of misunderstanding is subsumed under what Austin calls "the doctrine of *the things that can be and go wrong* on the occasion of such utterances, or the doctrine of the *Infelicities*" (1962, 14, his italics). Austin thus lays great stress on norms and conventions: "Speaking generally, it is always necessary that the *circumstances* in which the words are uttered should be in some way, or ways, *appropriate*" (1962, 8, his italics). When a performative goes wrong, we know this to be the case only because of some breach in an accepted conventional procedure having a certain conventional effect, like launching a ship or getting married. All conventional acts which have the general character, in whole or part, of ritual or ceremonial will therefore be exposed to the risk of infelicity of one kind or another.[4] Statements, it should be noted, can be subsumed under the category of conventional acts in this respect, for they, too, are exposed to every kind of infelicity (1962, 136).

The felicitous performance of an act, then, requires attention to the context. Austin cites the examples of the statements "France is hexagonal" and "Lord Raglan won the battle of Alma" as suitable to some contexts and not to others (1962, 144)—the standards of a general are not the same as those of a geographer, and a banal statement which might be appropriate in a school history textbook would be unjustifiable in a serious work of scholarship. Although Austin admits this plurality of possible contexts, as we have just seen, he appeals to what he calls "ordinary circumstances" as the touchstone for deciding whether utterances are felicitous or not. This appeal to conventionality and dictionary definitions, however, will hardly do as a working definition of an appropriate context. In particular, it would rule out important uses of language, such as that used by an actor on a stage, introduced in a poem, or spoken in soliloquy, on the grounds that they fall under the "etiolations of language" or constitute a "parasitic" use of language (1962, 22), in which the normal conditions of reference are suspended. There is surely some inconsistency in this disregard for the use of language in joking, for example, by this most Sternean of all philosophers. After all, it was the same Austin who thought up examples like the following: "Trapped on a branch against the moon, we decide to pretend to be owls: you give a colourable hoot while I pull up my legs and hunch my shoulders up to my ears" (1979, 265). Although many of his examples derive explicitly from parlor games, where the rules of play are laid down and known to all players beforehand, this assumption of a uniformity of interpretative procedures is precisely what *cannot* be assumed when we are dealing with different persuasive definitions which operate performatively in their attempt to authenticate, often in implicit opposition to one another, each vying for its own claim to authenticity. At this point, Austin's hopeful claim that "our common stock of words embodies all the distinctions men have found worth drawing, and the connexions they have found worth marking, in the lifetimes of many generations" (1979, 182), based as it is on a subservience to historical evolution and the principle of the survival of the fittest, fails to offer insights into ways of dealing with a multiplicity of discourses in which some discourses are dominant and others subaltern.

While expressing his recognition of the fertility of Austin's patient approach, Derrida has also attacked the conventionality of the notion of context in Austin's work, though from a different angle (Derrida 1972a, 1990a).[5] For Derrida, the conventional notion of context is theoretically inadequate: "A context is never created *ex nihilo;* no mark can create or engender its context by itself, let alone control it fully. This limit, this finitude is the condition for the permanent openness of the contextual transformation" (1990a, 149). The written sign, he argues, involves a rupture with its context as the totality of presences which organize the moment of its inscription: "It is always possible to remove a written syntagma from the chains in which it is caught or presented, without depriving it of every possibility of functioning, but precisely of every possibility of 'communication.' It may be given others by inscribing it or grafting it onto other chains. No context can enclose it" (1972a, 377). Of course, this critique of the conventional notion of a context does not mean that there are no contexts, nor that any context will do, but that there are only *provisional* contexts, contexts without anchorage in an absolute center (1972a, 381). There can be no determination of meaning outside of a context, but no context can lead to saturation (Derrida 1986, 125). Here Derrida comes closest to Austin's practice, for the latter's discussion of the performative begins with the words: "Everything said in these sections is provisional, and subject to revision in the light of later sections" (Austin 1962, 4 n. 1).[6]

As is suggested by the origin of Austin's infelicities in the practical experience of performatives, this discussion is not limited to the analysis of written signs. As Derrida stresses, his conclusions apply both to written words and to spoken ones (1972a, 376). Moreover, they apply to every kind of sign and to all languages in general. In all these cases, the possibility of weaning the mark from a point of reference within a specific context applies both to writing in the restricted sense of the term and to the spoken word (Derrida 1972a, 378).[7]

In shifting the focus from the appropriateness of a specific context to the provisional nature of the context, we raise the issue of possible contexts and of the linkage between them. Various writers have used the image of chains or threads. For instance, in responding to the question "What significance do you think historians will in the future attribute to 'the Derrida affair' at Cambridge in 1992?"[8] Derrida stresses that, as other historians follow "other threads, other causal chains," there is a wide range of different histories which could be written: "to approach it one would need to pull on some tenuous and rather peculiar threads, to follow their trajectory through the chain of 'general conditions'" (1995, 419). Wittgenstein also uses the metaphor of the thread, in which fiber is twisted on fiber: "the strength of the thread does not reside in the fact that some one fibre runs through its whole length, but in the overlapping of many fibres" (1958, sec. 67). He describes the resulting pattern as "a complicated network of similarities overlapping and criss-crossing: sometimes overall similarities, sometimes similarities of detail" (1958, sec. 66). Austin talks of overlapping with similar connotations when he refers to "families of related and overlapping speech-acts" with wide possibilities of marginal or awkward cases and overlaps (1962, 150).

Derrida himself concentrates either on the relatively limited field of written and spoken words or on the vast field of what he calls the *mark*. Can we apply these insights to the field of visual representations, too? Can one or more of the elements contained within a specific painting, say, be grafted onto threads or chains of images that extend outside the frame? The question is answered in the affirmative by Wills (in a discussion of the late-nineteenth-century canvas *A Holiday at Mentone* by Charles Conder). According to Wills, "if an utterance, such as a figure in the center of a painting, can be grafted onto another context, this means that it has no 'natural' place, never did have, and that the relations it forms with subsequent contexts inevitably reinscribe that fall out of naturalness" (1995, 45).

However, the emphasis on similarities between elements caught up in such a network of different contexts is at the expense of the specific but provisional context of each unit. This has serious implications for a very influential method of analysis of visual representations: the so-called iconographic or iconological approach elaborated from the 1920s onward. Because this approach is largely about discovering the appropriate context for the interpretation of a visual work of art, we shall have to reconsider this notion of the appropriate context in the light of the above considerations.

The Undecidable in Iconography

> Once again an iconographical reconstruction which gives the impression of a puzzle of which one of the pieces, and one of the most important, is irretrievably lost.
>
> Lugli, *Naturalia et Mirabilia*

In 1932 Erwin Panofsky first published a methodological article best known to English readers in its revised form as the introductory chapter to his *Studies in Iconology* (1962, 3–31).[9] Iconography is there defined as "that branch of the history of art which concerns itself with the subject matter or meaning of works of art, as opposed to their form" (3); "a correct iconographical analysis in the narrower sense presupposes a correct identification of the motifs" (7).

Panofsky proceeds to illustrate the method with the familiar example of a painting of a young woman with a sword in one hand and a charger in the other, on which rests the head of a decapitated man. There are two contenders for the identification of the scene: it represents either Salome with the head of John the Baptist or Judith with the head of Holofernes. In either case, however, there is a problem in the identification—an infelicity, we could say. If the female figure is Salome, she should not be holding a sword, since John the Baptist was decapitated at Salome's request, but not by her hand (Matt. 14.10). On the other hand, if the figure is to be identified as Judith, the head of Holofernes should be in a sack rather than on a charger.

At this point, Panofsky goes to work like a detective. The choice of the potential suspects must be narrowed down from two to one. Since the biblical sources alone are not sufficient to arrive at a conclusion, Panofsky resorts to what he calls the *history of types*. There are several sixteenth-century paintings from Germany and northern Italy of what he regards as "unquestionable" portrayals of Judith with a charger, but it proves impossible to adduce a single example of an unquestionable portrayal of Salome with a sword. The case is closed: the painting in question must represent Judith with the head of Holofernes (1962, 12–13).

The historical types function in Panofsky's argument as appropriate contexts that lay down a rigid protocol. Because there is no unquestionable *type* of Salome with a sword, the argument runs, a painting which was published as a portrayal of Salome with the head of John the Baptist cannot be regarded as an exception to the rule. There is some degree of circularity in the argument, as Panofsky was well aware (1970, 32–33), since the function of the types as a protocol depends on their prior constitution through individual acts of identification which cannot therefore appeal in turn to a history of types. Overdependence on the rule of the types excludes the possibility of individual deviations from the rule, and *a fortiori* the existence of visual *hapax legomena*—such as the existence of a representation, but not a type, of Salome with a sword.[10]

If a painting is to communicate at all—as the pioneer in the application of information theory to the interpretation of works of art, Ernst Gombrich, has argued[11]—then the range of choices open cannot be unlimited. However, the alternatives of an unlimited field of choices, on the one hand, or a single interpretation, on the other, do not exhaust the entire range of possibilities. Without necessarily calling into question the rightness of this particular Panofskian interpretation, it is worth concentrating in a little more detail on some of the implications of this detective-like quest for the single, right interpretation of the facts.

One of the reasons for Panofsky's need to arrive at a single solution is connected with the iconological program to which his iconographic method was tied.[12] Iconology, or iconography in a deeper sense, treated the work of art as "a symptom of something else which expresses itself in a countless variety of other symptoms." The following passage is typical: "A really exhaustive interpretation of the intrinsic meaning or content might even show that the technical procedures characteristic of a certain country, period or artist, for instance Michelangelo's preference for sculpture in stone instead of in bronze, or the peculiar use of hatchings in his drawings, are symptomatic of the same basic attitude that is discernible in all the other specific qualities of his style" (1962, 7–8). This "something else" expressed in various symptoms is the homogeneous Hegelian totality, each of whose elements is symptomatic of the same unified entity.[13] In other words, this symptomatic relation is one not just of analogy, but of homology. The unified nature of this totality presupposes that its symptoms can be distinguished from one another as separate entities, albeit each with the same relation to the whole. In certain cases, Panofsky admits, a discrepancy may arise. For instance, he argues that the Christian Middle Ages were unable to comprehend the figures of classical antiquity unless they were presented in a Christian guise—Venus as the Virgin Mary, for example. He treats this discrepancy as a failure—"the failure to realize the intrinsic 'oneness' of classical *themes* and classical *motifs*" (1962, 28). The argument here is normative, with the Italian Renaissance acting as a factor of reintegration to do away with this disjunction between theme and motif (30). In another case—the place of the bust of Brutus within Michelangelo's post-1534 work—Panofsky simply labels this awkward piece of evidence as an exception (229) in an attempt to discount documentation which does not square with the preconceived intuitive scheme (cf. Ginzburg 1990, 40).

As Vanbergen notes, there is also a kinship between Panofsky's theory of expression and the physiognomic theories of Lavater, according to which an individual's character could be read from his or her external physiognomy (1990, 21–22).[14] The physician who can interpret symptoms, the detective who can interpret clues, the art historian who can interpret physiognomy—all of these elements are present in Panofsky's program for iconographic analysis in both the narrower and the deeper sense (i.e., iconography and iconology).[15] The iconological argument, however, is just as circular as the argument in terms of the history of types; it involves just as much 'reading into' if the 'something else' which is constructed on the basis of 'symptoms' is at the same time that on which the symptoms are supposed to depend for their meaningfulness (cf. Ginzburg 1990, 35–36).

If we instead stress the existence of pluralities rather than totalities; the absence of an overruling, transcendent schema acting as a protocol on the appropriateness of a specific work of art within a history of types, let alone within a history of cultural symptoms; and the potential of the work of art to subvert such overriding orders—then there is no need to reject the iconographic method itself. What changes is the emphasis on the relative weight of the work of art vis-à-vis its place within a history (or rather, histories) of types. In other words, instead of trying to narrow down the interpretation of a painting of a young woman with a sword to a single type, it might be more useful to consider the particular painting as the point of intersection at which a plurality of chains of resemblances meet. And these resemblances do not have to be complete; it will be enough to indicate the existence of one or more points in common, despite the existence of differences, just as one can refer to a family resemblance between cousins despite a difference in the shape of their noses.[16]

The suggestion here, then, is that, by reversing the direction of the iconographic argument, as it were, the rigor of the method can be retained but be put to a different end: the reconstruction of morphological chains that may be found to resonate within a single work of art. There is a family resemblance between Judith and Salome. Although this may be less relevant for the question of strict iconographic identification, it is highly relevant for the (re)construction of patterns of family resemblance to which both types belong. In the last resort it may be necessary to narrow down the possible candidates to one and to acquiesce in Panofsky's exclusion of the possibility that the woman is Salome; in terms of the protocol of literary sources, however, as he himself admits, there is no need to make such an exclusion. For present purposes, this last resort will be postponed for as long as possible.

The shift in emphasis which results from this displacement of the center of gravity of the Panofskian system has been formulated by Vanbergen as follows (1990, 32):

> The interpretation of a representation should proceed from a critically justified corpus of works, selected from that genre to which the work of art belongs . . . This genre, however, is not a clearly defined class of representations. Genres should rather be determined in terms of series of characteristics and their mutual configurations (types). Most of these series are more or less complex combinations of elements from other series. Although such series develop chronologically, it is primarily their synchronic typology which requires study. It is above all the ambiguous and shifting character of these configurations which makes interpretation so difficult. They give the work of art the appearance of a stratified, complex and polycentric order.

The shift from Panofsky's viewpoint to such an emphasis on a complex, stratified order is perhaps nowhere clearer than in Panofsky's strictures on the ambiguity of content caused by the superimposition of contradictory meanings within a single work of art. Although Vanbergen stresses the dynamic character of the work of art as a signifying complex which resists articulation in an unambiguous and definitive way (1990, 36), Panofsky puts his hope in the overcoming of ambiguity or even in its becoming an added value "if the conflicting ingredients are molten in the heat of a fervent artistic temperament" (1962, 6 n. 1). In this respect, the position advocated here can be seen as a return to Aby Warburg's emphasis on a dynamic, conflicted, heterogeneous entity in contrast to the fixity of Panofsky's approach (cf. Iversen 1993).[17]

The result of the reversal of Panofsky's priorities comes very close to a phenomenon which Panofsky himself also took into consideration, the *pseudomorphosis*. He applies this term to the Renaissance practice of reviving a classical character while retaining some of the attributes it had acquired during the Middle Ages. The result is a reputedly classical character which proves on examination to be something of a hybrid, compounded of heterogeneous classical and medieval elements, and invested with a meaning that had not been present in its classical prototype (Panofsky 1962, 70–71). Panofsky himself provides two case studies of pseudomorphosis in his treatment of Father Time and Blind Cupid (71–128).[18] Such figures, by their very hybridity, can never be reduced to a single unitary interpretation; they are the points of intersection of at least two distinct morphological chains, and in their heterogeneity they may evoke the most diversified generic contexts.

Incidentally, the emphasis on morphological chains and family resemblances rather than on the unique work of art makes it easier to include representations that may not be deserving of the status of high-quality works of art as such and where the fervent artistic temperament may not have reached melting point. Many of the representations discussed in the following pages are the works of what are generally considered to be minor artists, at least as far as the traditional canons are concerned. All the same, the participation of such a work of art in one of the genres under consideration can still make it worthy of investigation, irrespective of the (thorny) question of its artistic qualities.

Sandwiched between Panofsky's methodological essay and his pseudomorphological studies is an essay on the work of such an artist, who, in Panofsky's words, "was not a 'great' master, but a most charming and interesting one" (1962, 33): the Florentine painter Piero di Cosimo (1461–1521). In his life of the artist, Vasari noted Piero's fascination with the shapes that appeared on walls against which people had spat and with the forms which could be discerned in clouds (Fermor 1993, 16, 34). This preoccupation with the "image made by chance," and the problematic relation between art and nature which it implies (Janson 1961), already links one of Piero's concerns with the organization of natural and cultural objects in the Renaissance collections of curiosities discussed in chapter 4. Moreover, as is stressed in Panofsky's essay, "The Early History of Man in Two Cycles of Paintings by Piero di Cosimo" (1962, 33–67), Piero displayed a lively interest in the early stages of humanity and was a passionate observer and painter of strange animals, plants, and other natural objects that were taken to accompany them. For instance, during the Renaissance the camel and the giraffe (probably painted from life)[19] in the background of one of the paintings in his Vulcan cycle were both understood to be domestic animals, despite their strangeness, and thus appropriate in a depiction of the early stages of civilization (Lazzaro 1995, 214–16).

Panofsky's discussion of Piero's images of early civilization displays a curious lack of interest in ethnographic matters. Subsequent scholars, such as

Ginzburg (1993), have stressed the importance of ethnographic discoveries on these representations, but Panofsky alludes in no more than a passing footnote to Renaissance paleontological and ethnological theories (1962, 55 n. 60). Although his great predecessor Aby Warburg traveled among the Pueblo Indians of New Mexico during his youth before turning to the study of fifteenth- and sixteenth-century astrology and magic,[20] Panofsky subsumed ethnography and ethnology to his own interpretative project (1970, 57–58):

> Ethnology, for instance, is defined as a "*science* of human races" by the same *Oxford Dictionary* that defines "ethnography" as a "*description* of human races" . . . So I conceive of iconology as an iconography turned interpretative and thus becoming an integral part of the study of art instead of being confined to the role of a preliminary statistical survey. There is, however, admittedly some danger that iconology will behave, not like ethnology as opposed to ethnography, but like astrology as opposed to astrography.[21]

The interpretative framework applied in the following chapters departs from the Panofskian project in two main ways. First, most of the visual representations under consideration have a high level of ethnographic content. Second, it will be argued that the degree of specificity required by a rigorously iconographic method is irreconcilable with works characterized as exponents of what we will call the "exotic genre." In considering a number of early European attempts to depict the New World as something rich and strange, I develop an historical iconography that tries to match the indeterminacy of certain types of exotic scenes.

2 THE EXOTIC GENRE

> The knee-length feather skirt is puzzling . . . In fact, the quills of the feathers would have made it a most uncomfortable, if not slightly perilous, garment for anyone not standing upright.
>
> Honour, "Science and Exoticism"

In attempting to establish a corpus of first images of America during the century after the "discovery" of the new continent by Columbus, art historians have understandably proceeded along iconographic lines. If a particular attribute could be said to characterize a visual representation as a portrayal of America, it could then be used to set up protocols which could subsequently be applied to a much wider body of material. In this way, hidden Americana might be brought to light.

One clue to the possible existence of such Americana is the ubiquitous feathered skirt, a stereotype of Amerindian dress which is taken to have become a stock iconographic attribute of Amerindia,[1] despite the fact that, according to Honour (1979, 277), "no such item of clothing is known to have been worn in America or indeed anywhere."[2] Honour goes on to make the ingenious suggestion that the origin of the feathered skirt in representations may lie in a misapprehension of an object detached from its ethnographic context. Pointing out that a feathered skirt, if opened out flat, comes very close to resembling a Central American featherwork headdress, such as that said to have belonged to Motecuhzoma, he states that a European confronted with such an object might well be excused for thinking that it was worn around the waist instead of around the head. It might be added that the feathered skirt also bears a resemblance to the feathered capes seen on the shoulders of some Amerindians in some prints.

This confusion is hardly surprising if one bears in mind the paucity of available artifacts against which representations could be checked. There were, it is true, some objects available in the form of the first gifts presented by Motecuhzoma to Cortés, including featherwork, and in the 1580s feather goods from South America were still to be found in a list of presents for a projected Spanish embassy to China (Spence 1985, 189). Nevertheless, most of the featherwork artifacts which reached Europe have not survived (Feest 1985). Moreover, it must have been difficult to be certain about the precise function of those featherwork artifacts which did arrive, detached as they were from their bodily support.

Nor was there much differentiation in what Europeans knew, or thought they knew, about the costumes of the various social and ethnic groups who inhabited America. Analysis of the European treatises on national costume compiled in the course of the sixteenth century reveals that the iconographic system to be found in these sources has very little to say about such niceties (Pellegrin 1987). On the contrary, the reduced stock of images on which the engravers of these books of costumes drew for these representations is indicative of the slow rate at which detailed information about the different regions of the American continent and their inhabitants was conveyed to the Old World.[3] The result is a stereotype of Amerindian dress (or the lack of it) which displays little variation.

Whether or not the earliest representations of feathered skirts are actually based on a misunderstanding of the function of an authentic Amerindian feathered garment of a different kind—whether a headdress or a cape—they obtained such a hold on the European imagination that they could easily cloud the vision of those who were able to view native Amerindians at first hand. Thus, some of the images in an early work on costume appear to have been influenced by European conceptions of the Amerindians, including those who wear feathered skirts, despite the fact that the compiler, the Augsburg draftsman Christoph Weiditz, benefitted from the opportunity of seeing real Mexicans on display in the court of Charles V during his visit to Spain in 1529 (Honour 1979, 281).[4]

The first representation of Amerindians wearing feathered skirts dates from 1505.[5] A colored woodcut from Augsburg or Nuremberg, probably by Johann Froschauer, accompanied by a four-line text based on Vespucci's letter on his third voyage to the New World, depicts a number of Brazilian men (three of whom are bearded), women, and children who are standing beneath a roof from which human limbs hang like hams, just as Vespucci had described them (Vespucci 1984, 102). All the adults are wearing feather headdresses and various feather ornaments. The men are wearing skirts consisting of long feathers bound to a belt at the waist. Although most of the feather ornaments may well be ethnographically accurate (the Tupinamba *enduape* worn as a bustle by the figure on the left, as well as the collars, anklets, and armlets), the skirts have no known parallel; Sturtevant suggested that they may be an invention of a European artist following verbal descriptions (1976, 420).[6] Though this woodcut is extremely rare (only two examples are extant), it appears to have been very influential on the later iconographic tradition.

Similar in form are the feathered skirts worn by both men and women in a woodcut by Hans Burgkmair to illustrate the triumphal procession of Emperor Maximilian I.[7] It dates from 1516–19 and was first printed in 1526.

This work, the "Leute von Calicut," contains not only Asians but also Amerindians, identifiable both by their feathered skirts and radial feathered crowns and by the ears of corn they bear, the monkeys and parrots which accompany them, and the Tupi clubs they carry (Sturtevant 1976, 421).

As Honour and Sturtevant in particular have both shown, one could go on extending this list of early representations of Amerindians clad in feather skirts (although they are absent from the illustrations to Staden, Léry, and Thevet). The feathered skirt and other feathered attributes recur in a great many representations of native Americans, including the allegories of the four continents, in which feathered apparel is regularly used to identify the American continent (Poeschel 1985).[8] All these examples confirm its persistence as an Amerindian icon, like cannibalism, right into the present century.

In view of this apparent association of feathered items of clothing with America, it is surprising to find American-style feather headdresses and ankle ornaments on the illustration of inhabitants of Sumatra which Jörg Breu the Elder made for Ludovico Varthema's *Itinerario* of 1515 (fig. 1). It may be possible to trace a tenuous connection with America; although there is no evidence for the transportation of Mexican featherwork to Europe before 1519, it is conceivable that similar artifacts from South America, and particularly Brazil, were available in parts of Europe at an earlier date. At any rate, Dürer was already able to draw a young man wearing a feathered skirt in Maximilian I's *Book of Hours* of 1515, though this human figure has no Native American features and stands in a classical contrapposto pose. If there was a limited stock of featherwork images available at this time (i.e., before the conquest of Mexico) to artists in southern Germany such as Dürer and Burgkmair (who exerted an influence on Breu in Augsburg),[9] the fact that Varthema's *Itinerario* was published in Augsburg might indicate that Jörg Breu the Elder was also drawing on this restricted pool of images.

As this example shows, the urge to establish an American connection with featherwork attributes can involve the researcher in very tortuous and fragile chains of reasoning. Indeed, the current tendency to expand the corpus of images of America to any illustration in which featherwork appears is a hazardous enterprise. Take the example of a late-sixteenth-century cabinet from the southern Netherlands. Besides its marquetry of exotic colored woods, it is also decorated with a complex pattern of exotic motifs which includes two torsos with skirts made of feathers or leaves. Fabri labels them "Indian torsos," executed in the style of Cornelis Floris and based on an unknown engraving (1992, 50, ill. 10). The Antwerp engraver Cornelis Floris is regarded as the initiator of the grotesque in the Netherlands, which underwent a particularly rapid stage of development toward the middle of the sixteenth century. A large part in spreading the influence of Floris's work was

Fig. 1. Natives of Sumatra
From Ludovico de Varthema, *Die ritterlich und lobwir dig rays . . .* , Augsburg: Hans Müller, 1515. Courtesy of Staatsbibliothek Bamberg (Geogr. It. q. 82).

played by Cornelis Bos (ca. 1510–55), and there is a good deal of confusion between the work of these two artists (cf., e.g., De Jong and De Groot 1988, no. 74). In his study of the origins of the Netherlands grotesque, Schéle suggested that the Mexican objects on show in Brussels in 1520 may have been a source for Bos's grotesques (1965, 79–80). If this were the case, the argument for an American influence on Cornelis Floris would also be strengthened, thereby lending greater plausibility to Fabri's identification of the torsos on the cabinet as Indian. However, at least two arguments can be raised against such an assumption. First, most of Bos's production of grotesques postdates his departure from Antwerp in 1546 and seems to have been influenced more by the work of his contemporaries in Paris or Germany than by any display of Americana.[10] Second, and more crucially, the case for an Aztec source for Bos's grotesques has been considerably weakened by Dacos, who pointed out that the source of the feather or metal strip arrangements which both Bos and Floris frequently use lies much further back in the leaf decorations of antique Italian, and particularly Etruscan, art; a revival of these themes in the early sixteenth century has more to do with the discovery of the Domus Aurea in Rome (Dacos 1969b)[11] than with the influence of Americana (1969a, 58–59).

Nevertheless, grotesques associated with Bos and Floris have been taken to have an American reference by a number of scholars. For instance, the four figures with feathered headdresses on a stone monument erected in the church of St. John Baptist, Burford, Oxfordshire, in 1569, after a cartouche designed by Cornelis Bos, have been identified as Tupinamba by various scholars, though it is hard to imagine what they are doing in Oxfordshire (cf. Mason 1998b). Similar figures on the borders of the Brussels-made arrases in Wawel Castle, Cracow, presumably connected with the circle of Cornelis Floris, have also been labeled as American (Piwocka 1996, 318–22), though once again there is no obvious reason why Sigismund II Augustus should have commissioned works with an American connotation. In the light of these considerations, the case for a specifically American source behind these South Netherlandish featherwork decorations is considerably weakened. The most we can say with any degree of certainty is that they are composed of exotic decorative elements.[12]

Another of the items of furniture from the southern Netherlands discussed in this connection by Fabri is an early-seventeenth-century desk inlaid with ebony and provided with ivory plates on which fishing scenes are depicted (1992, 51, ill. 13). According to Fabri, "American exotic fishing methods were displayed together with European fishing techniques on the front panels." The front panels of two of the drawers do indeed depict what was considered as a typically Brazilian method of fishing. Indians dressed in feathered skirts and headdresses shoot arrows into the backs of the fish from the shore. They then dive into the water, chase after their prey, and collect the fish in nets.

In this case we do have the source for the scene: a print by Hans Bol, engraved by Philips Galle from the series *Venationis, Piscationis et Aucupii Typii* (Antwerp 1582). Because the caption to the print identifies the scene as Brazilian (Fabri 1992, 50 n. 14), we can be certain that these exotic figures are indeed to be identified as Amerindians. However, in this connection it is worth adducing a scene of whale fishing in which the natives concerned are also dressed in feathered skirts and feathered body ornaments (fig. 2). They are the "Indianer unnd Eynwohner der Insel *S. Maria*" depicted in a volume published by De Bry. This particular scene, however, is meant to illustrate the account of Jan Huygen van Linschoten's journey to the East, published in Frankfurt in 1599, and the "Indians" are probably situated off the coast of Madagascar (Barthelmess and Münzing 1991, 160). Remarkably, if we turn to one of the publications by the De Bry family that explicitly refers to the Americas, volume 9 of the *Great Voyages* (1601), we find an illustration of whale fishing in the same manner, but the human figures identified as Indians in this engraving are not wearing any items of feathered clothing at all (fig. 3).

Fig. 2. Whale fishing off the coast of Madagascar
From *Wie die Wilde Barbarische Leute in der Insel* S. Maria *die Wallfische fangen,* copper engraving, 13.3 × 17.5 cm, Jan Huyghen van Linschoten, Indiae Orientalis, Frankfurt: De Bry, 1599.

To return to the seventeenth-century inlaid desk, Fabri has identified "Latin American shell divers" on the left front panel (1992, 50–51). In this case, too, the source is a print by Bol engraved by Galle, but the accompanying text makes no mention of a specific geographic locality. Because pearl fishing was practiced off the coast of Venezuela, Fabri assumes that the scene is an American one. However, pearl fishing was by no means confined to American waters. Awareness of the Oriental location of pearls as a source of wealth is vividly displayed in various of Columbus's marginal annotations to Plinius and others (Flint 1992, 54, 70). Long before the discovery of the new continent, pearl fishing was being carried out off the coast of Ceylon (De Silva and Beumer 1988, 385–87), in the Persian Gulf, and in the Red Sea. Moreover, we can adduce a parallel scene of mussel fishers dressed in feathered skirts and wearing turbans. They are to be found in one of the 104 engravings after Johannes Stradanus in the hunting compendium *Venationes Ferarum, Auium, Piscium: Pugnae Bestiariorum et Mutuae Bestiarum,* which dates from the end of the sixteenth century. The location of these natives, however, is identified in the accompanying text as the Red Sea (*mare rubrum*) (Achilles 1982, ill. 162).

Fig. 3. Whale fishing in America
From *De Indorum mira piscationis ratione, Idaea vera et genvina, praecipuarum historiarum omnium . . .*, copper engraving, Frankfurt: De Bry, 1601.

At the risk of losing the reader in this flurry of feathered items of clothing, it is necessary to refer to a work of ca. 1580 by Jacopo Zucchi depicting *The Riches of the Sea* (Exh. Cat. Berlin 1982, ill. 31). This oil painting on copper depicts three seminude female figures in the foreground receiving coral, shells, and pearls, while the background contains scenes of pearl fishing. Honour has suggested that the inspiration behind this painting may have been Varthema's *Itinerario*, with its report of pearl fishing in the Persian Gulf, but he goes on to suggest that two dark-skinned figures "were surely intended to depict American Indians" (1979, 294). However, dark-skinned figures were generally connected with Africa rather than America, and the parrot and monkey in the painting could be African rather than American as well. There is, therefore, no compelling reason to interpret the scene in *The Riches of the Sea* as one of Venezuelan pearl fishing.

Another fishing scene in the collection of engravings after Stradanus illustrates the use of pelicans in fishing (fig. 4). The use of birds (although cormorants, not pelicans) for fishing is first documented for China in the early fourteenth century by Odoric of Pordenone.[13] Since most of the scenes in the Stradanus collection are taken from Africa or the Far East, there is no particular reason to assume that we are dealing with an American scene here. However, the presence of feathered skirts has been taken to indicate that this is in fact an American scene (Achilles 1982). This possibility cannot be ruled out entirely; in leafing through the pages of some missionary account covering travels both to America and to the Orient, Stradanus may have inadvertently become the victim of a continental shift and have attributed to America a well-established fishing practice that was documented only for the Orient. All the same, it should be evident by now that the presence of feathered skirts is by no means incongruous in an Asiatic setting.

Zucchi's *The Riches of the Sea,* which incorporates elements drawn from a variety of geographic settings, is a precursor of the work of Jan van Kessel (1626–79), in whose exotic paintings the geographic origin of the items on display is of minor importance. This tendency continues into the eighteenth century. For instance, Vandenbroeck (in Exh. Cat. Antwerp 1992, no. 199) describes a piece of Delft faience from the first quarter of the eighteenth century which is mainly taken up with a Dutch version of a Chinese subject. This piece of chinoiserie, however, includes what Vandenbroeck refers to as "three black Indians" on the grounds of their featherwork attributes. He is undoubtedly correct in referring to the "ethnographic eclecticism" of the

Fig. 4. Fishing using pelicans
Karel de Mallery, after J. Stradanus, *Venationes Ferarum, Auium, Piscium, Pugnae Bestiariorum et Mutuae Bestiarum*, ca. 1600.

scene, intended to heighten the exoticism, but there is no need to see these Blacks as Amerindians rather than Africans. Moreover, there were good precedents for depicting natives of the Far East in a guise resembling that of the Amerindians. In his report on the embassies of the Dutch East Indian Company to China (published in Amsterdam in 1674), the armchair traveler Olfert Dapper included a scene depicting inhabitants of Taiwan as half-naked men with feather headdresses, one of whom holds a decapitated head in his left hand (fig. 5). Cannibalism and feather headdresses, as we have seen, were featured in the 1505 woodcut of Amerindians. Were it not for the schematic pagoda in the background, this Taiwanese scene could be construed as an American one (König 1988, 72).

This survey of some alleged cases of American scenes, identified as such on the basis of featherwork headdresses, skirts, or body ornaments, is intended to show that these artifacts, which at first might seem to justify an American attribution, are not sufficient by themselves to warrant the labeling of a scene as American.[14] There is a high degree of interpenetrability between Asiatic and American iconography such that, in many cases, we are faced with a construct that cannot be pinned down to a specific continent at all. On this reading, the presence of both American and non-American attributes within a single scene defies categorization in terms of geographic specificity.

Furthermore, it may be concluded from this survey that ethnographic eclecticism is not limited to the taste of a particular era. It is already rife in the sixteenth century and shows no signs of dying out in the seventeenth or eighteenth centuries. As Vandenbroeck notes (Exh. Cat. Antwerp 1992, no. 199): "Already in the early sixteenth-century tapestries (*carabara, calcou*) were mixing elements from various cultures. Ethnographic eclecticism also dominated later artistic representations: 'Moors' were painted with 'Indians' feathers' [*sic*], members of mutually hostile Indian tribes were shown together as idyllic companions, or Asiatic and African motifs were combined in one and the same scene with those from Egypt and antiquity."

The latter point—the combination of elements from the newly discovered countries with elements from antiquity[15]—comes to the fore in a particularly tantalizing example: Raphael's *Repulse of Attila*, a fresco from a series in the Stanza d'Eliodoro in the Vatican Palace in Rome, which was completed by 1513. In this representation, which depicts the encounter between Pope Leo I and Attila in the year 452, the barbarians accompanying Attila are dressed in a variety of exotic costumes. One of these figures, who is wearing a feathered bonnet over his helmet, has been singled out for special attention by Colbert, who asks: "Was it Raphael's purpose to allude to the inhabitants of the New World by means of this particular attribute?" (1985,

Fig. 5. Native of Taiwan
From Olfert Dapper, *Die zweite und dritte Gesandschaft der Niederländischen Ostindienkompagnie nach China,* Amsterdam: Jacob Meurs, 1674. Courtesy of Staatsbibliothek Bamberg (Geogr. It. f. 15).

184). Answering in the affirmative, Colbert then ingeniously proceeds to connect the painting with contemporary political events and, in particular, with debates on papal policy toward the Amerindians.[16]

As Colbert admits, however, "if Raphael did intend to depict an American Indian, he leaves a great deal to be desired in terms of anthropological illustration." The only identifying feature in the fresco is the feathered headdress.[17] Yet the very combination of feathers with a classical helmet has little "ethnographic" about it.[18] Feathers are a regular feature of plumed helmets,[19] and feathered headdresses of various kinds appear regularly on the heads of Orientals in European art well before the arrival of Americana in Europe.[20]

A clear-cut case of the depiction of Americana at this early date can be seen in the inclusion of American birds within the grotesque decorations of the Loggetta of the Cardinal of Bibbiena and the Vatican Loggias.[21] In fact, the colibri and *colinus Californicus* in the paintings for Raphael's Loggias executed by Giovanni da Udine derive from the exotic gifts presented to Pope Leo X by the envoy of Emmanuel I of Portugal in 1514 (Dacos 1969a).[22] Yet these exotic gifts were not confined to Americana. On the contrary, on the basis of these ornithological representations, one could argue that Raphael displayed no particular reluctance to represent what were presented as exotic gifts, rather than specifically American ones, and the same is true of the depictions of exotic birds that figure prominently in subsequent pergola paintings in sixteenth-century Rome by Matthew Bril and others (Negro 1996, 51ff.). This indifference to geographic provenance, as we shall see in chapter 4, characterized the collections of curiosities, the donations that led to their formation, and the visual representations of those curiosities. With hindsight, we can label Raphael's birds as American. There is no reason to suppose, however, that they were regarded as any more specifically American than other exotic fauna at the time.

The various elements considered thus far point toward the existence of what we might call the *exotic genre*. Though drawing at times on information made available during the age of discovery, the works corresponding to this category cannot be taken to represent any specific geographic locality. They conjure up what is exotic, and what is exotic, in turn, can be applied to a variety of distant locations. To gain a better idea of the content and workings of this exotic genre, we shall now consider what has been presented in the scholarly literature as the first painting of the New World, Jan Mostaert's *West Indian Landscape*, because discussion of this painting raises many of the questions associated with the representation of the exotic.

West Indian Landscape?

> There is also a landscape, a West Indian one, with many naked people, a curious cliff, and a strange construction of houses and huts; but it was not completed.
>
> Van Mander, *Het schilder-boeck*[23]

The best-known example of a large-scale representation from the sixteenth century that has repeatedly been connected with the New World is the painting by Jan Mostaert known as *West Indian Landscape* (fig. 6; see following p. 112). Since the discovery of this painting in a private collection in Scheveningen in 1909, scholars have followed its discoverer, Ernst Weiss, in assuming that it is related to a painting which Karel van Mander describes in the above terms.[24] Since 1909, various attempts have been made to interpret the painting in relation to a historical event, ranging from Columbus's landing on Goanin in 1492–93,[25] Cortés's conquest of Mexico in 1521–23, Vásquez de Coronado's exploits near a Zuni village in 1540–42, to even the Portuguese invasion of Brazil in the middle of the century. With more circumspection, the author of an entry in the catalog to an exhibition on "The Age of Brueghel" cautiously referred to "an episode in the discovery of America" (Exh. Cat. Brussels 1963).

Eighty years after Weiss's discovery, in 1989, Cuttler published a short article entitled "Errata in Netherlandish Art: Jan Mostaert's 'New World' Landscape," in which he calls the West Indian, or American, attribution of the painting into question. After reviewing the opinions on the various geographic and historical settings which have been proposed, he brings forward arguments which lead him to the conclusion that "We must truly doubt that this painting is specifically intended to be a West Indian, or American, landscape" (1989, 195). In what follows, I propose to present several purely art historical considerations relating to the work and then to concentrate on the iconographic analysis, dealing with each of the items discussed by Cuttler in turn.

To start with the epithet "West Indian," this need not necessarily be taken to mean the West Indies, for the name could be used for the New World at large to distinguish it from the East Indies.[26] Moreover, it is not known when the painting acquired its current title, so there is no guarantee that this title goes back to Mostaert. It is certainly present in Van Mander's reference to a West Indian landscape, as we saw, but there are some problems in matching Van Mander's description to the painting now on display in the Frans Hals Museum in Haarlem, The Netherlands. For instance, though Van Mander refers to an unfinished painting, our picture has every appearance of being complete. Besides, if we accept a rough dating for the painting somewhere in the second quarter of the sixteenth century, there are two generations intervening between the creation of the work and Van Mander's description—time enough for possible distortions, influenced in particular by later political events in the Netherlands during the second half of the century, including a northern version of the Black Legend, to have had an effect on Van Mander's reading of the painting.

As for the word *landscape,* its adoption as a convenient way of designating a multitude of background details in depictions of natural scenery took place only on a gradual scale during the course of the sixteenth century, and it could refer both to a geographic region and to pictorial subject matter (Gibson 1989, 53). The juxtaposition of a topographic epithet ("West Indian") with the word *landscape* is thus a combination of two elements which were both in a state of development, if not flux, in the sixteenth century. Moreover, at a time when landscape painting itself was only just coming into its own, the representation of specific *national* landscapes (as in the work of Jan van Scorel, for example) had by no means hardened into a firm iconographic tradition. Instead of representing an urge to express the uniqueness of a place, depictions tend to dwell on the need to convey what a place was essentially like. Myers (1993) sees a resemblance in this respect between Patinir's multiperspectival style of landscape painting and the organization of Columbus's description of Hispaniola in his letter to Luis de Santangel of 1493 (Colón 1984, 141). The organization of Columbus's description, Myers argues, is not psychological, logical, or pictorial. Columbus's answer to the question "What kind of a place is Hispaniola?" is it is a place of uncultivated pleasantness, a *locus amoenus*. For most of his original readers, that is probably all they needed or wanted to know. In the case of Van Mander, then, while he no doubt had a clear idea about what he took the term to mean, it is questionable whether we can say the same about a painter of Mostaert's generation.

To turn to the figure of Jan Mostaert himself, Pierron began his study of the Mostaert family in 1912 with the words: "There are not many painters of the old schools of the Low Countries who have been the object of so few studies as the Mostaert family" (1912, 1).[27] Thanks to the meticulous investigation of the Haarlem archives by Thierry de Bye Dólleman (1963), we are now much better informed about the painter's biographic details. Born into a family of millers in Haarlem around 1472,[28] Jan Jansz. was already active as a painter by 1498, soon after his upwardly mobile marriage to a widow, Angnyese Martijnsdr. As a painter with a high reputation, Mostaert was elected deacon of the guild of St. Luke in Haarlem on various occasions. There is no evidence to support the claim that he was attached to the court of Margaret of Austria; the archival sources indicate that he was present in Haarlem on a number of occasions when she was at court in the southern Netherlands.[29] Mostaert himself probably died in 1555, and most of his works were destroyed by the fire of Haarlem on 23 October 1576, though an important collection was saved in the house of his grandson, Niclaes Suycker, sheriff (*schout*) of Haarlem.[30] There is nothing to suggest that the painter ever went to America, as the seventeenth-century Netherlandish painters Frans Post and Albert Eckhout (discussed in detail in the following chapter) were to do. Thus, if the painting refers to the New World at all, it must be based on visual or written sources available to the artist in Europe.

There were indeed ways of bringing the New World to Europe for those who were unable to make the trip from Europe to the New World. In particular, as we know from Dürer's enthusiastic account of the treasures of Motecuhzoma which Cortés sent to Europe and which were displayed in the palace of Margaret of Austria in Brussels in 1520 (Panofsky 1971, 209), American artifacts made an immediate and deep impression on European artists. Within five years or so, they were already influencing the decoration of the capitals in the Palace of the Prince-Bishops in Liège (Dacos 1969a). Whether Mostaert himself actually saw the artifacts in Brussels or not, he could hardly have been oblivious to the fact that America was in the air.[31]

One of the artists whom Dürer met in Margaret's court was Joachim Patinir of Antwerp, who was to play a crucial role in the development of landscape painting.[32] Some critics have associated elements of Mostaert's work with that of Patinir. Stylistically, Mostaert's landscape conforms to the Flemish color scheme of brown to green to blue as the eye recedes into the distance, suggesting a date in the 1520s.[33] Thus, in terms of both style and patronage, a date for the painting of *West Indian Landscape* in the 1520s would be plausible.[34]

There is, therefore, nothing in the art historical setting which definitely excludes an American reference for the work. Cuttler's main arguments against an American reference, however, are of a strictly iconographic kind. It is, therefore, time to consider the iconography of the painting in more detail.

The narrative action of the painting passes from right to left. On the right, we see a sailing ship far out to sea, while canoes can be seen near the shore. An army of men is seen advancing, some of them chasing off the animals on the far right. The main body, armed with pikes and firearms, are advancing behind two cannon. In front of the cannon, three men in cloaks advance.

Then comes the point of contact between the invaders and their opponents, as one of the invaders attacks a native with his sword in front of one of the native dwellings. In the foreground, a native archer aims his bow at the assailant. Two women, one of them with two small children, flee in the direction of a large group of men advancing from the left. Most of these figures are arranged in pairs, and they are looking to the front or the rear. Some of them are running with their hands behind their backs, suggesting that they are prisoners with their hands bound. They display a variety of types: some are bearded, some have light-colored hair, one has large, pointed ears and a pair of horns. One of them is wearing a turban, two of them are wearing red hats trimmed with white, another has a floral band in his hair. Some are unarmed, others carry agricultural implements (pitchforks and flails), clubs, lances, (round or oval) shields, or longbows, and one carries armor.[35] Two of them are blowing elongated trumpets.

On the left, a woman appears to be trying to restrain a man armed with a club from leaving to join in the fray. Three dwellings are visible, and in one of them a woman and child are left behind as a man leaves to fight.

The fauna include sheep, parrots or macaws, cows, a monkey, a hare, and rabbits. The landscape is dominated by a rock formation, where ladders propped against the stone lead up to a roof supported on twisted stakes. Standing in the open doorway of this structure is an old man, who is looking away from the invaders in the direction from where the natives are coming.

Even this brief description indicates the presence of so many narrative elements that the painting must be telling a story. But is it an American one?

We begin with the numerous nude figures, apparently the only nudes in works by this artist. Cuttler argues: "Had Mostaert intended to show the savages of the New World, who were well known by the 1520s through prints, drawings and even from actual Indians brought to Europe, he could very quickly and easily have made his figures more specifically identifiable by the addition of arm-bands or feather-headdresses, if nothing else" (1989, 195).

However, a glance at the list of depictions of Amerindians compiled by William Sturtevant in 1976 reveals that there were in fact very few prints or drawings of the "savages" of the New World circulating at this period. Moreover, a significant number of those which did exist depict naked males and females. For instance, the earliest portrayal of American Indians that exists, the woodcut frontispiece to the metric version of Columbus's letter by Giuliano Dati (*La lettera dell isole che ha trovato nuovamente il Re di Spagna*) of 1493, depicts King Ferdinand II in the foreground and a mass of naked men on land. This woodcut was recycled to illustrate Vespucci's very influential *Lettera delle isole nuovamente trovate,* published in 1504–5. Other woodcuts that accompanied editions of Vespucci, many of them based on the European iconography of the Wild Man and the Wild Woman (Colin 1987; Mason 1990, 43–50), similarly depict naked human figures.[36] A woodcut of a male and a female cannibal butchering their human victim, which is used to illustrate the section entitled *Von den neüwen inseln* in Sebastian Münster's *Cosmographia* (first published in German in 1544), portrays both figures stark naked. Besides these visual sources, it should be borne in mind that Columbus's initial reaction to the Amerindians was that "They were all naked as their mothers had born them, including the women" (Colón 1984, 30; cf. Mason 1998a). Indeed, it was the nudity of the women which fascinated voyeurs like Amerigo Vespucci and Pero Vaz de Caminha (Mason 1991b).

As we have seen, the presence of feathered skirts in a representation does not necessarily imply an American frame of reference. To make the same point in reverse: the absence of feathered skirts does not necessarily imply the lack of an American frame of reference.

The same logic applies to another of the points raised by Cuttler, the question of skin pigmentation. Mostaert could obviously not draw any information on this score from monochrome prints or drawings (Bucher 1981, 35). Written sources, however, which are notoriously difficult to interpret when color terms are at stake, had little to offer either. At any rate, it was advisable not to portray the Amerindians as dark-skinned as the Ethiopians, the traditional Blacks of the written sources. Hence, while a lightish complexion did not necessarily point toward America, it did not point away from it either.

Another of Cuttler's objections is that, while some of the naked natives in Mostaert's painting have beards, the Indians of the New World were at the time immediately remarked as being beardless (1989, 193). However, the Dati and Vespucci woodcuts referred to above depict bearded men, deriving no doubt from the Wild Man imagery. The Amerindians depicted working for the brazilwood trade on a wooden plaque from Rouen dating from the middle of the sixteenth century (Hamy 1907a; Exh. Cat. Paris 1976, no. 8) have European-style beards and moustaches. The frontispiece to book 9 of De Bry's *Great Voyages* (1601), dealing with Sebald de Weert's expedition to the Strait of Magellan, depicts a bearded Indian with feathered headdress and skirt (Bucher 1981, 121ff.).[37] Incidentally, both this frontispiece and the Vespucci woodcuts also corroborate another of the iconographic attributes in Mostaert's painting, confirmed as an item of Americana by the texts of Columbus, Vespucci, and Vaz de Caminha: the bow and arrow.[38]

However, there are other iconographic elements which are more disturbing within an alleged American setting. First are the two older men with beards, who are wearing white-trimmed red caps and who seem to be elders of the community, since several natives appear to be deferring to them. If we look for a parallel to this headgear, it can be found in the figure of a Tartar taken from A. de Bruijn's collection of national costumes, *Omnium pene Europae, Asiae, Aphricae atque Americae gentium habitus* (Antwerp, 1581).[39] The question then arises: What is it doing in America?

The answer to this question lies in a process that was commonly employed during the sixteenth century to fill in the details of ethnographic accounts, which might be called *reading off*. As a function of Eurocentric discourse, it worked on the assumption that those who were not Europeans were barbarians and that one barbarian was more or less like another. In other words, if you wanted information about the barbarians of the New World, all you had to do was to turn up the sources on the barbarians of the Old World—the Thracians, Scythians, and so on. These resemblances were not purely morphological, however; many authors used the similarities to argue theories of descent. In fact, in the course of time, more than twenty different ancestors were put forward in the scholarly disputes over the Amerindians' ancestors (Ryan 1981, 533).[40]

Vespucci was the first to note that, in his opinion, the Amerindian men do not have very beautiful faces because they have long eyelids, which make them look like Tartars. In the second half of the century, long black hair, broad faces, flat noses, and a tawny color were considered distinguishing features which allowed the Eskimos captured by Frobisher to be regarded as resembling Tartars (Sturtevant and Quinn 1987, 71). Tartars, Chinese, and Scythians tended to get treated as if they were one Oriental people, and some authors sought to derive the origins of the Amerindians from this ethnic amalgam during the course of the sixteenth century.[41] In his survey of theories which appeared at the beginning of the following century, the *Origen de los indios de el nuevo mundo, e Indias occidentales* (1607), Gregorio García examined the pros and cons of a derivation from the lost tribes of Israel, the Carthaginians, the Greeks, the Spaniards, and others, including the Tartars, mainly basing his argument on physical appearance and customs. By this time, in fact, the hypothesis of an Asian origin for the Amerindians had already gained solid ground. In the eyes of a large body of the learned public of the sixteenth and seventeenth centuries, there was thus no contradiction between an American frame of reference and the presence of a Tartar feature in one and the same composition.

Another obstacle to an American point of reference might be seen in the presence of European-looking sheep, cows, and a hare, even though they are combined with a monkey and a parrot. Yet it should not be forgotten that the earliest chroniclers tended to treat New World fauna and flora as if they were no different from those of the Old World. Hernán Cortés's first letter from Mexico refers to lions and tigers (Cortés 1972, 29). In the early years of the seventeenth century, the sugar planter Ambrósio Fernandes Brandão did not know what to call a jaguar except a tiger, and he referred to the New World crop maize as sorghum (1986, 278, 198). Toward the end of the same century, when Hans Sloane voyaged to Jamaica in 1687, his close friend and correspondent John Ray still asked him to be particularly observant of similarities in plants on both sides of the Atlantic (MacGregor 1994, 12, 16). As for the parrot, it appears on maps as one of the first icons of America (George 1969, 56ff.). Columbus was determined to find parrots in America and to take them back to Spain as evidence that he had reached his Oriental destination (Colón 1984, 80).[42]

Similar considerations apply to the clothing of the Europeans in the painting. While attempts to find a historical point of reference for the painting would lead one to expect Spanish or (less likely) Portuguese intruders, Cuttler argues that the moderately slashed costumes and short breeches of the invaders are consonant with Netherlandish dress of the 1520s and 1530s, as opposed to the long hose of the Spanish. However, although interest in the different national costumes of the peoples of Europe did begin to develop in the sixteenth century, it was not until the second half of the century that individual prints and costume books began to circulate on a wide scale, and then it was mostly in Germany and Italy (Defert 1987; Du Mortier 1991, 403). Hence, it would be anachronistic to stress the national character of the dress of the Europeans in a painting of the 1520s or even 1530s.

Another iconographic item in Mostaert's painting which at first sight jars with an American setting is the fact that two of the natives are portrayed blowing long classical trumpets (*tubae*) to rally support against the invaders.[43] Another detail which seems to be derived from a classical source is the pointed, faunlike ears of one of the human figures. Taken in combination with the agricultural implements that some of the natives are carrying, this might suggest a connection with some bucolic scene from classical antiquity.[44]

A classical detail could have a function similar to that of the Tartar red caps already discussed. Eighteenth-century writers like Fontenelle and Lafitau were to make much of the alleged parallels between the "savages" of the New World and the inhabitants of the world of the ancient Greeks, but the tendency to see the New World through the eyes of classical antiquity was present from the first. The parallel was uncomfortably close after the sack of Rome in 1527, and after the conquest of Peru the same parallel could be drawn between Rome and Cuzco (Zinser 1982; MacCormack 1995, 80–86). A weaker version of the argument simply assumed that "noble savages" in America or anywhere else looked something like the heroes of antiquity;[45] the stronger version explained this similarity by theories of descent. For instance, Pedro Sarmiento de Gamboa, author of a *Historia de los Incas* which was completed in 1572, argued that the Amerindians were descended from the ancient Greeks, substantiating his theory with alleged parallels between Greek words and certain elements in Yucatán vocabulary. "Historically," Odysseus must have sailed across the Atlantic to Yucatán after the sack of Troy (Huddleston 1967, 30). Sarmiento combined this with the theory that the Indians of Peru were descended from the inhabitants of the westernmost part of the Greek world, the lost city of Atlantis. Such an Atlantean origin was already implied in the highly influential poem *Syphilis*, written between 1510 and 1512 by the prominent sixteenth-century Veronese poet Fracastoro (?1478–1553) and published in 1530 (Eatough 1984). Moreover, the connection between the Old and the New Worlds was implied in the search in the Americas for the so-called Plinian races, who had played such a prominent part in the ethnographic imagination of the Greeks and Romans (Mason 1990, 1994; Egmond and Mason 1997, 105–32).

To sum up this treatment of the individual iconographic elements: strange though it may seem, the presence of Tartarian caps, classical trumpets, Netherlandish costume, and European fauna in the painting does not rule out the possibility that it may refer to what the painter imagined a "West Indian landscape" to look like. As a corollary, the absence of feathered attributes—which might have made the human figures "more specifically identifiable" (Cuttler 1989, 195)—should not be taken as evidence that they are not Amerindians. It only shows that the painter was not interested in, or capable of, this degree of specificity.

Indeed, to suppose that he could have attempted it at such an early date is an anachronism. As the early history of the personification of America in allegories of the four continents shows, there was no established iconography of the continent before the volumes of De Bry's *Great Voyages* began to appear in the last decennium of the century. Thus, when Giovanni di Vecchi set out to portray the four continents in a series of frescoes for the Sala del Mappamondo of the Palazzo Farnese in Caprarola in 1572–74, he had to include the globe with America to make it evident which continent he was portraying (Poeschel 1985, 92). Moreover, as we have seen, at a time when landscape painting itself was only just coming into its own, there was certainly no iconographic tradition of *national* landscapes, let alone an *American* landscape. The presence of stylized palm trees in such paintings as the *Entry into Bethlehem* or the *View of Antwerp with Scenes from the Life of Christ,* both painted by a follower of Lucas Gassel, is no doubt intended to evoke the exotic flora of the Holy Land (Gibson 1989, 21, pls. 2.16 and 2.18). Like the camels to be found in some depictions of St. Jerome in the wilderness, however, the primary point of reference of these elements is to an exotic landscape as such, and not to a geographically specific one. A similar point can be made in relation to the implausible collection of sixteen kinds of animals, ranging from Asian giraffe to north European brown bear, in the setting to a biblical story—the gathering of the manna—in a painting by Francesco Ubertini (il Bacchiacca) dated c. 1540–55; these animals suggest "not the precise geographic setting, but the generic one" (Lazzaro 1995, 209).

Thus far, then, the present argument is intended to demonstrate that there is no reason to deny an American reference to Mostaert's painting. A painting containing the ingredients of an exotic landscape must in fact have appeared particularly suitable as a representation of the New World to Mostaert's contemporaries. At a time when geographic knowledge about America in the Netherlands was still in a state of flux,[46] and when the iconography of the New World had not yet been consolidated,[47] "America" was a free field of fabulation—though within certain constraints. The next stage in the argument thus bears on these constraints: What were the iconographic options which were open to Mostaert, supposing that he did indeed set out to portray a New World landscape?

We start with a suggestion made by Cuttler. He finds a model for Mostaert's painting in Jacopo de' Barbari's woodcut, *Battle of Men and Satyrs,* dated around 1497–1500. There is a connection between Barbari and Mostaert in that the former was also a member of the court of Margaret of Austria in Malines from 1510 and followed her in her constant movements through the country (Duverger 1980, 136–39). There certainly are some points of resemblance between Barbari's woodcut and Mostaert's painting: the hurling of rocks and the blowing of classical trumpets, the craggy landscape including a rock with a hole in it, the huts and barriers, and the platforms made of living tree limbs and branches. Cuttler proceeds to draw far-reaching conclusions from this supposed parallel (1989, 197): "Such is the subject of our painting. Bartsch gave Jacopo de' Barbari's woodcut the title: Battle of virtue against vice and the final conquest of the latter. Mostaert borrowed ideas and forms from that classicizing Italian artist's woodcut of men battling evil satyrs to create an equally moral theme more pointed and relevant to his own day."

Before examining the individual iconographic items in more detail, it is necessary to raise an objection of a more fundamental kind to Cuttler's interpretation. Curiously, he does not mention the fact that the woodcut he reproduces is one of a pair, the second of which is known as the *Triumph of Men over Satyrs.* The program of these woodcuts requires further study to elucidate their precise meaning, but that it is a moralizing one is evident from the inscriptions they bear: "How it is done rightly is (or will be) seen" on the first; "Lofty virtue subdues Cupid, ruling with money" on the second. The pair of woodcuts, therefore, treats the advance of civilization in terms of moral progress. The satyrs represent the race of primitive beings whose barbarous community is doomed; as personifications of vice, they are also personifications of greed. Cupid, the debased lord of the satyrs, has succumbed to the nobler Apollo (Kaufmann 1984, 77–79). If we suppose that Mostaert was following Barbari, he appears to have got it all wrong, for while the Italian artist portrays the satyrs in negative terms, Cuttler would have us believe that the natives in Mostaert's painting are to be seen in a positive light, living in "a world of peace and harmonious domesticity under assault by forces equipped with weapons far more effective than those of the society under attack" (1989, 197). Such a "Black Legend" interpretation is completely at odds with Barbari's moralizing praise of the advance of civilization.

Scrutiny of the individual iconographic items also fails to substantiate the alleged parallel with the Barbari woodcut. To take the use of rude tree limbs or branches as building materials, they are derived from a motif which was widespread at the time. As Panofsky pointed out in his essay on Piero di Cosimo (1962, 44), the style of building using unsquared tree trunks interwoven with twigs is a stock feature of an early phase of civilization as described by Vitruvius and can be found in woodcut illustrations to his *De architectura libri decem* from the first half of the sixteenth century.[48] The parallel between these depictions of primitivism, whether of a "soft" or "hard" variety, and the condition of the peoples in the newly discovered lands—as well as that of marginal groups like gypsies on the European continent (Holberton 1995)—was already being drawn at this time. Thus, Cesare Cesariano, the Italian translator of a 1521 edition of Vitruvius, added a caption to Vitruvius's passage on the invention of fire in which he compared those early human beings to the people whom Spanish and Portuguese travelers had recently found living in grottoes in southern Asia (Ginzburg 1993, 129–30). We may suppose that Mostaert would have been aware of this motif and realized its appropriateness to his purposes.

As for the unusual features of the landscape, Van Luttervelt (1948–49) ingeniously compared the rock with a hole in it to rock formations in Arizona, thereby hoping to add support to his theory that the painting represents Coronado's activities in the American southwest. However, the landscape is obviously an imaginary landscape; there is nothing in it which could either confirm or refute an association with America.[49] Moreover, there are sufficient parallels for such an imaginary landscape without our having to fall back on Barbari. The natural arch formed in a rock formation by the forces of erosion was one of the favorite geologic forms of Joachim Patinir (Gibson 1989, 5), and it can be found in many works by other Flemish landscape painters of the early sixteenth century, such as Cornelis and Quentin Massys, Cornelis van Dalem, Joos van Cleve, Herri met de Bles, and Matthys Cock, as well as the Ferrarese artist Benevenuto Garofalo.[50] A particularly interesting example is the presence of such a natural arch in the background to the Thomas and Matthew retable by Barend van Orley, another of Margaret of Austria's court painters,[51] since it has been suggested that this painting includes other "Indian" motifs as well.[52] A natural arch also occurs in another painting by Mostaert himself, *Portrait of a Lady* (Rijksmuseum, Amsterdam), where the background to the portrait includes a scene from the life of St. Hubert[53]—a fitting theme both for a courtly painting and for the idyllic landscapes in which deer hunting was supposed to take place.

Landscapes of this kind are often the setting for paintings of St. Jerome or other hermits in the wilderness;[54] scenes of the rest of Joseph and Mary during the flight into Egypt; Christ carrying the Cross; the Sermon of St. John; and landscapes with St. Christopher. Van Mander could have had such landscapes in mind when he referred in his *Den grondt der edel vrij schilderconst* (VIII, 31g) to "shepherds' huts and peasant hamlets,/In rocky caves, hollow trees and on stakes."[55] In his commentary on this passage, Miedema (1973, 2:554) refers such a setting not only to hermits but also to the surroundings of the primitive, first human beings, citing both the Mostaert painting and Cornelis van Dalem's *The Dawn of Civilization* (fig. 7; see following p. 112).[56] In view of these iconographic connections with the dawn of humanity, one can follow Snyder (1976) in noting the resemblance in mood between Mostaert's *West Indian Landscape* and Piero di Cosimo's portrayals of primitive humanity.[57] For instance, the presence of the faunlike figure with pointed ears among the human figures in Mostaert's painting has a parallel in Piero's *The Hunt* (ca. 1495–1505), a scene of a forest hunt conducted during a brutish stage in human development, which includes satyrs and centaurs among the human figures. This and others of Piero's paintings include rocky landscapes (particularly in his depictions of St. Jerome in the wilderness; cf. Fermor 1993, 199–205), an interest in both domestic and exotic animals and plants, and the portrayal of a primitive stage of humanity before the use of metal weapons. Incidentally, there is nothing incongruous about the presence of these weapons in an idyllic landscape, for the original friendship between humans and animals is related to a lack of exploitation of domesticated animals, not to the absence of the weapons used for hunting. It is thus only natural that, when this way of life is attacked from without, its members should defend themselves with every available means.

Honour regards the Mostaert painting as "one of the most beautiful and fascinating of all paintings on an American subject" (1979, 282). Comparing the background with Mostaert's *Expulsion from Eden,* he interprets the *West Indian Landscape* as a modern counterpart, seeing in it a contrast between the "pastoral pre-lapsarian or Golden Age way of life" of the naked Indians and "the Spanish age of steel represented by armed men advancing into the peaceful landscape."[58] Two opposite tendencies in the interpretation of the painting—the urge to link it with a specific historical event in the conquest of America, on the one hand,[59] and Cuttler's denial of an American frame of reference at all, on the other hand—both have in common the fact that they deny the existence of a continuous to-and-fro movement between the prelapsarian, Old World past and the idyllic elements which many of the first observers of the New World saw there. It was this cross-fertilization of elements from two different worlds which produced the kind of pseudomorphoses of which Mostaert's *West Indian Landscape* is an example.

Mostaert's *West Indian Landscape* can be considered as an exponent of the utilization of a stock of elements drawn from different sources which could be combined with one another to create an exotic result. Artists who

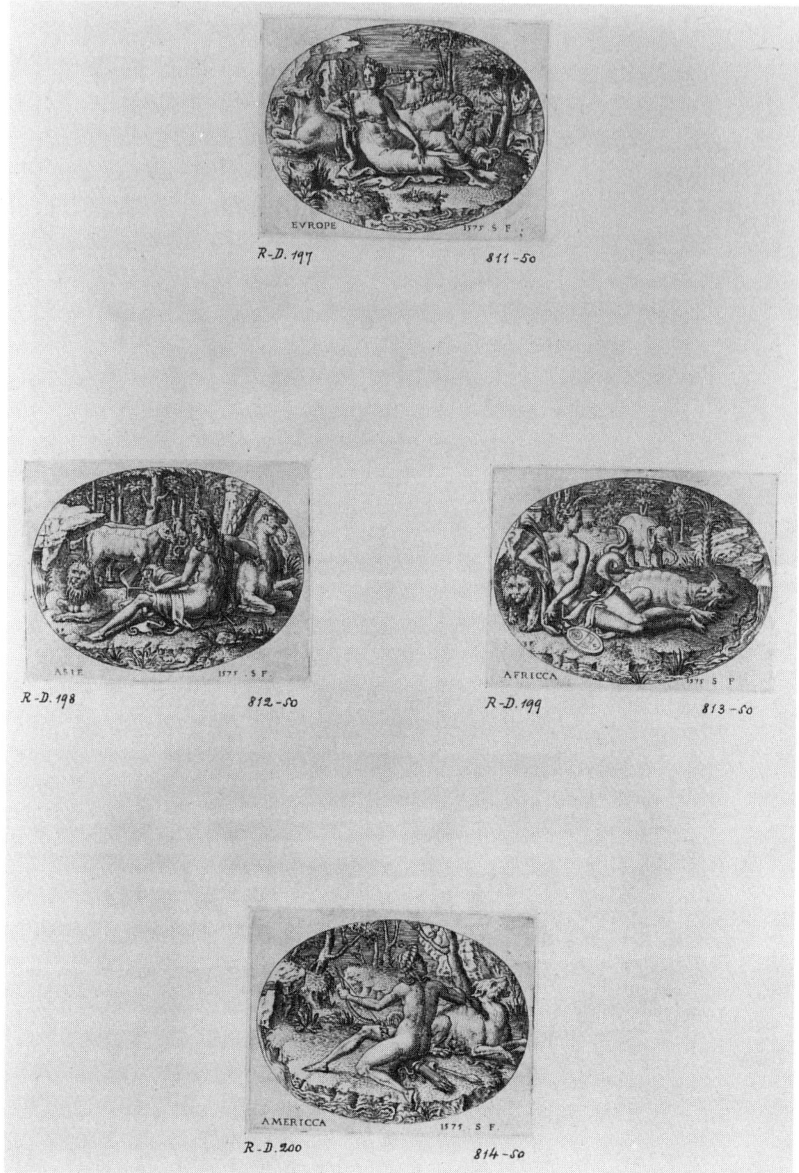

Fig. 8. *The Four Continents*
Etienne Delaune, 1575, copper engraving, Kupferstichkabinett Staatliche Museen zu Berlin-Preussischer Kulturbesitz, Kat./Inv. nos. 811–50, 812–50, 813–50, 814–50. Photograph by Jörg P. Anders.

set out to make representations relating to America could feel free to draw on this stock of geographically undifferentiated items as being in some way appropriate to their image of America. The present-day researcher can certainly inquire, like an archaeologist, into the origins of these individual items, but it would be incorrect to retroject these analytic concerns and standards of accuracy to an earlier period when they were, if not attainable, at any rate irrelevant. For the most salient characteristic of the exotic genre is the fact that it is diffuse. The elements of which it is composed have not yet been broken down analytically into separate, specific items.

After Babylon

There is an interesting parallel to this to-and-fro movement between the Old and the New Worlds in an engraving by Etienne Delaune (1518/19–83?), a member of the school of Fontainebleau. Delaune is better known in studies of the iconography of America for his copperplate engravings of the four continents dating from 1575 (fig. 8), but at an earlier date he executed a series of twelve prints of *combats et triomphes.*[60] The seventh of this series depicts a combat of naked warriors, whose feathered clothing, distended lower lips, and clubs mark them unmistakably as Tupinamba (Lestringant 1991c, 108).[61] This is the only one of the twelve prints which is not taken from Greco-Roman mythology, for the other themes include a centauromachia and the triumph of Bacchus, as well as four scenes of combat between horsemen and infantry. However, a certain degree of contamination has taken place between the scenes of the Old World and the New World, so that Romans and Ottomans fight as the Brazilian Indians do. While the Old World reference remains dominant, it is not exclusive. In commenting on this series, Lestringant remarks: "The series of combats declines the variations of a theme, but without distinguishing between the successive stages of a sequence. In this glorious chaos, unified by the work of the engraver alone, the boundaries are abolished between animal and human, between brute nature with its strange productions and the refinements of civilized war, between the primitive violence of an emergent world and modern ritualized frenzy" (1991c, 110).

Lestringant's term *beau désordre* (here rendered as "glorious chaos") is equally applicable to Mostaert's painting.[62] Not only is there nothing in Jan Mostaert's *West Indian Landscape* which stands in the way of its representing an American scene; the example of the contamination of Old and New World iconography evidenced by Delaune's series of prints indicates that Mostaert was not the only sixteenth-century artist to combine the historical remoteness of the Greeks and Romans with the geographic remoteness of the Americans and other exotic peoples to produce a new amalgam: the exotic genre.

A representation from the very end of the sixteenth century could be regarded as emblematic of the exotic genre in this sense. It is the copper engraving *Confusio Babylonica* by Zacharias Dolendo, after Karel van Mander. Against the looming tower of Babel in the background, which is still intact, we see a panorama of various peoples of the world. The etching was included in the 1992 Antwerp exhibition "America, Bride of the Sun" because of the presence of two women and a child in the left-hand corner, who have been identified as Amerindians (Exh. Cat. Antwerp 1992, no. 108) by their feathered headdresses. This is their only distinctively "American" feature. One of them is holding a tablet, which is inscribed with Arabic script and Egyptian hieroglyphics (Wendt 1989, 172 n. 4).

This print apparently depicts the moment when God "confounded the language of all the earth; and from thence did the Lord scatter them abroad upon the face of all the earth" (Gen. 11.9). The act of God—the Confusion of Tongues—creates linguistic plurality. A number of scholars in the sixteenth century attempted to show that a particular language of their time was a vestige of the pure and universal language which had preceded the Babel episode. Joannes Goropius Becanus, for example, a physician from the Dutch province of Brabant,[63] used far-fetched etymologies to demonstrate that the language of his homeland was a derivative of primitive Hebrew.[64] Moreover, the discovery of the New World raised the possibility that its inhabitants might be descended from a tribe—one of the descendants of Noah, for instance—which had been exempt from the Confusion of Tongues. Since the humanist Van Mander must certainly have been aware of these contemporary debates, it is plausible to take both the presence of foreign scripts and the presence of "American" headdresses as allusions to such theories.

The various peoples illustrated in the print are already setting off in various directions. The distinctive features of the different peoples can therefore be considered proleptic: the distinctions embodied in the print are *in the process of* being marked off from one another. The exotic genre precedes the confusion of Babel, and it consists of what can only be defined as different strands after the event. Thus, the feathered skirt as an attribute of America is an anachronism: it is an element which belongs to the exotic genre, scattered among the peoples of Africa, America, and Asia after Babel and before national distinctions had become established. The corollary is ethnographic interchangeability: in one of the painted copies of Van Mander's print,[65] the "Amerindians" have been replaced by a procession of Germans in contemporary dress.

Ten years after Van Mander's death, the Leiden historian Philipp Clüver contrasted the tight-fitting garments of the German nobility with the wide trousers of the Gauls. The latter were so universal a fashion that they must go back to the time of the tower of Babel (1616, 141). The exotic genre was as accommodating as the baggy trousers of the Gauls.

3 ETHNOGRAPHIC REALISM AND THE EXOTIC PORTRAIT

Eckhout was not a great painter.

Whitehead and Boeseman, *A Portrait of Dutch Seventeenth-Century Brazil*

Between Cracow and Copenhagen

Prolepsis also characterizes a small oil painting on paper (fig. 9; see following p. 112), one of the thirteen representations of human subjects that make up almost one-quarter of the third volume of a seventeenth-century compilation of natural historical paintings and drawings known as *Theatri Rerum Naturalium Brasiliae*. The painting itself has covered a remarkable trajectory: produced by a Dutch artist in Brazil during the years in which Count Johan Maurits van Nassau-Siegen was governor-general of the Dutch colony in northeastern Brazil (1637–44), it formed part of a gift made by Johan Maurits to the Elector of Brandenburg in 1652 in exchange for noble titles and land in the proximity of Cleves. Within a decade it had been incorporated into volume A 34 of the series of *Libri Picturati* compiled by the Elector's physician Christian Mentzel. Evacuated from Berlin during World War II, it was transferred to the Benedictine monastery in present-day Krzeszów. Thanks to the efforts of the late P. J. P. Whitehead, the whereabouts of this material was discovered in the late 1970s in the Jagiellon Library in Cracow, leading to the publication of a facsimile edition of *Libri Picturati* A 32–38 in 1995 (Brasil-Holandês 1995).[1]

In their fundamental study of the products of the Dutch artists in the retinue of Johan Maurits, Whitehead and Boeseman refer to this figure as "Negro girl holding sugar loaf" (1989, 171). Though none of the Brazilian drawings and oil sketches is signed or dated, the same authors go on to state that this figure "is clearly an earlier version of the negro woman in Eckhout's Copenhagen painting" and thus attribute it to the Dutch artist Albert Eckhout. The painting to which they refer in Copenhagen (fig. 10; see following p. 112) is undoubtedly the work of Albert Eckhout, as it is signed *Æckhoût fe 1641—brasil* on the lower right. Though there are only seven extant paintings by Eckhout which are signed, there is nothing exceptionable in the attribution of the oil sketch to this artist.

Little is known about the artist Albert Eckhout (ca. 1607–65). In the words of Whitehead and Boeseman: "Even now, the number of securely attributable works is few and his life is almost as poorly documented as is Shakespeare's" (1989, 168).[2] We do know that both he and Frans Post (1612–80) were chosen to accompany Johan Maurits van Nassau-Siegen to Brazil in 1636, though whether other artists were included in the company is a matter of debate. Besides the works of natural history that he produced in Dutch Brazil, Eckhout's oeuvre includes a series of remarkably large oil paintings of human figures, which now hang in the National Museum of Copenhagen (figs. 10–17; see following p. 112). These eight paintings are all more or less the same size, measuring no less than approximately 265 cm by approximately 160 cm. They consist of four pairs: two pairs of Brazilian Indians (figs. 12–13 and 16–17), two half-bloods (a mameluc woman and a mestizo man) (figs. 14–15),[3] and one Black African pair (figs. 10–11).[4] All of these paintings, except that of the mestizo (fig. 15), are signed by the artist and dated between 1641 and 1643, during his stay in Brazil. A ninth painting (fig. 18; see following p. 112), a horizontal composition (168 cm × 294 cm), depicts an Indian dance.

These paintings were probably intended to hang in the great hall of Vrijburg, the residence which Johan Maurits had built to the east of Mauritsstad in Brazil, completed in 1642. Johan Maurits returned to the Netherlands in May 1644, where the Mauritshuis in The Hague was complete and waiting for him. However, none of the halls in the Mauritshuis was large enough to accommodate the entire series, and Johan Maurits had to make do with a number of frescoes painted along the walls of the staircases depicting "life-like, all the heathen and barbaric nations, male and female Moors, negroes, Brazilians, Tapuyas, Hottentots and other savage nations who are all God's creatures" (De Hennin 1681). They formed the backdrop to a feast organized to celebrate the return of Johan Maurits to the Netherlands in 1644, at which the pièce de résistance was a dance executed by naked Indians, to the horror of certain preachers and their wives among the guests.[5] No doubt some of these painted frescoes were based on the Eckhout paintings. They were all destroyed when the Mauritshuis was gutted by fire in 1704.[6]

The redundancy of the large-scale Brazilian paintings in the Mauritshuis may have been one of the factors which prompted Johan Maurits to present them in 1654 as part of a gift to his cousin Frederick III, the king of Denmark, who took a lively interest in art and ethnographica (Gundestrup 1985). The gift, apparently negotiated on the initiative of Admiral Lindenov, who had assured Johan Maurits that the gift would be acceptable to the king (Whitehead 1987, 154), comprised not only twenty-six paintings,[7] but also some of the exotic artifacts and natural curiosities that Maurits had brought back from Brazil, including native artifacts, exotic plants, a caiman, a python or boa, tortoises, a rhinoceros, a sea lion, an elephant, and various smaller animals, as well as minerals, corals, and shells (cf. Whitehead 1979, 429). The Eckhout paintings appear in the 1673–74 and later inventories of Frederick's *Kunstkammer* (Dam-Mikkelsen and Lundbæk 1980, 42; Gundestrup 1991, 2:125) and have remained in Copenhagen to the present day.[8]

The large oil painting in Copenhagen (fig. 10) with which the small oil sketch in Cracow (fig. 9) has been compared, that of the Negro woman, presents her in a frontal pose. Her only items of clothing are a blue and white skirt, wrapped at the waist with a red sash, and a broad hat. She wears pearl-drop earrings tied with red ribbons, a pearl necklace and a red necklace, a bangle on her left wrist and a bracelet of beads on her right wrist. Her other attributes are the basket she is holding in her right hand and the pipe tucked in her waistband. Her left hand rests on the head of a lighter-skinned boy, naked except for a necklace and earrings, who is holding a maize cob in his right hand and has a small bird perched on his left hand. By comparison, the Negro woman in the earlier sketch is characterized by Whitehead and Boeseman in terms of lack: "she has no hat, no necklaces, no pipe, no bracelets, there is no child beside her" (1989, 77). We could add that, apart from the sandy foreground and the sea behind, there is nothing in her natural surroundings corresponding to the luxuriant vegetation of the later painting.

Lack, however, is the product of hindsight. If we consider the earlier sketch, not looking back from the later painting on canvas, but looking forward—proleptically—we can see it preparing the way not for one composition but for a series of compositions. The basic structure of a human figure, the right arm bent at the elbow to support an object, applies to five of the eight large vertical paintings (figs. 10, 11, 13, 14, and 17). In two cases the object supported by the right hand is a basket (figs. 10 and 14), while baskets also appear in two more of the eight paintings (figs. 12 and 16). If we look for a match for the color of the skin of the Negro woman in the earlier sketch (fig. 9), it is not the black of the Negro woman in the Copenhagen oil painting (fig. 10) but the lighter coloring of the Brazilian Indian subjects (figs. 16 and 17). As for the bent position of the right leg of the Negro woman in the earlier sketch (fig. 9), we find this not in the later portrait of the Negro woman (fig. 10) but in the portrait of a 'Tapuya' woman (fig. 16).

In short, the earlier sketch of the Negro woman seems to contain the germs of a number of the later paintings, and not just those with Negro subjects. It is broken down by the artist into separate elements that are subsequently combined in different configurations. This implies a high degree of indeterminacy, a relatively unspecific form which becomes increasingly specific through the addition of further detail (the jewelry, the child, the vegetation, the basket and hat, etc.). Like the *Confusio Babylonica* discussed at the end of the previous chapter, these paintings conform to the exotic genre, to a stage in which clear-cut distinctions have not yet emerged.

From Exotic Genre to Ethnographic Portrait

Let us look more closely at the way in which the transition from indeterminacy to specificity takes place. First, what Whitehead and Boeseman identify as a sugar loaf seems a curious attribute for the woman to be holding. What is it? After close examination of the oil sketch in Cracow in June 1997, I suggest that we should refer to it as an indeterminate object—there simply are not enough clues to identify it, whether this was the artist's intention or not. He felt that the woman must be holding something, and in the later oil painting we can see that it has become a basket, but there is no need to project this degree of specificity back onto the earlier sketch.

The basket in the large oil painting in Copenhagen (fig. 10) loosely resembles a basket from the mouth of the Congo which was once in the collection of Ole Worm and is now in the Nationalmuseet in Copenhagen (Dam-Mikkelsen and Lundbæk 1980, 50; Gundestrup 1991, 2:143). As for the hat in the same painting, decorated with shells and peacock feathers, it is apparently "of an oriental type which Dutch merchants had brought from Asia to their allies in the Sohio kingdom at the mouth of the Congo" (42). There is something incongruous about the combination of this elegant item of headgear with a woman who may be supposed to be of slave status.[9] The artist seems to have done the same in the case of the male counterpart of the Negro woman. The large sword with a sheath of polished ray skin that can be seen in the painting of the Negro man in the Nationalmuseet in Copenhagen (fig. 11) has a very close match among the ethnographic objects in the same museum (Dam-Mikkelsen and Lundbæk 1980, 56; Gundestrup 1991, 2:100), but such a ceremonial weapon would have been worn by important dignitaries, not by the near-naked man in the large oil painting.

As Whitehead and Boeseman suggest, it seems likely that Eckhout added these objects brought over from Africa (1989, 75). Since the objects themselves are ethnographically identifiable, their addition to the human support introduces ethnographic distinctiveness to the composition as a whole. By virtue of the increased degree of specificity, the indeterminacy of the exotic genre gives way to the verisimilitude of the "ethnographic portrait." The culmination of this process is the application of an ethnographic label, like the (misleading) title "Tapuyarum mulier" that is applied to the earlier oil sketch in the *Libri Picturati*.[10]

A contemporary of Eckhout, Zacharias Wagener (1614–68), who started out as a common soldier for the Dutch West India Company in Brazil in 1634 and later became quartermaster to Johan Maurits, also produced representations of Brazilian wildlife and people, though not in oils but in watercolors. The version of the Negro man in his *Thier Buch* is clearly based on Eckhout's portrait of the same man (fig. 11), but Wagener added a long oval shield which is similar but not identical to a shield in the Copenhagen Nationalmuseet (Dam-Mikkelsen and Lundbæk 1980, 59; Exh. Cat. Schleswig 1997, 2:337). As Jones suggests, this would also appear to be an object imported from West Africa (1990a, 105). In other words, Wagener is applying the same technique as Eckhout in the construction of an ethnographic "portrait" on the basis of ethnographic artifacts.

The technique of combining more or less accurate renderings of exotic clothing and artifacts with more fanciful depictions of the human figures who are wearing or carrying them goes back to the earliest images of Native Americans. As we saw in the previous chapter, two drawings of people presumably meant to be Brazilian Tupinamba, attributed to Hans Burgkmair and dated to the second decade of the sixteenth century, which were in Sir Hans Sloane's collection of Americana, contain detailed renderings of identifiable Brazilian and Aztec artifacts, but the physiognomy of the human figures themselves is negroid. Dürer's marginal illustration of a Brazilian Indian in Emperor Maximilian's *Book of Hours,* dated 1515, betrays a familiarity with Brazilian weapons combined with an ignorance of their users (Massing 1991b, 515–16). The notion of ethnographic convention as defined by means of costume and adornment followed by the art historian Bernard Smith in his study of European images of the Pacific (1992, 80) is thus too narrow: the Dürer and Burgkmair figures can hardly be classified as ethnographic portraits given the lack of contact with and information about the actual human beings depicted.

The reality effect that the observer undergoes when confronted by representations of this kind is brought about by the realistic rendering of authentic exotic artifacts, whose authenticity is then (unjustifiably) assumed to extend to the representation as a whole. Incidentally, this is not a technique that is confined to visual representations, for analysis of the early textual record on alleged anthropophagy in America leads to a similar conclusion: descriptions of the practice of cannibalism are embedded in accurate accounts of the everyday lives of Native Americans in Brazil and the Caribbean written by eyewitnesses, and the veracity of the other, accurate details is then (unjustifiably) projected to include the accounts of cannibalism as well (Menninger 1996, 128; cf. eadem 1995).

Bassani and Tedeschi (1990) have drawn attention to a collection of drawings from the Carte di Castello, comprising eighty-two items, which is now in the Biblioteca Laurenziana in Florence. They identify four of these drawings as the work of an anonymous Dutch artist from around the middle of the seventeenth century and suggest the addition of a further two watercolors (now in Dresden) to the corpus. The drawings in question are all figural representations of Hottentots, portrayed either singly or, in one case, combined in a dance.[11] Despite the uncertainties surrounding the authorship and date of these drawings, Bassani and Tedeschi show that they had a profound influence on the image of the Hottentot in the seventeenth and eighteenth centuries. The exotic artifacts in the drawings prove to be accurate depictions of authentic Hottentot articles, which presumably came under the eyes of the Dutch artist among the flood of objects from distant lands, especially the Dutch East Indies, which reached the Dutch port through the mediation of the East India Company. In other words, there is no need to assume that the artist actually went there in order to explain the ethnographic accuracy of the African objects that he portrayed. The human figures themselves, however, appear to be based on the conventional images of exotic peoples to be found in costume books of the late sixteenth century and after. In short, the artist seems to have created an image of Africans which combines conventional depictions of exotic human figures with a high degree of authenticity in the portrayal of exotic objects, despite the fact that there is no evidence for his having "been there."[12]

The same practice has been documented in the case of Rembrandt. Rembrandt was a collector of curiosities in his own right (Scheller 1969), and he also could draw on his large collection of exotic objects (horns, shells, weapons, Oriental porcelain, bird of paradise, etc.) as a basis for his paintings and drawings. It is thus noteworthy that a sword similar to that of the Negro man in Eckhout's portrait can be found in Rembrandt's painting of *St. Paul in Meditation* (now in the Germanisches Nationalmuseum, Nürnberg) from around 1630 (Whitehead and Boeseman 1989, 74).

A similar case is presented by a watercolor by or after the English artist John White,[13] which is generally taken to depict a fight between Martin Frobisher and Eskimos on Baffin Island in 1577. The details of this scene have been taken to be so realistic that Hulton has argued: "it would have been impossible for anyone to reconstruct this Arctic scene with its Eskimo clothing, tents and kayaks in such convincing detail if he had not himself witnessed it and recorded it on the spot" (1984, 8). He even suggests that this display of White's abilities may have helped him to secure the position as artist on the 1585 expedition to Virginia. This is pure speculation. We cannot be certain that White drew the original, and there is no independent evidence that White ever went to the far North with Frobisher. Moreover, it is hazardous to base hypotheses on the alleged ethnographic accuracy of the watercolor, for the accurate details of most of the artifacts, especially the kayak, could have been derived from observations of the Eskimo captives who were on display in England in 1576 and 1577 (Sturtevant and Quinn 1987, 108; cf. Rowlands 1994, 249–50). The presence of native artifacts in a representation is in itself no evidence that the artist had ever visited the spot.

To move on to the eighteenth century, the realism of an engraving of the death of Captain Cook by Bartolozzi (after an oil painting by John Webber)[14] is certainly in no small measure due to the accurate depiction of the Hawaiian cloak made of the feathers of various birds. The cape worn by Cook's assailant was copied from the specimen in Webber's own collection (Joppien and Smith 1988, 127).[15] All the same, realism in the depiction of an artifact does not necessarily make the composition as a whole an accurate historical record. Rather than following Sahlins (1985, 130), who draws far-reaching conclusions about the identity of Cook's assailant on the assumption that the man who killed Cook is exactly represented in this engraving, we should consider both Webber's painting and Bartolozzi's engraving, both of which were made after the voyage, in the context of the European mythologization of Cook (cf. Smith 1979, 1992; Obeyesekere 1992; Howe 1995) rather than as eyewitness documents of the fateful events of 14 February 1779.

The use of realistic details to suggest the authenticity of a painting as a whole can be documented down into the nineteenth century.[16] During a trip to the American West as part of the Lander survey in 1859, Albert Bierstadt took photographs, completed sketches, and collected Indian clothing and artifacts. The objects did more than testify to his status as eyewitness; in drawing on them for representations of Indian life, Bierstadt successfully turned the status of his paintings from aesthetic objects into sources of documentary information. The "truth" of the parts led viewers to believe in the "truth" of the whole (Anderson 1992, 8–12).

"Being There"

If we consider the reception of Eckhout's paintings, especially in the twentieth century, the emphasis has been on the fact that, since he had "been there," his "ethnographic portraits" must be taken at face value as ethnographic *portraits*. In the case of exotic portraits, scholarly discussions have tended to divide their subject matter up in terms of an opposition between realistic portrayal and imaginative fantasy or the constraints of artistic tradition. Couched in terms of the problem of authenticity, the procedure followed in these discussions is usually as follows. First the identifiable exotic artifacts in the representation are compared with the material record as contained in present-day ethnographic museums. Second, the manner of portrayal of the human figure(s) is set within what is supposed to be the appropriate historical context. Finally, reference is generally made to the almost overpowering effects of artistic tradition in conditioning perception—an admissible datum in itself, of course—to draw the conclusion that the work in question reveals a limited assimilation of the new to the old, of the exotic to the familiar. Those concerned with the use of visual representations as ethnographic sources are thus expected to pare off the artistic accretions in order to arrive at the "authentic" ethnographic record.[17]

Eckhout's paintings have thus tended to be seen as authentic ethnographic records rather than as works of art. "No one would claim that Eckhout is a great artist" is the verdict of Peter Whitehead (1985, 134). His paintings have always attracted interest and admiration for their ethnographic accuracy rather than any intrinsic artistic worth. Alexander von Humboldt admired their descriptive quality, and William Sturtevant called them "the first convincing European paintings of Indian physiognomy and body build" (1976, 419), a view which was received favorably by another expert in the field of American iconography, Hugh Honour (1979, 295; cf. idem 1975, 83).[18] Commenting on the Copenhagen paintings, Joppien asserts: "All eight portraits are of immense ethnographic interest, not only for representing natives at a period from which very few records are known, but also because they allow for detailed examination of artifacts, their construction and function" (1979a, 303). He lavishes similar praise on Eckhout's representations of Africans: "The importance of Eckhout's sketches of African people, to which we have to add a number of oil sketches of slaves,[19] can hardly be overrated. There is no other material of the time which can compare with it in accuracy and animation. Little known, it would be rewarding if all the representations of African people by Eckhout were placed together and given the ethnographic discussion which they deserve" (1979a, 307).

Whitehead (1985) argues for the priority of Eckhout as a New World portraitist, demarcating his work sharply from the "idealized types" of his predecessors, who did little more than to produce a vision of how a European might look if he painted his body, adorned himself with beads, and stuck feathers in his hair. This view is echoed by Jacobs, who singles out the painting of the 'Tapuya' dance in particular as "not only the earliest painting of native people in a ceremonial act, but also perhaps the first western work of art to capture the movements and postures of such people without resort to classical prototype" (1995, 113). As we have seen, the Copenhagen paintings are one remove from Eckhout's own preliminary sketches, on which Whitehead and Boeseman have the following to say: "Eckhout's ten pencil sketches of Tapuyas stand as the first life studies of Amerindians, whether in North or South America, or at least the first that we know of, the first attempt by a competent European artist actually to record what he saw, virtually unsullied by European precepts of pose, body proportions or physiognomy" (1989, 203). As for the relationship between the sketches and the paintings, the same authors state that the paintings "did not greatly distort the honesty of the first-hand observation" (ibid.). The tone is the same in Whitehead's verdict on an anonymous painting of Greenlanders in the same Copenhagen museum, which "should be placed, together with the John White drawings and the Albert Eckhout paintings, in the very highest ethnohistorical category by those explaining the original people of the New World" (1987, 155).

Incidentally, Eckhout was not the first artist to produce full-length figure representations of exotic people in European art. The credit for this must go to the whole-length figure drawings made by John White, whose watercolors of Algonquin Indians apparently followed sketches made in the 1580s, a good half century before the Eckhout paintings (Hulton 1984). Of course, the tradition of graphic representations of the peoples of the New World goes back much further. Gonzalo Fernández de Oviedo y Valdés had already turned to visual illustration when faced with his inability to describe what he saw in words. Of the four woodcut illustrations in his *Sumario de la natural y general historia de las Indias* (1526), two were of an ethnographic nature; of the twenty-eight woodcuts in his *Primera parte de la Historia general y natural de las Indias* (1535), eight are concerned with the various customs and practices of the natives of Hispaniola, Central America, Peru, and Patagonia. Moreover, there are indications that he produced many more illustrations which did not find their way into his printed works (Pardo Tomás 1998b). The originality of his drawings is certain; indeed, no previous models are known for any of them (Sturtevant 1976, 424). Mention should also be made of the drawings by Jacques Le Moyne de Morgues made in 1564–65, some of which were apparently copied by John White (Hulton 1984, 8–9), although only a single Le Moyne original is extant—a miniature portrait of the son of a Timucuan chief (Hulton 1978, 198)—and even the attribution of this painting to Le Moyne has been questioned (Feest 1988). All the same, Eckhout was the first to make full-length paintings (Joppien 1979a, 302 n. 37).

The enthusiasm for the ethnohistorical accuracy of the Eckhout paintings is occasionally heightened by contrasting them with other work. For instance, Honour (1975, 83) contrasts them with the conventional figures in

Bonaventura Peeters's scenes of imaginary America painted in the late 1640s, and Kopplin (1987, 318) contrasts the objectivity and lack of pathos or romanticism in the Eckhout portraits with the bizarre exoticism of the work of a contemporary who knew Eckhout's work, Jan van Kessel (1626–79).

If we take this alleged ethnohistorical accuracy of the Eckhout paintings seriously, we are bound to ask who and what is being portrayed, particularly as far as the portraits of Amerindians are concerned. This question was tackled by Ehrenreich in an article published a century ago, in which his examination of the pictorial, literary, and linguistic evidence led him to conclude that "The portraits left us by Maurits van Nassau are the oldest artistic representations of a wild people. The Tapuya were a Gê tribe, were known as Tarairyou or Otschucayona, and were probably related to the Patasho or Koropo, although they were by no means identical with them" (1894, 90).

Whether these are in fact the oldest representations is a debatable issue. Ehrenreich, after all, was not familiar with the collections of drawings and sketches from Eckhout's hand when he made this assessment. But to concentrate on the problems of ethnographic classification, we can first ask who the Tarairyou are to whom Ehrenreich refers. In his article on the Tarairiu in the *Handbook of South American Indians,* Lowie explains that the Tarairiu are only one among a group of "Tapuya," so we have to turn our attention to the 'Tapuya' (1963b).

Today doubt has been thrown on the identification of the 'Tapuya' with the Gê (Maybury-Lewis 1965). The 'Tapuya' tend to be identified with the modern Canela or Krahó as a people of hunters and gatherers who are noted for their swiftness of foot (Hemming 1984). The word *Tapuya* itself is a Tupi term, which is supposed to mean "Westerners" or "enemies," according to Martius. It is thus not a self-ascription, but a label attached by one group (the Tupi) to refer to those who are definitely beyond the pale in their (Tupi) eyes. That is to say, *Tapuya* means simply "non-Tupi." Consistently with this, the 'Tapuya' are denied any form of agriculture, which may simply be a reflection of the fact that they cultivated other plants than the manioc on which the Tupi depended. The allegation that they slept on the ground and not in hammocks is another feature which is not borne out by the early sources. In short, the profile of the 'Tapuya' is little more than a negative image of the Tupi: they are what the Tupi are not. It is therefore doubtful whether it makes any sense to look for a unified 'Tapuya' ethnos at all. As Lowie sums up: "It seems hopeless to assign a definite linguistic meaning to the term 'Tapuya' . . . ethnographically, there is hardly more warrant for considering all Tapuya in one category" (1963a). In other words, there is no

'Tapuya' culture. The term has no place in scientific usage, it should only be written between single quotation marks, and its use should be confined to citations from writers of previous centuries.[20] We are thus not dealing with self-ascriptions, but with a Tupi term that has been incorporated into European nomenclature and subsequently imposed on non-European regions in accordance with European preoccupations.

Initially, the first European observers of the New World do not know into which categories the native population as a whole is to be fitted, and both textual and iconographic representations waver between the positive and negative possibilities: noble savage or inhuman barbarian. Gradually the distinction is transported within the body of the Amerindian peoples themselves, as the "binary surface" of the self/other distinction reveals elements of a tripartite classification whose three constituents are self, relatively civilized other, and totally uncivilized other (Mason 1994, 152–53). In the case of Montaigne's well-known essay "Des cannibales," for instance, Rawson (1994) has suggested that behind the dominant opposition between "civilized" Tupinamba and "barbaric" French lies a tripartite division in which the Amerindians are further subdivided into virtuous and depraved cannibals.

Civilized and *uncivilized,* of course, are loaded terms which reflect the vision of the colonizers. *Civilized* means for them docile and amenable to European domination; *uncivilized* means putting up a spirited resistance to this colonial endeavor. In the Caribbean area, the people labeled *Arawaks* are those who are prepared to accept the Spaniards, while the people labeled *Caribs* are those who defend their own territory and way of life (Hulme 1986, 72; 1994, 165ff.). The anthropological nomenclature is thus a work of Realpolitik; it does not necessarily correspond to linguistic, cultural, ethnic, or other categories. In the Brazilian situation, the same principle is at work in the application of the term *Tapuya.* While Marc Lescarbot, part of whose work was translated into English as propaganda for the Virginia Company of London in 1609, had already singled out the tribes of Brazil as being beyond hope of civilization (Pennington 1978, 185), a comparison of Eckhout's portraits of Tupi Indians (figs. 12–13) with those depicting 'Tapuya' (figs. 16–17) shows that the humanity of the latter is stunted or incomplete. The contrast is between wildness and savagery on the one hand and a cultivated habitat and elementary civility on the other. The series of Eckhout's paintings can thus be seen as showing the different grades of civility, ranging from the 'Tapuya' via the Tupi and Blacks to the mulattoes and mestizos.[21] The message behind the paintings would then be: "These are our Tupi, blacks, mulattoes and mestizos, recruits to civility who show some promise; and those are the Tapuyas, our irredeemable, infernal allies" (Van den Boogaart 1979, 538).[22] In this way it becomes possible to compare the "message" of the paintings with the actual problems faced by the employees of the Dutch West India Company in their dealings with the Brazilian Indians, as Van den Boogaart has shown in detail (1979).

Portrayal and Betrayal

Representations of nature can only be called true or accurate within a particular context agreed upon by the creator and the receiver (Ackerman 1991, 203 n. 5), and such a context inevitably changes over time. We have seen how Eckhout and his contemporaries could make use of exotic artifacts to construct their representations of exotic peoples. We have also seen that, at least in the case of the 'Tapuya', it is problematic to regard the paintings as portraits of an ethnos if no such ethnos exists. After all, the lack of existence of a 'Tapuya' culture as such entails the lack of a *presence* which the Eckhout paintings might be supposed to *represent.* In both respects, what is called into question is the alleged transparency of the portraits. In a discussion of this phenomenon in relation to representations of Renaissance women, Simons writes (1995, 264–65):

> Portraits can be enunciations of cultural display rather than of private subjectivities; they can be readable as ideological apparatuses rather than as aesthetic units reporting referential truth; as a medium of exchange between art and society, object and viewer, sitter and artist, patron and artist, sitter and spectators . . . , in a rich conversation of overlaid, even competing and conflicting voices, rather than as singular objects with one universalized and static, authoritative interpreter.

Though she concentrates on portraits connected with a courtly setting, the same refusal to take portraits as passive reflectors of simple, preexisting appearances should be applied to the ethnographic portrait. This stress on the rhetoric and politics of various forms of representations, which characterizes much recent work in the humanities and social sciences as well, involves a shift from a stress on the documentary value of these representations to one on how they articulate cultural values.[23] In visual terms, we might speak of a related shift from portrayal to betrayal: it is not what representations purport to represent which is the focus of attention, but what the eye as a performing agent constructs. The visual images we confront are not just portrayals; they betray the activity of the eye and the gaze in the construction of worlds which, however their problematic relation to "reality" is to be thematized, are by definition "imaginary" worlds. In the case of the exotic portrait, it is not the relation of the representation to what is represented which is at issue; instead, the aim is to show how various elements, irrespective of their relation to empirical artifacts, are combined in the work of producing the exotic portrait.

An approach of this kind means that we can bracket the problem of a possible fit between the Eckhout paintings and some Brazilian Indian tribe and turn our attention to the forms of representation which are articulated by the paintings. In the rest of this chapter, they will be considered in relation to the conventions of natural historical illustration, the typical landscape, the coexistence of realistic and moralizing forms of representation, and the special filter exercised by gender.

Natural historical illustration has always been marked by a tension between the urge to approximate the perception of a momentary visual experience, on the one hand, and the need for a didactic image to conform to a recognizable type and not to an individual specimen, on the other hand. Thus, although Dürer's famous nature study *Large Piece of Turf* depicts a living complex of organisms in their natural beauty, Pliny had already stressed that it is not enough for each plant to be painted at one period only of its life because plants alter their appearance with the fourfold changes of the year (*Historia Naturalis* 25:4). Credit is usually given to Hans Weiditz for "the first botanical studies of the Renaissance that can hold a claim to being properly scientific in their concern for unmediated descriptive accuracy and completeness" (Landau and Parshall 1994, 252). On the other hand, the woodcuts in Leonhart Fuchs's *De historia stirpium commentarii insignes* (Basel, 1542) include a plant depicted as flowering and fruiting simultaneously, more than one species of a plant springing from a single root, and the presence of both sexes on a single plant, the *Canabis sativa* (Landau and Parshall 1994, 255; cf. Swan 1995). In other words, conceptual or taxonomic concerns could sometimes prevail over the intense observation of individual phenomena under precise lighting conditions and in a specific environment—what Renaissance artists called *accidentals* (Ackerman 1991, 191).

This is what we find in the natural historical setting to Eckhout's portrait of the Tupi man (fig. 13).[24] The plant depicted on the right is a manioc, but Eckhout has added some trimmed stems (implying that the root has not yet been removed from the ground). In the foreground on the right, a large manioc root can be seen, cut in two to provide a view of both the outside and the inside.

The painting thus depicts three stages in the cultivation of manioc. A still life in the Nationalmuseet in Copenhagen, also attributed to Eckhout (Dam-Mikkelsen and Lundbæk 1980, 37; Gundestrup 1991, 2:134), depicts the same three stages as well as a fourth: a calabash containing manioc flour refers to the final stage in the preparation of manioc. This is documentary painting, with science prevailing over art.

The same resolve to represent diverse stages or aspects of Brazilian botany can be seen at work in a number of the large Copenhagen paintings.[25] The painting of the Tupi woman (fig. 12) follows a similar pattern to that of her male counterpart; next to the banana tree on the right is the stump of a felled tree. In the painting of the 'Tapuya' woman (fig. 16), we see a native *Cassis grandis* tree on the right and in the right foreground a long seedpod that has been cut to reveal the cross-section, like the manioc in the painting of the Tupi man (fig. 13). In the case of the mestizo man (fig. 15), the papaya on the left bears both male and female flowers and fruits. Like Leonhart Fuchs's draftsmen, Eckhout seems to be producing a composite to illustrate the flowers and fruit of both the male and the female trees. As for the mestizo's female counterpart (fig. 14), the castor oil plant on her left is depicted in two different stages to indicate the formation of the seeds.

Examination of the botanical details in the Eckhout paintings, then, confirms the conclusion that has already been drawn from consideration of the human figures: these paintings are portraits in which the intellect prevails over the eye, furnishing what the eye could not take in at any one moment. The attempt to describe, to make a true *conterfeit* (Parshall 1993), marks the Eckhout paintings as bearers of visual facts rather than as direct records of observation at any point in time.

It is not just the botanical setting that is congruous with the representations of human figures, but the ecological setting as a whole. For some who described the New World in the sixteenth century in word or image, the study of natural history included the study of human beings as part of their natural environment (Mason 1998b). For instance, a late-sixteenth-century manuscript now in the Pierpont Morgan Library in New York, which contains almost two hundred watercolor drawings by at least two different artists of not only American fauna and flora but also Native Americans, is entitled *L'histoire naturelle des Indes* (1996). As we have seen, earlier in the same century Gonzalo Fernández de Oviedo y Valdés decided to compensate his inability to describe the indescribable in words by including woodcuts of ethnographic subjects as well as of animals and plants in his *Sumario de la natural y general istoria de las Indias* (Toledo, 1526). At a much later date, recognition of the implicit connection between a species and its habitat implied the need to place plants, animals, and "primitive" peoples in an appropriate environmental setting. The *typical landscape,* as it has come to be known, is a genre whose emergence has been connected with the voyages in the South Seas during the second half of the eighteenth century. It was given particular stimulus in the practice and writings of William Hodges, who served under Captain Cook aboard the *Endeavour,* and received its theoretical underpinning in the writings of Alexander von Humboldt (Smith 1988, 4).

The choice of environment was sometimes dictated by aesthetic rather than ecological considerations: for example, in the botanical illustrations by various hands to Robert Thornton's *Temple of Flora* (1799–1807), the illustrated plants were set against backgrounds which, rather than being connected with the ecological locale of the species depicted, assisted in conveying the "spirit" or "personality" of the blooms (Kemp 1996, 218; Kemp 1998). Nevertheless, what mattered was the appropriateness of the background to the illustration, no matter whether this appropriateness was based on artistic or scientific criteria. A special kind of typical landscape which developed in the first half of the nineteenth century was the prehistoric landscape, setting creatures from "deep time" within an appropriate natural setting (Rudwick 1992). With the development of the natural sciences, this endeavor to present a coherent whole was extended to the geologic formation, atmospheric conditions, and climate. The implications of the emergence of such a genre for ethnographic illustration are well illustrated in the work of Charles Alexandre Lesueur, an artist who accompanied Nicolas Baudin on his voyage to the South Pacific from 1800 to 1804. In Lesueur's work, landscape was used to convey certain facts about the construction of native canoes and their form of navigation. He drew native dwellings amid typical vegetation to reveal the form of their construction. He added a native group together with a heap of shells in the foreground to indicate their diet (Smith 1988, 199). The result was a typical landscape in which the level of development of a society could be 'read off' from its cultural artifacts and from the natural environment which conditioned them.

The period discussed by Smith is roughly that between 1750 and 1850, when he considers the typical landscape to have achieved its most complete expression. However, in a note he admits the existence of important predecessors in seventeenth-century topographical and ideal traditions in landscape (Smith 1988, 199 n. 21), and in a later publication he regards Post's Brazilian landscapes as an anticipation of the typical landscapes of the nineteenth century (Smith 1992, 20). As we saw in the previous chapter, the landscape as a genre does not emerge in European art before the sixteenth century, but already at that time we can detect the germs of one of the elements of the typical landscape: the search for variety in landscape corresponding to the wide variety of human activities which can take place in it. Nor is this concern limited to painters alone, for Golson (1969) has noted the relevance in this respect of printmakers from the School of Fontainebleau such as Etienne Delaune, who prepared the way for the seventeenth-century idyllic and heroic landscapes.

Chronologically, then, there is no need to rule out the possibility that Eckhout's Brazilian paintings might in some respects betray features of the typical landscape. For instance, when the pink oyster shell decorating the sword of Eckhout's Negro man reappears among the collection of shells scattered at his feet, does this not imply a high level of integration between the human figure and his natural surroundings?

In his discussion of the influence of the Pacific voyages on artistic conventions, Smith formulates the issue in terms of a tension between neoclassical theories of art, with their stress on the unity of mood and expression,[26] on the one hand, and the tendency of analytical and empirical observation to disrupt such a unity, forcing the artist to look at the world as a mass of isolated, though interconnected, entities. Was Eckhout's choice primarily dictated by what he saw, or were his principles of selection guided by the desire to produce a harmonious whole in which the isolated elements corresponded with one another to produce a typical landscape?

At this point it is essential to introduce a second, related notion, which has been the subject of controversy among historians of seventeenth-century Dutch art for decades: the debate on *disguised symbolism.* Starting with Panofsky's suggestion that everyday objects in some late medieval religious works might have a specific symbolic meaning, the presence of such symbolism was soon detected in sixteenth- and seventeenth-century Dutch still lifes, genre painting, and portraits, although the combination of an analytic interest in detail with an allegorical framework in the work of Ulisse Aldrovandi and in paintings by some his sixteenth-century contemporaries (Olmi 1992, 110) shows that this was not an exclusively Dutch phenomenon. Naturally enough, it was also extended to landscape painting on the grounds that, if moralizing symbolism was a feature of the other types of seventeenth-century art already mentioned, it was only logical to expect to find it in landscape painting as well (Bruyn 1987). Hence, the landscape could be seen to lend itself for moralizing Christian messages, particularly the notion of life in this world as a pilgrim's progress through a world full of temptation. Sometimes the message conveyed was more prosaic: elements in the landscape, such as cows, might symbolize the well-being of a thriving agricultural economy (Exh. Cat. Dordrecht/Leeuwarden 1988). Cheese might carry the same message; or it might evoke rotting, disease, and death (Bruyn 1996). In short, moral lessons might lie behind seemingly naturalistic, or naturalizing, scenes.

Paradoxically, though, the concern of Northern humanism to infiltrate classical and Christian wisdoms into the business of daily life depended on the artist's skill in depicting everyday reality. As Schama notes, "It is this delicate tension between necessary means and required ends that makes the judgement of motivation in genre painting so difficult" (1987, 413). Not just landscape and genre painting, but still lifes too could operate in the same way. Thus, Georg Hoefnagel, who was court painter to Rudolph II, used highly naturalistic portrayals of flowers and butterflies to convey moral messages about the soul's emergence from the body (Ritterbush 1985, 151; Hendrix 1997). In a way, the debate on the admissibility of this kind of symbolic interpretation recalls a hoary anthropological controversy, which we might paraphrase: Are still lifes good to think with or good to consume?

Ashworth has argued that the single most important factor in determining late Renaissance attitudes toward the natural world is the "emblematic world view," the essence of which is "the belief that every kind of thing in the cosmos has myriad hidden meanings and that knowledge consists of an attempt to comprehend as many of these as possible" (1990, 312). Ashworth takes this emblematic world view to extend down to the middle of the seventeenth century. Although he claims that New World natural histories lacked this emblematic significance because they introduced new fauna and flora which had no known similitudes (1990, 318), it is legitimate to wonder whether the carefully depicted flora and fauna to be found in the Copenhagen Brazilian paintings are necessarily devoid of emblematic significance. Despite the novelty of the New World, right from the start persistent attempts were made to assimilate the new to the old. In this process, there is no reason why some of these animals could not have been endowed with some of the animal semantics associated with Old World fauna in the emblematic literature.

The iconological approach is open to criticism on a number of counts. For example, the texts on which Bruyn's interpretations of landscape imagery are based are far fewer than the books of emblems on which the interpretation of still lifes drew. Moreover, almost half a century ago Gilbert had argued that "pure" landscape, an apparently subjectless production, existed in the sixteenth and seventeenth centuries (Gilbert 1952).[27] This is not the place to go into these controversies in any detail,[28] but an awareness of the existence of this controversy among art historians might help to make us aware of the possibility that the naturalistic effect produced by the Eckhout paintings need not necessarily exclude a possible symbolic interpretation.[29] If the realism of Eckhout is not dispassionately observed and secularized naturalism, what are the moral connotations of his paintings?

We can start by comparing the portrait of a 'Tapuya' woman (fig. 16) with the portrait of a Tupi woman (fig. 12). The Tupi woman is clad in a short white skirt; the 'Tapuya' woman is naked, except for an arrangement of leaves covering her pubic area. This opposition between nakedness and some degree of dress is already an indication of different degrees of civility. Indeed, one of the sixteenth-century travelers to Brazil, André Thevet, had regarded the possibility of teaching the Indians to dress in a European style as the possibility of their improvement to the Christian values of the Old World (Pellegrin 1987, 512). In the moral code conveyed by dress, its elaboration or its absence, then, the Tupi woman is assigned a position on a higher rung than her 'Tapuya' counterpart.

To turn from what they wear to what they carry, the Tupi woman carries a child on her arm, from which there also hangs a gourd, while the other arm supports an ornamental basket on her head. The 'Tapuya' woman carries a different load; the basket on her back suspended from a band over her head contains a severed human foot, while in her right hand she holds a severed hand by the wrist. The contrast between the two figures is further accentuated by the landscapes in the background. While the Tupi woman stands in front of an orderly plantation, the 'Tapuya' woman finds herself in a wild, uncultivated landscape. Furthermore, the armed Indians on the skyline behind her seem intended to relate to warfare and the dismembered limbs that she bears, contrasting with the scene of agricultural prosperity and peace in the Tupi background. The allegorical use of landscape as a form of *paysage moralisé* (cf. Panofsky 1962, 64) points up the opposition: the relatively civilized (i.e., westernized) Tupi versus the wild and savage 'Tapuya'.

If we look at the male counterparts, a similar opposition emerges. The 'Tapuya' man (fig. 17) is naked, while the Tupi man (fig. 13) wears wide-legged shorts. The 'Tapuya' man is armed with four spears, a spear-thrower, and a club,[30] whereas the Tupi man has a bow and five arrows and carries a wooden-handled metal European knife tucked into his waistband. The 'Tapuya' man is adorned with facial ornaments, a feather headdress, and sandals, which create a more primitive appearance than the unadorned, European-looking body of the Tupi man.

The opposition is not just a binary one between civilized and uncivilized, for the other paintings in the series—the portrait of a mameluc, a light-skinned woman wearing a long white robe and carrying a bowl of flowers (fig. 14), and the portrait of a Negro woman and child (fig. 10)—introduce the possibility of other gradations. As we have seen, the Negro woman also carries a basket laden with fruit and is dressed in a short skirt, with a Dutch clay pipe tucked into the sash, a hat, and a pearl necklace. The existence of the half-blood creates a triad of relations: the 'Tapuya' are wilder than the Tupi, who are in turn less civilized than the mestizos. And the criteria for measuring this wildness are precisely their distance from the invisible European eye which perceives them (cf. Harbsmeier 1994a, 195f.).

Thus far, we have left the horizontal painting (fig. 18) out of account. It shows a group of eight 'Tapuya' warriors arranged in a circle, stamping the ground and brandishing their spears and clubs, while two women watch from the side. There was much in this painting for European observers to disapprove of. Dancing was frowned upon by Calvinists and others in the Netherlands in the seventeenth century, despite the precedents provided by the Greeks and the Biblical examples of Miriam and David. The nudity of the two women on the edge of the painting carried a similar negative connotation, recalling the nudity of the familiar representations of witches by artists like Hans Baldung Grien and Dürer. At any rate, Zacharias Wagener had no difficulty in attributing devil worship to the 'Tapuya'. The two women on the right appear to be pinching their nostrils; ethnographic parallels suggest that this represents an attempt to protect dangerous forces from gaining entry into their bodies.[31] Consonant with the negative connotations of the 'Tapuya' dance is the animal depicted in the right-hand corner, the armadillo. One of the most well-known representations of this creature was in the allegory of America by Marten de Vos dating from the last decade of the sixteenth century, where the female personification of America is supported on a gigantic armadillo, whose grim aspect has been enhanced by the addition of a pair of devilish horns.[32] Indeed, another of the Netherlanders in Brazil, Willem Pies, records that the armadillo was used by Brazilian witches for its magicomedicinal properties (Baumunk 1982, 194). Another of the fauna in the Eckhout paintings is heavily laden with moral connotations. Whatever relation the boa constrictor in the portrait of the 'Tapuya' man (fig. 17) may bear to real-life Brazilian serpents, Eckhout must have realized that the placing of a serpent in an uncultivated and primitive landscape was bound to have biblical implications in addition to its exotic connotations. It was as if Columbus's vision of having reached the terrestrial paradise had come true.[33]

Besides this tradition of European representations of witchcraft and devil worship, there is another contextual chain into which the paintings can be inserted. The period from the 1580s onward saw the appearance of a spate of publications in the Netherlands relating to the "primitive" ancestors of the Dutch, the Batavians (Schöffer 1975). This interest in Nordic ancestors was not confined to printed sources, for it is also implied by the series of pictures commissioned from Dutch artists by Christian IV of Denmark in 1637 to display the heroic achievements of his ancestors in Kronborg Castle. The forty-five drawings which have survived are based on various Dutch works of cultural history, ethnography, topography, and geography (Schepelern and Houkjær 1988). Not only is the project more or less synchronous with the plan of Johan Maurits to commission the Eckhout paintings for the great hall in Vrijburg, the fact that the paintings are now in Copenhagen is itself a reflection of the close ties between Johan Maurits and his cousin, Frederick III, to whom the Eckhout paintings were given in 1654. It is therefore plausible to suggest that elements of a "Batavian" iconography may well have been at the back of Eckhout's mind as he set to work to portray the native peoples of Brazil.[34]

The Eckhout paintings thus seem to combine exoticism and primitivism in linking the Indians of Brazil with marginal groups on the European continent. What these groups have in common is that they *are* what Europe is *not*. To be more precise, they are a negative self-definition of the European ruling class (Vandenbroeck 1987). The close juxtaposition of animals and humans in the Eckhout paintings may also imply some kind of mental bracketing in which the colonial I is separated off from the exotic, animal-like, primitive Other.[35] Certainly, the juxtaposition functions in this way within the genre of the typical landscape: one can 'read off' the nature of the people depicted from the nature of the plants and animals with which they are associated, and vice versa.

Thus far, we have treated the representations of men and women in the same way, as if the same message could be 'read off' from either sex. However, there may be a particularly strong connection between the typical landscape and *female* principles. Bewell (1994) has argued that, when English explorers entered the Pacific during the eighteenth century, they sought to establish a social correlation between Pacific women and Pacific landscapes, observations which were inevitably structured by their own attitudes toward English society and women. In other words, from the eye of the male observer and agent, both land and women bore the imprint of his cultural activity. As we have seen, there are grounds for dating the emergence of the typical landscape earlier than the eighteenth century. Do we find a social correlation between Brazilian landscapes and Native American women in Eckhout's Brazilian paintings?

It is therefore necessary to examine the articulation of gender *within* each of the human pairs in the Eckhout portraits to determine in what ways 'Tapuya' femininity is articulated with 'Tapuya' masculinity, Tupi femininity with Tupi masculinity, and so on. Of the four portraits of females, two include a child. To take the Negro woman first (fig. 10), we can note that her erotic power is explicitly accentuated. Her frontal gaze offers her to the eye of the beholder. The firm, bared breasts and the short skirt convey an erotic invitation that is confirmed rather than denied by the presence of the half-blood child, who presumably serves as a reminder of the past sexual activities of his mother. Iconographically, the maize cob carried in the child's right hand points literally toward the woman's vagina in an unmistakably phallic gesture. This has its match in the image of the Negro woman's adult male counterpart (fig. 11), on which Whitehead and Boeseman comment: "the phallic appearance of the date palm trunk and the virility of the negro's pose seem exactly to compliment [*sic*] each other, much as the character of the mameluc woman is set off by the objects in the background" (1989, 74). The bird perched on the boy's left hand (fig. 10), a red-faced lovebird (*Agapornis pullaria*), points to the use of the bird as a symbol of lasciviousness and lust in Dutch seventeenth-century genre representations (De Jongh 1995, 21–58; Exh. Cat. Amsterdam 1997, 85–89).[36] The tobacco pipe tucked into her red waistband,[37] too, is an allusion to sexual activity in Dutch genre painting (Schama 1987, 204–15).

The portrait of the mameluc woman, "this dusky Brazilian Flora" (Whitehead and Boeseman 1989, 73), represents a more Europeanized sensuality (fig. 14). Her body is fully clothed, with a hint of eroticism in the drawing up of the robe to reveal an ankle, in contrast to the brazen eroticism of the Negro woman. The mameluc has no disturbing features to break the flow of assimilation to European canons of female beauty. Unlike the Tupi and 'Tapuya', who are surrounded by wild animals, she is in the company of frivolous and harmless guinea pigs.[38] Her main attributes—the floral bowl and headband—could just as easily be found in European portraiture. Whether the only non-European feature of her attire—her jewelry—is from the East Indies or Ottoman Empire (Whitehead and Boeseman 1989, 73), it is at any rate not American.

The Tupi woman (fig. 12) is a mother, like the Negro mother, but her child is a girl. The woman herself wears a tunic; her ample breasts are bare, but the presence of the child at the breast deflects their erotic stimulus to replace it with a maternal one.[39] The round forms of the breasts are echoed in the round form of the gourd. By contrast, the phallic gesture in the Negro portrait is reflected in the vegetation too, which is strikingly phallic as well. In short, the aggressive sexuality of the Negro woman that invites the penetration of the male gaze is contrasted with the soft, maternal eroticism of the Tupi mother.

The male counterpart of the Tupi woman is also her complement (fig. 13). As the virile male, he bears the attributes of the hunter (bow, arrows, and [European] knife) and has facial hair, while the similarity between his dress and that of the Tupi woman also serves to identify their complementarity as a pair.

Finally—and crucially—we come to the 'Tapuya' woman (fig. 16). She is not frontal, but in the three-quarter pose that derives from the Cracow oil painting with which this chapter began. This involves a deflection of her gaze—she does not offer herself to the observer—and gives her added substantiality by stressing the third dimension. She has no child, but the amputated hand that she carries in her right hand has an unnaturally erect position in line with her genitals which gives her a phallic aspect, emphasized too by the upward-slanting direction of her "fig leaf." Moreover, she is in motion. Unlike the static frontal poses of the other women, her poised position suggests the movement befitting a goddess of the chase (the dog at her feet recalling the hounds that accompanied the classical huntress Diana)—in short, a classic representation of the phallic, castrating, aggressive female familiar from the psychoanalytic literature. And the alleged presence of Amazon-like women in Brazil, an inversion of European mores,[40] could be taken to imply that intervention by Europe was needed to restore the proper balance by turning everything the right way round.[41]

But it was not long before the Dutch world itself seemed to have been turned upside down, when the militia in The Hague delivered the De Witt brothers up to a mob that tore them limb from limb on the flagstones of the Buitenhof in August 1672. This situation was mirrored in language evocative of the Dutch colonial adventure in Brazil. Soon after the murder and dismemberment of the brothers Jan and Cornelis de Witt, a collection of verses by diverse hands compared the Dutch butchery to a "Tapuyan meat market." The poet "thought he was in Brazil, but found himself in The Hague."[42] In these verses, as in Albert Eckhout's Brazilian paintings, Dutch Brazil provides the terrain on which predominantly European preoccupations are played out.

European discourse could not get a hold on America before the opacity of the New World was broken. The New World had to learn to speak the same language and play the same game. Eckhout's Brazilian portraits belong to this historical juncture. In portraying the 'Tapuya' in resistance to European sexual mores, Eckhout conjured up a vision of what Europe could not tolerate, neither among its "inner Indians" (Mason 1987a) nor among its overseas contacts. The portrayal of the 'Tapuya' betrays the thrust of colonial desire, eager to reduce the Other to Self, bent on using its eye to extend the dissemination of its power. Hence, there can be no exotic without the prior desire to produce it. In other words, exoticization is predicated on (sexual) power.

4 PRESENTATIONS OF THE EXOTIC

> For what else is this collection but a disorder to which habit has accommodated itself to such an extent that it can appear as order?
>
> W. Benjamin, *Illuminations*

Few Europeans actually traveled to the New World during the sixteenth century, and even fewer returned to Europe to provide visual or textual information on what they had seen and experienced there. Moreover, from the first there were doubts about the very possibility of producing an adequate visual or textual representation of the New World (Mason 1990, ch. 1). The gap between the object and its representation was thought to be too wide.

There was an alternative for those who could not travel to the New World and who had insufficient faith in the veracity of representations. This was to bring America to Europe. If representations were not to be trusted, direct presentations might be seen to derive increased veracity from their visible and tangible connection with the New World. Fragmentary though they inevitably were, such partial glimpses of America, their legitimacy shored up by the presence of eyewitnesses who had been there to collect them, might be reassembled to form a recreation of the American continent by the totalization from part to whole that is generally known as *synecdoche*.[1] Each functioned as a *pars pro toto*. Freed from the representational constraint of having to stand for something else, they could simply be themselves: not *representations* of America, but *presentations* of the new continent, piece by piece.[2]

One of those who went to the New World and returned to Europe with Americana was André Thevet (1516–92), cosmographer to the last of the Valois French kings. Thevet accompanied Villegagnon on his voyage to Brazil in 1555 and spent exactly ten weeks (15 November 1555 to 31 January 1556) on American soil—or rather, above it, since he was soon taken ill and spent most of his time there in a hammock (Lestringant 1991a, 89). Despite the limitations imposed by the brevity of his stay and by his illness, Thevet's *Les Singularitez de la France Antarctique,* first published at the end of 1557, assured him of a place as an authority on the New World. Born of relatively humble origins, like the Huguenot potter Bernard Palissy, the surgeon Ambroise Paré, and other writers of his day, Thevet used his authority as an eyewitness to pit his version against the combined strength of the learned tradition.[3] The fact that he had actually visited America gave him, as *homme nouveau* and representative of a *savoir prolétaire*, a weapon with which to contest the sacrosanct position of the humanist scholars of his day (Lestringant 1991b).[4]

Besides returning with the authority of an author, however, Thevet brought back some actual objects. After describing the first Patagonians that Magellan had seen as dressed from head to foot in animal skins, he states that he himself had had two of their cloaks made of the same animal skins and of an indescribable color (Lestringant 1987b, 476), though they were too large for him. In the case of Thevet's two cloaks, there is no way in which we can verify his statement, since he notes that his possession of them was already a thing of the past. In the case of the Patagonian arrows, made with the use of bones and stones instead of metal, Thevet claims to have recovered some of those fired into the vessel of the French and to have taken them back to France with him (Lestringant 1987b, 482). Such objects could be used to win the favor of the monarch, like the maracas and various multicolored skins of birds brought from Brazil which reached Henri II through the intermediary of the royal geographer Nicolas de Nicolay, who was later to become a rival and personal enemy of Thevet (Thevet 1997, 209; Lestringant 1991a, 260), or the Patagonian bow and arrows which Thevet presented to "Anthoine Roy de Navarre." Thevet even seems to have offered the English king Edward VI a moonstone and his services (Lestringant 1990, 213; 1991a, 81). Besides ethnographica, Thevet also displayed an interest in natural curiosities. He was fascinated by the Brazilian toucan and brought back with him both a specimen of the bird itself and an item of headgear made from toucan feathers, which he presented to the king (Thevet 1997, 186).

Thevet's activities as a collector certainly preceded his Brazilian expedition, for during his trip to Egypt in the winter of 1551–52 he was given an ebony vase from India, purchased on the shore of the Red Sea, which had the power to counteract the effect of poison (Lestringant 1991a, 24). His Oriental journey also furnished him with a serpent's tongue or *glossopetra* from Malta (cf. Thevet 1985, 208), which he sent to the German naturalist Conrad Gessner and which earned him a mention in book IV of the latter's *Historiae Animalium* (Lestringant 1991a, 67). As Thevet was aware, the way to a wider audience lay in publication. The fossilized shark's tooth which he sent to Gessner reached a much wider audience through its inclusion in Gessner's natural history than the exotic artifact itself could ever have done within the extremely limited confines of Thevet's *cabinet de curiosités*.

Besides the evidence relating to these and other exotic objects—a crocodile hide, a rhinoceros horn, the feet of a mummy, Egyptian idols—which can be culled from Thevet's voluminous texts (Lestringant 1987b, 480; Pellegrin 1987, 517), there is one exotic artifact that certainly passed through

Thevet's hands and is still extant. This is the so-called *Codex Mendoza,* a work commissioned by Antonio de Mendoza, first viceroy of New Spain, to portray the history and culture of the natives of Mexico to his sovereign. This codex, which is now in the Bodleian Library in Oxford, came into Thevet's hands in the middle of the century and passed into Hakluyt's possession by 1587 at the latest (Mason 1997a).

The circumstances under which these various objects came into Thevet's possession are not always clear. Indeed, some of the Americana may have been acquired during his sedentary occupation as royal cosmographer rather than directly in America. At any rate, we do know that he was on cordial terms with some French collectors, such as Michel de l'Hospital (Lestringant 1990, 56 n. 44). Although he was himself in charge of a chamber of curiosities, he was extremely reluctant to admit visitors, with the exception of a few public figures like King Charles IX or the archbishop of Rouen (Lestringant 1987b, 480). In Thevet's case, then, his collection could not have had a direct effect on many people. Indirectly, however, through the way in which Thevet himself could draw on his collection for the descriptions of objects that appear in written and published works (for an example, see Lestringant 1990, 177), the collection did have an effect on a wider audience.[5]

Other writers of the time, like Ambroise Paré or Pierre Belon, bear witness to the taste of the sixteenth-century French monarchs for collections of exotic animals and plants (Schnapper 1988, 180–81).[6] The French navigator Jacques Cartier brought back weapons, clothing, and Indians to François I in the 1530s, and Jean Moquet, apothecary to Henri IV, crossed the Atlantic on several occasions to collect plants and rarities for the *cabinet de singularitez* at the Tuileries. The French royal collections entered a period of decline toward the end of the sixteenth century, but mention should also be made of collections among the nobility. In Montaigne's castle, for example, one could see the following American objects: "the form of their beds, their ropes, their swords and the wooden armbands with which they cover their wrists in combat, and the large canes, open at one end, which they use to beat out the rhythm of their dances" (Montaigne 1962, 206). As in the case of Thevet, Montaigne's collection of American artifacts may be presumed to have had less of an effect in the castle of Saint-Michel than through its dissemination in his essay "Des cannibales" (1580), from which the above citation is taken. As Ginzburg has stressed (1993, 140):

> Montaigne's astonishing readiness to understand the New World natives on their own terms was part of a larger fascination with the bizarre, the distant and the exotic, with novelties and curiosities, with works of art aping nature . . . and with populations that he regarded as especially close

to nature. In his essay on cannibals Montaigne unfolded what we may call the moral and intellectual implications of the *Wunderkammer.*

Presentation therefore rapidly yields to representation, and the form of that representation itself may be determined at least partly by the form of presentation. It is, therefore, to the form of presentation of exotic artifacts in Renaissance collections of curiosities that we now turn.

Collections of Curiosities

> The genealogical tree of the Croixmare family took up the whole back of the door. On the reverse panels the pastel of a lady in Louis XV costume matched the portrait of Bouvard père. The mirror's casing was decorated by a black felt sombrero, and a monstrous clog, still full of leaves, the remains of a bird's nest. Two coconuts (Pécuchet had had them since boyhood) stood on the mantelpiece, flanking an earthenware barrel with a peasant astride it. Nearby, in a straw basket, was a coin brought up by a duck. In front of the library stood a chest of drawers made of shells, with plush ornaments. Its lid supported a cat with a mouse in its jaws, a petrifaction from Saint-Allyre, a workbox also made from shells, and on this box a carafe of spirits contained a bon-chrétien pear.
>
> G. Flaubert, *Bouvard et Pécuchet*

The collection as such can be traced back for millennia (Pomian 1987, 15–19), but it is the sixteenth century in particular which witnesses the rise of the *Kunstkammern* or *Wunderkammern* in northern and southern Europe. Julius von Schlosser's classic 1908 study (1978) concentrated on the princely Austrian collections, especially that of Archduke Ferdinand in Schloss Ambras, Innsbruck.[7] Since then, studies have been devoted to collections in France (Pomian 1987; Schnapper 1988), the Iberian peninsula (Morán and Checa 1985; Vassalo e Silva 1992), Italy (Benedictis 1991; Olmi 1992; Findlen 1994), and the northern Netherlands (Bergvelt and Kistemaker 1992; Van Gelder 1993).[8] At various times, scholars have stressed the relevance of such collections to contemporary art practice. In the foreword to a catalog of the contents of Schloss Ambras published in 1977, Klauner attributes interest in them to a growing familiarity with abstract, nonfigurative art (Scheicher et al. 1977, 8). Less than a decade later, Morán and Checa suggested an affinity with postmodernism (1985), and an exhibition held in Bonn in 1994, *Wunderkammer des Abendlandes* (see Exh. Cat. Bonn 1994), implied parallels with the surrealists. Some of the curious juxtapositions found in the collections now have a strangely familiar look about them.

The objects which belonged to these collections were of various kinds. Besides works of art proper (classical or classicizing paintings and sculpture, ancient coins, gems, and inscriptions; cf. Schnapper 1994), they could include natural wonders such as eaglestones, coral, fossils, petrified objects, mandrakes, barnacle geese, birds of paradise, sharks' teeth, flying fish, mermaids, the horns of unicorns, chameleons, the bones of giants, and armadillos, as well as objects crafted by human hand, such as canoes, weapons, Egyptian mummies, feathered headdresses, musical instruments—to name but a few. Ordinary animals—the pelican, the crane, and the stork—were also to be found in some *Wunderkammern.* The singularity of these birds lay not in their provenance but in their emblematic significance: the pelican stood for parental devotion, the crane was emblematic of vigilance, and the stork stood for filial devotion (Ashworth 1991, 132).

Interest in wonders of this kind was nothing unusual during the sixteenth century. Dürer's enthusiastic reaction to the sight of the objects from Mexico which were on display in Brussels in 1520 has often been quoted (Honour 1975, 28):[9]

> I saw the things which have been brought to the King from the new golden land: a sun all of gold a whole fathom broad, and a moon all of silver of the same size, also two rooms full of the armour of the people there, and all manner of wondrous weapons of theirs, harness and darts, wonderful shields, strange clothing, bedspreads, and all kinds of wonderful objects of various uses, much more beautiful to behold than prodigies. These things were all so precious that they have been valued at one hundred thousand gold florins. All the days of my life I have seen nothing that has gladdened my heart so much as these things, for I saw amongst them wonderful works of art, and I marvelled at the subtle *ingenia* of men in foreign lands. Indeed, I cannot express all that I thought there.

Some of the appeal of these artifacts can be gauged from the fact that Dürer's most cherished possessions at the time were a large tortoiseshell, a buckler made of fish skin, a long pipe, a long shield, a shark's fin, and two little vases of preserves and capers (Panofsky 1971, 207; cf. Massing 1991a).

Many such objects had already decorated the interiors of churches in the Middle Ages (Schlosser 1978, 11–27; Lugli 1983, 12ff.).[10] Curiosities such as whale ribs or jawbones also came to adorn the facades of secular public buildings, such as town halls (Barthelmess 1989, 245 n. 10; Egmond and Mason 1997, 31). A principal courtyard of Whitehall Palace, designated Whalebone Court because of the display of whalebones there, was one of the sights of London (MacGregor 1989a, 413), and the large bones of a rhinoceros, a whale, and a mammoth were suspended above the portal of Wawel Cathedral in the Royal Castle in Cracow (Firlet 1996, 94–95). There is also evidence for an interest in curiosities on the part of private collectors toward the end of the Middle Ages. Schlosser had already stressed the importance of collectors like Jean Duc de Berry (1340–1416) in France (1978, 29–41). If the inventory of Doge Marin Falier of 1351 is not a forgery, it provides evidence for a *Wunderkammer*-like assortment in Venice during the fourteenth century (Brown 1996, 63–64). A similar collection was that possessed in Spain by Cardinal Mendoza at the end of the fifteenth century, which consisted of coins, antiquities, and *naturalia.* A *cédula* of Juan II from 1428 also bears witness to an interest in exotic objects, which were usually kept in *cámaras del tesoro* (Morán and Checa 1985, 31–32). The value attached to such curiosities at the time may strike the modern reader with amazement. In the famous auction held after the death of Lorenzo il Magnifico in 1492, the horn of a unicorn was valued at 6,000 florins, while a painting by Van Eyck did not fetch more than 30 florins (Schnapper 1988, 9). It is indicative of the same system of values that the representatives of Margaret of Austria in Italy during the first quarter of the sixteenth century had little to report on the work of the masters of Italian art, but they displayed a lively interest in the birth of monsters, a phenomenon which they believed to be rife in Italy (Duverger 1980, 127–28).

It is in the sixteenth century that the phenomenon of the private collection of curiosities really emerges, whether they were stored in cabinets (like the objects in Thevet's collection) or put on display for a (select) public. Schlosser posited the existence of a geographic distinction between the aristocratic collections of bizarre objects in northern Europe, on the one hand, and the scholarly collection of antiquities and objects for scientific purposes by the humanists of southern Europe, on the other (1978, 201). This distinction can no longer be regarded as valid, for there are many exceptions to such a geographic classification, and the same applies to the distinction he posits between aristocratic and humanist collections.[11] Given the emphasis on the plurality of possible contexts which runs throughout the present volume, the approach in this chapter is closer to that advocated by Kemp (1995), who argues that the role of these items is characterized by complex fluidity, ambiguity, and diversity of meaning which undermines any propensity to categorize them neatly within rigidly delimited parameters.

A number of studies have concentrated on the sociological aspects of the collections and their audience, revealing that the status of the collectors themselves could indeed range from monarchs and aristocrats to humanist scholars, but that it could also extend to doctors and apothecaries—many of the objects in their collections, such as the horn of a unicorn, were believed to have medicinal properties—or even to the relatively humble sixteenth-century Dutch beachcomber Adriaen Coenen (Egmond and Mason 1996; Egmond 1997). Similarly, the status of the visitors whom they admitted and the extent of the collection as a display of wealth have also been carefully documented. With the exception of Lugli (1983), however, few scholars have paid much attention to the nature of the collection itself, the principles—or lack of them—by which it was arranged, and in particular the role of Americana within such collections.

First, we note the effects of the removal of artifacts from cultural areas which were completely foreign to the cultural milieu of the collection itself. Drawing attention to the Mannerist fondness for fragment and quotation, Kirshenblatt-Gimblett has noted (1991, 388):

> Like the ruin, the ethnographic fragment is informed by a poetics of detachment. Detachment refers not only to the physical act of producing fragments, but also to the detached attitude that makes the fragmentation and its appreciation possible. Lovers of ruins in seventeenth- and eighteenth-century England understood the distinctive pleasure afforded by architectural fragments, once enough time had passed for a detached attitude to form. Antiquarian John Aubrey valued the ruin as much as he did the earlier intact structure . . . A history of the poetics of the fragment is yet to be written, for fragments are not simply a necessity of which we make a virtue, a vicissitude of history, or a response to limitations on our ability to bring the world indoors. We make fragments.[12]

Many collectors had to make do with fragments—the tooth of a shark, the penis of a whale, the saw of a sawfish, the horn of a unicorn, the beak of a toucan, the head of a walrus.[13] Sometimes they created fragments, as when they cut off the feet of birds of paradise to make them conform to the mythical descriptions of this bird, whose footlessness came to be emblematic of the eternal unrest of one who is footloose (Harms 1985). To go one stage further, they could combine different fragments from different creatures to come up with a new, composite creation. This is the origin of the so-called Jenny Haniver, in which the dried bodies of skates and rays, in particular, were combined to produce dragonlike curios (Exh. Cat. London 1990, 85–86). Adriaen Coenen was an old hand at the construction of these monsters, which hung in many a home of a well-to-do compatriot (Egmond and Mason 1995). Although in the same century Rondelet was sceptical and Aldrovandi was aware of how these monsters were made, monsters could still form the object of dispute as late as the nineteenth century—witness the controversy surrounding Barnum's exhibition of the Feejee Mermaid in Charleston, South Carolina, in 1843 (Greenberg 1990).

Another way of compensating for the fragmentary nature of the collection was to fall back on representation as a supplement to presentation. Although Rudolf II's collection of *naturalia* in Prague was vast, he commissioned artists to supplement it with images of what could not be contained within the imperial storerooms. The landscape artist Roelandt Savery was sent to Tyrol to search for rare wonders of nature, such as bizarre rock formations, rainbows, and alpine waterfalls, and bring them back to Prague in the form of drawings after nature (Spicer 1997). Savery may have been one of the artists who collaborated to produce the 179 folios of nature studies in Rudolf's collection, which thus combined both wondrous natural objects and a paper museum of drawings of the wonders of nature (Hendrix 1997).

Detachment implied a loss of cultural meaning for the object in question, but this loss was compensated by an emphasis on the material nature of the object itself. Hence, catalogs of collections lay great stress on the materials from which the objects are made, which sometimes served as a principle of classification, like the Plinian principles on which the arrangement of the collection of Archduke Ferdinand II at Schloss Ambras was based (Scheicher 1985). The use of precious metals or of unusual natural materials, such as ostrich eggs, asbestos, byssus, coral, horns, bones, and coconuts, was worth recording. Particularly striking were those objects which combined natural with artificial materials, such as bezoars mounted in gold or silver settings or nautilus shells or coconuts mounted on silver standards to be used as goblets.[14] Some of the best examples of such composite creations are the pictures executed on the polished surfaces of strongly veined stones, in which the veins form part of the composition. Such "images made by chance," which held a fascination for Piero di Cosimo, were often collected in *Kunst-* and *Wunderkammern* during the first half of the seventeenth century (Janson 1961).

Besides raising issues of the boundary between what is natural and what is artificial, attempts at the classification of many of the objects in the collections called into question the divisions between different realms of nature. The stone with an animal bone growing inside it owned by the Count of Benavente, don Rodrigo Alonso Pimentel, bordered on the line separating the animal from the mineral (Morán and Checa 1985, 26). Petrified plants and animals, including fossils, seemed to partake of both the animal or vegetable and the mineral world; a consensus on the origin of fossils, and with it a more or less clear dividing line between the organic and the inorganic, did not emerge until around 1700 (Thackray 1994, 123). These links in the Chain of Being could even extend to the human world, as can be seen from the case of the petrified child acquired by Frederick III of Denmark in 1654 (Schnapper 1988, 18). Coral, which featured prominently in many collections,[15] was variously classified as animal, vegetable, or mineral. As for the eaglestone, folklore associated it with eagle nests, thereby linking the animal and mineral worlds again. The mandrake seemed to be both human and vegetable, and the barnacle goose (Heron-Allen 1928; Egmond and Mason 1995) and the Tartary lamb straddled the boundary between plants and animals.[16] Shells were also difficult to classify, since the claim that some of them were decorated with the letters of some alphabet (Hebrew, Greek, etc.) raised the question of whether they were to be classified as natural or artificial.

The special attraction of these objects was based on the principle of contiguity. Because they had been contiguous to a highly charged exotic setting, these objects reestablished a tangible contact with a distant reality as parts of a larger whole. The objects from Montaigne's cabinet can be cited to illustrate this principle: the bamboo sticks used to beat out a rhythm on the ground during dances evoke the "savage dance" which was such a popular subject in depictions of the early contact between Europe and the non-European world (Joppien and Smith 1988, 35; cf. ch. 3, n. 11), while the Brazilian clubs evoke the man-to-man combat illustrated in the woodcuts accompanying Thevet's account of the French Antarctic (cf. Lestringant 1990, 142).

Exotic artifacts could thus serve to evoke an exotic culture by virtue of the principle of *pars pro toto:* the exotic culture was the whole of which they were the (fragmentary) parts. There were certain practical limitations imposed on the choice of objects for this purpose. Featherwork, for instance, was not very durable, so that most of the items of featherwork which reached Europe from America perished before gaining entry to a *Wunderkammer* (Feest 1985). The choice of fauna was dependent on the techniques of preservation, so that it was easier to introduce the armadillo to European cabinets because of the relatively uncomplicated techniques required to preserve it. In the case of many other animals and plants, however, even if they entered a collection intact,[17] they were not likely to stay that way for long. The catalog of Antonio Giganti's museum tellingly refers to a crocodile which is not quite complete, a porcupine with only two quills left, an almost completely mangy beaver skin, and threadbare fish and birds (Olmi 1993, 241).[18] Only fragments of them could be kept, which had the function of Mannerist "quotations" (cf. Olmi 1985).

In view of the ability of the artifact to evoke something bigger, a typically Mannerist play of the gigantic and the miniature came to form a regular feature of the *Kunstkammern* (cf. Stewart 1984). Characteristic of this is the interest attaching to giants and dwarfs, such as the playing cards for giants and dwarfs in Schloss Ambras (Scheicher 1985), the portrait of a giant and dwarf there (Lugli 1983, 113), or even the presentation of live giants and dwarfs in one of the centers in Amsterdam to which exotica gravitated in the late seventeenth century, the Blauw Jan tavern and its menagerie. The same interest in degrees of scale is witnessed by the examples of an egg-within an egg, the virtuoso examples of wood-turning consisting of a seemingly endless regression of polygons enclosed inside polygons, or the even more extreme cases in which an ostrich egg is used as the material in which to sculpt an ostrich, a rhinoceros horn is given the shape of a rhinoceros, or a whale is carved or painted on a piece of whalebone.[19] The "tautological" nature of these objects (Lugli 1983, 16) lies in the project of representing a rhinoceros by—a rhinoceros. An even more complex example is the coconut beaker (now in the Bayerisches Nationalmuseum in Munich) inscribed PERNAMBUCA and decorated with a view of Mauritsstad and Recife (Exh. Cat. The Hague 1979, 214; Fritz 1983, ill. 109b), thought to have been the work of a Dutch goldsmith whom Johan Maurits took with him to the Dutch colony in Brazil. In this case the colony there is condensed in a representation on a coconut, while the coconut itself is assumed to bear a relation of contiguity with Brazil; a representation of Brazil is carved on—a piece of Brazil.[20]

The individual objects in a collection evoked more than what they were themselves, conjuring up an elusive whole of which they were all parts. In addition, the collection itself could be organized according to a symbolic scheme which indicated its place within a wider setting. In this microcosmic form of representation, the collection is a scaled-down model of the world at large, and the mechanism of synecdoche is replaced by that of metaphor. Not all collections were of this kind; though Von Schlosser's characterization of Rudolf II's museum in Prague as Barnum-like (1978, 124) is less likely to find approval today, many collections did indeed consist of a disorderly presentation lacking any systematic purpose (Schnapper 1988, 11; cf. MacGregor 1996, 152–54). After all, the emphasis was on the selection of objects rather than on exhaustiveness, coinciding with a period in which science was more preoccupied with accidents than with laws (Ginzburg 1990, 96–125). The accumulation of exotic artifacts, an endless replication of the exotic Other, is a Tantalus-like attempt to encompass what cannot be encompassed. In this sense the *Wunderkammer* is the antithesis of the museum: the categorical will to knowledge of the latter is precisely what is absent in the former (Mullaney 1983, 40–43; cf. Herklotz 1994, 134). It is sometimes difficult to assess the extent to which a symbolic ordering can be detected because of the nature of our sources. For instance, the printed catalog of the collection of Lodovico Settala in Milan written by Lorenzo Legati displays a taste for the bizarre, while Settala's own manuscript notes contain condemnations of the more superstitious errors. Moreover, neither of these sources is in harmony with Fiori's engraving of the Settala collection, which should be seen as a stylized arrangement rather than a realistic description (Aimi, De Michele, and Morandotti 1985). Nevertheless, there certainly are cases of private collections which do appear to have had some kind of symbolic arrangement, such as the *studiolo* of Francesco I de' Medici (cf. Lugli 1983, 45; Olmi 1985) or the arrangement of the Mauritshuis in The Hague as a *domus cosmographica* (Lunsingh Scheurleer 1979). The Dutch, it has been suggested, were particularly prone to giving their collections a moralizing impulse (Lunsingh Scheurleer 1975, 1985). Aesthetic considerations seem to have affected the arrangement of Antonio Giganti's collection in Bologna, where the *theatrum naturae* was characterized by the principles of alternation and symmetry (Laurencich-Minelli 1985). Sometimes a *studiolo* could have a special iconographic program, such as the decoration of Leonello d'Este's *studiolo* outside Ferrara with a cosmic mythology of Apollo and the Muses. Piero de' Medici's *studiolo* was decorated with astrological signs, hours of the day, and so forth (Lugli 1983, 45).[21] The cycle of paintings of illustrious men and the elaborate trompe-l'oeil intarsia in the *studiolo* of Federico da Montefeltro in Urbino seem to have commemorated the major intellectual disciplines of the day, indicating Federico's combination of a life of action with a life of contemplation (Cheles 1991). Italian humanism influenced the *studiolo* in Spain as well, as can be seen from the example of that of the Duke of Calabria in Valencia (Morán and Checa 1985, 45).

It is in line with the symbolic potential of the collection as a whole that the individual objects could also have their own symbolic value. The public display of whale bones antedates their importance as economic products of the whaling industry; the whale bones, elephant's tusk, and crocodile which Thomas Münzer saw in Guadalupe in the late fifteenth century, for instance, were examples of what is marvelous, curious, and extraordinary, which could have an apotropaic function (Lugli 1983, 12; Morán and Checa 1985, 24–25). Certain fish, such as the sucker fish (or remora) and the electric ray (or torpedo) were also accredited with magical powers (Copenhaver 1991). The unicorn was associated with a rich mythology going back to Ktesias, which lent added luster to the presence of a unicorn's horn in a collection. For instance, its connection with moral purity (it could be tamed by nestling its head in a virgin's lap) may help to explain the presence of a "unicorn" horn almost one and a half meters long in the *studiolo* of Isabella d'Este, where the program of paintings by Mantegna and others was also focused on the triumph of virtue over vice (Franchini et al. 1979, 115–21; Exh. Cat. Vienna 1994, 372). Giants' teeth or giants' bones carried heavy symbolic connotations in relation to theories of the flood and human origins. In a letter of 1586 in which he describes the collection of the apothecary Filippo Costa in Mantova, the physician Giovanni Battista Cavallara wrote that the "denti di giganti" it contained must be from some large marine creature;

although giants have been reported in Brazil, he continues, the teeth in Costa's collection would require an owner two or three times the size of an average human being in the sixteenth century. And now that all the parts of the world are known, he concludes, it is impossible to affirm that giants still exist.[22] Within contemporary theories of human origins, credence in American giants was tantamount to placing the inhabitants of the American continent in the distant past. Moreover, if huge bones were actually found on the American continent, they could be taken as added proof of the existence of gigantic humans because of the impossibility that such relics might simply be elephant bones or tusks, given that elephants were not to be found in the New World (Schnapper 1986, 1988, 103; Pregliasco 1992, 108ff.; Bolens-Duvernay 1991, 1995; Mason 1990, 105–10).

The collection underwent changes over time, and we should be wary of projecting data from the (better documented) seventeenth-century collections onto those of the previous century. One change is the tendency for inscriptions on stone to supplant coins as a source of information on antiquity, which can already be traced in the seventeenth century and which gets under way in the second half of the eighteenth (Pomian 1987, 118; Schnapper 1988, 164–65). Another indication of a change in taste can be seen in the tendency to organize specialized collections and to separate curiosities from works of art.[23] Spanish examples of mixed collections are the collection of paintings and curiosities by Juan Hurtado de Mendoza, who died in 1624, and the (rejected) plan presented to Felipe II by Juan Páez de Castro for a room to contain scientific and natural objects as well as a portrait gallery with Cortés, Columbus, and Magellan "with the discovery and objects of the New World" (Morán and Checa 1985, 95–97, 184). In Italy, the seventeenth-century collection of Cassiano dal Pozzo and his younger brother Carlo Antonio in Rome contained originals and copies of paintings, statues, scientific instruments, and natural curiosities;[24] although some parts of the collection seem to have been arranged along systematic lines, others betray a greater degree of heterogeneity (Sparti 1989, 1992).

On the other hand, the history of the reorganization of the Habsburg art gallery in Vienna during the eighteenth century demonstrates a desire to introduce distinctions. The original Schwarze Cabinet contained natural curiosities such as coral, a shell, and the horn of a unicorn, but the plans for a reorganization of the picture gallery in the Stallburg during the last decennia of the century envisaged a renovation of the Schwarze Cabinet and a relegation of the curiosities to a different location (Meijers 1995, 21, 63). Although some scholars regard the systematic nature of the *Encyclopédie* as marking the end of the encyclopedic collection (Lugli 1983, 118), Meijers

(1993b) has pointed out the emergence of a new type of encyclopedic collection in the eighteenth century. There was no linear development from the chamber of curiosities to the picture gallery.

Americana in European Collections

It has been estimated that, of the thousands of American artifacts carried to Europe before the eighteenth century, fewer than three hundred have survived to the present (Feest 1993). Moreover, there are numerous problems of interpretation in the attempt to match existing objects in museums with early catalogs and other sources. For example, in attempting to connect some of the ethnographic objects now located in museums with the name of André Thevet, Métraux (1932) tentatively suggested that a Tupinamba club now in the collection of the Musée de l'Homme in Paris might be the one given Thevet by Quoniambec and might therefore derive from Thevet's collection of curiosities. However, the artifact in question does not bear any indication that it ever belonged to Thevet (Lestringant 1990, 140 n. 30). There are similar Brazilian clubs in other European collections; Feest (1985) records ten which have survived in modern museum collections. The same applies to Métraux's suggestion that a Brazilian cloak of feathers in Paris might go back to the cloak which Thevet gave to Bertrandi, the future cardinal, who in turn presented it to Henri II. Despite its resemblance to Thevet's account of such a cloak, there are no grounds for assuming it to be the same object.[25]

The attempts to attribute certain surviving artifacts to the collecting activities of Thevet can be seen as illustrations of the general principle of collecting that items connected with memorable persons have enhanced interest. A well-known example is "Powhatan's Mantle," now in the Ashmolean Museum in Oxford, which is unlikely to have been a garment at all and cannot be connected with Powhatan.[26] Feest draws a similarly pessimistic conclusion from his examination of the Mexican treasures in Vienna: "The combined histories of these pieces afford an illuminating illustration of the trade and exchange between collections in 16th century Europe, rather than evidence for a direct transfer of 'Moctezuma's presents' to Austria along Habsburg family lines" (1990, 32). With the possible exception of two items,[27] Feest considers it impossible to trace any of the items in the 1519 shipment of Motecuhzoma's gifts in any European collection after 1530 (1990, 47).

In considering lists of the American artifacts which found their way to European *Wunderkammern*, it is important to bear in mind that both the choice of objects to represent America in the collections and the constraints imposed by their mode of presentation there were to affect European attitudes toward the artifacts themselves and—more importantly—toward the

New World. Besides a limited number of items of featherwork, there are shields, masks, inlaid skulls, knife handles, mirrors, stone figurines and pendants, spear-throwers, pottery, codices, belts, necklaces, wooden bowls, bows, clubs, axes, musical instruments, combs, hammocks, pipes, and ceremonial batons (Feest 1985, 1995a, 1995b). Schlosser's pioneering study contains only scant references to Americana: the featherwork shield and headdresses now in the Vienna Ethnological Museum, which are all recorded in the 1596 inventory of Schloss Ambras (Schlosser 1978, 88; Vandenbroeck 1992, 103–4), and the weapons of "Indian" origin in the sixteenth cabinet of Ferdinand's collection (Schlosser 1978, 108–9). However, more recent studies enable us to document the diffusion of Americana through Europe in more detail.

Naturally enough, there was a lively interest in Americana in the Iberian peninsula from the first, as can be seen from their inclusion among the gold jewels and other items sent by Isabel to Maria of Portugal in 1504 (Morán and Checa 1985, 34). In Spain, Carlos V's collection in Simancas included "a gold and silver casket with an Indian couple carrying a halberd, a golden cane 'displaying the wheat of the Indies,' two shoes of the Indians of Peru, a green cotton crown with coloured feathers, an Indian flag, necklaces, multi-coloured feathers, precious stones, Indian jewels and a section comprising 'Indian swords,' including an enormous quantity of green stones set in gold" (Morán and Checa 1985, 51). In the later half of the century, the collecting of exotic objects was discouraged, since the Holy Inquisition regarded native artifacts as diabolically infested (Feest 1984, 86). Nevertheless, Amerindian themes continued to appear in Spanish tapestries and jewelry. Felipe II, whose collection in El Escorial included an American armadillo, commissioned a vast work on the natural history of America from Francisco Hernández,[28] and Nicolás Monardes, who had a botanical garden and collection of curiosities in Sevilla, drew on the objects at his disposal in writing works on the medicinal properties of American flora (Morán and Checa 1985, 149).[29] Moreover, Spain occupied an important position as an entrepôt for American items on their way further afield. For instance, in 1575 Elisabeth de Valois, Queen of Felipe II of Spain, was requested to send exotic objects for the *Kunstkammer* of Albrecht V in Munich, which contained a large number of Mexican antiquities (Seelig 1985, 85; cf. Heikamp and Anders 1970). Spanish interest in Native American artifacts subsequently dwindled until the late eighteenth century, when, in the wake of the voyages of Cook and others, Mexican antiquities and early Plains Indian material came into Spanish possession (Feest 1984, 90).

It is difficult to trace Americana (or Africana, for that matter) in French royal collections before the middle of the eighteenth century. After the dispersal of Thevet's cabinet, the French monarchs of the seventeenth century displayed little interest in exotica (Schnapper 1988, 108), although North American canoes were a feature of many collections in France and elsewhere.[30] As for Switzerland, we can note that Felix Platter, who was studying in Montpellier, took great pains to send an American cactus to his father in Basel in 1554; America features primarily in the texts of Felix Platter in terms of its fauna and flora (Le Roy Ladurie 1995, 305, 309).

In England the development of collections lagged behind that of continental Europe, and although curiosities and rarities were present in the royal collections of the early Stuarts, they seem to have had little effect (MacGregor 1989a, 418). The main North American material found its way to the collections of the Royal Society and the private collections of the Tradescants and Ralph Thoresby (1658–1725).[31] Though there is no evidence that John Tradescant the elder ever visited the New World, his son made three visits, in 1637, 1642, and 1654 (Allen 1964, 162; Leith-Ross 1984, 101ff.). The catalog of the *Musaeum Tradescantianum* contains many entries of American treasures, sent or brought back to the Tradescant home, aptly named the Ark, in South Lambeth, although it is not certain exactly which items were introduced as a result of the voyages and which derived from third parties.[32] Besides numerous botanical items,[33] the catalog includes the beaks and feathers of various Brazilian birds, some whole Virginian bitterns and hummingbirds, specimens of the sloth, a Virginian wild cat, various armadillos, various Brazilian fish, insects and reptiles, "the Indian lip-stone which they wear in the lip," "Indian morris-bells of shells and fruits," "Indian musicall instruments," "Indian Idol made of Feathers, in the shape of a Dog," "Indian fiddle," "Instruments which the Indians sound at Sun-rising," "A Canow and Picture of an Indian with his Bow and Dart, taken 10 leagues at Sea," "A bundle of Tobacco," "Indian Conjurors rattle, wherewith he calls up Spirits," various weapons, Virginian coats made of feathers, bear or raccoon skins, Amazonian and other Indian "Crownes," shoes from Peru and Canada, "Black Indian girdles made of Wampam peck, the best sort," "Variety of Chains, made of the teeth of Serpents and wilde beasts, which the Indians weare," Indian utensils and furniture, an "Indian dish made of excellent red earth, with a Nest of Snakes in the bottome," tobacco pipes, and the "Knife wherewith Hudson was killed in the North-West passage, or Hudson's Bay."[34] When the Ashmolean Museum in Oxford opened in 1683, a substantial part of the collection was that of the Tradescants.[35]

The relatively small number of contributions available at first engendered particularly intense rivalry among British collectors of Americana. The London-based collector John Woodward had a collection of objects from all over the world, which he used to prove the universality of the biblical flood.

Woodward is mercilessly mocked in John Gay's *Three Hours after Marriage* (1717), where Woodward appears as Fossile. When Fossile discovers the true character of the woman he has just married, he exclaims, "Whom has thou married, poor Fossile? Couldst thou not divert thyself still with the Spoils of Quarries and Coal-pits, thy Serpents and thy Salamanders, but thou must have a living Monster too!" (I.142–45). More generally, Gay parodies such collections of eccentricities as a whole in another passage in this play (II.274–79):

> FOSSILE. Do you know of any Hermaphrodites, monstrous Twins, Antidiluvian Shells, Bones, and Vegetables?
> PLOTWELL. Vat tink you of an Antidiluvian knife, Spoon and Fork, with the Mark of Tubal Cain in Hebrew, dug out of de Mine of Babylon?

Yet, despite the insinuations that Woodward had become a living anachronism, he could depend on a wide network of like-minded individuals to supply him with objects from abroad, including North America. For instance, in 1697 he received a large cargo from America which included shells, bones, and teeth of fishes (Levine 1977, 98 n. 25). Woodward's Americana were drawn from Barbados, Jamaica, Newfoundland, Carolina, Virginia, Maryland, Guatemala, Brazil, and Peru (Price 1989, 91).

Woodward's great rival, both within the Royal Society and as a collector, was Sir Hans Sloane (De Beer 1953; MacGregor 1994, 1995), whose *Voyage to the Islands of Madera, Barbados . . . and Jamaica with the Natural History of the last of these Islands,* based on the fifteen months that Sloane spent in Jamaica from December 1687 to March 1689 as personal physician to the Second Duke of Albemarle, was the first monograph on the natural history of an island in the New World.[36] Sloane always maintained an interest in expeditions across the Atlantic, and the extant items from Sloane's Latin American and West Indian collections include a Mesoamerican painted gourd, a Central American ax, a Mesoamerican pot and penis sheath, as well as a Mesoamerican (Toltec?) stone head and three Peruvian pottery vessels (King 1985, 1994). In addition, Sloane possessed drawings of Dutch Brazil by Frans Post, drawings of the plant and insect life of Surinam by Maria Sibylla Merian, and copies of John White's drawings not only of Virginian birds, beasts, and reptiles but also of ethnographic scenes covering Brazilian and Inuit subjects, as well as Carolina Algonquians (Rowlands 1994).

In the Netherlands, America was also well represented in the collection of Bernardus Paludanus (1550–1633) in Enkhuizen, enriched by objects brought back from the East by his fellow townsman Jan Huygen van Linschoten. Part of Paludanus's collection was purchased in 1651 by the Duke of Gottorp for his collection in Schleswig (Schepelern 1985), where the librarian Adam

Olearius showed a particular interest in natural and ethnographic curiosities (Drees 1997). It is likely that some of the American artifacts now in the ethnographic collection of the Nationalmuseet in Copenhagen derive from the collection of Paludanus, such as a leather and mother-of-pearl loincloth (probably from the southeast of North America, cf. Exh. Cat. Schleswig 1997, II, item 209), a South American bone flute, and a Brazilian club (Dam-Mikkelsen and Lundbæk 1980, 20–36).[37] Nor should the Dutch collections in Leiden be forgotten, where the exotic animals included a snake from Surinam with Arabic letters on its back (Schupbach 1985).[38] Collections of Americana in the Netherlands were enriched after the return of Johan Maurits van Nassau from Brazil in 1644; besides the princely collection itself, the collections of lesser figures such as the astronomer, cartographer, and zoologist George Markgraf, a member of Maurits's Brazilian retinue, also included their share of Braziliana (Whitehead 1979, 432). A good picture of the role of Americana in the later collections in the northern Netherlands can be gained from the account of the travels to Holland, Belgium, France, and England by the German philosopher, theologian, and jurist Christian Knorr von Rosenroth in 1663 (Fuchs and Breen 1916). Knorr von Rosenroth gives a detailed description (in Latin) of the contents of twelve collections in Amsterdam, where he saw the following Americana: a sloth, a club "used by the Americans before they discovered iron," an American belt, various armadillos,[39] American iguanas with and without beards, an American wind instrument made of bone, West Indian spiders, a parrot from Greenland, gum from Guyana, American cacao, American duck, American laurel, a Virginian autumn hyacinth, and a Peruvian balsam tree "with the scent of sweet Asia."[40] Even the collection of Chinese objects of the amateur sinologist Royer (1737–1807) in The Hague included an American club, a West Indian bow, and Mexican featherwork (Van Campen 1995, 19).

Italy was a source of inspiration for many collectors in northern Europe during the sixteenth and early seventeenth centuries. The wealthy Reynst brothers in Amsterdam, whose collection of curiosities included an urn with the ashes of Aristotle (!), the horns of a gemsbok, lamps, fishes, shells, Egyptian figurines, and *petrefacta,* were also the proud possessors of the largest collection of Italian paintings, antiquities, and *naturalia* in the Netherlands in the middle of the seventeenth century (probably purchased en masse from Andrea Vendramin in Venice) (Logan 1979, 98). The presence of featherwork capes in Florence can be documented as early as 1539 (Feest 1985), and the collections of Ulisse Aldrovandi, Ferdinando Cospi, and Antonio Giganti in Bologna also had their share of Americana (Heikamp 1976; Laurencich-Minelli 1982, 1985; Shelton 1994, 200). Aldrovandi's museum includes an Amazonian ceremonial anchor ax, two Aztec knives, and two feathered headdresses given him by Giganti, as well as a picture made of feathers and a mask decorated with mosaics. The most notable item of Americana in the collection of Ferdinando Cospi (1609–86), who was born four years after the death of Aldrovandi, is the precolonial Mixtec screenfold that he acquired in 1665 (Laurencich-Minelli 1992). Out of doors, botanical gardens like that of the physician Marcello Donati in Mantova contained plants from America, and his fellow townsman Filippo Costa had American resins, plants, fruit, and beans which were used for medicinal purposes (Franchini et al. 1979, 41–62).

Italian collectors were well aware of the important role that visual documentation could play in recording nature. In Bologna, Ulisse Aldrovandi commissioned illustrations of items in other people's collections, such as the American items in Tomasso de' Cavalieri's collection in Rome, and had them copied for his own natural historical compilations (Olmi 1992, 238). Crucial figures in this respect are artists like the Mantovan painter Teodoro Ghisi (1536–1601). As a court painter, Ghisi had access to the ducal collections for his paintings of birds and animals, while his own collecting activities included the beak of a toucan from Brazil (Franchini et al. 1979, 24–27, 228; Olmi 1992, 245).[41] In the early seventeenth century, the collector Cassiano dal Pozzo played a key role in the project of the Accademia del Lincei to publish a *Tesoro Messicano,* containing a wealth of material on the fauna and flora of the Americas (Freedberg 1993).[42]

This brief survey indicates that the geographic distribution of Americana throughout the collections of Europe was by no means confined to certain countries. Moreover, it should be borne in mind that many of the collectors belonged to international networks of like-minded individuals, so that national boundaries and affiliations were constantly overstepped. As we saw in the previous chapter, dynastic and other ties facilitated the transfer of Americana (and of images of Americana)[43] among the Netherlands, Germany, and Denmark. The renowned Danish physician Thomas Bartholinus, who studied extensively abroad, including a period in Leiden, made use of a network which included the Dutch chronicler of the New Indies Johannes de Laet. It was through the offices of the latter that Bartholinus was able to attend the dissection of a *homo marinus* found off the coast of Brazil by merchants of the Dutch West Indian Company and taken to Leiden for dissection by Pieter Pauw.[44] The incredulous could examine the skeletal hand and rib of this "siren" in Bartholinus's own collection; readers of his work could make do with an illustration (Bartholinus 1654, 171; reproduced in Egmond and Mason 1997, 130). Bartholinus's network also included the Italian Cassiano dal Pozzo, who also had a *homo marinus* in his collection and who advised the Dane on the medicinal properties of merman's rib

(Schnapper 1988, 64). Cassiano dal Pozzo, in turn, was a member of a network that included Peter Paul Rubens in the Spanish Netherlands, Nicolas-Claude Fabri de Peiresc in France, and members of the circle associated with Cardinal Francesco Barberini in Rome and Padua (Jaffé 1989). Such networks were already in existence during the sixteenth century. The intense scientific ties between scholars in Italy and Germany during that century can be documented from the letters addressed to the German physician Joachim Camerarius by the Italian naturalists Ulisse Aldrovandi, Francesco Calzolari, Giuseppe Casabona, and Ferrante Imperato (Olmi 1991; cf. Findlen 1994, 129–32). At a more humble level, it is also possible to trace the network into which the Dutch beachcomber Adriaen Coenen managed to insert himself (Egmond 1997). The career of the miniature painter Daniel Fröschl is indicative of the international nature of such contacts: born in Augsburg, he worked in the 1590s as an illustrator at the Botanical Garden in Pisa and at the court of Ferdinand I de' Medici in Florence. His work came to the attention of Aldrovandi, who published Fröschl's illustration of a cardinal in his *Ornithologia* (1600). Fröschl visited Prague in 1601, was appointed imperial miniature painter in 1604, and became keeper of Rudolf II's *Kunstkammer* in 1607 (Hendrix 1997, 163).

Though the relatively even distribution from country to country imposed few constraints of a geographic nature—and the international circulation of images (said to have been made) *ad vivum* also played an important part in this exchange of spectacular information (Swan 1995)—there were certain limitations on the display of the items, which in turn affected their mode of presentation. The most striking such limitation is the fact that admittance to view such a collection was, by and large, the privilege of the wealthy or the noble (Findlen 1994, 132–46), although the introduction of an admission fee in certain cases lowered the threshold to those who could afford to pay, irrespective of rank or class. In an episode in Defoe's *Moll Flanders* (1989, 105), after marrying a *nouveau riche,* Moll and her new spouse "have a mind to look like Quality for a Week" and decide to visit Oxford in a coach and six, pretending to be nobility. Their stay includes talks with the Fellows of the colleges, and they also visit the rarities there, which is presumably a reference to the collection in the Ashmolean Museum. Despite the fictionality of the episode (Defoe could have visited the museum, which opened in 1683, but such a visit was an anachronism in the case of Moll Flanders), it hints at the connection between being seen in a collection of curiosities and the hope that this would enhance one's status.[45] Von Uffenbach, on the other hand, who visited the Ashmolean Museum in 1710, recorded his shock at the admission of "all sorts of country-folk" to the museum, as well as to the Bodleian Library (Findlen 1994, 147–48).

The system of social manners affected not only the choice of the public admitted, but also the mode of presentation of the artifacts in which that public might be expected to take an interest. In the case of Montaigne's collection of Braziliana, the inclusion of musical instruments and weapons is faithful to the aristocratic tradition which saw combat and music as the privileged activities of the upper classes (Schnapper 1988, 111), and the appreciation of the warrior-like qualities of the Brazilian Indians at the end of "Des cannibales" implies that the native peoples of the New World are the last representatives of values which were already declining in Montaigne's Europe.[46] Not surprisingly, that courtier of four kings André Thevet shared Montaigne's inability to conceive of any other image of royalty than the traditional construction in which the king is above all commander-in-chief of the armies. Thevet's portrait of Quoniambec, a Tamoio chief, as king of Brazil therefore meant that his feather diadem could be seen as a crown, his ornaments and jewelry as tokens of a royal costume, and the lodge or *maloca* as a palace (Lestringant 1987a). Although it transports us to a later era, the same aristocratic filter on Americana is betrayed in Gibbon's recollections of an ancestor who had spent a year in Virginia. His passion for heraldry found satisfaction in the decoration of the bark shields and naked bodies of the native Indians in what he took to be the colors and symbols of his favorite science (Kiernan 1989, 89).

In collecting and presenting exotic artifacts from distant lands, the European collectors were undoubtedly guided by the ingrained habits of their own sense of taste and aesthetics. Exotic objects could, therefore, come to function within aristocratic contexts which were very different from their original setting. Thus, Pagden writes that "Such items as the greenstone Aztec mask which one of the Medici had set with rubies and mounted in a gilded copper frame is wholly incommensurate with its original purpose, function or value, as either cultural symbol or object of exchange" (1993, 33).

As we saw in chapter 2 (n. 18), Archduke Ferdinand II included some feathers from one of the pre-Columbian feather headdresses inherited from his father in the helmet that he wore on the occasion of his second marriage (Scheicher 1985, 34). Another case of the quasi-heraldic use of Americana in an aristocratic context may be detected in the pattern of ostrich feathers on the mantle and hat of a portrait of Lady Elizabeth Pope, painted to celebrate her marriage to Sir William Pope in 1615.[47] Since Elizabeth was the only child of Sir Thomas Watson, one of the largest investors in the Virginia Company, the feathered pattern—as well as the bracelet of pearls and coral—might be an allusion to the riches of America, as well as a tacit allusion to the analogy between England's possession of the New World and Sir William's possession of his wife (Chirelstein 1990).

Another aristocratic figure whose Americana were interwoven with the fabric of courtly life was the humanist prince Johan Maurits von Nassau-Siegen, governor of the Dutch colony in Brazil from 1637 to 1644. The residence of Vrijburg that he had constructed there on the island of Antonio Váz was the palace of a humanist prince, complete with a botanical garden (the first botanical garden in the New World), zoo (with both Brazilian and African animals), and museum (Whitehead 1979, 429). Maurits gave away numerous items before his return to the Netherlands,[48] many of which must have enriched private collections of curiosities, but it was above all in the Mauritshuis in The Hague where Brazilian feathers, ivory, various kinds of wood, and animal skins, set amid the Brazilian paintings by or after Albert Eckhout and Frans Post, brought Brazil to the attention of numerous distinguished visitors. One of those who visited the Mauritshuis in 1644 even attributed the natural objects a higher status than that of the works of art on display, for while works of art had the secondary status of representations which referred to an absent reality, the exotic objects on display themselves partook of that very reality.[49] Another way of trying to bring Brazil to life in a Dutch setting was the execution of a dance by naked Brazilian Indians mentioned in the previous chapter. However, no proper description of the interior was made during Johan Maurits's lifetime, and the sole reminder in the Mauritshuis of the two shiploads of Braziliana which he brought back with him is the splendid painting of two South American tortoises (see ch. 3, n. 18).

Such courtly settings for the display of Americana passed them on to a select public through an aristocratic filter, reinforcing the values of the princely *Kunst-* and *Wunderkammern.* Within this mode of presentation, the New World was displayed inextricably linked to the colonial adventures of the French, Dutch, and English in Brazil and North America. Although the effect of such presentations must have been considerable, those who had access to them were relatively few.

That the Americana were destined for collections of curiosities affected the selection of objects collected, as well as their display; to feature among other rarities, they had to be precisely that—strikingly unusual or singular. This was one of the paradoxes of the cosmological collections: on the one hand, they set out to display the rich variety of the world in all its facets; on the other hand, the fact that each object on display was marvelous tended to enhance the differences between objects, making the task of building up a representative collection impossible. To cite Céard (1977, xi):

> The order of the world can only evade the confused monotony of identity through the existence of differences. There are no two creatures or

> things which are absolutely the same. In this sense, each creature or thing is a rarity. This rarity may seem unimportant to us if it is only a question of a distinctive feature which does not appear to affect its nature; and yet, since the order of the world only exists by virtue of differences, the most tenuous distinctive feature has its place within this order. It is precisely one of the functions of extreme rarities, monsters, prodigies, marvels to make us aware of these differences. Nature, which is not a simple given, but a living being engaged in constant activity, does not cease to multiply differences in order to perfect its order and to maintain its coherence at the same time: differences are thus marks (and, in this sense, signs) of this activity.

The exotic object might be striking as a paragon of its kind (like the animals displayed in zoos), or it might be striking as a deviation from its kind (like the animals displayed in freak shows and fairs). On both counts, however, the collection created a context in which each object was deemed to have importance (otherwise it would not be there)—to be in some way representative of the wonders of the world (the collection as *theatrum mundi, liber mundi*, or microcosm) and to be in another way singular (the collection as a cabinet of curiosities).

As we have seen, the detachment of the fragment from one cultural setting and its display in an entirely different one was accompanied by an enhancement of the symbolic efficacy of the object. As a striking metonym, it could have more force than the whole of which it was a part. At the same time, this exotic quality of the object in a collection of curiosities was contagious, for if every object on display was a curiosity, each of the objects might be supposed to be equally curious. This leveling effect of the presentation was an elevating one, which tended to make everything more rather than less exotic.

The principle that exotic objects belong with other exotic objects further created a notion of the globe as the source of wonder which exceeded geographic boundaries. It was not the specific geographic provenance of the artifact which was important, but its capacity as a singular object to partake in the world of exotica in general within a cabinet of curiosities. This can be illustrated from the collection of the Amsterdam merchant Levinus Vincent (discussed in more detail in the following chapter). In the 1706 catalog of his collection, Vincent writes that a large cabinet in his *Theatrum Naturae Mundum* contained the following items (1706, 26): "Indian rarities, artfully made, consisting of jewelry, clothing, ornaments made from beautiful and strange feathers and other materials, cleverly constructed baskets, a rifle, tools and weapons, as well as many other curiosities which have reached us from diverse shores and which brevity prevents us from citing here." The word *Indian* in such a context could mean Asian as well as North or South American.[50] On the accompanying engraving, at any rate (fig. 19), we can distinguish a string of wampum from North America, Indian featherwork, and a bow and arrows, as well as a toucan preserved in a jar, but the weapons on display also include an Indonesian kris, which may be assumed to have reached the Netherlands via the Dutch East India Company.

This striking lack of geographic specificity—related to the rules of the exotic genre discussed in chapter 2—is another main feature of all the curiosity cabinets. In this respect there is a remarkable disparity between the imprecisions in the specification of provenance and the geographic knowledge that had been acquired by European travelers of this time. The title of a seventeenth-century catalog of the Sieur de Bernonville's cabinet in La Rochelle is revealing in this respect: *Recueil des pièces curieuses apportées des Indes, d'Egypte and d'Ethiopie and de plusieurs autres lieux. Avec des raretés servant à la personne d'un général des Sauvages* (Paris, 1670). Although the author gives the Antilles, Madagascar, Java, Bantam, and other places as the provenance of his grains and fruits, he fails to specify where this "savage general" came from (Schnapper 1988, 109, 226). In his survey of the presence of artifacts from Mexico and South America in the *Wunderkammern* of Europe to which reference has already been made, Feest (1985) provides many examples of such geographic incongruities. For instance, an early colonial Mexican obsidian mirror from the Vienna *Schatzkammer*—like the one used for magical purposes by John Dee—was originally thought to be Chinese, as were the characters on Mexican codices; a club from the Brazilian Tarairiu in Munich was acquired in 1913 as having come from the "South Seas"; the Brussels "Montezuma's mantle" is Brazilian, not Mexican; a "Brazilian" pipe in the catalog to the collection of Ole Worm has a North American provenance; and so on. Objects collected among the Taino of the Greater Antilles seem to have been particularly resistant to classification (Feest 1986).

Amid this welter of geographic guessing, there is a dominant tendency: the assumption that Brazil can serve as an iconographic model for the Americas as a whole. Hence, allegories of the four continents, which replaced the triad of Europe, Africa, and Asia after the discovery of the New World and which make their appearance at the same time as the first European *Wunderkammern,* are based primarily on Brazil, with hardly any reference to Mexico or North America (Poeschel 1985, 186ff.). As Poeschel notes, "the iconographic characteristics of the personifications of America are thus very restricted by comparison with the sources, and remain such for centuries" (1985, 187).

The European iconography of the Amerindian was thus not based on the

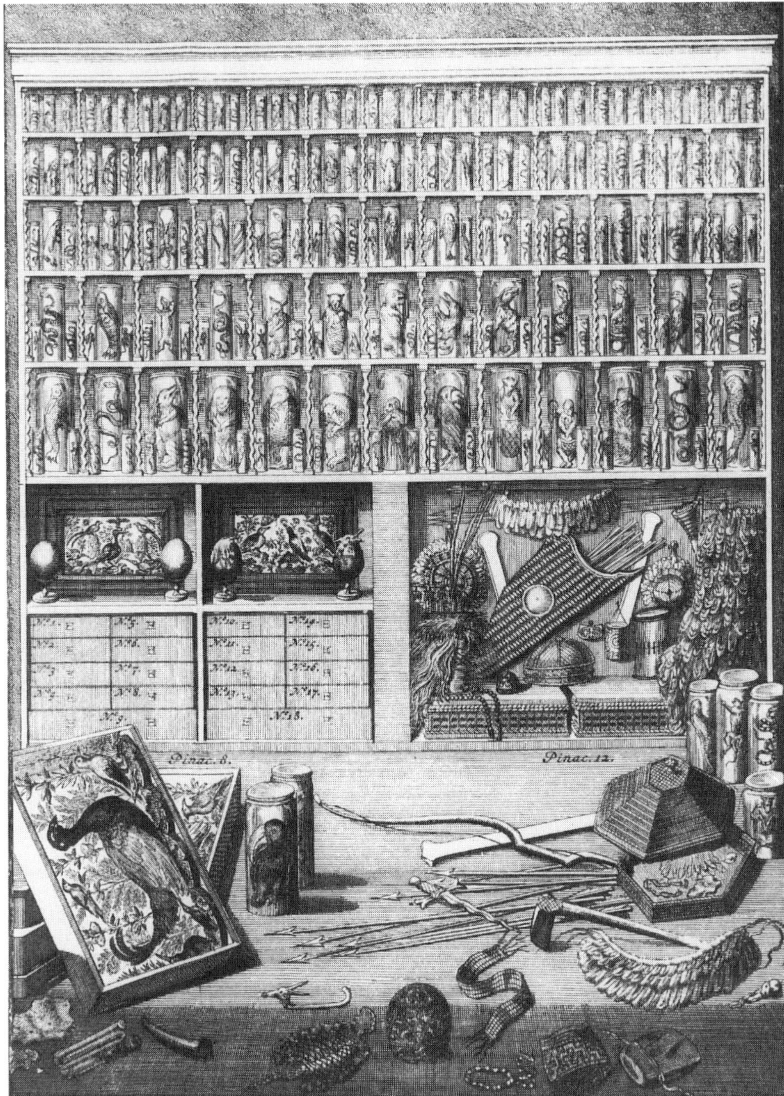

Fig. 19. *Americana* in the collection of Levinus Vincent in Haarlem
From Levinus Vincent, *Wondertooneel der Nature,* Amsterdam, 1706.

Caribbean population which Columbus encountered in the Antilles, but on the Tupinamba of Brazil encountered by Juan Cabral and Amerigo Vespucci around 1500, only to disappear in the course of the seventeenth century. Montaigne was only following this privileged position of Brazil in 1580 when he claimed to have based the American observations contained in his essay "Des cannibales" on the evidence of a man who had spent years in Brazil as an interpreter and on three Brazilian Indians whom he had met in Rouen after the siege of 1562. In the later essay "Des coches," first published in 1588, Montaigne returns to the New World to describe the magnificence of Peru and Mexico, but the apparent contamination of his account by some of the themes of "Des cannibales" suggests that the portrayal of the states of Mexico and Peru through Brazilian eyes can best be seen as a case of "discrete Tupinambization" (Lestringant 1990, 251). By the 1590s the word *Tupinamba* was even being used as a synonym for Amerindians (Lestringant 1990, 247, n. 43).[51] Since Montaigne's collection of Americana seems to have been confined to objects from Brazil, he is thus deprived of visual supports for his account of the Aztecs and the Inca, and his Brazilian "reading" of America moves in to fill this vacuum. In fact, Lestringant's characterization of Montaigne's geography as "aleatory" is very apt (1990, 144), since it is very hard to imagine what Montaigne thought corresponded precisely to what he called the *païs infini* of the New World.[52]

This notion of an aleatory geography is as accurate a description of the collections of curiosities as it is of Montaigne's textual representations of the New World. Moreover, if we move from strictly textual representations to visual representations of the same period,[53] the same lack of attention to geographic precision can be discerned. Of course, the phenomenon is not confined to the process of Tupinambization, as the following citation makes clear (Sturtevant 1976, 418):

> Artists lacking appropriate models often assumed that all non-Europeans resembled each other, and transferred images from known cultures (classical, Oriental, or African) to the New World setting. More common still was the assumption that Indians and their artifacts vary little: Brazilian Indians appear in Mexico, Patagonians are found in central New York, Florida Indians hold Brazilian clubs, Natchez Indians in Louisiana use a North Carolina temple, and Pocahontas wears a Tupinamba feather costume.

In the illustrations of book 2 of the collection of travel accounts known as the *Great Voyages,* published by Theodor de Bry in 1591, the images of the Timucua of Florida, based on drawings by Jacques Le Moyne de Morgues,[54] include material drawn from at least three different geographic provenances. European conventions lie behind the depiction of hoes, trees, vines, and scenes of field cultivation (Sauer 1971, 206–7). Lowland South America is represented in the profusion of Tupinamba clubs—it is not clear whether the artist copied them from illustrated works or from collections of exotic objects in Paris or London (Lestringant 1990, 186–88). And Mesoamerican urban culture is represented in the Aztec headgear and a curious version of an Aztec tunic. Le Moyne not only Tupinambized Florida—he Aztecized it, too.[55] In the process, "America" seemed to be becoming more distant than ever.

This apparent indifference to ethnographic accuracy is often due to the fact that many of the visual representations were embedded in discourses whose motive was primarily theological rather than ethnographic (Shelton 1994, 201–3). For example, it was in line with the religious thrust of Protestant texts on the Americas to align the alleged anthropophagy of its natives with what Protestants regarded as the cannibalism of the Catholics. This explains why the artist John White represented the carved posts of the Algonquians as resembling "the faces of Nonnes couered with theyr vayles," a similarity which was emphasized even more in De Bry's engraving after White's original (Hulton 1984, pl. 39, fig. 22; Greenblatt 1991, 8 n. 8).

White was an artist who had "been there"—yet, as we saw in the previous chapter, the perceiving eye is not free of preconceptions. Other artists might have to make do with objects from an exotic continent that were on display in a collection of curiosities—and the aim of the present chapter has been to demonstrate just what distorting tendencies this setting could involve. More often, artists even further removed from reality had to rely on representations of such objects. The further removed they were from "ethnographic reality," the more work the trope of "ethnographic realism" was required to do, incorporating ethnographic realia within representations that were themselves based on representations. Both the metonymy of presentation and the metaphor of representation are founded on an absence: the absence of the rest of the whole of which the metonymic presentation is a part or the absence for which the representation is a substitute. In the gap marked by this absence—in the process of the transfer of the objects to a collection or in that of their translation to a representation—they are exoticized. The exotic quality of both collections and representations does not reside in the nature of the objects (re)presented. Not only do we make fragments; we make exotic fragments, and we make fragments exotic.

5 INCORPORATIONS OF THE EXOTIC

> La représentation *supplée* régulièrement la présence.
>
> Derrida, *Marges*

We have already seen how the inclusion of ethnographically accurate details in a painting could be used to suggest the authenticity of the representation as a whole (ch. 3). The presentation of such ethnographic artifacts in collections also affected the way in which they appeared in representations (ch. 4). But what happens when the representation in question is patently non-realistic? Is there a tension, as Smith (1988) has argued, between neoclassical theories of art, with their stress on the unity of mood and expression, and the tendency of analytical and empirical observation to sacrifice such aesthetic unity to the considerations of realism?

In the present chapter we shall examine a few classicizing representations in which the exotic plays a significant part to see whether attention to ethnographic accuracy is necessarily at odds with aesthetic predilections. Once again, the story starts with De Bry's *Great Voyages.* The engravings in the early volumes of De Bry's publication, along with the woodcut illustrations to Thevet's *Singularitez de la France Antarctique,* can probably be counted among the iconographic sources of the *Album des habitans du Nouveau Monde* by Antoine Jacquard, a French engraver from Poitiers active between 1613 and 1640 (Hamy 1907b). This set of engravings (fig. 20; see following p. 112) represents men, women, and children of the New World, each figure or pair of figures set within a classicizing architectural framework. The scenes of children depict them playing in pairs. These scenes are followed by scenes of naked women and children dancing together in pairs. The majority of the illustrations, however, are of men, each occupying a separate niche, depicted in a variety of aggressive poses. Some of them are engaged in acts of cannibalism; others carry human or animal victims over their shoulders; one is flayed, his skin dangling over his shoulder; and one has been reduced to a macabre skeleton.

The artist was drawing on artistic tastes of the end of the sixteenth century in the elongated female figures, and the skeleton and flayed man are derived from Vesalian anatomic illustrations (Mason 1992; cf. Cazort 1996). For present purposes, however, it is not the human figures themselves which concern us, but the objects portrayed in their vicinity. Among the flora depicted are palms and pineapples; the fauna include a flying fish, a serpent with a forked tongue, and a toucan. Among the cultural artifacts are various maracas and a hammock. The following identifications of the weapons wielded by the men have been made: a Tupinamba club, a *boutou* from Guyana, an Antillean or Gê club (Hamy 1907b, 236; Lestringant 1991c, 224 n. 23), Tupi shields, and weapons from Florida and the Upper Amazon. The hairstyles seem to be variously Huron, Tupinamba, and Virginian.

It is possible to match the toucan and maracas with those illustrated in the *Jardin et Cabinet poétique de Paul Contant,* one of the poetic catalogs accompanied by reproductions of the plants and animals from the collection of curiosities of Paul Contant, a French apothecary and fellow townsman of the engraver Jacquard. Contant received numerous curiosities from his circle of friends and acquaintances, such as a one-eyed lamb, armadillos, swordfish, and a thirteen-foot-long crocodile. In particular, the arms dealer Moriceau, from a family which had been trading with America for generations, was able to provide him with exotica from the New World (Schnapper 1988, 223–25). Among his Americana we can note the presence of a Micmac or Beothuk birchbark canoe, described as "Cimba Canoe dicta 18. Pedibus longa ex unico cortice arboris Indiae Ceiuas nomine" (Feest 1992, 74). Contant's wampum belt and string may be the earliest known examples to have entered a European collection (Feest 1992, 89).

There was a lively interest in Indians after the arrival of the Tupinamba brought from Maranhão by the French officer Razilly and displayed in Paris in 1613 (Hamy 1908), but Hamy has argued that there is no reason to suppose that Jacquard borrowed the ethnographic attributes of his engravings from them (1907b, 234). It is more likely that he took them from the collection of curiosities of Paul Contant. In that case, the Jacquard engravings can be added to the corpus of representations of America based on the presentation of Americana in the European curiosity cabinets.[1]

The mode of presentation of exotic objects in the collections may be seen to have influenced the mode of representation practiced by the engraver in a number of ways. First, there is the same lack of geographic precision in both cases. Despite the presence of a strong Tupinamba coloring, the artifacts associated with the human figures are taken from a variety of American provenances. Second, the combination of the presentation of material artifacts in the apothecary's collection with a written commentary in a literary form has its parallel in the way the engravings combine a realistic portrayal of human figures, fauna, and flora with Mannerist references to classical and Vesalian iconography. Third, in the case of both presentation and representation, the presence of certain bizarre objects has the effect of increasing the exotic quality of each and every object presented or represented. This is the leveling effect of collections of curiosities described in the previous chapter. In the case of Contant's collection (as we know it from the catalogs), the juxtaposition of a canoe, bat, toucan, or swordfish implies that they share an equal degree of strangeness. Relatively normal lizards become exoticized when they feature in the same context as a one-eyed lamb or an eight-footed anomaly. The armadillo becomes even more exotic when juxtaposed with a dragon and a two-headed pigeon. The same tendency can be seen to be at work in Jacquard's engravings. The relatively innocuous scenes of children playing or of women and children dancing are rendered more exotic by their disposition in the same sequence of representations which contains the savage male cannibals. The sparring matches of the children acquire the sinister undertones of early lessons in the grim combats practiced by the male adults, and the lively poses of the dancing women, once they are viewed within the whole sequence, bear too close a resemblance to the aggressive thrusts of the males.

Reading the Frontispiece

The engravings by Antoine Jacquard are a form of representation of the New World in which the conventions of Mannerist artistry go hand in hand with the representation of ethnographically realistic artifacts. The textual frame—the title *Album des habitans du Nouveau Monde*—makes it clear that some kind of a link is presupposed between the engravings and the inhabitants of the New World. The break with ethnographic realism seems to be absolute, however, when we turn to allegory. Allegory has no need to posit a relation of direct representation, for it is free to function at a purely metaphoric level. In other words, since the allegory by definition narrates a different story, the allegorical representation itself is not obliged to include any of the elements to which it alludes within its own frame. Nevertheless, the allegorical frontispieces to be discussed in this chapter *do* resort to ethnographic realia as part of their iconographic content. Discussion of them will therefore have to begin with an iconographic analysis.

The Dutch merchant in drapery Levinus Vincent (1658–1727), whom we encountered at the end of the previous chapter, moved from Amsterdam to Haarlem in 1705, providing him with a reason to have the first catalog of his collection of rarities published the following year.[2] The frontispiece to his *Wondertooneel der Nature* [Wonderful Theater of Nature] (fig. 21) was executed by Jan van Vianen, whose life span corresponds almost exactly to that of Vincent himself and who had previously done the same for the cabinet of curiosities of the Huguenot Nicolas Chevalier in Amsterdam (cf. Schnapper 1988, ills. 69–72). The design of the frontispiece was by Romeyn de Hooghe (1645–1708), a prolific illustrator of seventeenth-century Dutch literature, who is best known for his depictions of historical themes. However, he was also familiar with more exotic topics, as can be seen from the example of a late-seventeenth-century collector's cabinet with chinoiserie scenes after De Hooghe (Exh. Cat. Amsterdam 1992, no. 83). Besides this frontispiece, we have various other sources on the content and arrangement of Vincent's collection: first, various catalogs, ranging from the *Wondertooneel der Nature* (1706) to the *Korte beschrijving* (1726); second, the prints to illustrate the contents of the various cabinets, which were included in the 1706 publication; and third, a unique drawing of the interior of Vincent's cabinet in 1703 by the amateur Jan Velten (see Exh. Cat. Amsterdam 1992, nos. 22 and 285n).[3]

Pomian has pointed out that, in interpreting depictions of the interiors of cabinets, one must take into account the fact that the artists who portrayed them did not hesitate to correct reality if they thought it necessary. They sometimes included works of art which are known not to have formed part of the collection in question, and they sometimes included identifiable visitors who are known not to have visited the cabinet on the same day. Pomian concludes that, "Although realist, the representations of the cabinets therefore have an allegorical significance, like the still lifes painted with the utmost respect for the physical appearance of objects but which are heavily symbolic at the same time" (1987, 66).

Rademaker's drawing and De Hooghe's print are both assumed to represent an imaginary interior (though it bears a curious resemblance to the interior of what is the oldest Dutch museum still in existence, Teylers Museum in Haarlem, which was not opened until 1784, sixty years after Vincent's collection had moved from Haarlem to The Hague). However, the arrangement of the cupboard corresponds more or less to Vincent's own written account of the disposition of his cabinet. In architectural terms, therefore, the idealized frontispiece nevertheless appears to bear some relation to reality, without being conceived as an accurate realistic portrayal of a particular interior.[4]

The nonrealistic aspect comes to the fore once we turn to the mythological and nonmythological figures in the scene. Here we can best follow De Hooghe's own explanation of the various figures (Vincent 1706, 7–10). The female figure standing on the left is Levinus Vincent's wife, whose decorative skills could be seen in the arrangement of the contents of her husband's drawers. She is here portrayed embroidering a box. A basket of beads hangs over her left arm; she holds the box in her left hand; in her right hand is the embroidery needle. As a pendant to this nonmythological figure (though we have no way of knowing whether it is in any way an accurate portrait of Vincent's wife herself) is a standing male figure on the right, Painting (*de*

Fig. 21. Frontispiece
From Levinus Vincent, *Wondertooneel der Nature,* Amsterdam, 1706.

Schilderkunst der Ouden), who is painting flowers and exotic animals from every region in watercolors. He is painting from life: in front of him is a stone vase containing plants from the East and West Indies. Resting on the vase is a rectangular painting of butterflies with their pupae, larvae, and eggs.

To turn to the figures in the foreground: to the far left is "the careful Investigator (*Naspoorder*)," wearing over his shoulder a zodiac belt to indicate his readiness at all seasons to carry out his collecting activity. He has his net at the ready to catch butterflies and other flying creatures which hatch out of pupae. With his right hand he raises the headdress of the goddess Isis to reveal the band around her neck. He kneels in wonder at the marvels which God has scattered through the universe. The plume on Isis's head symbolizes the inscrutability of the divine godhead. The citadel of the earth which she bears on her head rests on a floral garland. The neckband is decorated with plants and acorns, "the first fruits of mortals." Her numerous breasts symbolize "plenty, procreation and sustenance of all creatures." Her skirts, embroidered with floral designs, "still cover some of the rest, to encourage the Love of Science (*Liefhebberij*) to progress in uncovering her other rarities and astonishing treasures in the rest of the world, on which the goddess Isis rests her arm for support."

The pendant to the Investigator/Isis group is the Love of Science, with a pen at the ready to describe it all and to dispatch her letters (alluded to by the staff of Mercury, the messenger-god). The glass flask in her left hand filled with aqua fortis stands for her passion to collect items from all over the world in this room. She has a book with illustrations of birds, plants, seeds, and flowers on her lap and another with illustrations of animals open in front of her. At her feet are a shell and a crab.

To her right is Voyage, an "Amazon" wearing a nautilus shell on her head, her hair loose in the wind. She wears a sail over her sturdy body. In her left hand she holds an oar for paddling along rivers and creeks. The results of her collecting activity can be seen in the two jars on which she leans, containing a spectacle cobra and a toad which gives birth in its back, as mementos of voyages to the East and West Indies, respectively. One of the rectangular drawers in the center of the foreground contains insects; the other contains seashells and other marine items.

In the background the viewer sees in the center a circular frame enclosing the bust of Anthony van Breda, brother of Jannetje van Breda, the wife of Levinus Vincent. Van Breda's collection, which he started in 1674 (Vincent 1706, 29), formed the basis of Vincent's own collection after the death of Van Breda in 1693. On either side of his bust are sculpted in niches the personifications of two of the continents from which he amassed the objects of his collection, America and Africa. (De Hooghe's text indicates that personifications of the other two continents were accommodated in the opposite niches, but they are not visible in the print). The personification of North and South America, wearing a feathered headdress, reclines in a hammock, with a basket of rarities under her left arm, while her right hand is ready to shoot down birds.[5] Africa, holding an elephant's tusk, is decorated with peacock feathers and armbands. She flies past the hot mountains and sparse woodlands to stop wearily at the Gold Coast, from where she dispatches the rarities she has found to Levinus Vincent.

Finally, standing on a pedestal in the center of the background is a Nymph. She is restless, eager to expand the collection, while the wings of reason on her head aid her in arranging it properly. In one hand she holds a beehive, symbol of her beelike activity in culling the best from every flower and bringing it together in a chamber of curiosities. She is accompanied by two attendants. The one on her right has a compass, water level, and map; the other has a drawing and a peacock's tail to show her eagerness to display all the treasures at their best.

The very fact that such an extended commentary is necessary to explain the iconography of the frontispiece is proof enough of its allegorical nature: it is because the isolated iconographic elements combine to tell a different story that their meaning has to be made explicit. Figures from mythology combine with relatives of Levinus Vincent himself to give him and his activities cosmic proportions. At the same time, however, a part of the support on which the allegory rests consists of realistically portrayed ethnographic objects. The references to the East and West Indies are intended to display the universal scope of the collector's activity, but this grand claim is backed up by actual realia from the Indies. The toad in a glass jar, the Surinamese *Pipa pipa,* was of a kind unknown in Europe. It aroused the curiosity of many other Dutch collectors,[6] and Vincent later devoted a tract to this creature. Vincent sent an (unidentified)[7] friend to America in 1700 to make watercolors of the flora and fauna and to collect rarities, and seven years later he referred to a contact in Brazil from whom he hoped to receive consignments of rarities (Van der Veen 1992, 58, 61).[8] The hammock on which the personification of North and South America reclines is also a native artifact, already illustrated in the Jacquard engravings.

The relation of elements in this allegorical frontispiece to genuine exotic artifacts is even more apparent if we pass beyond it to the catalog itself, for it included not only engravings of the individual cupboards and their contents, but also detailed descriptions of these engravings. For instance, the rectangular painting of the butterflies in front of the mythological figure of Painting recurs in one of these engravings; both the combination of flora and fauna in books and the fauna preserved in glass jars which are associated with Love of Science in the frontispiece can be found in another of those engravings; and the contents of each cupboard as illustrated in an engraving are further commented on by Vincent himself (1706, 26–30). However, while the presentation of the curiosities in these individual engravings of cupboards stresses their variety and strangeness, their inclusion in the company of the classicizing mythological figures of the frontispiece tends to "deexoticize" them, now that the emphasis falls on their place within the cosmic creation. The artist thus had some degree of freedom in the extent to which the exotica could be made more or less exotic. Their exotic quality was not something intrinsic; it was something that could be added or subtracted.

In view of the way in which the exotic and the erotic tend to attract one another, it is also worth noting how the artist chooses to associate or dissociate these two elements. First, virtually all of the mythological figures are female. It is only the Investigator who is male. Moreover, the language used by De Hooghe to describe the partial stripping of Isis is nothing if not erotic, drawing heavily on the trope of geographic and scientific exploration as penetration, which is by no means confined to the era of the Enlightenment. Exposure to the eye of the beholder affects not only the objects themselves, represented as being looked at by the visitors to the cabinet of curiosities, but the scene composed by visitors and objects themselves, which is exposed to the gaze of the beholder. Pomian concludes that this double gaze transforms the image of a cabinet, however realistic it may be, into an allegory of the human apprehension of the works of nature and art (1987, 66).

If we go on to ask to whose gaze the scene contained in the frontispiece is exposed, the answer must be Levinus Vincent himself.[9] Though absent from the representation, it is his gaze which proudly falls on his wife (to the left); his deceased brother-in-law, from whom he inherited a substantial part of his collection; two of the continents (Africa and the Americas) which bring him their rarities; the Amazon Voyage, who is at his service; the Love of Science, engaged like him in the work of cataloging and coordinating the international network with the center of its web in Vincent's Haarlem; even Painting, a pendant to his wife, appears to be engaged on his behalf, coloring plates which will eventually find their way into the drawers of his cabinet. If Vincent can be identified with any figure at all, it is with the voyeur Investigator, tugging at Isis's clothing. Godlike, the owner surveys his microcosmos as the divine demiurge surveys his cosmos.

This absent presence of Levinus Vincent himself explains a peculiar feature of the frontispiece: the large, empty space in the center. At the end of his explanatory text, De Hooghe concludes with a reference to "the cupboards and cabinets on each side, which can be continuously rearranged like screens, which are packed with overabundance, the utterly astounding combined works of nature, which can be understood better in thought than in words" (Vincent 1706, 10). Yet there is little of this cornucopian abundance to be seen in the frontispiece, where the cupboards and cabinets present an extremely orderly arrangement. This almost static impression is reinforced by the pendant figures of Jannetje van Breda and Painting, engrossed in their

Fig. 22. Frontispiece
From J.-F. Lafitau, *Moeurs des sauvages ameriquains comparées aux moeurs des premiers temps,* Paris, 1724.

own handicrafts. If anyone's eyes are on anyone else, it is the couple Investigator/Isis which is the center of attention, to whom both Voyage and Love of Science turn their gaze. The emptiness of the center shifts the focus of attention toward the left-hand figures in the foreground: the Investigator peeping at the female goddess.

Having considered a frontispiece to a book which centers on the collection of curiosities and in which America plays only a small part, we now turn to a frontispiece to a book which centers on America, but in which curiosities play a by-no-means-marginal part. The frontispiece to Joseph François Lafitau's *Moeurs des sauvages amériquains comparées aux moeurs des premiers temps* (fig. 22) has already attracted some attention in the scholarly literature,[10] and Lafitau himself is a better-known figure than is Levinus Vincent. James Clifford, for instance, launches chapter 1 of his *The Predicament of Culture* with a comparison between this frontispiece and that to Malinowski's *Argonauts of the Western Pacific* (1988, 21–22):

> The 1724 frontispiece of Father Lafitau's *Moeurs des sauvages amériquains* portrays the ethnographer as a young woman sitting at a writing table amid artifacts from the New World and from classical Greece and Egypt. The author is accompanied by two cherubs who assist in the task of comparison and by the bearded figure of Time, who points toward a tableau representing the ultimate source of truths issuing from the writer's pen. The image toward which the young woman lifts her gaze is a bank of clouds where Adam, Eve and the serpent appear. Above them stand the redeemed man and woman of the Apocalypse, on either side of a radiant triangle bearing the Hebrew script for *Yahweh* . . .
>
> Unlike Malinowski's photo, the engraving makes no reference to ethnographic experience—despite Lafitau's five years of research among the Mohawks, research that has earned him a respected place among the fieldworkers of any generation. His account is presented not as the product of firsthand observation but of writing, in a crowded workshop.[11]

Joseph-François Lafitau was born in 1681 to a rich merchant family in Bordeaux. He spent five years in Canada among the Algonquin, Huron, and Iroquois, attached to the Jesuit mission in Sault-Saint-Louis, where he collaborated with Julien Garnier, an expert in Indian languages. Lafitau's observations on kinship terminology led him to anticipate Bachofen in assuming the existence of a matriarchy. His *Moeurs des sauvages amériquains comparées aux moeurs des premiers temps* was published in two simultaneous editions (one in quarto and one in octavo) in Paris by Saugrain and Hochereau in 1724.[12]

The frontispiece is the work of E. L. Creite.[13] Like the Vincent frontispiece, this one also is accompanied by explanatory remarks on the iconography:

> The title print shows a person in the act of writing, who is engaged on making a comparison between various antiquities, such as pyramids, obelisks, statuettes, temples, coins and ancient writers, and various descriptions, maps, voyages and other things from America. Two genii compare these objects with one another, and demonstrate the similarity between them both to the writer. Time, who alone reveals all, makes the comparison clearer, shows the writer the origin of all things, and enables him to grasp the connection of all these antiquities with the first creation, with the foundation of our religion, and with the entire system of the revelation, after the sin committed against our forefathers, shown to the writer as a concealed face.

To begin with the mythological figures, the central one—Time—conforms to the Renaissance iconography of Father Time, a "pseudomorphosis" of classical prototypes combining the figures of Kronos (the Roman Saturn) with Chronos, the Greek expression for time (Panofsky 1962, 69–93).[14] The scythe was interpreted as a symbol of the cyclical nature of time, bending back on itself like the curve of a blade. On the other hand, it conjures up the sickle that appears in Greek mythology as an instrument of castration. Kronos, according to the version narrated by the archaic Greek poet Hesiodos in his *Theogony,* had used the sickle given him by his mother Gaia to castrate his father Ouranos during the act of copulation. Moreover, Kronos was warned that he would be usurped by one of his children and thus consumed them immediately after their birth. Zeus escaped this fate and later did in fact usurp his father Kronos with the aid of the Titans. Once this myth was interpreted symbolically, it yielded the image of time as the great devourer, the consumer of what it brings forth. In his iconographic handbook, Vincenzo Cartari (1581, 36) interprets it as follows: "The scythe that Saturn is holding shows that time harvests and reaps all things . . . All things born and produced by time are also devoured by time." At the same time, it is hard to resist the suggestion that the cannibalism of Kronos is appropriate here in view of the fact that cannibalism was the most important iconographic attribute of Native Americans in European representations from the very first.

The right-hand figure is identified as "a person in the act of writing" (*une personne en attitude d'écrire*). Clifford's phrase "the ethnographer as a young woman" accentuates the strangeness of this figure, for if it is intended to represent the ethnographer Joseph François Lafitau, why is he portrayed as a woman?[15] The allegory is here making use of an intermediate mythological figure who substitutes for the ethnographer and writer. From her antique costume, it seems reasonable to look for an analogue in classical iconography, such as Kleio, the muse of history, who was occasionally depicted with a writing implement, although a scroll is more common. The figure of Historia is regularly found in association with Saturn, and it is to Historia that the latter figure is subordinate: it is the writing down of the past which transmutes it from isolated events into history (Bätschmann 1990, 58). Whatever the precise identification may be, the figure in question bears witness to the same process of mythologization which was shown to be at work in the Vincent frontispiece.

Having established the mythological character of the main figures,[16] we can now turn to the realia depicted in the foreground, behind the genii, and in their hands.[17] Next to a globe and a few books, we see the figure of Artemis of Ephesus with the many breasts, taken from de la Chausse, who is also the source of the medallion with the figure of Isis Mammosa encircled by symbols of the four elements to the right. Further to the right are a statue of Hermes (which reappears among the Egyptian figures behind the genii), two medallions representing Astarte with a cross, a medallion featuring Isis and Osiris as serpents, a sistrum, and a map. The genius to the observer's left kneels in front of a statue of Hermes and a Horus Apollo with hieroglyphic symbols, a conical and a pyramidal stone, and a Canopus on a griffin. He holds in one hand an American winged pipe of peace and in the other the caduceus of Mercury. The other genius holds an Egyptian rattle of Anubis in one hand and a North American rattle in the other.

The many-breasted goddess Isis and the staff of Mercury are already familiar from the Vincent frontispiece, but in the case of the Lafitau frontispiece the structure of the print is different. Many of the forty-one plates in Lafitau's two volumes display a binary structure, in which artifacts from the New World and artifacts from the Old World are compared and contrasted. For instance, the eighth plate depicts "the musical instruments of the first times, compared with those of the Americans," where the reader can observe an Egyptian rattle of Anubis, a Brazilian *maraka,* and a North American *chichikoué,* as well as a comparison of the North American tortoiseshell with the lyre of the Greek god Apollon. Sometimes the link between the frontispiece and the other plates is even one of literal citation: the statue of the Ephesian Artemis with the many breasts is repeated in one of the later plates (plate 4, fig. 2).[18] One of the sources for these illustrations is Bernard de Montfaucon's *L'Antiquité expliquée et representée en figures* in five volumes, published in Paris five years before Lafitau's work. In Montfaucon's work, in which the Egyptians appeared as the barbarian precursors of the Greeks and the Romans, the monuments of antiquity were divided into two groups: books, on the one hand, and visual sources (statues, reliefs, inscriptions, and coins), on the other (Schnapper 1988, 119). The artifacts could be considered to supplement the history contained in the books; they might even provide information on matters which did not appear in ancient literature at all.

Lafitau's interest in these antiquities marks him as a product of his era, but the interest in ethnographic objects is more closely related to a development among the tastes of collectors in which interest in coins began to wane in favor of an interest in *naturalia,* particularly shells. For Parisian collections, Pomian has estimated that the percentage of coins dropped from 39 percent in 1700–1720 and 21 percent in 1720–50 to 8 percent in the second half of the century. Inversely, the corresponding percentages for objects of natural history are 15, 21, and 39, respectively (1987, 143).[19] A similar tendency seems to have been at work in London, at least if the case of Woodward can be regarded as typical, for the virtual absence of coins and medals from his collection is—paradoxically—evidence of their popularity at the time: it was because of their popularity that he could be sure of being able to barter them for the fossils to which he himself attached much more attention and scientific interest (Levine 1977, 128). Within the context of the history of collections, Lafitau's frontispiece may therefore be considered as poised on the watershed between two eras of collecting. On the one hand, it bears witness to the Egyptomania of the beginning of the eighteenth century (Syndram 1989);[20] in particular, the figure of Isis found in both the Vincent and the Lafitau frontispieces derives its importance from the head crowned with a tower which was found in Paris during the reign of Louis XIV and which was taken to confirm the iconographic assimilation of Cybele, Isis, and Io (Schnapper 1988, 175). On the other hand, the frontispiece already bears the marks of the subsequent shift in interest from antiquities to curiosities of natural history.[21]

Despite the explicit concern of Lafitau's work with the Americas, then, it also betrays a close connection with the trends in collecting that were in fashion at the time. It is this context which throws light on the treatment of the exotic artifacts from the Americas in the frontispiece. They are, in fact, de-exoticized by bringing them into relation with the artifacts of Greco-Roman and Egyptian antiquity. This visual message is in line with Lafitau's theory of an original matriarchy, for his "fieldwork" in North America found its confirmation, he believed, in a passage from Herodotos's *Histories* (I.173) asserting that in Lykia men received the name of their mother instead of that of their father. Herodotos's claim has not been substantiated by twentieth-century scholars (Pembroke 1965), but Lafitau was content to assume the existence of a parallel style of human development among the ancient Greeks and in the Americas.[22]

The culmination of the process of deexoticization at work in the Lafitau frontispiece can be seen in the frontispiece designed no later than 1815 by François Gérard and engraved by Barthélemy-Joseph-Fuloran Roger for volume 18 of Humboldt and Bonpland's *Voyage* (fig. 23). There we see the personification of America, portrayed with pre-Columbian artifacts—the *ichcahuepilli, coa*, and feathered headdress (Von Kügelgen Kropfinger 1983, 577)—subsumed within an allegory which includes the Greco-Roman deities Athena-Minerva, bearing an olive branch, and Mercury-Hermes, the god of commerce (Exh. Cat. Paris 1976, no. 244; Pratt 1992, 139; Pagden 1993, 9; Mason 1998b). In this compilation of Greco-Roman and Mexican mythology, all the negative elements of the iconography of America have been removed; the reference to decapitation that is so common in other representations of the continent is here reduced to an upturned bust of an "Aztec priestess."[23] Every trace of savagery has been effaced as pre-Columbian cultures are brought within the same framework as the classical models of antiquity.

The Lafitau frontispiece can be compared with that from a contemporary work, the *Travels* of Aubrey de la Motraye in Europe, Asia, and Africa, first published in London in 1724 (fig. 24).[24] Here too we see a female figure engaged in writing the *Voyages d'A. de la Motraye* as she follows the directions of another female mythological figure who can be identified as Wisdom (Sapientia) by the sun on her breast.[25] In the foreground we see the familiar globe and compass, together with an antique bust, vase, and coins. In the background are Egyptian obelisks, as well as scenes of Lapland life based on engravings by Hogarth. Once again, the frontispiece is poised at the transition from antiquity to contemporary ethnography. Indeed, the frontispiece to the second edition of this work, published in 1732,[26] contains ethnographic additions, such as the mines of Brunswick, an Egyptian pyramid, and extra obelisks, while the classical bust has disappeared.

The choice of a female figure for the writer in the Lafitau frontispiece is thus conventional.[27] All the same, a convention has its effects, and we are therefore bound to inquire what effects this choice has on the reception of the frontispiece. The female gender of the writer seems to eliminate the actual historical writer—Joseph-François Lafitau—from the scene. Like Levinus Vincent, his presence is marked and mediated by his absence. If we follow the direction of his and our gaze, it undergoes a process of refraction. Moving from the foreground to the genii, whose eyes are fixed on the writer, the viewer's gaze at first falls on the writer (whose quill almost, but not quite,

Fig. 23. Frontispiece
From volume 18 of *Voyage de Humboldt et Bonpland,* Paris, 1814, engraved by Barthèlemy Roger after a drawing by François Gérard.

touches the tip of Father Time's scythe—history and historiography fail to meet), before following her gaze to Father Time himself, who in turn gesticulates toward the biblical scene behind him, where the angel in the clouds gesticulates toward Adam and Eve, and from them to the divine godhead, whose presence can only be marked by the Hebrew characters for his name. The gaze is—definitively—deferred.

Fig. 24. Frontispiece
From *Voyages du Sr. A. de la Motraye en Europe, Asie & Afrique,* The Hague: T. Johnson & J. van Duren, 1727.

Gender and Accessibility

Thus far we have been dealing with personifications or allegories in isolation. However, there is another set of representations of the American exotic which cannot be left out of the present discussion, the allegories of the four continents.

To deal with the question of terminology first, it is debatable whether the representations in question should be labeled *allegories* at all. As Wendt points out (1989, 156 n. 1), the allegory is often a means of giving visual form to some abstraction, whereas what she refers to as the personifications of the four continents tend to be oriented toward specific material objects capable of direct representation. However, the representation of "Europe," for example, is surely also the representation of an abstraction. Besides, it may be permissible to use the term *allegory* in the expanded sense claimed for it by Paul de Man. Though formulated in terms of the textual allegory, the following remarks by de Man apply equally well to visual allegories: "Allegory is sequential and narrative, yet the topic of its narration is not necessarily temporal at all, thus raising the question of the referential status of a text whose semantic function, though strongly in evidence, is not primarily determined by mimetic moments" (1981, 1). De Man's work calls into question the very possibility of nonallegorical description (closely allied with the romantic search for unmediated meaning). In line with the thrust of his argument—and of its application to ethnography by Clifford (1986b, 100) and others—the label "allegory of the four continents" will be used here to draw attention to the stories told by these personifications.

Allegories of the four continents, which replaced the triad of Europe-Africa-Asia after the discovery of the New World, make their first appearance at the same time as the emergence of the *Wunderkammern* in the middle of the sixteenth century.[28] The earliest appearance of the allegory of the four continents is in the civic procession (*ommegang*) held in Antwerp in 1564.[29] Six years later we find the first occurrence of the allegory of the continents in a permanent form in the frontispiece to Abraham Ortelius's widely circulated *Theatrum orbis terrarum,* accompanied by an explanatory text.[30] Other artists soon followed, often drawing on travel accounts,[31] cosmographies, costume books,[32] and bestiaries for the iconographic details (Poeschel 1985), and by 1603 the four continents had been assigned fixed representational conventions in the woodcuts by Cavalier d'Arpino for the first illustrated edition of Cesare Ripa's *Iconologia.*[33]

The continents could appear singly, in series, or combined in a single composition. As an example of the latter, we can take Frans Francken II's *Allegory on the Abdication of Charles V,* signed and dated to 1636.[34] This large painting, which is now in the Rijksmuseum Amsterdam, combines an allegorical depiction of the four continents with the detailed portrayal of typical *Kunstkammer* objects, including porcelain, shells, and Indian weapons (cf. Poeschel 1985, 113–16). Such paintings reveal the lavishing of a good deal of attention on the details of the artifacts, resembling still lifes in their "realism." However, this realism is combined with a lack of interest in geographic specificity as realia drawn from regions thousands of miles from one another are juxtaposed in strange company with one another. It is remoteness which is important, not specificity.

In these allegories some of the figures of the continents themselves display a remarkable turning away from the observer. In the earliest French series of allegories of the four continents, a set of prints from 1575 by Etienne Delaune (1518/19–95), each of the four figures is turned away from the spectator (see fig. 8). If a full frontal view may be considered as offering a maximum of accessibility,[35] we can arrange these four figures in terms of a scale of decreasing accessibility:

full frontal view > three-quarter frontal view > three-quarter dorsal view > full dorsal view

In the Delaune prints Europe and Africa both present three-quarter frontal views; Asia's head is in profile, while her body presents a three-quarter dorsal view; and America is the most averted of the four, combining a three-quarter dorsal view with a rear view of the head looking away to the rear of the scene. America therefore presents minimal accessibility in this context.[36]

In most of the allegorical representations of America, usually presented as a woman,[37] the human figure appears in profile, looking away, as in the influential sketches made by Marten de Vos for the entry of Archduke Ernst of Austria to Antwerp in 1594 (Exh. Cat. Paris 1976, no. 88). The gaze is averted even more by its upward and outward shift in Jan Sadeler's print of America from 1581 (Exh. Cat. Berlin 1982, pl. 286), in which the seated figure pays no attention to the idyllic scene in the center of the illustration, but seems to be gazing up at the sky. In the mid–eighteenth century, the figure of America in Tiepolo's Würzburg frescoes is characterized by a strong rotational movement that once again eludes the spectator's grasp (Alpers and Baxandall 1994, 130). Indeed, the relative fixity of the Europe fresco (and of its iconography) by comparison with the frescoes of America, Asia, and Africa in Würzburg suggests the rightness of a Eurocentric perspective, as if one were supposed to look from Europe (154). Three-dimensional versions follow the same pattern, as in the female seated on a crocodile-like monster from a mid-eighteenth-century design by Bouchardon for the sculptural decoration above an arch (Exh. Cat. Berlin 1982, pl. 291). The most radical of these variants is to be found in an oil painting of America from the same period by Jean Dumont, where all the spectator sees is the back of the human figure. There could be no clearer statement that America—the exotic par excellence in this context—is elsewhere.

The Atypical Landscape

We have already encountered the notion of the *typical landscape* in connection with the Eckhout portraits discussed in chapter 3. The representations considered in this chapter, which set Native Americans within an allegorical setting, might be said to constitute the *atypical landscape.* In this genre—if it is a genre at all—the presence of exotic natural and artificial objects, fauna, and flora is influenced by their presence and display in the European cabinets of curiosities. Any direct synecdochal relation that they might have with distant lands is mediated by their accommodation within the European collections.

Discussions of early representations of America have generally tended to operate in terms of the degree to which they accurately represent an absent ethnographic reality. Thus, in presenting a list of 268 depictions of Native Americans up to 1590, Sturtevant introduces it as "the catalogue of extant illustrations prior to de Bry and having some claim to ethnographic accuracy" (1976, 420; cf. idem 1991). Hamy's comment on the Brazilian figures on a bas relief in Rouen from the middle of the sixteenth century was that "one should not demand of them that ethical verisimilitude which escapes most artists, painters and sculptors of the time" (1907a, 6). Similarly, in a study of representations of the New World from 1493 to the volumes published by De Bry a century later, Falk (1987) has drawn a distinction between those representations of poor artistic quality but high ethnographic value, on the one hand, and those of good artistic quality but little ethnographic value, on the other hand—an opposition which more or less overlaps with Smith's distinction (1988) between neoclassical aesthetics and close observation of empirical detail. Within this period further distinctions may be made between inaccurate anatomic portraits of Amerindians and relatively more accurate portrayals of hammocks, weapons, and other ethnographic objects (Hamy 1907b, 226) or between the relative ease of assimilation of botanical and zoological objects in the eyes of Renaissance artists, on the one hand, and the difficulty they encountered in reproducing crafted objects from the New World, on the other (Dacos 1969a).

All of these accounts imply an opposition between aesthetic considerations and fidelity to the ethnographic context. There is a fundamental difference involved in the transition from the contiguity with which an American artifact that partook of the New World could metonymically present a part of that world to the inevitably secondary nature of a visual representation which could and can only stand for a world it will never actually touch. Nevertheless, even though presentations imply a visible and tangible connection of the objects in collections with the totality of which they are fragments, it would be hazardous to suppose an enhanced fidelity to ethnographic reality on the basis of this contiguity.

In view of the explicitly allegorical nature of both allegorical frontispieces and allegories of the four continents, no one need be supposed to have taken these representations to be ethnographically realistic. Nevertheless, they often do make use of ethnographic realia to a surprising degree. Since allegory sets out to achieve a transformative effect on the viewer, inviting or compelling him or her to confer fullness of meaning (cf. Stewart 1984, 3–5), these allegorical representations must have had a considerable influence on the creation of European images of what was to be found in distant lands. In trying to 'read' the impact of the discovery of America, we have to look not only at learned texts and at collections of American artifacts (Mason 1996, 115), but also at metaphorical and allegorical representations.

6 EXOTIC SPECTACLES

> Were I in England now, as once I was, and had but this fish painted, not a holiday fool there but would give a piece of silver: there would this monster make a man; any strange beast there makes a man: when they will not give a doit to relieve a lame beggar, they will lay out ten to see a dead Indian.
>
> Shakespeare, *The Tempest*

Thus far we have considered the presentation of the exotic in the Renaissance collection of curiosities and its representation in genres which made no pretense of being realistic, such as the allegorical frontispiece, as well as in genres which set out to convince the viewer of their realism (the ethnographic portrait). Besides the stasis of the *Wunderkammer* and the confines of the two-dimensional representation,[1] there is another mode of representation: the dramatic. The sixteenth century, after all, was a period in which cultural activity was so theatrical that it becomes hard to treat the theatrical metaphor as a metaphor at all. For both critics and defenders of the Elizabethan theater, it has been claimed, things in general fail to exist apart from their own theatricalizations, and theatricality is "simply the constitutive condition of existence itself" (Levine 1994, 71). As Mullaney points out: "We find the same audience, the same suspension of cultural decorum and blurring of xenophilia and phobia, in attendance at madhouses, royal entries, and wonder-cabinets as we find at the popular playhouses of Elizabethan London" (1983, 50). In a world like this, a female sovereign like Cleopatra in Shakespeare's *Antony and Cleopatra* exhibits the same attitude toward theatricality as does the female sovereign on England's throne. Power had to be enacted to be believed, making trials public events that could draw large crowds; on the continent it was the public execution which seemed to have combined spectacle with the dramatic display of power (Maus 1991, 32).

Other areas in which this practice was found were the Baroque theaters of experiment and the anatomy theaters (Findlen 1994, 208–20), another focal point of this "culture of dissection" (Sawday 1995). The word *theater* should be taken literally, for so-called anatomy lessons became grisly spectacles of both popular and learned entertainment, where European audiences could be regaled with the sight of the dissection of the corpses of executed criminals (Mason 1992).[2] The carnival-like aspects of these spectacles of dissection could even be enhanced by timing them to coincide with carnival itself, allowing the entry of spectators wearing (carnival) masks, and providing music to accompany the macabre performance (Ferrari 1987; Lazzerini 1994). Visitors to the Amsterdam house of punishment, the Rasphuis, could pay to gloat at the sight of men turning as red as Amerindians as they rasped the brazilwood imported from the New World (Schama 1987, 20–21). In this spectacle of suffering (Spierenburg 1984), where the act of dissection was at the same time an extreme and total act of punishment (Barker 1984), texts and actions that register the compelling powers of the real, with anything but theatrical intentions, are nevertheless revealing of a mimetic practice in which the imagination is at work rather than at play (Greenblatt 1991, 23; cf. idem 1980). It is therefore fully compatible with this state of affairs that representations of the exotic should also take a dramatic turn.

It is commonly assumed that exhibitions of live human beings were predominantly a nineteenth-century phenomenon, although Carl Hagenbeck was still exhibiting humans as well as animals in his Zoological Garden near Hamburg as late as 1910 (Reichenbach 1996; Flint 1996, 106–8).[3] To modern sensibilities, it seems hardly credible that such antics could still go on today. This incredulity is well conveyed in the following remarks by Kirshenblatt-Gimblett: "Imagine being installed in a room at an exhibition in, say, Bangladesh, where one's only instruction was to go about one's daily chores just like at home—making coffee, reading the *New York Times*, working at the computer, talking on the phone, walking the dog, sleeping, flossing, opening the mail, eating granola, withdrawing cash from a money machine—while curious visitors looked on" (1991, 409). The oddity of such displays has been brought out in an artistic setting in various venues in the 1990s by the performance artists Guillermo Gómez-Peña and Coco Fusco, who posed as aboriginal inhabitants of an island in the Gulf of Mexico that Columbus had somehow overlooked. They were exhibited in an iron cage "for the last stage of their world tour." Wearing skirts of straw and an imitation panther skin, they spent their time watching television, drinking Coca Cola, and working on the laptop computer. Two guides in khaki uniform offered visitors an explanation. An "authentic Amerindian Dance" cost fifty cents; the price for a display of the male's genitals was five dollars. While some members of the various audiences who saw them were horrified and canceled their museum membership, others were apparently completely taken in.[4]

Nevertheless, human displays of the kind mimicked and mocked in this installation did continue in the twentieth century. A poster from 1951 was still advertising the Dutch Circus Strassburger with Sioux Indians from Dakota in the "Hallo Texas" Wild West Show, as well as "Prince Kari-Kari and his Somali Negro tribe from dark Africa"; visitors were invited to observe the latter during their visit to "our menagerie with animals from every continent."[5] In 1994, a village from the Ivory Coast reconstructed in Nantes included live Africans as exhibits. And some critics see present-day festivals such as the Festival of American Folklife as perpetuating the tradition of displaying exotic others in important ways (Price and Price 1994). When groups of tribal people accompany touring exhibitions of art from their area, are we to interpret this as a way of expressing that the art belongs to them, as an act of empowerment, or is their presence simply part and parcel of the display itself, recapitulating the long history of European voyeurism? In retracing the development of this form of dramatic representation, we are dealing with a phenomenon extending over a number of centuries and well into the twentieth century.

The capture and display of exotic humans as objects can be traced back at least to the late medieval period,[6] though the dramatic content of human displays at that time is rather low. One of the earliest cases from northern Europe is that of the "wild woman" who was allegedly fished out of a Dutch lake (the Purmermeer) around 1403 and subsequently exhibited to the "many people who came to see this woman from many foreign countries."[7] Columbus's delivery of the six "Indians" who survived the journey back to the Spanish king upon his return from his first voyage is the paragon and precedent that initiated the practice of kidnapping Amerindians and taking them to the European continent.[8] It was followed by the removal of Newfoundlanders to Portugal and England in 1501 and 1502, the taking of Brazilians to England and France in 1532 and 1505, respectively, and the presentation of ten Hurons kidnapped by Jacques Cartier to the court of François I in 1536 (Honour 1979, 279). Trinculo, who reflects on the possibility of displaying Caliban to some "holiday fool" in *The Tempest* (II.ii.28–34), is not the only character in this play for whom the idea of kidnap seems to be more or less a reflex, for Stephano's reaction to the appearance of Caliban is equally characteristic: "This is some monster of the isle with four legs, who hath got, as I take it, an ague. Where the devil should he learn our language? I will give him som relief, if it be but for that. If I can recover him, and keep him tame, and get to Naples with him, he's a present for any emperor that ever trod on neat's leather" (*The Tempest* II.ii.66ff.).

Many of the early displays of Amerindians included a dramatic component of some kind. The Aztecs displayed by Cortés before the court of Charles V in 1529, which have come down to us in the earliest known representations of American Indians taken from life in the colored drawings which Christoph Weiditz made at the time, engaged in various games, feats of acrobatics, and juggling for their audience. The first dramatic performance in which native peoples took part as actors,[9] however, was the spectacle held

Fig. 6. *West Indian Landscape.*
Jan Mostaert, ca. 1520–1530, panel 86.5 × 152.3 cm, Frans Hals Museum, Haarlem. Courtesy of Rijksdienst Beeldende Kunst from a photograph supplied by the Frans Hals Museum.

Fig. 7. *The Dawn of Civilization.*
Cornelis van Dalem, ca. 1565, panel 88 × 165 cm. Courtesy of Museum Boijmans Van Beuningen, Rotterdam.

Fig. 9. Negro woman.
Albert Eckhout (attr.), ca. 1641, oil on paper, 36.1 × 24.0 cm, Libri Picturati A 34, f. 21.
Courtesy of Jagiellon Library, Cracow.

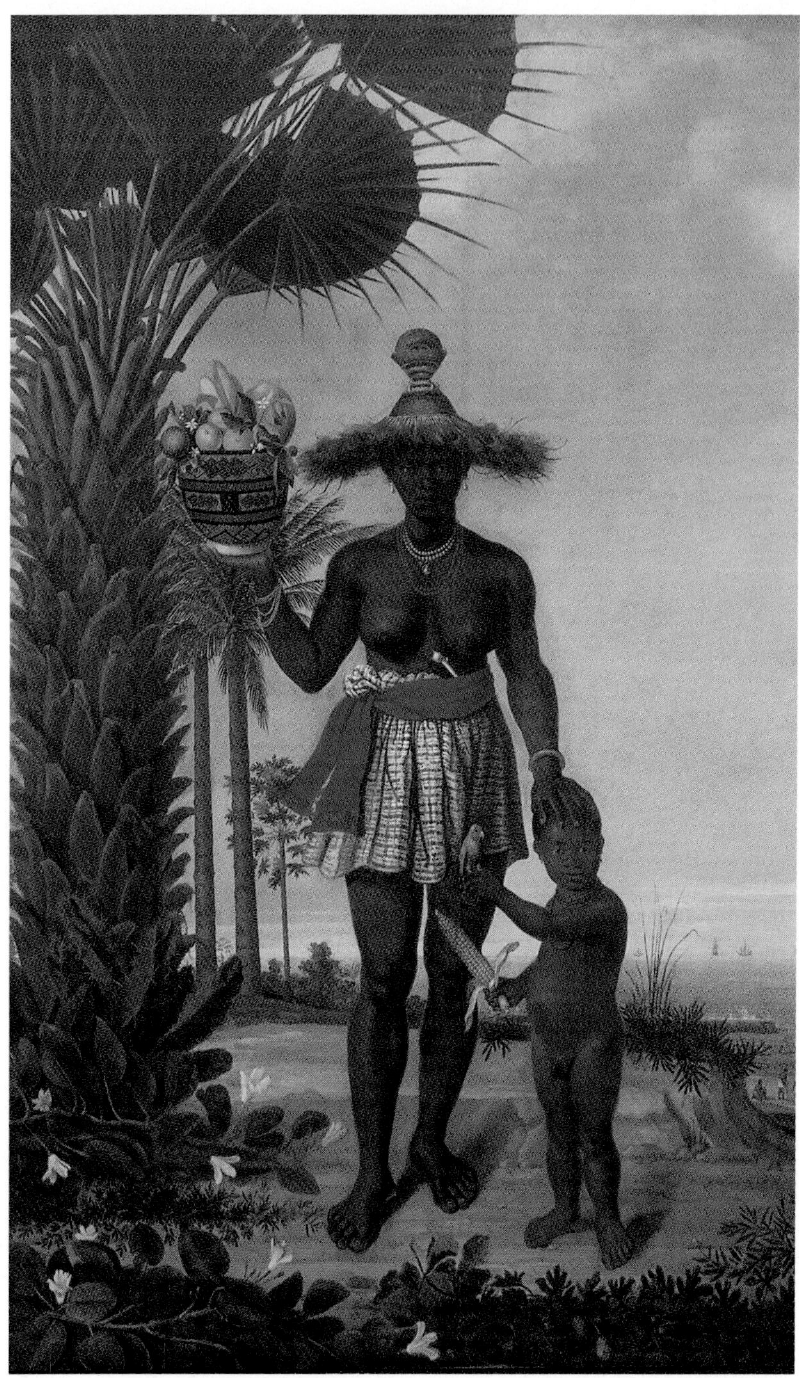

Fig. 10. Negro woman and child.
Albert Eckhout, 1641, 267 × 178 cm, Etnografisk Samling, Nationalmuseet Copenhagen.
Courtesy of the National Museum of Denmark, Department of Ethnography.

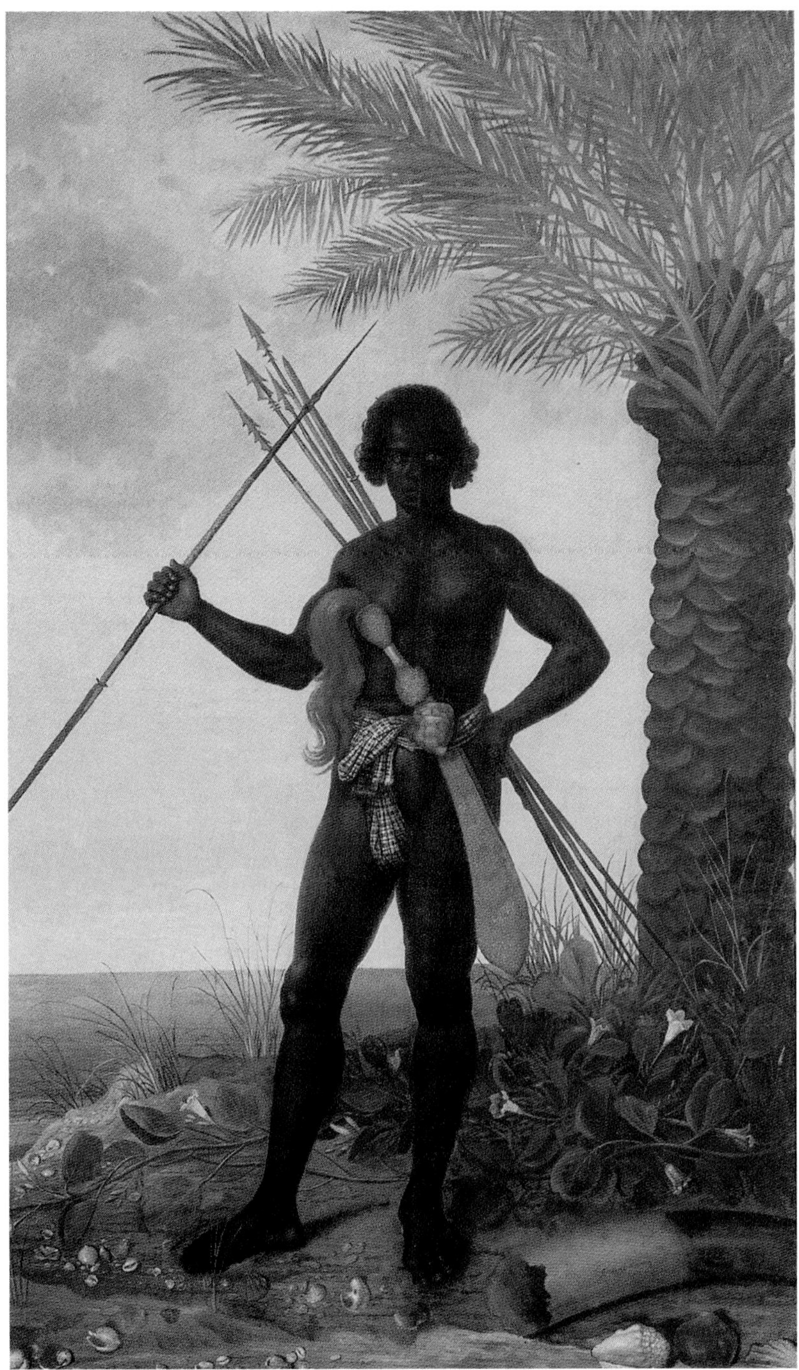

Fig. 11. Negro man.
Albert Eckhout, 1641, 264 × 162 cm, Etnografisk Samling, Nationalmuseet Copenhagen. Courtesy of the National Museum of Denmark, Department of Ethnography.

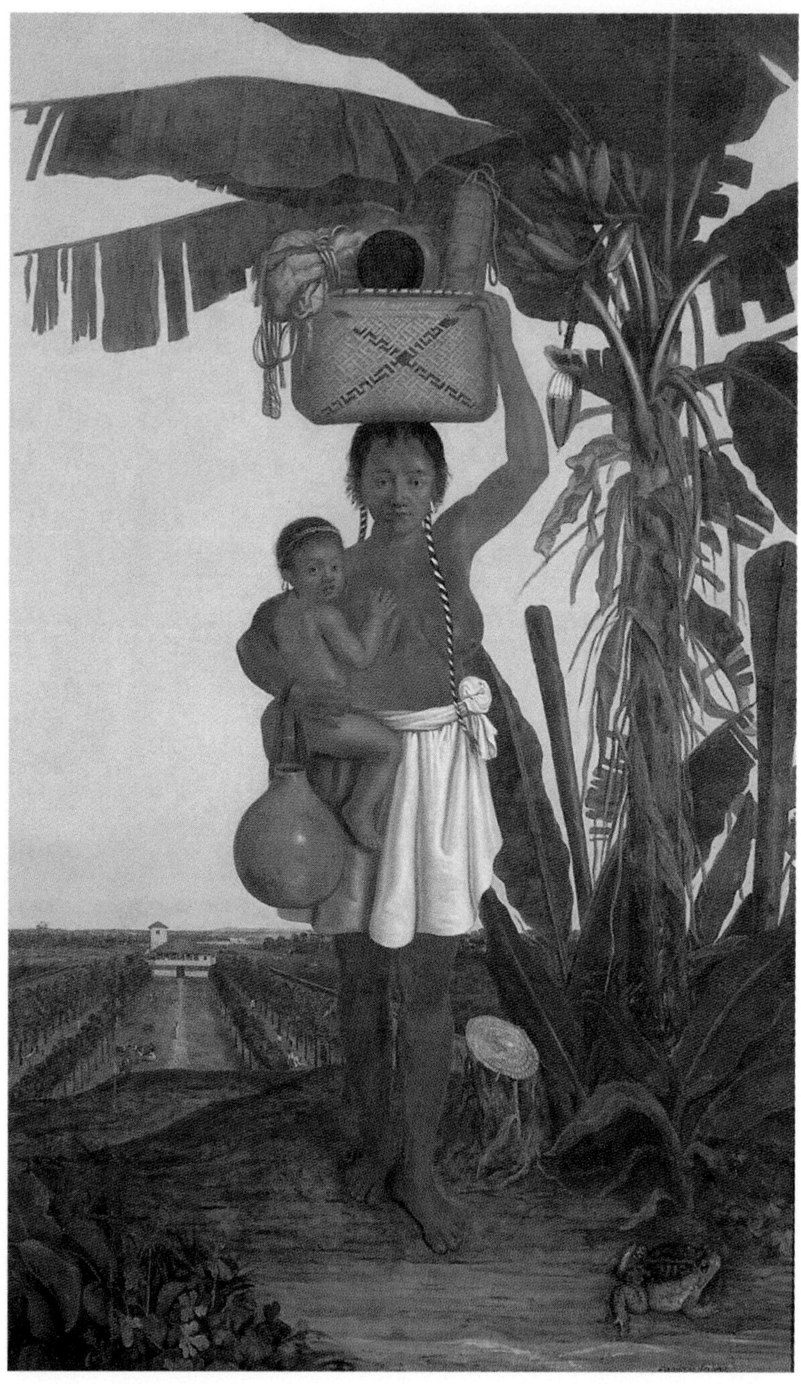

Fig. 12. Tupi woman.
Albert Eckhout, 1641, 265 × 157 cm, Etnografisk Samling, Nationalmuseet Copenhagen.
Courtesy of the National Museum of Denmark, Department of Ethnography.

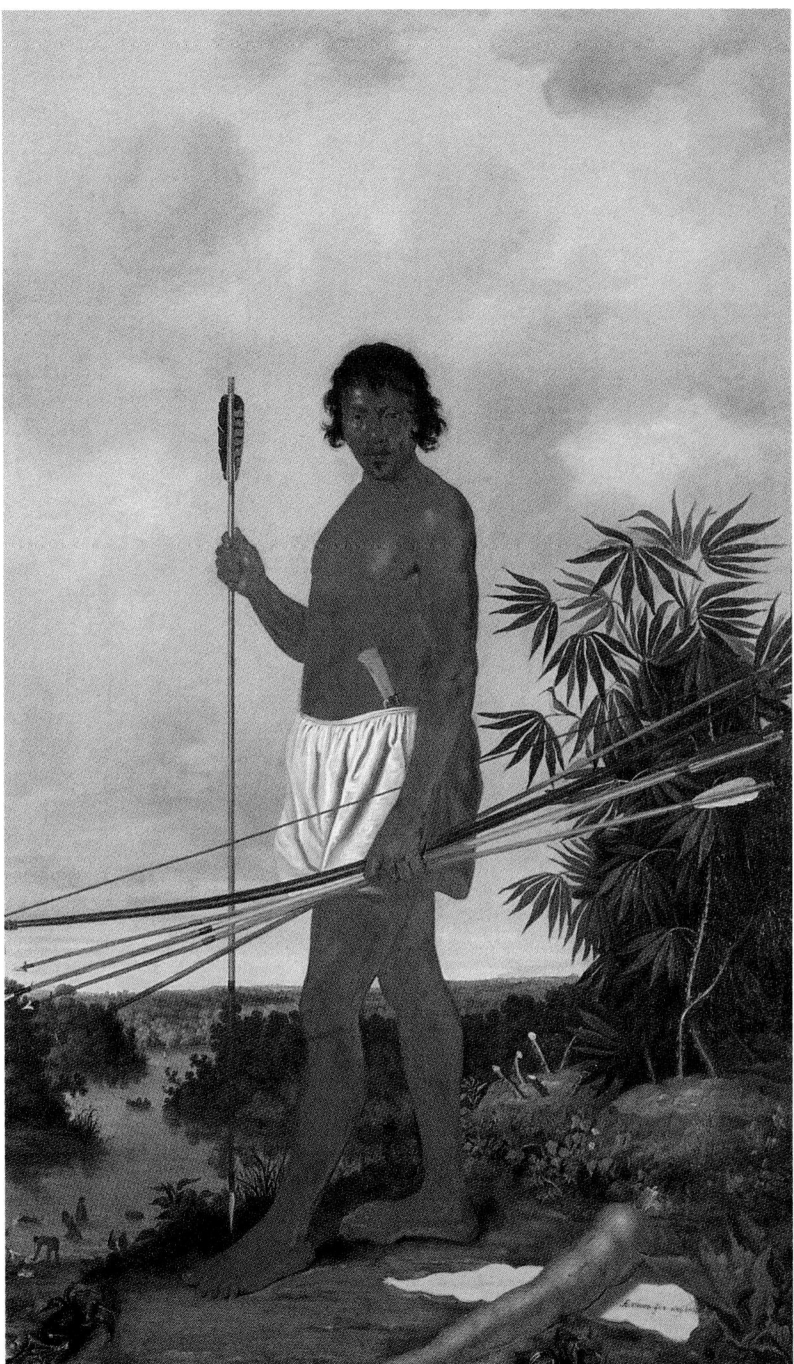

Fig. 13. Tupi man.
Albert Eckhout, 1643, 267 × 159 cm, Etnografisk Samling, Nationalmuseet Copenhagen. Courtesy of the National Museum of Denmark, Department of Ethnography.

Fig. 14. Mameluca.
Albert Eckhout, 1641, 267 × 160 cm, Etnografisk Samling, Nationalmuseet Copenhagen.
Courtesy of the National Museum of Denmark, Department of Ethnography.

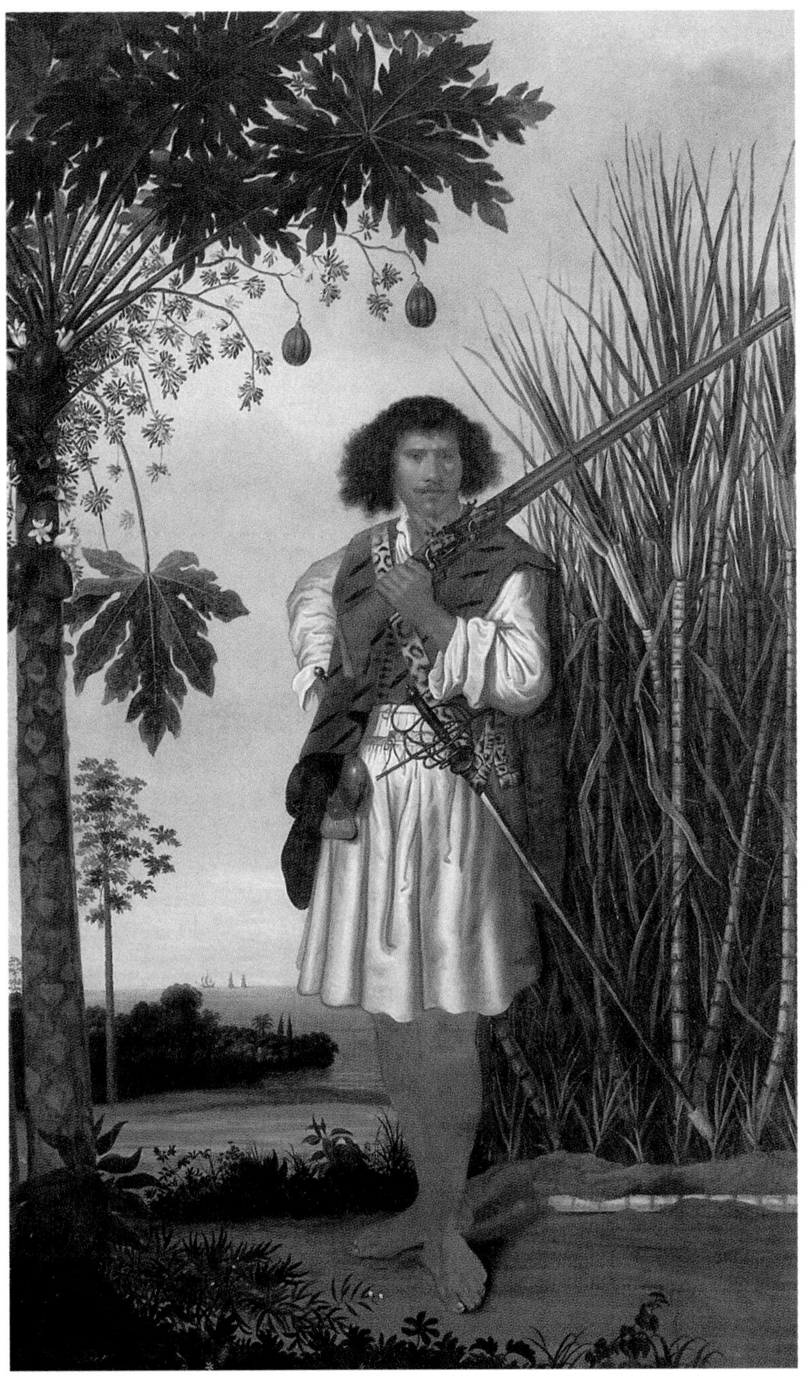

Fig. 15. Mulato.
Albert Eckhout, ca. 1641–1643, 265 × 163 cm, Etnografisk Samling, Nationalmuseet Copenhagen. Courtesy of the National Museum of Denmark, Department of Ethnography.

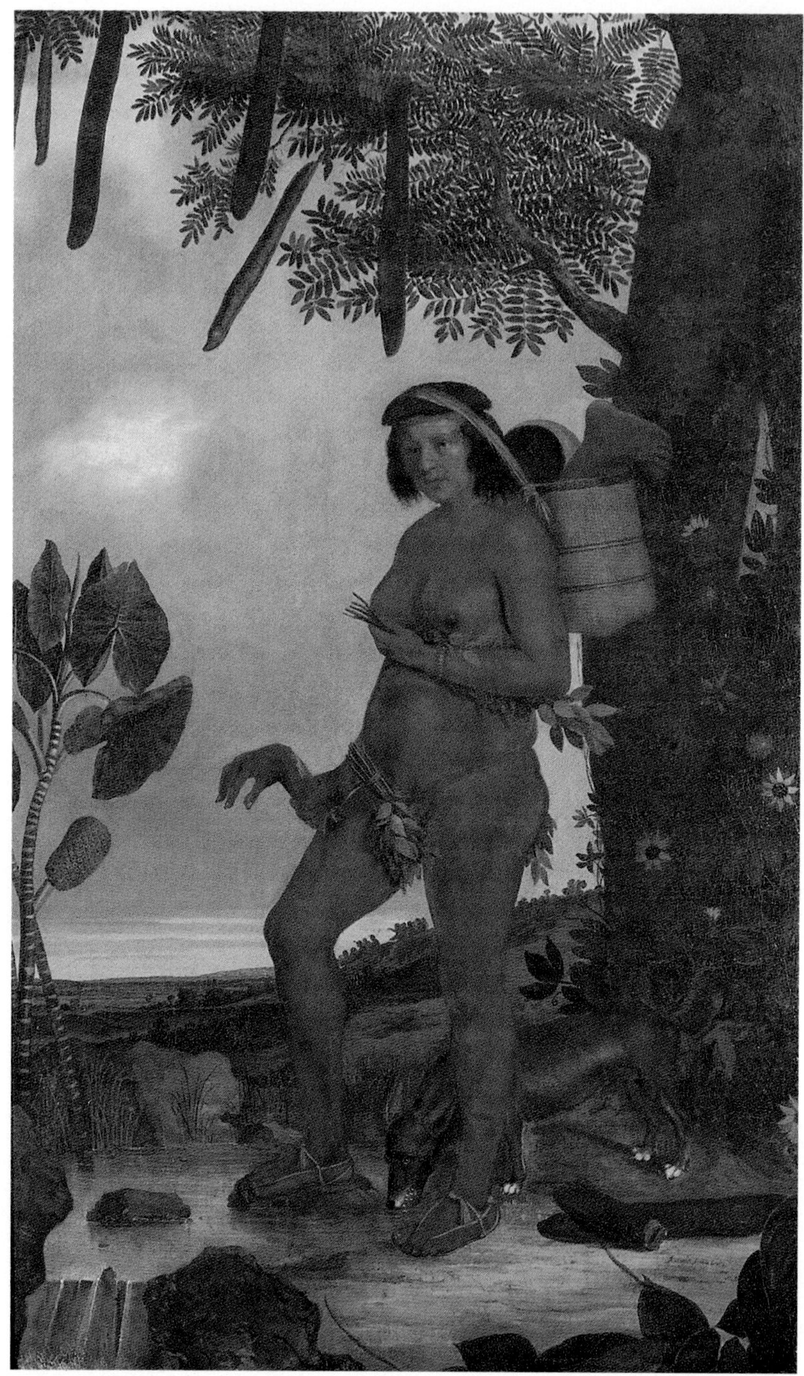

Fig. 16. 'Tapuya' woman.
Albert Eckhout, 1641, 264 × 159 cm, Etnografisk Samling, Nationalmuseet Copenhagen.
Courtesy of the National Museum of Denmark, Department of Ethnography.

Fig. 17. 'Tapuya' man.
Albert Eckhout, 1643, 266 × 159 cm, Etnografisk Samling, Nationalmuseet Copenhagen.
Courtesy of the National Museum of Denmark, Department of Ethnography.

Fig. 18. 'Tapuya' dance.
Albert Eckhout, ca. 1641–1643, 168 × 294 cm, Etnografisk Samling, Nationalmuseet Copenhagen. Courtesy of the National Museum of Denmark, Department of Ethnography.

Fig. 20. Peoples of the New World.
From *LES DIVERS POURTRAICTS et figures faictes sus les meurs des habitans du Nouveau Monde,* Antoine Jacquard, ca. 1620, Cabinet des Estampes, Bibliothèque Nationale, Paris. Courtesy of Cliché Bibliothèque nationale de France, Paris.

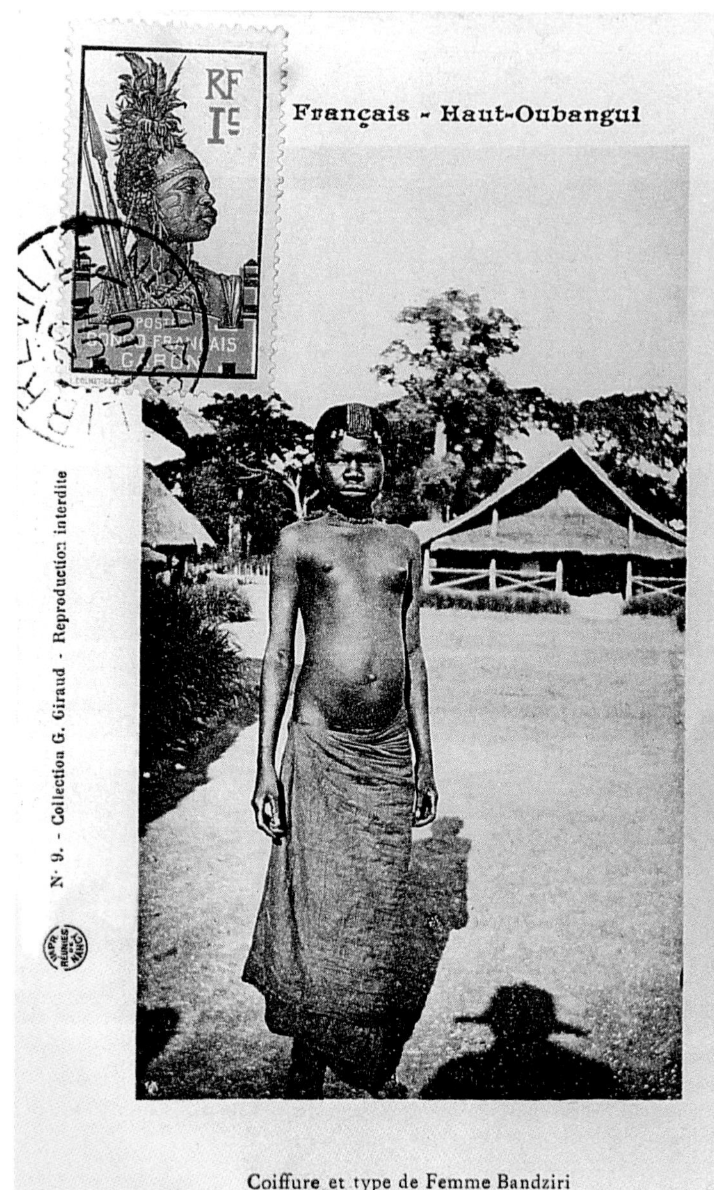

Fig. 25. "Coiffure et type de Femme Bandziri."
From Gabonese postcard, ca. 1900–1925, private collection.

Fig. 26. Overmodeled skull, 27 × 15–17 cm, Sepik.
Museu de Antropologia da Universidade do Porto (84.01.071).

Fig. 27. Sychnecta, Mohawk displayed in the Blauw Jan inn in Amsterdam in 1764. Etching by A. Smit after drawing by P. Barbiers, 26 × 19.5 cm, Dressmann Collection (Dr. pr. 1436, neg. no. D6839), Department of Prints and Drawings, Gemeentearchief, Amsterdam.

in Rouen (the main French center for trade in brazilwood) for the French king Henri II and his wife Catherine of Medici on 1 and 2 October 1550. French ceremonies of possession enacted in the New World were marked by a strong sense of the dramatic in which the local natives were also involved (Seed 1995), and the same was true of this event staged on French soil. Some fifty Brazilian Indians were supposed to give a display of life and battle in an Indian settlement, a task in which they were assisted by 250 French sailors, merchants, and adventurers dressed—or undressed—as Indians. The setting was a meadow which had been planted to resemble what a Brazilian forest landscape was expected to look like, including huts carved from tree trunks. Before the main action began—a fight between the two tribes—the royal procession about to enter the city of Rouen was allowed to enjoy the spectacle of everyday life in a Brazilian village: scenes of hunting and gathering, tree felling,[10] native dances, and open sexual activities, all under the eye of a naked "royal" couple who observe the scene from a hammock.[11] The staged action of the defeat of the "Tabagerres" by the "Toupinabaulx" and the subsequent burning of the village of the former was repeated on the second day of the celebrations, though with the roles of the two tribes reversed.[12]

Some features of the Rouen festivities reveal a continuity with the more static presentations of the exotic in the *Wunderkammern*. First, the same aristocratic filter, by which individuals like Montaigne could idealize and admire the noble and generous mode of warfare of the Amerindians, can be seen in the predilection for battle scenes.[13] Moreover, the highlighting of this particular activity inevitably reinforced the stereotype of the aggressive Indian, which could always be used to justify European aggression in the name of retaliation. Second, the presentation of scenes of "everyday life" involved an attempt to recreate life in Brazil by what were regarded as its salient characteristics. This inevitably entailed a static presentation of a stereotype in which individuals and individual acts were generalized. Indeed, the question of what constituted typical traits of a society was itself a question of representativeness. Dance, which was particularly singled out as a marker of the primitive both in early representations and in the nineteenth-century world expositions (Hinsley 1991, 361), naturally belonged to the repertoire, as it still does today in many tourist displays of "staged authenticity."[14] We might regard this stereotypical presentation as a dramatized version of the "typical landscape": not just the natural historical setting, but also the cultural setting is recreated to convey the impression of activities which are appropriate to, and revealing of, the "primitive" people in question. The turning of everyday activities into spectacle required that the exotic be transplanted to a different spatial context—the exotic is never at home—which accounts for the presence of a fence, platform, stage, or reconstructed village to mark the scene of the action off as something which is more exotic than everyday domestic life (cf. Kirshenblatt-Gimblett 1991, 407–9). Third, the plethora of activities depicted in the woodcut corresponds to the impulse to cram the exotic to overflowing. Like the profusion of exotic artifacts in later allegories of the four continents, the simple amassing of items substitutes for a grasp of their intrinsic meaning. It is the blankness of the exotic to the outside gaze to which this *horror vacui* is a response. Finally, the drama combines both genuine and nonauthentic exotic items; as far as the latter are concerned, it is enough to refer to the acting out of supposed Brazilian scenes by French sailors on French soil, in a setting which had been devised to function as a typical landscape.

Another illustration of the scene even alluded to how the native Brazilians came to find themselves on French soil by including the French merchant ship which brought the captured natives from the New World to the Old.[15] Such a reenactment of the subjugation of Amerindians by the natives themselves has its parallels in colonial theater as practiced in New Spain. At roughly the same time that this spectacle was being enacted in Rouen, the theater of spectacle was being used in Mexico to "recall past native humiliations, to create memories of present failures, both native and Iberian, and to project future images of these colonized peoples" (Trexler 1984, 190). Thus, native Indians were recruited to perform in military triumphs commemorating St. Hippolytus, the saint on whose day the Spaniards had conquered Tenochtitlán and its empire, and St. James, the captain of the Spanish armies. Dressed as Spaniards, native Indians had to ride out to welcome genuine Spaniards with the cry of "Santiago!" More humiliating still, the Indians, whose long hair had been cut by the Spaniards, were now dressed in long-hair wigs to imitate their former state. Moreover, it was not just ordinary Indians who acted out these humiliating roles, for Motolinía emphasized that it was the "signors and principals" of Tlaxcala who played the roles in the celebrations held in 1539. In Tlaxcala it was an army of Indians playing Indians who enacted what the Spaniards hoped would soon be history: the conquest of Jerusalem from the Moors (cf. Gutiérrez Estévez 1993).[16]

There is also a strong dramatic element in the public display of the Eskimos whom Martin Frobisher captured on his second voyage in 1577.[17] A man, woman, and child who were captured and taken to Bristol in October of that year were soon put on public display. The man, Kalicho, paddled his kayak on the River Avon and demonstrated his skill in hunting ducks. On another occasion he demonstrated the use of dogs to draw sleighs. Dramatic display of a different kind was envisaged when the female and male captives were brought together "in what the English seem to have regarded as a theatrical spectacle" (Greenblatt 1991, 117). Though there is no evidence that they were man and wife, the audience hoped to catch a glimpse of primitive mating habits—in vain.[18] This seemed to set a pattern for Eskimo displays. At any rate, when the Dutch entrepreneur Adriaen Leverstyn brought an Eskimo from Davis Strait to lend support to the claims of his "Little Northern Company" in the 1620s, the man was expected to put on a similar display of kayak maneuvering and hunting on the lake known as the Hofvijver in front of the Dutch seat of government in The Hague.[19] Besides hunting fish and waterfowl, the man also gave displays of eating them raw. The Danish expeditions to the North Atlantic in the early seventeenth century also brought back Eskimos who were displayed in public (cf. Whitehead 1987; Harbsmeier 1997). No doubt some of the Eskimos and others who were kidnapped to take part in exhibitions of this kind managed to escape, and some of those Eskimos sighted off the Scottish coast might have been abducted Eskimos on the run (Idiens 1987).

Besides their involvement in the Renaissance culture of spectacle, the captive Eskimos were also made the subject of ethnographic portraits.[20] The first of Frobisher's captives to be brought to England, in 1576, described at the time as a trophy ("new prey"), died a fortnight after arriving in London. Cornelis Ketel, a Flemish painter resident in London at the time, was commissioned to make portraits of the man, none of which has survived.[21] Nevertheless, we can gain some idea of their content from contemporary records and from some of the eighteen depictions by other hands which are still extant (Sturtevant and Quinn 1987, 88ff.). Greenblatt classifies them in accordance with three distinct approaches to the Other. First, the full-size portraits featuring native dress as well as the presence of a kayak bear witness to cultural otherness—the ethnographic portrait with the unfamiliar cultural artifacts functioning as a typically exotic "landscape." In this form, these portraits of named individuals entered the sets of costume types of exotic peoples, thereby ending up as typifying whole populations. Second, the portrait of the Eskimo in English dress would seem to be doing the opposite: the ability of clothing to effect a transformation brings about an equivalence between European and non-European. Third, the portrait of the Eskimo without any clothing, according to Greenblatt, suggests both an opaque, unreadable body and a Shakespearean "bare, forked animality that is the common condition of all men and women" (1991, 112).

In addition to their role in dramatic spectacles and ethnographic portraits, the Eskimos also made an early contribution to the development of the allegory of the four continents. This can be seen from the copper engraving "America," one of a set of four by Philipp Galle after a drawing by Marcus Gheeraerts the Elder (Exh. Cat. Antwerp 1992, no. 74). This engraving, which features standing figures of an Eskimo man and woman with baby, must have been created more or less immediately after the display of the Eskimos in question (Sturtevant and Quinn 1987, 93).

Finally, there is a direct relation between the Eskimos and the collections of curiosities. Some of the items in the catalog of John Tradescant's collection in London, which mentions "A Canow & Picture of an Indian with his Bow and Dart, taken 10 leagues at Sea. *An.*° –76'" (Allen 1964, 266), may well have derived from Frobisher's Eskimos (cf. Sturtevant and Quinn 1987, 73). In a similar fashion, three items associated with the three Mohawks and a Mahican who visited England in 1710 found their way to the collection of Sir Hans Sloane (Feest 1984, 89); in 1712 Ralph Thoresby owned a knife "taken from one of the Mohawks at London, An. 1710" (Feest 1992, 82). Many other collections included portraits of non-European peoples and illustrations of their artifacts, as well as the artifacts themselves.

The live display of Eskimos is attested for the seventeenth century in Germany and continued there well into the nineteenth century (Feest 1984, 86). In France, a fever of curiosity was aroused by the arrival of six Brazilian Tupinamba in April 1613, who performed dances with maracas for the young French monarch (Hamy 1908). As in the case of Frobisher's Eskimos, the portraits that have survived show a range of attitudes to cultural difference. While the engravings made by Joachim Duviert present the Tupinambas in courtly dress, with their maracas and extravagant hairstyles as the only exotic features (Exh. Cat. Paris 1976, 21–22), other engravings depict them clad only in a minimal feathered apron, their bodies almost entirely covered by tattoos, wielding a club, bow, and arrows (Vitart 1992, 118–19).

These events in Paris coincided with a wave of interest in Amerindians in the British capital. While Pocahontas was being presented to the British Queen in 1616,[22] two other native Virginians were on display along with domestic and foreign animals in the zoo in St. James's Park in London (Feest 1984, 87–88). Incidentally, the latter attitude, which places non-European peoples on a par with animals, can be documented from a host of other examples.[23] Oblivious to any distinction among human beings, plants, and animals, the prefect of the Farnese gardens in Rome, Tobia Aldini, included in his description of the curiosities (*mirabilia*) of the cardinal's court a certain Arrigo Gonzalez; this native of the Canary Islands,[24] whose face was completely covered with long hair because of a hereditary condition of hypertrichosis, had been given by the Duke of Parma to Cardinal Odoardo Farnese (Zapperi 1985, 310). Later, in the eighteenth century, both humans and animals were displayed in the Blauw Jan inn in Amsterdam, including a giant from Finland and a dwarf from the Dutch province of Friesland (Hamell 1987; Pieters and Mörzer Bruyns 1988). At roughly the same time, Joseph Banks was harboring plans to bring an islander back with him as a souvenir of his trip to the South Pacific on Cook's first voyage; he explicitly refers to keeping him "as a curiosity, as well as some of my neighbors do lions and tygers at a larger expense than he will probably ever put me to" (Guest 1992, 104). The same telling juxtaposition of human and animal forms is displayed in a colored drawing from Adolf von Mentzel's 1885 sketchbook, *The Zulus*, in which wildly dancing Negroes on a cabaret stage repeat the forms of exotic animals on the curtain behind them (Lloyd 1991b, 104).[25]

The fact that non-Europeans were displayed in settings appropriate to both popular and courtly entertainment does not exhaust all the possibilities, for in the nineteenth century other interests became involved as well. The dramatic presentation competed with ethnographic collections in the nineteenth and twentieth centuries as a site for the production of knowledge about exotic lands, particularly those which were also tied to some European country by colonial bonds. Although the allegorical nature of the frontispieces and the personifications of the four continents was explicit, the colonial allegory that was narrated in these spectacles was often masked behind their designation as scientific, international, trade, or colonial exhibitions. In their use of tangible human and inanimate ethnographic realia, these dramatic representations served to shape and to reinforce European images of the exotic.

Many of the grand schemes for the display of exotic peoples in the nineteenth century were not put into effect, such as George Catlin's plan for a floating museum of mankind (Poignant 1992, 51) or Joseph Fayrer's proposal that the Asiatic Society of Bengal should organize an ethnological exhibition "with typical examples of the races of the old world," who were to submit to be photographed, painted, and taken in casts (Pinney 1990, 255), but among those who were brought to Europe from the colonies were Eskimos, North American Plains Indians, Australian Aborigines, "Aztecs," members of Bantu races, Batwa pygmies from Africa, and Ainu from Japan (Street 1992, 122). Their appearance helped to reinforce the values of the dominant powers, both abroad and at home. This latter aspect explains the easy elision which took place between non-European peoples and members of the European lower classes: both categories shared the fact that they were excluded from the central structures of power.[26] Symptomatic of this isomorphism is a pair of photographs of Batwa pygmies in London, taken in 1905; while the first shows them dressed on the terrace of the House of Commons with members of Parliament, emphasizing both the civilizing role of the colonial power and the gulf separating civilizer and civilized, the second shows the same pygmies undressed in what is supposed to be a fitting habitat—a working-class backyard (reproductions in Street 1992, 129). A similar merging of the notions of class and race can be seen in the fact that the modeled figures of the peoples of Imperial Russia displayed at the Moscow Ethnographic Exhibition in 1867 included both "non-Russian races," such as the Samoyed, and "classes" of people engaged in various professions (Poignant 1992, 47–48).[27]

The emphasis on habitat as an index of civilization was driven home in the Exposition Universelle in Paris in 1889, where no less than thirty-nine houses of different types were constructed to illustrate the diversity of dwelling arrangements (Greenhalgh 1989, 91). Such a "History of Human Habitation" implied a general unity of humankind, in that all of its members lived in some kind of habitation. On the other hand, the juxtaposition of anthropological "survivals" and "primitive" cultures might serve precisely to highlight their difference. For example, in the reconstruction of both an Irish village and a Senegalese village at the Franco-British Exhibition in London in 1908, the supposedly simple European communities were still intended to show the self-evident superiority of the European peoples in relation to those whom they colonized.[28] It is characteristic that the guidebooks produced for the occasion referred to the ancient traditions of the Irish and the Scots but assumed that the Africans were a people without tradition or history (Coombes 1991, 206–7).

Yet another possibility was to imply an affinity between European aristocrats and their non-European counterparts. When the Khedive of Egypt paid a visit to Paris in 1867 to attend a universal exposition, he was accommodated in an imitation palace which had been built as a copy of medieval Cairo. In fact, he became a part of the exhibition, with the palace functioning as his "typical landscape" (Mitchell 1989, 220). The implied affinity between aristocrats throughout the world (cf. Tamplin 1992) was not always of a complimentary nature. Thus, it was considered possible to see a parallel between the allegedly wild practices of the Mohawks and those of a class of aristocratic ruffians in eighteenth-century London by dubbing the latter "Mohocks" (Fuller 1983, 3–4; Hamell 1987, 189). The name derived its topicality from the Mohawk chiefs who visited London in a colonial deputation early in 1710.[29]

Like the objects in collections, the authenticity of the people on display might have seemed to have bypassed the doubts raised by the representation. After all, were they not the real thing? As a journalist commented on the panorama "Le Tour du Monde" at the Paris Exposition Universelle in 1900: "To animate the authentic decor, we need the inhabitants. And it should not be immobile, cardboard or wax figures—nor supernumeraries recruited in Paris and dressed in fake exotic costumes" (cited in Exh. Cat. Antwerp 1993, 48). Nevertheless, entrepreneurs sometimes had recourse to fakes. For example, at a time when French illustrated mass magazines were reporting the raising of the French flag over Timbuktu in January 1894, the interest in the defeated Africans was fed by the exhibition of Tuaregs in the Champs-de-Mars during the same year. However, it was soon discovered that these "Tuaregs" had been recruited among the inhabitants of Constantine province in Algeria (Schneider 1982, 146). Captain Samuel Hadlock, one of the nineteenth-century entrepreneurs to take Eskimos to Europe, displayed a similar resourcefulness: when one of his Eskimos succumbed to a European disease, as was often the case,[30] Hadlock simply replaced him with a gypsy, who was dressed up in sealskin and exhibited as an Indian (Wright 1987). Another entrepreneur, George Catlin, began a traveling show in England in 1840 which included scenes of Indian life acted out by European actors dressed up as Indians. When the potential of these make-believe Indians had been exhausted, he employed nine Ojibwa Indians, to be succeeded by other Ojibwa and Iowa Indians in the next few years (Mulvey 1987). Authentic Indians were not used in Buffalo Bill's show until 1877, and in the early twentieth century Hans-Stoch Sarrasani did not hesitate to supplement the cast of his circus with natives of Dresden disguised as Indians (Conrad 1987). Under the name of "interpretive theater," the Canadian Museum of Civilization in Quebec now employs a troupe of professional actors to provide "supportive interpretation of specific exhibits" (MacDonald 1992, 171).

Botocudos in London, Bella Coolas in Bremen, Seneca in Manchester, Sioux in Budapest, Sioux at Windsor—there seemed to be no end to Europe's thirst for exotic human exhibits. Interest in them came from both popular and learned circles. This can be well illustrated from the late nineteenth century, although there are earlier precedents.[31] For instance, the exhibition of thirty-four African skulls in the university of Leipzig in 1885 has its popular parallel in the display of an "Anthropological Cabinet" on the Michaelismesse in the same city in 1862; the cabinet included eight men and women from various parts of Africa (Exh. Cat. Leipzig 1995, 5). The presence of Bella Coola Indians in Germany in 1885 was utilized by scholars interested in musicology, anthropometry, and material culture, including Franz Boas (Feest 1984, 94), who was later to include North American Indians in the World's Columbian Exposition in Chicago in 1893 (Hinsley 1991). The anthropologist Prince Roland Bonaparte took advantage of the presence of natives from Surinam at the Amsterdam World Exposition in 1883 to carry out a systematic work of physical anthropology, including the inevitable craniometry. Two years earlier, one of the members of the Anthropological Society who visited the exhibition of Tierra del Fuegians in Paris five times complained that, though he had been able to take fifty measurements of each, he had been unable to examine and measure their genitals (Schneider 1982, 131). In an address delivered in 1900, the British anthropologist W. H. R. Rivers called for more use to be made of the opportunities for the inspection of colonized peoples that such exhibitions presented (Coombes 1994, 88). As late as 1928, Géza Róheim could practice doing "fieldwork" on a Somalian troupe which spent a month in Budapest (Goldmann 1987, 90).

We even find some scholars actually operating as showmen: the nineteenth-century comparatist Max Müller and another colleague of his from Oxford made use of natives from the East to illustrate the delivery of their papers at a notorious congress of orientalists in Berlin (Mitchell 1989, 218). A meeting held at the Anthropological Institute in London in 1885 combined an exhibition of Roland Bonaparte's photographs of Lapps, papers on the physical anthropology and ethnography of the Sami, and the presence of a Sami group as living exhibits (Edwards 1995b, 318–19). In general, however, colonized subjects were not available in the flesh for educational settings like the museum, which had to make do with photographs, casts, skeletons, and skulls, even though ethnographic displays still made ample use of patently theatrical gestures and techniques to display people and things (Kirshenblatt-Gimblett 1991, 397ff.).

It remains doubtful whether this form of contact ever yielded any insight into Indian lifestyles—a "jumble of foreignness" (Hinsley 1991, 351) was usually enough. One of the clearest examples of this jumble can be seen from the performances expected of the Creek "princes" displayed in the 1720s by Captain John Pight: they had to juggle with rubber balls and logs like the Aztecs who had been displayed in Spain in 1529; paddle their kayaks like Eskimos; drill fire, throw their spears, or shoot with their bows and arrows; and flash their scarlet cloaks open to reveal (upon payment) their extensive tattoos (Feest 1987, 615). Evidently, they conformed to the fairly clear understanding on the part of the spectators as to what they expected to see—the exotic. A revealing piece of evidence in this respect concerns the six Osages who arrived at Le Havre in 1827 and were the rage of Paris for a couple of years, until interest fell off and funds eventually had to be raised for their repatriation (Honour 1975, 231). During their stay in Europe, an enormous blue whale which had stranded off the Belgian coast was brought to land in Ostend and put on display to the public in 1828.[32] The event was celebrated in a litho which appeared in the Brussels weekly *L'Industriel* of that year, depicting *La baleine d'Ostende visitée par l'Eléphant, le Giraffe, les Osages,* and the monthly *De Arke Noach's* even published a fictional correspondence between the Osages and the giraffes (Keyser 1993, 60).

The Osages, then, were regarded as exotic exhibits of the same kind as elephants and giraffes, animals usually found in a zoo. In the second half of the century, when a new kind of exhibition was presented in the Jardin d'Acclimatation in Paris to attract a larger audience, the display included not only African camels, giraffes, exotic species of cattle, elephants, miniature rhinoceros, and ostriches, but fourteen Africans into the bargain. The addition of humans to the animal display as an afterthought was such a success that it was repeated with different ethnographic exhibitions in the subsequent years to boost gate receipts (Schneider 1982, 128ff.).[33]

The European audiences were disappointed that the Bella Coolas did not look like Indians (Haberland 1988a) and that the Cayuga chief who spent a year in Geneva in the 1920s, in the vain hope of gaining from the League of Nations recognition for the Six Nations as an independent state, did not have an aquiline nose (Rostkowski 1987, 445). When the entrepreneur Johan Adrian Jacobsen was engaged in hiring a troupe of Oglalas for the summer show of Hagenbeck's zoo in 1910, he took pains to exclude anyone who spoke English or who had short hair (Haberland 1988b). A member of the Anthropological Society complained that the Tierra del Fuegians on display in the Jardin d'Acclimatation in Paris in 1881 did not look like the people described in accounts he had read by travelers who had been there (Schneider 1982, 131).[34] North American Plains Indians were expected to have tomahawks, blankets, and tepees, whereas Native Americans from the Andes were expected to have a poncho, blanket, and hat (Scherer 1992, 35).

On the other hand, audiences did not seem to mind that the Botocudos were wearing Hawaiian feather cloaks and North American attributes in addition to their Brazilian lip and ear plugs. In fact, the presentation of the Brazilian Botocudos clad in material that was mainly derived from North America constitutes a reversal of the process of "Tupinambization" by which North American Indians were portrayed with the attributes of their South American, particularly Brazilian, counterparts. The fact that these Botocudos were exhibited in London together with William Bullock's Lapps indicates that what counted was a superficially and immediately recognizable exotic appearance, no matter where the various accoutrements originated.[35] As has been pointed out with respect to Conrad's *Heart of Darkness,* "the erasure of a precise location and of historical and ethnic specificity gives to the native peoples he represents the appearance of the near-mythic" (Fothergill 1992, 51). The resulting composite image, "primitive man," can then readily be inserted within an evolutionary scheme of history on a lower rung to that of the observer.[36]

From Entertainment to Edification?

During the course of the nineteenth century, it is possible to chart a growing process of diversification and fragmentation as the different forms of presentation went their separate ways. The Renaissance chamber of curiosities and works of art had already undergone a transformation in the eighteenth century, when the two types of collection began to part company, or at least the relations between them shifted (see ch. 4). From this time on, rarities were generally banned from the collection of works of art. Their place was now in natural historical or ethnological museums, firmly separated from the museums which housed the cultural heritage of Western art. At the same time, a further division arose between the private collections of amateurs and more academically organized collections, often attached to scientific institutions. This development can be illustrated, for instance, by the contrast between Sir John Soane's semipublic house-museum in London, preserved in its 1837 form by an Act of Parliament, and the British Museum built around the original bequest by Sir Hans Sloane, which was rising in its present form at the same time. The former not only served as a visual history of art, architecture, decoration, and design, but also continued the tradition of the *Kunst- und Wunderkammern* by including such objects as pieces of elm bark shaped like Ionic volutes, an old wooden-and-leather clog, part of the horn of a deer, gemstones, a Sumatran fungus, and so forth; the latter, informed by a spirit of rationalism and professionalism, stands for what we now regard as the canonical museum.[37]

Within this tendency toward diversification, it remains to be seen whether some of the distinguishing characteristics of the Renaissance collection of curiosities and the Renaissance displays and dramas continued to exert an influence on these later, more divergent modes of presenting the exotic. That the lines of demarcation were not always strictly drawn can be deduced from the history of Hampton University in Virginia, where students were encouraged to handle and try on the objects in the ethnographic collection. These artifacts were used in pageants during the early years of the twentieth century in ways which recall the Rouen festivities. For instance, all but one of the actors dressed as African warriors in a Hampton Folklore Pageant in 1913 were American students (Zeidler and Hultgren 1988, 104). There is even a reminiscence of the theater of humiliation in the acting out of the transformation of an African village from savagery to civilization by the return of the Hampton-educated chief's son (106).[38]

Many of the features of the Renaissance presentation of the exotic can be traced in the history of another North American ethnographic collection, that of the American Museum of Natural History. The aristocratic filter, for instance, was still at work in the hall of African ethnology, where a photograph from 1910 displays ethnographic artifacts and mounted animal trophies side by side, "giving it the appearance of a grand trophy hall in the mansion of a nineteenth century sportsman" (Schildkrout 1988, 158). Indeed, the combination of hunting trophies and native weapons in decorative arrangements was common enough at the time, not only in European and American museums and expositions but also in private settings (Arnoldi 1992, 447). It was not until the 1930s that the presentation of the history of humanity in the same way as the history of animal life fell into discredit in this museum, at last marking a break with the time-hallowed tradition of displaying humans and animals together. The same process seems to be at work in the presentation of the famous bear ceremonies of the Ainu of Japan to a London audience at the Japan-British Exhibition of 1910. While little remains of the complex ritual of the killing of bears, the postcard of "The Bear Killer" which accompanied the event presents an old man and a bear head in a pose that is reminiscent of European conceptions of the hunter and his trophy (Street 1992, 126).[39] Not surprisingly, the same image of the collector as hunter crops up in the discourse of colonial administrators. One such figure remarked that collecting figures of Hindu gods brought him some of the delights associated with securing a specially good head or meritorious skin (Breckenridge 1989, 210).

It is hardly surprising that, in the case of those whose claim to status was based on wealth rather than on lineage, the aristocratic filter was replaced by a plutocratic one. Thus, in the plans for a museum and art gallery in Port Sunlight, U.K., W. H. Lever intended the largest part of the premises to be taken up by ethnographic exhibits, operating as a symbolic link between his activities as a collector and his commercial interests. In fact, the trips on which Lever did his collecting were always associated with business opportunities (West 1992).[40]

With the shift from a collection of curiosities to an educational institution (cf. Coombes 1991, 194),[41] the museum was bound to resort to the display of a smaller volume of exhibits, combined with an increase in accompanying documentation.[42] A novel feature of the African Hall in the American Museum of Natural History was the use of color transparencies mounted in window boxes to create a context for the objects on display. This was followed by the creation of large mammal dioramas, a technique which was later extended to the ethnological exhibits.[43] When a shift from geographic to ecological ordering took place (under the aegis of the anthropologist Colin Turnbull), dioramas continued to be used in the later displays (Schildkrout 1988, 158).[44] This example shows, once again, the familiar bracketing together of humans and animals, combined with the desire to set them against a typical landscape[45]—all techniques familiar from the ethnographic portraits of Brazilian Indians painted by Albert Eckhout in the seventeenth century (see ch. 3).

The use of photographs to document the isolated artifacts on display in museums like the Blackmore Museum in Salisbury or the Pitt Rivers Museum in the 1880s is characteristic of the need to provide an appropriate narrative structure in which the artifacts can be embedded. Photographic realism is used to bridge the gap between the site of collection, its human reality, and the object on display in the museum. Outside the museum, in the art gallery, we can detect a similar process at work in some nineteenth-century presentations of works of art. When Frederic Church's *Heart of the Andes* was displayed to the paying public in a special, one-picture exhibition in 1859, this vast canvas was placed in an elaborate wooden structure with parted draperies to give the illusion of looking out of a window onto the exotic landscape, and the exoticism was probably heightened by the addition of dried tropical plants which Church had brought back from South America.[46] Five years later, the exhibition of Albert Bierstadt's equally enormous *The Rocky Mountains, Lander's Peak* (which he painted at the same time and in the same place in which Church was working on *The Heart of the Andes*; see Anderson 1990, 74) in the picture gallery of the Metropolitan Fair in New York was accompanied by a *tableau vivant* in front of a painted backdrop in the nearby India Department; Onondaga Indians from upstate New York were brought in to impersonate the Shoshone represented in the painting (Sandweiss 1992, 118). These displays recall the combination of items of natural history from a foreign country with artistic representations of the same country in connection with the events in the Mauritshuis after the return of Johan Maurits von Nassau from Brazil (see ch. 4). They betray both a loss of belief in the illusionist quality of the paintings and a feeling that their confinement to two dimensions requires some kind of three-dimensional boost to bring out their narrative content.

By this time the technique of photography had been developed, and a new challenge to painterly realism was issued from this quarter, although Smith's claim (1988, 256) that the invention of photography brought the close alliance between art and science to an end overstates the case.[47] Isolated anthropological photographs, of course, cannot provide a narrative in the strict sense, since they lack sequence. Nevertheless, a series of photographs can have narrative pretensions, and accompanying texts may also fill the observer in on what is supposed to be the appropriate background.[48] Nomenclature can fit the photograph into a colonial narrative, particularly when a title of a generic kind suggests a timeless, static existence outside the dynamic West. The labeling of one of E. H. Man's photographs as "Andamanese Shooting, Dancing, Sleeping and Greeting" (Edwards 1992b, 110) betrays Man's eagerness to conform to the guidelines laid down in *Notes and Queries* and reveals an approach to native culture similar to that we saw in the case of the Rouen festivities: the labeling of particular activities as typically everyday and thus generic.

There is a degree of continuity between the anthropological photograph and the forms of ethnographic realism characteristic of the prephotographic era—and indeed of the yet earlier traditions of anatomic representation.[49] For example, as Edwards has pointed out (1992a, 8), the anthropometric systems devised in the 1860s were absorbed into a more general realistic aesthetic; they may be alluded to both in photographs intended to show or display culture and in portrait types. Francis Galton experimented briefly with the use of composite photography in craniometry, and the use of composite portraits to analyze racial types was applied both to Jews and to American Indians (Green 1985, 12 n. 27). Similar theories of racial types underlay Pitt Rivers's interest in the paintings of South American Indians executed by Edward Goodall during the British Guiana boundary expedition of the Schomburgk brothers in 1841–43 (Mowat 1993). As far as portraits are concerned, there is also continuity in the way in which the focus on (male) dress and personal adornment tends to present a very narrow segment of material culture, both in the prephotographic portrait (cf. Kasprycki 1990, 115) and in the photographic portrait. The continuing importance of the dance as a marker of the primitive, and the ease with which it lent itself to sensationalism and romanticism, can be seen in the fascination that native dance ceremonies held for Western photographers.[50] For example, although dance among the Kuba of the former Congo was tied to the exercise of authority, Western photographers elicited staged dances to reinforce the stereotype that "Africa dances" (Vansina 1992, 198). In the case of Richard Baxter Townshend, who witnessed and photographed a Hopi snake dance in 1903,[51] we can see how his tampering with the negatives led to a loss of high-definition detail, indicating that it was the exotic drama of the dance, rather than its particularities, which appealed (Gidley 1987). By contrast, when a Native American photographer, Freddie Honhongva, presents a Hopi ceremonial performer, it is emphatically not at a dramatic moment (Gidley 1992a, 69).

Another area in which continuity can be detected is in the more general field of the presentation of the exotic through a familiar aesthetic, often taken from the classical world. A sixteenth-century example is provided by John White's drawing of an Indian conjurer (Hulton 1984, pl. 49), which seems to be influenced by Giambologna's famous bronze statue of Mercury. Many instances of this process can be found in eighteenth-century representations of the peoples of the South Pacific. Under the influence of the Italianate style that dominated English taste at this time, it was thought appropriate to apply a grand style to the portrayal of the events of Cook's voyages. A particularly striking example is provided by Johann Zoffany's canvas of the death of Captain Cook, painted around 1795: Cook himself is portrayed in a pose borrowed from the iconography of the Dying Gaul,[52] while his killer is shaped after another figure of classical iconography, the Discobolus (Smith 1988, 120; 1992, 235). Another model from classical antiquity, Polykleitos's figure of the ideal warrior, Doryphoros, served as the iconographic framework for Piron's drawing of an Admiralty Islander (Smith 1988, 149). And the artist who accompanied Cook on the third and fatal voyage, Webber, modeled his representation of Tongan boxers on the images of the Borghese Gladiator to be found in a late seventeenth-century book of anatomy for artists (Joppien and Smith 1988, 30; Smith 1992, 182).[53] Besides these South Sea examples, one could cite "Europe supported by Africa and America," one of the sixteen plates which William Blake engraved for the *Narrative of a Five Years Expedition against the Revolted Negroes of Surinam* by John Gabriel Stedman in the 1790s,[54] which draws on the iconography of the Three Graces.[55] Although this use of classicizing models might be regarded as an instance of false perception, Smith argues that its ennobling effect on representations of non-Western peoples implies a critique of Eurocentric artistic standards (1992, 60). We know from Blake's writings where his sympathies lay, but in other cases the classical or classicizing framework may have been used ironically to point up the contrast between, say, white canons of beauty and black bodies. Something of the kind seems to be at work in Joshua Reynolds's famous portrait of the Tahitian Omai (as colonial discourse called him; in fact, this islander from Raiatea was called Mai), brought to England by James Cook in 1774. While the pose of this figure in the painting is that of a "self-confident patrician" (Smith 1988, 80–81), recalling the grandeur of the Apollo Belvedere, the fact that the tattoos on Omai's left hand are so prominently displayed in the center of the painting implies a discrepancy between the dignity imparted by the classical pose, on the one hand, and the barbarian savagery of which the tattoos could be taken to be symptomatic, on the other (Guest 1992, 106).[56]

The deployment of classical or classicizing conventions in ethnographic presentations and representations persisted in the nineteenth century. Thus, the Ojibwa whom Catlin brought to Europe were drawn by Eugène Delacroix, but in poses suggestive of a Greek mode (Honour 1975, 236–37). The presence of such classicizing models, particularly that of the Graces, was to become commonplace in ethnographic photography, overriding geographic or ethnic boundaries (Edwards 1992a, 9). George Catlin frequently borrowed from the poses of classical statuary for the oil paintings in his Indian Gallery, and after the discovery of photography his successors did the same, draping standing figures to resemble Roman orators or setting them in reclining poses reminiscent of orientalist fantasies. As Dippie (1992) points out, these photographers had read their *Hiawatha.*

Presentations of the exotic through the medium of photography follow the same rules of increasing or decreasing exoticism—"laying it on thick" or "toning it down"—which can be found in earlier representations. For example, a photograph of Swampy Cree people from around 1925 includes one woman wearing a rabbit-skin robe, although they were not used as items of dress at the time—she put it on for the occasion (Edwards 1992a, 12). Although this woman apparently chose to appear in this way in the photograph, Edward S. Curtis chose how he wanted his subjects to look for them, photographing "traditional" Native Americans after issuing wigs to cover shorn hair, providing costumes, and removing signs of the mechanical age (Gidley 1992b, 103–4). One could also contrast the highly aestheticized photographs of Australian Aborigines made in J. W. Lindt's studio in the early 1870s (Quartermaine 1992), where they were set within a constructed romantic landscape with authentic plants, with the contemporary images of Aborigines by Fred Kruger, who photographed them mainly in European dress, playing cricket and fishing (Poignant 1992, 54). The fact that Lindt's photographs are represented in virtually every ethnographic archive in Europe, while Kruger's are very rare, tells us a lot about the construction of the anthropological object. There are similarly contrasting images of the Todas of southern India: although some photographs portray them in a manner suggestive of a Jewish patriarchal family or of toga-clad Roman senators, W. H. R. Rivers strove to attain a documentary realism and to break with the picturesque arcadian visions of these inhabitants of "a sort of tropical Switzerland" (Pinney 1992a, 84).

The idealizing aesthetic is often the product of awareness that the image may well be one of the last to be made of a disappearing world—hence its pastoral and nostalgic tones. In one case, that of the portraits of Trucanini, the last of the Tasmanians, the predominance of this aesthetic has meant that Woolley's photograph of a melancholic woman living on after the desecration of her husband's corpse has displaced earlier Tasmanian portraits by colonial artists whose accurate representations of Tasmanians and their culture embodied an aesthetic different from the deceptive official discourse (Rae-Ellis 1992, 232–33).[57] This aesthetic requires that the people being portrayed are clearly demarcated from the standpoint of the observer. Both the methodological detachment of a Rivers and the detachment from everyday existence implied by the romantic images are functions of the same urge to remove the people being portrayed from contact with the observer and present them in what is often a timeless setting—a characteristic of photography in general, it might be added.[58] In this respect, the anthropological photograph functions in the same way as the ethnographic present, for while the latter sets the ethnographic (human) object within a static temporality of its own, divorced from that of the observer, the photograph by its very nature suggests a cult of remembrance that mourns for what is no more (Benjamin 1968, 226). This aesthetic also implies the need to erase any marks of the impingement of the observer's presence on the image if it is to correspond to an unblemished primitivism. One rarely finds evidence of the photographer's presence in the anthropological photograph: "The photographer, invisible beneath his black cloth as he eyed the world through his camera's gaze, in this respect typified the kind of presence desired by the European in the Middle East, whether as tourist, writer or indeed colonial power . . . The representation of the Orient, in its attempt to be detached and objective, would seek to eliminate from the picture the presence of the European observer" (Mitchell 1989, 230). Where the presence of the photographer has not been elided, as in the framing of a scene from the doorway of the anthropologist's tent, the effect is generally artistic—a framing device—rather than documentary. The exotic is never at home—so any traces of "home" have to be erased.

In his publication of a series of late-nineteenth-century African postcards, Corbey (1988, 1989) provides many examples of an increased exoticism through increased eroticism, as the fantasies of orientalist painting found their way into the medium of photography for postcard production.[59] Inasmuch as the dynamic and control of the production of these postcards was a commercial affair, other factors may have played a part in the choice of the images selected or created, but they still reveal a continuity with the images discussed above. For instance, the scanty dress of the women portrayed in these photographs, especially the extremely low position of the clothing they wear on their hips, conforms less to ethnographic authenticity than to the instructions of the photographer. In some cases, what are presented as images of "the African woman" are in fact photographs of prostitutes, and the European poses have been studiously copied from the conventions of European erotic photography. The packaging of such photographs in works with academic pretensions in no way affected the nature of the poses required of the women; the language of science is here being used to legitimate the popular gaze—to the extent that it is possible to separate the two. For example, the arid caption "Gestalt und Körperbau" to accompany a photograph of Wahima/Watussi women, instructed by Oberleutnant Max Weiss to strip and stand in a row for the photographer, hardly does justice to Weiss's claim that it would be hard to find more attractive female bodies in Europe (Corbey 1989, 33). Sometimes the caption attempts to deflect attention away from the bodies on display: a photograph published in 1900 in *Reliquary,* a serious antiquarian journal, displayed five nearly nude women's bodies under the precarious alibi of "Benin girls with aprons of Bells" (Coombes 1994, 12–13, where the photograph is reproduced).

In a sense, photography itself can be seen as a symbol of this colonial relationship (cf. Edwards 1995a, 50), in which technological superiority and control are vested in the hands of the male colonial authority. In the exercise of that authority by directing shots and setting the scene, the colonial administrator functions rather like a film director. At the same time, like the allegorical frontispiece to Levinus Vincent's catalog analyzed in the previous chapter, the representation itself is articulated in terms of presence and absence: on the one hand, the very fact of the photograph's existence bears witness to the presence of the photographer on the scene; on the other hand, the nature of the medium itself excludes the photographer from the picture. One of Corbey's African postcards is exceptional in this respect (Corbey 1988, 87; 1989, 160).[60] We see a girl illustrating "Coiffure et type de Femme Bandziri," while the shadow of a male figure wearing a colonial helmet (the photographer?) is visible in the foreground (fig. 25; see following p. 112). Very different in kind are the shadows which fall over some of the photographs taken by the Reverend Harold Dauncey among Motuan people in Delena, Papua, at the turn of the century (Macintyre and MacKenzie 1992, 160). In the latter, the presence of the photographer's own shadow, like the lack of interest in controlling background detail, is a trace of familiarity. The shared space of photographer and photographed is a metaphor for their shared humanity.

The Muted Voice of the Exotic

Swift's Gulliver tells the reader what it was like to be put on display among the Brobdingnag for months on end, but in few of the representations discussed in this chapter do we gain any idea of the perceptions of those perceived (cf. Harbsmeier 1994b and 1995), although there is now a growing awareness that the totalizing power of the dominant culture could itself be partially shaped or even constituted by the culture on show (Hansen 1996). That representatives of another culture were capable of abandoning the subservient role allocated to them and protesting against the more unpleasant aspects of their "employment" is demonstrated by the case of the Somalis who inhabited the Somali Village at the 1904 Bradford International Exhibition and who demanded compensation for losses they had suffered (Coombes 1994, 107). Occasionally we gain a glimpse of how exotic people brought to Europe viewed their hosts. For instance, the Lakota taken to England in Buffalo Bill Cody's Wild West show present an amusing account of the entry of Queen Victoria to the Golden Jubilee celebrations: "Grandmother England" in a golden wagon is seen as "like a fire coming" (Napier 1987, 388), although the enthusiasm of the Lakota for British royalty seems ironic if we bear in mind the role that British imperialism was playing at the time. The Egyptian delegation to the Paris World Exhibition of 1889, who enjoyed more freedom to express their opinion of what they saw, did not conceal their disgust at the Egyptian exhibit there and stayed away (Mitchell 1989, 217).

Most of the members of the public who paid to see exotic presentations were little concerned about the feelings of those on display; they were usually more disturbed by the possibility that some of the visual experiences might be offensive to members of the weaker sex (Goldmann 1987). Besides, the display of peoples from other cultures was a decidedly one-way affair—as one reporter on the ethnographic photographs included in the photographic exhibition in Vienna in 1864 eloquently put it: "No one here thinks of compiling a complete collection of Austrian costumes and racial types" (cited in Theye 1995, 17).

In general, because communication between cultures was only in one direction, the exotic presented in drama, spectacle, and photograph, whether the setting was courtly, popular, academic, or a mixture, was dumb; it was not expected to answer back, let alone to raise any questions. As we shall see in the following chapter, the one voice that was never heard in discussions of the relation between Native American art and European or Euro-American modernism was the voice of any Native American artist (Rushing 1995, 40). Moreover, museum labels and museum displays in general knew what they wanted the exotic to say and would brook no contradiction. Why this is the case—why the process of exoticization had to be stifling—will be left for discussion until the question of the authenticity of the exotic has been handled. For the exotic might be supposed to have a voice of its own, but if the exotic is pseudoexotic—a thesis advanced in the concluding chapter—then it can have no authentic voice at all.

7 DISPLAYING THE EXOTIC

CEREMONY, SPIRIT FIGURE, MAGICIANS AND SORCERERS, SACRED ART, SPEAR THROWERS, STONE AXES AND KNIVES, WOMEN, BOOMERANGS

labels in the Hall of Pacific Peoples, New York

True to the Object, True to the Context

As we have seen in the previous chapters, the exotic is produced by a process of exoticization. Like a cosmetic, the exotic comes in a variety of thicknesses. Roughly speaking, the distance between the original context and the new context into which the exoticized object is inserted is a measure of its degree of exoticism. And it is the concerns of the host context which are overriding.

In the case of the dramatic displays discussed in the preceding chapter, the exoticized human beings on show were presented to the public within various formats, which were not of their own choosing. In the present chapter, we consider the formats available to those who set out to display exotic objects, rather than human beings, in the aesthetic or edifying context of the artistic or museum setting.

This process can be seen at work during the early years of this century in relation to a particular type of the exotic: the *primitive*. As we shall see, scant attention was paid to what the makers of exotic artifacts had to say about the interpretation of their products, for what counted, in the "primitivist" discourse by which they were appropriated, was how they could be deployed within a particular moment of *European* art.

Though the exact details are still obscure, it seems that André Derain, Maurice de Vlaminck, and Henri Matisse were among the first to grasp the relevance of the non-European arts for their own artistic work in 1906, followed soon afterward by Pablo Picasso. These artists saw "the primitive" as a way of breathing new life into a moribund system of values. Obviously, this sudden interest in primitivism can hardly be called a discovery of these arts. In the same way that the Americas had been populated for millennia before Columbus "discovered" them in 1492, Africa and the other continents had been producing works of art long before the Fauves "discovered" them. Primitivism is clearly in the eye of the beholder: these objects appeared primitive, they could be labeled as "primitive," they could be taken to be representative of the primitive, only because of the way in which they could be viewed as an alternative to the specific canons of Western art—precisely those canons which were being called into question at the end of the nineteenth century.

The myth of the discovery of primitivism (leaving aside the contradictions in Vlaminck's various accounts of what he later liked to refer to as a "revelation") has it that Vlaminck's attention was attracted by three African objects on a shelf behind the bar in a bistro in Argenteuil; he bought them for the price of a round of drinks (Flam 1984, 213–16). One of the first places in which we see the juxtaposition of primitive and modern art to bring out their formal resemblance is in Derain's studio. An extremely revealing document in this respect is a photograph of Derain, taken in the winter of 1908–9, showing the artist holding a primitivist sculpture, *Cat,* while the larger carving in the right foreground has been described as "an imitation or pastiche of a tribal object—its head resembling certain Fang masks, and its body a Polynesian Tiki" (Flam 1984, 218).[1] On the wall behind Derain is a reproduction of Cézanne's *Five Bathers.* The juxtaposition of primitivist sculpture and Cézanne is new, soon to be given a far more radical treatment in the hands of Picasso.

Such mixed arrangements were not confined to the modernists. The sculptor Herbert Ward, who lived for five years in what is now Zaire and was an avid collector of African objects, installed them together with his own bronzes of African subjects on the upper floor of his Paris studio in 1906. His sculptures of African human figures, however, were executed in accordance with the bourgeois taste of the time that characterized the annual Paris Salon; there are no indications that Ward's collection of African objects in any way affected his academic style of work as an artist (Arnoldi 1992, 437).[2]

"Primitivism" in the sense in which Robert Goldwater used it in his 1938 classic *Primitivism in Modern Art* (1986) is a Western phenomenon, associated in art-historical terms with the end of the nineteenth century and the beginning of the twentieth. However, the primitivist impulse in modern art goes beyond a contact with ethnographic artifacts to include prehistoric cave painting; popular, folk, and peasant art; the paintings of children; the artistic products of patients in mental institutions (so-called outsider art); naive art; graffiti; and so forth (Rhodes 1994, 23–67)[3]—though a notable outsider to primitivism, in many cases, is the work of non-European artists who live in Europe (López 1993). Primitivism is thus an impulse "broader than that suggested by the current fixation on Picasso's discovery of African masks" (Brett 1991, 124). This upsurge of interest in the primitive was not confined to the personal histories of a handful of artists. Many of the same principles at work in it can also be found in the wider cultural context of the late nineteenth century. For instance, in her demonstration of the parallels between artists' studios and the displays in department stores in the United States in the late nineteenth century, Burns (1993) draws particular attention to their shared aesthetic principles and to the decontextualization which they effected on the objects on display.

As Coombes points out (1994, 5), the attribution of aesthetic value to material culture from the colonies was not confined to, or indeed initiated by, modernist artists. The display of so-called primitive art in an aesthetic setting has its roots in the last decade of the nineteenth century. The presentation in Europe at that time of a mass of "bronzes" seized in the Kingdom of Benin in 1897 highlighted the Western recognition of the art-historical as well as ethnographic interest of African material culture (Coombes 1994, 7–28 and 43 n. 1). Ironically, art conventionally thought of as typically African came from areas exposed to external influence, whereas the Kuba art brought to the British Museum in the first decade of the century, which came from one of the remotest corners of the continent, was considered to look *un*-African (Mack 1990, 81). At the Exposition Universelle held in Brussels in the same year as the Benin exhibition, African objects were displayed alongside sculptures and tapestries by Western artists (Arnoldi 1992, 447).

Art dealers, collectors, and museum directors were not slow to develop the implications of this phenomenon. The Ruhr collector Karl Ernst Osthaus, a devotee of Expressionism and Jugendstil, combined European and non-European art(ifacts) in the Folkwang Museum in Hagen in 1912 (Lloyd 1991a, 96; 1991b, 8–12), and this approach was continued in the arrangement of the new premises in Essen in 1929, where paintings by Emil Nolde, African masks, and figures of ancestors from the South Sea islands were put on display in the same room (Flacke 1993). The most influential, though not the earliest,[4] of these "mixed" exhibitions was that of "Statuary in Wood by African Savages: The Root of Modern Art," organized by the Mexican caricaturist Marius de Zayas and held in Alfred Stieglitz's 291 Gallery in New York City from 3 November to 8 December 1914, where works by Picasso and Braque were juxtaposed with eighteen objects from the Ivory Coast and Gabon.[5] From 1920 on, the Society of Independent Artists in New York began to exhibit Pueblo painting side by side with paintings by non-Indian contemporaries (Rushing 1995, 15). The principal force behind these exhibitions was the society's president, the painter John Sloan, but art dealers also played an important role in providing the stimulus (and objects) for such exhibitions. A key figure in this respect is the Hungarian art dealer Joseph Brummer, whose clients included Osthaus (Paudrat 1984, 143ff.). The art dealer Sidney Burney was displaying African and modern art in London in the 1920s.[6] The same presuppositions lay behind the controversial exhibition "'Primitivism' in Twentieth Century Art: Affinity of the Tribal and the Modern," held in the Museum of Modern Art in New York City in 1984. The essays in the catalog which accompanied this exhibition parade the names of those twentieth-century artists who succumbed at one time or another to the spell of art(ifacts) from exotic places and sought ways of using this knowledge and material in their own works (Exh. Cat. New York 1984). Besides the Parisians mentioned above, Brancusi, Giacometti, Epstein, Klee, and Nolde are among the best known.

Although much of the discussion on primitivism has centered on art from Africa and Oceania, it is one of the implicit arguments of the present book that the arts of the Americas have not received their proper share of attention in this debate, a revisionist view shared by Rushing (1995), who documents the influence of native American art on the New York avant-garde. Braun (1993) also tries to redress the balance by extending the primitivism debate to the importance of American art on modern artists who were underrepresented or ignored in the Museum of Modern Art exhibition. She illustrates the influence of arts from the pre-Columbian courtly cultures on figures like Paul Gauguin, Henry Moore, Frank Lloyd Wright, Diego Rivera, and Joaquin Torres-García. An important figure in the development of American modernism, Arthur Wesley Dow, came to Native American design through studies of Aztec art and ornament. Among artists of a later generation, Barnett Newman stressed the need for an aesthetic rather than ethnographic reception of pre-Columbian work, which was evident in the exhibition of pre-Columbian stone sculpture that he organized in New York in 1944 (Braun 1993, 304 n. 18).

A particularly interesting figure in this connection, though one who has been virtually ignored in the "revisionist" works by Braun and Rushing, is Wassily Kandinsky, who was already drawing the distinction between the art of "primitive" peoples, on the one hand, and primitivism in modern art, on the other hand, in 1921 (Weiss 1995, 130 n. 33). Kandinsky was attracted by Native American art at various periods. In 1931 he was using motifs like the tomahawk, cactus, and tepee, and one of the works from his late Parisian period may draw on an Apache amulet (Weiss 1995, 174 n. 60 and 197 n. 38).

Kandinsky was not only an artist but also an ethnographer. In 1889 he did six weeks of fieldwork among the Zyrians (McKay 1994), and the experiences of this trip were to persist in the artist's eidetic memory right up to his death (Weiss 1995). Indeed, it has even been suggested that Kandinsky's rejection of realism in his artistic practice was connected with his rejection of contemporary anthropology's obsession with the deviant body (McKay 1996).

While Kandinsky's particular interest in phenomena like shamanism gave his work a strongly ethnographic slant, the modernists frequently used the term *primitive* indiscriminately to cover both the products of what were seen as less developed cultures ("tribal" art) in sites which are distant in space and the products of more highly organized cultures ("archaic" or "theocratic" art) which are distant in time. Hence, the arts of the ancient civilizations of Africa, Asia, and America were brought into the debate on primitivism, often under the label of "archaic." Where a distinction was made between the primitive and the archaic, it was usually with regard to the extent to which these arts seemed to offer something radically new, for in many respects the familiar canons of Egyptian, Greek, and Roman art seemed easier to apply to archaic art than to tribal art.

The contrast becomes clear if we compare the aesthetic attitude of a late-nineteenth-century bourgeois, Sigmund Freud, with that of, say, Georges Braque. Freud's personal collection of antiquities consisted of more than two thousand Egyptian, Greek, Roman, Etruscan, Mesopotamian, Chinese, and Japanese objects, which were regarded as anything but primitive (Gamwell and Wells 1989). Braque, on the other hand, an avid collector in his early years, appreciated African masks for their ability to open up new horizons and to shake off the inhibitions of what he regarded as a false tradition (Rubin 1984b, 307). All the same, the contrast should not be overstated: Picasso took a lively interest not only in tribal art but also in archaic Iberian art and commented that Assyrian bas-reliefs retained a purity of expression similar to that of primitive art. Likewise, while the juxtaposition of Giacometti's elongated human sculptures with New Ireland malanggan figures in the Museum of Modern Art's Primitivism exhibition was meant to suggest an affinity with tribal art, some of the works from his Surrealist period have been connected with Meso-american courtly games (Krauss 1984), and Giacometti himself confessed that the pictures which seemed most true to his sensations of reality were certain stylized Egyptian paintings of trees (Sylvester 1994, 33). Many of those who admired Pueblo Indian art in the 1920s, such as Edgar L. Hewett, Walter Pach, or Alice Corbin Henderson, were struck by parallels with Egyptian or Persian art (Rushing 1995, 23, 32). In the case of objects from the ancient civilizations of the Near East and from the courts of pre-Columbian America, "discovery" amounted to a renewed awareness of something that had been there for centuries or even millennia; what changed was the attraction which works of art from these cultures held for the European artistic vanguard.

The exotic, then, covers both of these kinds of art—"tribal" and "archaic," to give them their conventional, albeit unpalatable labels. Emblematic of this fusion of the primitive and archaic in the exotic is Paul Gauguin's *Spirit of the Dead Watching,* which he painted in 1892, the year after he left Paris for the first of his two trips to Tahiti. Whether the sinister figure in the left background of the painting is derived from Egyptian sources (Varnedoe 1984a, 199) or from a Peruvian mummy (Braun 1993, 88 n. 64),[7] the canvas as a whole combines these archaic influences with the tribal world of contemporary Polynesia, just as Gauguin himself applied the epithets "primitive" and "savage" not only to Polynesia but also to the different styles of Persia, Egypt, India, Java, and Peru (Rubin 1984a, 2). Indeed, many of those who talked or wrote about "primitivist" modern art were equally vague about geographic precision. Carl Einstein's influential *Negerplastik,* first published in 1915, included Oceanic pieces in what was presumed to be a presentation of African art. Attempts to remedy the error in the second edition (1920) were only partly successful, and neither edition included captions on ethnographic attributions or on the identity of the owners. A similarly catholic interpretation of *art nègre* can be found in the album of reproductions of African and Polynesian objects entitled *Sculptures nègres,* published with a preface by Apollinaire in 1917 (Paudrat 1984, 155). Those who practiced primitivist art were liable to be just as indifferent to ethnographic specificity. Thus, a chief's stool modeled on one from Africa was introduced into a Micronesian setting in Max Pechstein's 1917 *In the Woman's House, Palau* (Gordon 1984, 392). Similarly, the North American artist Marsden Hartley, a protégé of Stieglitz who was already interested in the theme of the American Indian before the outbreak of the First World War, combined motifs from various Indian tribes which would never have been found together in real life, such as Plains Indians tepees and Pueblo pottery (Levin 1984, 459). Dilworth describes this process as follows: "Hartley appropriated a vocabulary of Indian decorative language and arranged it according to his own formal syntax" (1996, 203). Rushing explicitly compares Hartley to the keeper of a curiosity cabinet in the way that he deracinates objects from their "primary" meaning without describing, or even intending to describe, a specifically Native American content (1995, 55).[8] It is as if the rules of the exotic genre have not changed since Jan Mostaert's *West Indian Landscape.*

The growth of interest in primitive art entailed a shift in what was seen as the appropriate context of display. What had been regarded as belonging to the material ethnographic record of a distant people was now credited with aesthetic value and appeal. Though the role of European ethnographers in cultivating an aesthetic appreciation of their objects is controversial (Williams 1985, 159–62), we can note the example of the ethnologist Frank Hamilton Cushing, who lived with the Zuni in New Mexico for five years (cf. Hinsley 1989). Cushing influenced Arthur Wesley Dow, who was in turn one of the teachers of Max Weber, painter, collector, and writer on primitive art in the first decennia of the twentieth century (Levin 1984, 453).

To turn from artistic creation to the practices of display, the debate on how to present the objects in ethnographic museums—whether against the background of the cultural settings from which they have been detached or in the same aestheticizing manner that is used for exhibitions of Western art—still continues (see, e.g., Leyten and Damen 1993; Froning 1996). In a sense, this is a problem of our own making, for the separation between art and ethnography that it implies prior to their subsequent juxtaposition or even conflation is a modern phenomenon. If we turn to the collection of Hans Sloane in the eighteenth century, there is such a degree of interpenetration between art and ethnography that modern scholars have difficulty in deciding what falls under the heading of an ethnographic collection and what belongs to the collection of works of art (King 1994; Rowlands 1994). In the nineteenth century, the way in which polychrome ethnographic busts like those by Charles-Henri-Joseph Cordier could be transferred effortlessly from salon to museum of natural history and back to salon again (Blühm 1996, 36) is indicative of the low threshold separating artistic from scientific institutions at the time. In other words, against the background of this failure to establish a meaningful distinction between the two fields, their rapprochement in the present century merely iterates their lack of separation in previous centuries.

Many of these issues regarding the plurality of possible contexts of the exhibition or museum display itself were raised by the exhibition entitled "Art/artifact."[9] This exhibition, organized by the Center for African Art, New York, could be seen in various North American museums between 1988 and 1990. Objects from Africa were displayed in a variety of museum settings and installation styles.[10] Some were given an overtly aesthetic presentation as a sculptural group in a way which was familiar to those who visit collections of modern sculpture in many museums of modern art. Others were given individual treatment, presented under Plexiglas and sanctified by spotlights. For instance, by displaying a repoussé brass head made in the royal court of Abomey (Benin) lying on its side, it could be made to evoke works like Brancusi's *Sleeping Muse*. The elongated stalks of three ivory hatpins from Zaire could be regarded as abstract sculpture or a graceful plant, though their original audience saw them as neither. A pointed barkcloth hat from Zaire could become an effective sculpture under the photographer's spotlights, arguably looking more interesting than when it was on someone's head.[11] Other display rooms followed the style of presentation of the museum of natural history, in which objects were exhibited without highlights as representatives of a specific material culture, with no distinction being made between ordinary objects and objects which might be seen as works of art (cf. Exh. Cat. New York 1988, 103). This natural historical style included the use of the diorama (157–58), intended to show simultaneously various aspects of material culture, social interaction, and environment. Finally, objects were presented in a nonchalant mixture of zoological and ethnographic curiosities in the style of a *Wunderkammer.* Like the natural historical setting, the latter style of presentation is democratic, assuming that whatever is on display in such a room is of equal interest.

Such an exhibition—about the ways Western outsiders have regarded African art and material culture over the past century—draws attention to the effects that the style of presentation has on the perception of the objects in question by a North American viewing public (Vogel 1991b). In foregrounding museum practices rather than the possible contexts of the objects within different African cultures—i.e., in treating the (ethnographic) museum context as a context in its own right (Durrans 1988, 162)—the multiplicity of possible 'readings' of those objects is stressed. This multiplicity was compounded by the fact that separate readings of the artifacts on display in the exhibition were presented in the catalog entries, as different authors dealt with the African use and meaning, the museum collection information, and the artistic qualities of each object. The way in which the claims of different voices compete with one another in such a pluralist setting is a frank admission of the fact that exhibitions are fields in which different interpretations and assertions are contested and in which different narratives strive to be heard (cf. Clifford 1988, 189–252; 1991). The synchronic presentation of different historical styles serves to remind us that each (museum) context reflects the state of knowledge, predominant concerns, and ideologies of a specific culture at a particular time. Every aspect of the use of space—lighting, use of display cabinets or not, juxtaposition of similar or dissimilar objects, the contents of the museum label itself (Baxandall 1991)—directs the viewer's gaze in a particular direction and toward a particular focus. It thereby exoticizes or deexoticizes the object on display.

The art/artifact exhibition was not meant to be chronological or arranged in an ascending order of legitimacy. Each style of presentation had its advantages and disadvantages, erring now on the side of overaestheticization, now on the side of overpoliticization. Nevertheless, despite the fact that it is possible in the *fin de siècle* of the twentieth century to present such a variety of styles within the synchronic framework of an exhibition, it should not be forgotten that, as we have seen, each of the styles in question has its own specific history and periodization (cf. Meijers 1993a). For instance, the classic museum of natural history, based on the theory of evolution to provide a framework for a historical narrative, is predominantly a nineteenth-century phenomenon. As for the collection of curiosities (the art/artifact exhibition included a reconstruction of the curiosity room in the Hampton Institute, Virginia, of around 1905), the *Wunderkammer* or chamber of rare objects is a phenomenon which goes back to the Renaissance (see ch. 4). In the Renaissance *Kunst- und Wunderkammer,* the visitor could perceive paintings side by side with actual artifacts; the representation of the exotic could take place simultaneously with the presentation of the exotic. Some of the twentieth-century artists mentioned above testify to this combination of presentation—and the realist aesthetic that it implies—with representation. A case in point is provided by the still lifes of Emil Nolde based on drawings of objects in the Berlin ethnographic museum: "They are modernist and primitivist, redeploying fragments of non-European cultures in formally experimental and subjectively arranged compositions, but they are also copies of objects and refer in this sense to a realist aesthetic" (Lloyd 1991a, 92–93).

According to Vogel, contemporary African museums repeat history by presenting their works as curiosities accompanied by relatively little explanatory information, thereby casting a haze of vagueness over the display (1991a, 235). The African "museumification" of traditional works of art, she claims, tends to neutralize rather than to elevate them—the opposite to what happens in Western art museums. On the other hand, critics (e.g., Cámara 1995) have accused her presentations of African art of trying to impose a Western classificatory grid on native categories.

These discussions make it clear that display involves both a politics and a poetics. In the hope that some of these issues may be made clearer through a more detailed examination of a particular example, the rest of this chapter will be devoted to an analysis of the plurality of contexts into which an unmistakably exotic object—an overmodeled skull—can be inserted. As we shall see, even at the microlevel of the museum label, the work of exoticization relentlessly continues.

Regimes of Authentication

> I remember one extraordinary exhibit in a small provincial museum in southern Bohemia: a bowl containing a heap of small iron objects. The label read: "What a hen pecked and swallowed in the yard of a master engineer."
>
> Fučíková, "The Collection of Rudolph II at Prague"

Among a collection of a little more than one hundred Melanesian artifacts now in the possession of Oporto University in Portugal is an overmodeled skull (fig. 26; see following p. 112). In a discussion of the various labels which have been attached to these artifacts—all of them drawn from a region which lay outside Portugal's colonial empire—during the course of the twentieth century, Mary Bouquet has traced various "archaeological strata" in the nomenclature applied (Bouquet and Freitas Branco 1988). The first label—in German, since the objects reached Portugal via Germany[12]—is the bare *Zierschädel* (decorated skull), which refers to the object in question as if it were a natural history specimen. One of the Portuguese labels, however, describes it as a *cabeça mumificada* (mummified head), thereby shifting attention from the natural state of the skull to the fact that it has been subjected to a cultural process. In fact, there is an implicit tension between the two words *cabeça* and *mumificada.* Overmodeling—a technique by which the skulls of slain enemies were overmodeled with clay, fired, and painted and their eyes were inlaid with shells—has nothing to do with mummification, a process by which the skull is dried out. The first term, recalling the fact that the skull is presumably that of an enemy, evokes the savagery imputed to the Melanesians. The second term, emphasizing the possession of a cultural skill going back to the civilizations of antiquity, lays stress on skill in the techniques of preservation and modeling.[13] It diverts the spectator away from Melanesia and above all evokes the world of ancient Egypt, thus implicitly performing the same elision of the primitive and the archaic that we have detected in the primitivism debate.

A second label, *crânio melanésio embelezado com conchas de marisco,* returns the Melanesian reference of the artifact, but only to juggle with the term *Melanesian* in a manner which in no way evokes a geographically specific area. It is more in accordance with Odilon Redon's dictum that the title is justified "only when it is vague, indeterminate and even tending to create confusion and ambiguity" (cited in Gombrich 1991, 181).[14] Indeed, the absurd character of this designation is aptly summed up by Bouquet as having "the flavour of one of Manuel Ferreira's fantastic *Cozinha Ideal* creations" (1988, 137). At a time when ethnographic museums were involved in a discussion on how to make it clear that what they presented were not curiosities but carefully selected objects illustrating human history, as discussed in chapter 6, such a deliberately wayward label placed the artifact firmly on the side of the curio.

A third label, *raça negróide do Pacífico,* introduces a racial distinction to supplant the geographic reference, based on the familiar nineteenth-century premise that there is an intimate connection between race and culture. In fact, the world evoked by this label is not a geographic one at all, but the authoritative textbook world of physical anthropology—one of the preoccupations of the Oporto School of Anthropology in the 1920s (cf. Durand 1991, 123–24; Mason 1997b).

This label also points the observer to Melanesia, but this time the geographic specificity is lost in the wider expanse of the Pacific Ocean.[15] To gain some idea of the connotations that this epithet could carry, particularly during the early part of this century, it is sufficient to note that the European artists who drew their primitivist inspiration from the Pacific were gazing through utopian spectacles, and the syncretic art that modernism produced was out to see the reflections of its own intentions in African and Melanesian art.

That the labels ostensibly point beyond themselves to artifacts and at the same time evoke a plurality of discourses is a movement associated with the exotic—its ability to deflect the gaze of the observer elsewhere. This movement of deflection is inextricably bound up with the theme of blindness/ blankness, itself a function of the blankness of the exotic.

The artifact has acquired another label through the intervention of Mary Bouquet herself: it is now exhibit 109, "*crânio sobremodelado*/over-modelled skull, Sepik, 27 cm (h), 15–17cm (w)" (Bouquet and Freitas 1988, 187).[16] Moreover, the act of reproduction of eight other "over-modelled skulls, Sepik" on the same page as examples of graphic arrangements indicates how the skull is to be 'read' this time: as an example of body adornment, carried to a degree of finesse lacking in New Ireland examples (119).[17]

There are a number of noteworthy features relating to this label. First, the inclusion of the precise measurements of the skull, a piece of information of no use to anyone who can actually see the skull in front of him or her, introduces the theme of absence.[18] Measurements are of interest only to the absent observer, unable to view the skull in person, condemned (as we are) to perceive it by means of its representation on the printed page. In other words, the painfully physical precision of "27 cm (h), 15–17cm (w)" has significance only when this physicality is absent. As Baxandall points out: "The nearest thing the label offers to a description is the numerical statement of the object's dimensions—something of which the viewer, who can see the object, is unlikely to make very active use" (1991, 38).

The label, therefore, calls attention to the representational nature of what is on display (the printed page) as nonauthentic. As a *semiophore*—to borrow the term used by Pomian to distinguish between things in themselves and artifacts which are collected as bearers of signification (1987, 15–59)—the overmodeled skull transcends the sphere of immediate sensory experience by establishing communication between the visible and the invisible. In the present case, what is invisible is both the world of the Sepik and the world of the dead. Or rather, they are revived as archaeology (i.e., as *dead*) (Pratt 1992, 134; Rabasa 1994, 246). The overmodeled skull can be said to elaborate and articulate their absence.

Second, like *raça negróide do Pacífico,* the inclusion of physical measurements evokes scientific precision, and with it the scientific authority of the discipline which relies on precision of this kind. Moreover, this particular resonance imparts its flavor to the whole label: since the measurements are incontrovertible, the rest of the information contained in the label may be regarded as beyond dispute.

Third, the inclusion of the word *Sepik* operates on a number of registers. It represents a shift away from the Egyptian overtones of *cabeça mumificada,*[19] from the geographic vagueness of *crânio melánesio embelezado com conchas de marisco,* and from the even vaguer (in geographic terms) *raça negróide do Pacífico*. However, it is itself imprecise on at least two counts. Historically, it eludes any reference to the existence of the skull in time; an undated artifact, appealing to a general sense of humanity at large (as the *memento mori* motif reminds us, one of the hallmarks of humanity is the possession of a cranium by each of its members), the skull partakes of the same temporality as the so-called ethnographic present. Geographically, it reduces the scope of *Melanesian* to *Sepik,* while obfuscating divisions within the term *Sepik* itself (Lower Sepik, Middle Sepik, etc.).[20] Furthermore, the detachment of the skull from a more precise historicogeographic context also conceals a very material factor[21]—the fact that both undecorated and decorated skulls were used as items of exchange with the Germans, which is the very raison d'être for its inclusion in the German shipment of wares which eventually found their devious way to Portugal (Bouquet and Freitas 1988, 119).[22]

This detachment also tends to help us to forget that the skull actually once belonged to a human being. Displayed in a way that would be unthinkable had it belonged to, say, a relative of the museum staff or curators, the skull could be put on show thanks to its distance, in time and place, from the novel exhibition setting. Through the notion of overmodeling, the idea of a crafted artifact displaces the idea of a relic of a person who was once alive. In this respect, the display of this (or any) skull in a museum setting places it within the longstanding tradition, both inside Europe and outside it, of putting human beings on display, dead or alive.[23] Like those animals which succumbed to their fate in a menagerie and could be transferred lifeless to a curiosity cabinet,[24] human beings were not necessarily free from a similar fate. At times, these human relics had the status and sanctity of a quasi-holy relic. The arm bone of the Habsburg Duke Herman, preserved by his descendant Archduke Ferdinand II in the cupboard at Schloss Ambras designated "bones" (Scheicher 1985, 35), perpetuates the medieval tradition of holy relics. But there is nothing numinous about the fact that, at a time when tattooed Native Americans were being displayed live in Europe, a late-seventeenth-century Native American visitor to Paris was flayed after his death at the Hôtel-Dieu to preserve his tattooed skin (Feest 1992, 94). The eighteenth-century *Kunstkammer* of Peter I in Russia included a young hermaphrodite (who escaped) and a peasant boy with only two digits on each hand and foot (who did not); after his death, the boy was stuffed and exhibited next to the skeleton of a giant (Neverov 1985, 60). At the end of the eighteenth century, Charles Willson Peale proposed exhibiting embalmed humans in his museum in Philadelphia, though his attempts to obtain an embalmed child from a church in New York were unsuccessful (Peale 1988, 15).

Of course, it is not that there is something *wrong* with the label "*crânio sobremodelado*/over-modelled skull, Sepik, 27 cm (h), 15–17cm (w)."[25] In the act of labeling an artifact, we perforce construct a meaning for it which is appropriate in one context and less appropriate or inappropriate in another. Thus, "while the understanding of context is crucial, the questions of what counts as a context, and how it relates to the art objects, are not always simple" (Thomas 1995, 36). Objects taken, purchased, or stolen from one place and put on display in another are subjected to a process of "creative recontextualisation" (Thomas 1991, 5). There is no standard of truth for weighing up one label against another, for they may all be in a certain sense appropriate, but the rhetorics (and politics) they employ vary. As Vogel points out (1991b, 201), *each* label, like each museum presentation as a whole, is indicative of the fact that "What it [the public] sees is not material that 'speaks for itself' but material filtered through the tastes, interests, politics, and state of knowledge of particular presenters at a particular moment in time . . . It could hardly be otherwise." It would be unacceptable to suppose that a label such as "*crânio sobremodelado*/over-modelled skull, Sepik, 27 cm (h), 15–17cm (w)" is normal, while a label such as "*crânio melánesio embelezado com conchas de marisco*" is an etiolation. There is no basic, primary, or authentic description of this or any other artifact which precedes the play of rhetoric and resonance. If proof of this thesis is needed, it can be found in the substance of the present chapter, for all of these labels appear in the present text as citations. The labels which appear here in print do not have any external, prior existence attaching to a specific artifact; they are all citations, fragments taken from a plurality of discourses which intersect in the figure of the overmodeled skull. In fact, in this sense the very photograph of the skull reproduced as figure 26, in a context that is neither Melanesian nor Portuguese, as well as its detachment from the exhibition/catalog context, is yet another means of facilitating the acts of conjuring within an anti-authoritarian mode (cf. Bouquet 1992, 199).

It goes without saying that the present remarks address issues which are European rather than Melanesian. Indeed, various anthropologists have drawn attention to the relative lack of verbal explanation of artifacts by Melanesians themselves, though O'Hanlon (1992) notes the importance of verbal assessment of Melanesian artifacts rather than their exegesis. In studying the discrepancy between text and image, we therefore already set ourselves within the framework of European rather than Melanesian preoccupations. Furthermore, the recent focus on how exotic objects were collected and by whom, within a colonial context, and on the need to make these histories explicit within museum presentations has itself been criticized by some commentators for being what they regard as a primarily European preoccupation (Jones 1992, 237). Some would even see the awkwardness of the fit between text and image as a sign of the resistance of the exotic to (Western) appropriation. At any rate, it is clear that the labels discussed here are not constitutive of identity, but that they intervene in a representational struggle involving the reinvention of different identities. A revealing instance of this attempt to represent the past for the future is provided by the scripting of ruined synagogues, doorposts carrying the impressions of long-removed mezuzahs, crumbling cemeteries, and death camps in Poland to provide Jewish monuments for consumption by U.S. Jewish tourists. Since almost no one in Poland, it is claimed, is capable of writing texts and labels for the country's Jewish monuments, recently composed commemorative plaques had to be written by outsiders and then translated—with varying degrees of success—back into Polish (Kugelmass 1992, 412 and n. 89). There is an obvious theatrical quality about these labels which defies any sense of what is basic or authentic.

This active role played by labels in the reappropriation of objects and in the generation of new meanings has been discussed in relation to exhibitions of primitive art in the United States in the late 1980s by Clifford (1988, 189–214; 1991). He describes his general aim as "To displace any transcendent regime of authenticity, to argue that all authoritative collections, whether made in the name of art or science, are historically contingent and subject to local reappropriation" (1988, 10).

The labels under examination operate within regimes of authenticity, too. For instance, the way in which certain labels elided the fact that the skull exists in historical time, bringing it in line with the timelessness of the ethnographic present, also helps to reinforce the authority of the voice which describes it, for "the present tense is a signal signifying a discourse as an observer's language" (Fabian 1983, 86). In fact, it would be more accurate to speak of regimes of *authentication* rather than regimes of authenticity; in their implicit polemic with one another, the labels are all caught up in a movement in which the very question of what is authentic is at stake. As so many persuasive definitions, each label offers an attempt at an interpretation of this particular artifact through a specific image of alterity. Each represents an attempt at the imaginative construction of meaning.

Consideration of the workings of the museum label thus raises once again the question of the plurality of discourses in which artifacts are embedded and which they in turn help to shape. The artifact cannot signify by itself. It can only acquire a signifying force by being inserted into a discursive chain by means of a label, for labels are representations,[26] while artifacts are not. This act of insertion itself raises the question of the context and with it that of the plurality of possible contexts. Given the impossibility of pinning the skull down by means of a single label, it seems more useful to stress the plurality of chains of signification into which it can be inserted rather than the lack of a proper fit between the exotic artifact and its (created) context. The argument here resembles the reading of Panofsky's iconographic method advanced in chapter 1: the reconstruction of different morphological chains, each of which is a possible context for the artifact under discussion.

As we can see from this example, the dominant modes of presentation are the academic and the aesthetic. While the various labels attaching to the overmodeled skull point it simultaneously in different directions as they evoke a plurality of contexts into which the skull can be inserted, the presentation of the skull itself, as a museum exhibit, is firmly rooted in the practices of the twentieth-century ethnological museum, with its stress on the presentation of artifacts as representatives of a material culture. These are the functions which the aestheticization of native artifacts tends to marginalize. This can be seen from the plates illustrating Captain Cook's second South Sea voyage, in which the careful layout and display of detail overshadow the various functions of objects like baskets or weapons. Such a decontextualized form of presentation evokes the authority, precision, and alleged disinterest of science rather than providing any insight into native lifestyles (Thomas 1991, 133–38; Thomas 1994b). Aesthetic juxtapositions of this kind also serve to mirror colonial relations more explicitly. Thus, the aesthetic display of native artifacts in the dining room of the British governor of Fiji could suggest a setting out, rigidifying, and totalizing of Fijian culture as seen through the eyes of those who sought to control it (Thomas 1991, 172–75). We can even see the effects of a transition from one of these modes of display to the other in the collection of African objects amassed by the British sculptor Herbert Ward at the turn of the century. On display above Ward's studio were symmetrically arranged patterns of arrows, ivory tusks, bracelets, knives, spoons, whistles, and headrests, flanked by animal trophies and bronzes by the sculptor himself. The dramatic effect of it all was to reinforce Ward's invention of an exotic Africa. When the collection was moved to the Smithsonian Institution and installed in the new National Museum Building in 1922, however, Ward's own academic bronze sculptures were detached from the rest of the collection, and the scientific claims of the museum were given precedence over Ward's more aesthetic motives by arranging specimens of African material culture and zoology in cases by type and material and by adding museum labels to the cases (Arnoldi 1992). These labels, then, were not primary designators of the nature of the objects on display; instead, they functioned to constitute new meaning, intervening in a shift of paradigms from the predominantly (colonial) aesthetic to the predominantly (colonial) scientific.

The exotic artifact itself is thus equally at home in scientific and in artistic collections, and we should be wary of assuming that the transition from one type of display to another is unilinear or irreversible. Had our overmodeled skull belonged to the Louvre collection, for example, Jacques Derrida could have included it in his "gallery" of seventy-one portraits, prints, and drawings related to the theme of blindness (Derrida 1990b). Or by elevating the modest cowrie shells to a higher status, we might even see the skull as an illustration of Ariel's song in *The Tempest:* "Those are pearls that were his eyes" (I.ii.401). Indeed, the action performed on the skull by the labeling is perhaps nowhere better summed up than in the following lines from the same song:

Nothing of him that doth fade,
But doth suffer a sea-change
Into something rich and strange.

8 THE ELEMENTARY STRUCTURES OF THE EXOTIC

> We were upon a Voyage and no Voyage, we were bound somewhere and no where; for tho' we knew what we intended to do, we did not really know what we were doing.
>
> Defoe, *Captain Singleton*

"A sea-change in special circumstances"—that is how the linguistic philosopher J. L. Austin, the theorist of the performative, described the use of a performative utterance in a situation which he regarded as out of context (1962, 22). The time has come to review the collection of infelicities that have been presented in the preceding chapters and to consider whether the term *infelicity* itself has not undergone a sea change in the process.

Without losing sight of the degree of differentiation involved in the histories and periodizations of the exotic which we have examined, the trajectory from the first chapter to the present one has taken in the museum label and the style of museum presentation, the ethnographic artifact and the work of art, presentation and representation. In the process, certain continuities have emerged in the presentation and representation of the exotic from the sixteenth to the twentieth century. In that we come after the modernist avant-garde of the first half or so of the present century, we are by definition postmodern. It remains to be seen whether this banal statement may be taken to imply much more: say, the notion that a historical development has taken place in which postmodernist thought can genuinely be regarded as epochal.[1] At the same time, the focus on the individual case and the reluctance to draw general conclusions return us, in some respects, to sixteenth-century practices (the notion of the *singularité*). And the Mannerism of the Renaissance collection of curiosities, as we have seen, has evoked the juxtapositions of postmodern artistic practice in the eyes of some critics. Such returns, if they may be seen as such at all, are iterative; post-Renaissance thought is hardly the same thing as Renaissance thought.

The time has come, then, to consider whether anything can be said on the basis of this corpus of material regarding the elementary structures of the exotic—which is tantamount to considering *how* one is to say anything about the exotic at all. As was made clear at the start of the enterprise, the exotic as such does not exist—it is the product of a process of exoticization. Rather than recapitulating material that has already been presented, I shall now adduce fresh material to illustrate five theses on the exotic which apply, to greater or lesser degrees, to the exotic as it has been produced during the past five centuries.

The Exotic Is Not at Home

In Alfred Stieglitz's 291 Gallery exhibition of African art in New York City in 1914, the Fang sculpture displayed in isolation on a pedestal had been stripped of bark and bones to strip it of its African cultural context (Vogel 1988, 13). Within colonial relations, the displacement of native peoples from their own land to function as exhibits in human zoos or as sitters in European photographic studios mirrors their detachment from their own land. In each of these cases, the presentation of the exotic necessarily entails displacement and detachment. The exotic is never at home: its very exoticism is derived from the fact that it has been detached from one context and inserted in another, to which it is to some degree refractory. This process of decontextualization and recontextualization is an act of translation; like all translations, it is characterized by varying degrees of transparency and opacity, of success and failure. As we shall now see, this applies in both two and three dimensions, on both the macro-level and the micro-level. The skull and Fang sculpture are three-dimensional objects; the museum label and paintings are two-dimensional artifacts. But the exotic itself is not confined to any fixed dimensions; it can be found at the level of the total, relatively large-scale representation—the exotic landscape or the reconstructed exotic village, for instance—but it can equally well be found at the micro-level of the single word.

To substantiate the latter point: the sixteenth century, it has been argued, witnessed a shift in linguistic theory from the dominance of the verb to the dominance of the noun (Certeau 1982, 171–74). The consequent multiplication of nouns and their heterogeneity relaxed the need to seek a correspondence between noun and object, for there now existed a world of substantives which far exceeded the perceptible world of realia. At the same time, this proliferation of nouns made more cogent the possibility of a word which might refer to nothing at all. Thus, at the level of the text, the most basic exotic element to be encountered is the exotic word, with the *hapax legomenon* standing for the most extreme form of opacity, that of the sign which has become so dense that nothing is transparent through it. In a passage from the second act of *The Tempest* (II.ii 170–72), Caliban promises:

I'll bring thee
To clustering filberts, and sometimes I'll get thee
Young scamels from the rock.

The awkward word here is *scamel*. It is not recorded elsewhere as a literary word (Kermode 1958, 68), and editors have the choice of suggesting emendations (such as *sea-mels*) or retaining *scamels* without knowing what it means. Either way, the opacity of the word fits the exotic figure of Caliban. His language has been contaminated by the arrival of Miranda, from whom he learned to curse;[2] perhaps *scamels* are intended to be refractory, as Greenblatt has suggested (1990, 31), a last vestige of Caliban's pristine diction.

This example is by no means an isolated instance of the phenomenon. Many other examples of the use of exotic words to introduce opaqueness can be found in travel accounts. Take the following exotic words from the text of Jean de Léry's *History of a Voyage to the Land of Brazil* ([1580] 1990, 182): "*Ouacan*. The chief of that place, that is, their headman. *Soouar-oussou*. The leaf which has fallen from a tree. *Morgouia-ouassou*. A big rattle or bell. *Mae-uocep*. A thing that has partly emerged from the earth or from some other place."

The whole of chapter 20 of Léry's account contains a colloquy in Tupi and French.[3] Both this chapter and the isolated native words scattered through Léry's text, breaking up the linearity of his discourse, betray what Whatley has called "an attentive respect for the alien language" (1990, xxxiv), though it can hardly be regarded as a basic vocabulary displaying typical situations in which foreigners find themselves.[4] "A thing which has partly emerged from the earth or some other place" or "It no longer hurts our grandchildren when we shave their heads" hardly reflect typical situations. On the contrary, the act of translation here creates obscurity rather than dispelling it. At a more abstract level, this might be seen as the essence of translation, an act which throws up a barrier of opaqueness, thereby thwarting the act of communication itself.

In the case of Jean de Léry's great rival, André Thevet, it is easier to see what the strategic use of exotic words could entail.[5] In taking native vocabulary from Pigafetta's *Motz des geans de Pataghone,* Thevet might be said to be reversing the flow of clarity; far from serving to decode the message of the other, Thevet uses the strange words to create an effect of opacity.[6] It is precisely the *lack* of communication which confers a privileged status on Thevet himself as the polyglot authority (Lestringant 1987b, 471).[7]

Sometimes it is not just the exotic word itself which is so mystifying, but the way in which it jars with its surrounding context. Take, for instance, an illustration from William Marshall's *A Phrenologist amongst the Todas* (1873), which was used by W. H. R. Rivers in his study of the Todas. Hockings has reproduced it to support a hypothesis on the yellow bough of the *tûdr* tree (1992, 182), but without drawing attention to the curious label, which runs: "The Tûde or Sacred Bush. Weapons, bow & arrow, used at weddings & funerals. Imitation buffalo horns." While the symmetrical arrangement of the objects themselves in the illustration suggests that they fit together to form a harmonious whole (within a holistic view of Toda culture), this seeming aesthetic unity is disrupted in two ways. One of these is the word Tûde—for it is hardly the case that the gloss "Sacred Bush" makes its meaning any clearer; the other is the—to our eyes, at least—whimsical oddity of the second item, for the place of weapons at weddings and funerals is by no means self-evident.

One of the effects of the introduction of such exotic words is an "exoticization" of the texts or contexts in which they are inserted. To take the example of Voltaire, in his *Mahomet* and *Zaïre,* for example, some degree of exotic flavor is imparted by words like *sérail, calife, shérif,* or *soudan.* Indeed, this provision of local color was regarded as appropriate for stories set in foreign parts; hence, in *Candide* one of the audience attending the performance of a play in Paris complains that "the author does not know a word of Arabic, and yet the scene is in Arabia" (Voltaire 1979, 202).[8] Voltaire's *L'Ingénu* also contains genuine North American Indian words; the Huron hero of the tale who finds himself in France is "tested" by seeing whether the three Huron words that he gives—*taya* for "tobacco," *essenten* for "to eat," and *trovander* for "to make love"—are to be found in a Huron dictionary of the period (Voltaire 1979, 288–89).[9] In *Zadig* we even find Voltaire changing the orthography of "Arnoult" into "Arnou" to give this Parisian peddler of cures for apoplexy a more Oriental flavor (Voltaire 1979, 61, with the editorial note on p. 770), just as in *Aline et Valcour* Sade exoticized the name of the anthropophagous king Grand-Macoro by turning it into Ben Mâacoro (Lestringant 1994, 261 n. 29).[10] The technique itself goes back to the Attic tragedian Aischylos, whose *The Persians* is suffused with oriental rhythms, words, symbols, and actions to make it "the first unmistakable file in the archive of Orientalism" (Hall 1989, 99; cf. Said 1978, 56–57).[11]

Besides the use of isolated exotic words or word clusters in the text or dialogues, we also find compilations or lists of words, drawn up in columns. For instance, Antonio Pigafetta, on whom Thevet drew, compiled four lists of foreign words: 426 Malay terms, 160 Philippine terms, 8 words from a Brazilian tribal language, and 90 words from the Patagonians. Word lists can be found in the works of Sebastian Münster, Peter Martyr, Francisco López de Gómara, John Davis, Sir Robert Dudley, and many others (Greenblatt 1990, 19 n. 12).[12] The act of compilation of such a list presupposes both a commensurability and mutual transparency on both sides of the vertical line, a procedure which necessarily eliminates all that is refractory to such an enterprise. Yet, at the same time, it presupposes a gap in communication of some kind, for without this gap in communication, this *différance*, there would be no translation possible or necessary. As Jacques Derrida has (intranslatably) put it: "L'à-traduire du traductible ne peut être que l'intraduisable" (1987, 60). The gap in communication therefore implies the existence of a genre of "antilexica," lists of terms which savages did *not* have (Pagden 1993, 127), as observers of the seventeenth and eighteenth centuries increasingly perceived the impoverishment of native languages to be an index of their relative lack of culture (Andresen-Tetel 1985).

Parts of the body might seem to be incontrovertibly translatable (though the precise contours of the human body can be the object of dispute, too). When the parts of the body are extended to include clothing, however, the difficulties of translation immediately become apparent, as can be seen from the difficulties faced by European observers in their attempts to classify American Indian body painting and feather ornaments (Pellegrin 1987). They are virtually insurmountable when the topic is family relationships, religion, or other abstractions of this kind. In such situations, the opacity of the exotic serves to mask the blankness of communication (cf. Mason 1998a).

The Exotic Is Empty

One possible strategy to cope with this blankness is to resort to (unconvincing) equivalences which deny the existence of a problem at all. In this respect, it makes little difference whether the other is taken to be a virtual blank or a virtual double (Greenblatt 1991, 95). Either way, a supposed cultural transparency is the result. For instance, many of the African representations of human figures which attracted the attention of the modernists contained distortions or exaggerations; these were interpreted as examples of Munch-like Expressionism and taken to betray states of extreme anguish or alienation (Rubin 1984a, 35–36); in this way, they could be assimilated to European canons. At the linguistic level, such presumed equivalences could be based on homophony, as in the following fragment of "dialogue" from Léry (1990, 178):

TUPINAMBA: *Mara-pé-déréré*? What is your name?
FRENCHMAN: *Lery-oussou.* A big oyster.

As Léry himself comments (162), "never did Circe metamorphose a man into such a fine oyster, nor into one who could converse so well with Ulysses, as since then I have been able to do with our savages."[13]

That which has the semblance of a mode of communication turns out to communicate nothing; hence, it may be plausible to suppose that "the supposed 'communication' between European and native was in effect a European monologue" (Hulme 1978, 119). The exotic has a specular structure, conveying nothing but the empty echo of itself.

This process is perhaps best described at work in an exotic context in E. M. Forster's *A Passage to India,* first published in 1924. This is how Mrs. Moore reacts to the echo in the Marabar cave (Forster 1985, 144):[14]

> There are some exquisite echoes in India; there is the whisper round the dome at Bijapur; there are the long, solid sentences that voyage through the air at Mandu, and return unbroken to their creator. The echo in a Marabar cave is not like these, it is entirely devoid of distinction. Whatever is said, the same monotonous noise replies, and quivers up and down the walls until it is absorbed into the roof. "Boum" is the sound as far as the human alphabet can express it, or "bou-oum," or "ou-boum"—utterly dull. Hope, politeness, the blowing of a nose, the squeak of a boot, all produce "boum." Even the striking of a match starts a little worm coiling, which is too small to complete a circle, but is eternally watchful. And if several people talk at once an overlapping howling noise begins, echoes generate echoes, and the cave is stuffed with a snake composed of small snakes, which writhe independently.

This dull acoustic echo is still going through Mrs. Moore's mind during the preparations for her trip back to England:[15] "What dwelt in the first of the caves? Something very old and very small. Before time, it was before space also. Something snub-nosed, incapable of generosity—the undying worm itself . . . The unspeakable attempt presented itself to her as love: in a cave, in a church—boum, it amounts to the same" (194).

This mocking failure of the exotic to be where one expects to find it functions as a means of luring the inquirer away. Another traveler to India, the painter William Hodges, who arrived there five years after he had been sailing in the South Pacific with Captain Cook, was struck by what he called "the great distinction" between Asia and his own country; yet his initial response to the difference between the Hindu people of Madras and his own culture was not to scrutinize the objects of his curiosity more closely. Instead, "the spectator wants to look through, look beyond, to the interior of the continent, and not to be detained by that initial apprehension of the coastal border with its great distinction" (Guest 1989, 37).

But it would be naive to suppose that this lure toward the interior is a lure toward truth, for the interior itself is ever elusive. Responding to the demystifying effects of the crusades on popular images of the East, an eyewitness to the first crusade, Fulcher of Chartres, claimed that "we who were Occidentals have now become Orientals." As a result of the Occident having become the Orient, it now became necessary to shift the imaginary geography and ethnography associated with the Orient further to the East. The "wonders of the East" were a fixed given; if they could no longer be found in the Holy Land, they must be situated elsewhere (Campbell 1988, 124, 133). The pattern becomes familiar in reports by those in search of the extraordinary (Mason 1990, 100). Thus, when Aeneas Sylvius Piccolomini (the later Pope Pius II) inquires during a visit to Scotland in 1435 about the whereabouts of a tree which is said to produce living birds (barnacle geese), he is informed that the tree in question does not grow in Scotland, but further north in the Orkneys. The lesson that he draws from this experience is that wonders are always elusive (*miracula semper remotius fugere*) (Heron-Allen 1928, 20; cf. Egmond and Mason 1995). The deferral of the exotic is a lure.

The Exotic Is Double

As the train rushing Mrs. Moore through central India follows its serpentine course, she experiences a visual echo (Forster 1985, 194):

> There was, for instance, a place called Asirgarh which she passed at sunset and identified on a map—an enormous fortress among wooded hills. No one had ever mentioned Asirgarh to her, but it had huge and noble bastions and to the right of them was a mosque. She forgot it. Ten minutes later, Asirgarh reappeared. The mosque was to the left of the bastions now. The train in its descent through the Vindhyas had described a semicircle round Asirgarh. What could she connect it with except its own name? Nothing; she knew no one who lived there. But it had looked at her twice and seemed to say: "I do not vanish."

When she is back on familiar Western ground in the city of Bombay—"the huge city which the West has built and abandoned with a gesture of despair" (195)—the Marabar caves and Asirgarh combine to frustrate any illusions that she might still entertain about having gained some insight into India: "Thousands of cocoanut palms appeared all round the anchorage and climbed the hills to wave her farewell. 'So you thought an echo was India; you took the Marabar caves as final?' they laughed. 'What have we in common with them, or they with Asirgarh? Goodbye!'"

The example of Asirgarh introduces us to an alternative strategy to deal with the blankness of the exotic: iteration.[16] The concept of iteration, it should be stressed, is not the same as that of repetition. While the latter refers to repetition of the same, iteration introduces difference into the same through the singularity of the event (Derrida 1990a, 215–16). Iteration, therefore, combines repetition with alterity, sameness with difference, at the same time. When Mrs. Moore perceives Asirgarh for the second time, this is not a repetition, for on the second occasion the mosque has changed position. And the problem of knowing whether this second Asirgarh is the same as the first—the question of identity—is baffled by the fact that it could not be connected with anything except its own name. Through the persistence of its name, it remains the same; through the shift in perspective introduced by deferral in time, it becomes different.

Furthermore, though we can refer to a second occasion in the temporality of the narrative, there is nothing secondary about the second appearance of Asirgarh, for each viewing of Asirgarh carries equal weight. Since there is nothing secondary about the second occasion, there is nothing original about the first one either (cf. Derrida 1980, 373). Whether one proceeds forward or backward in time, the iteration itself can be reiterated *ad infinitum.* The attempt to impose a meaning on the exotic results in a series of acts of superimposition as signification is heaped on signification, this accumulation itself being permitted by the blank refusal of the exotic to admit any of the proffered meanings as its signification. The paradoxical logic at work here has been aptly summarized by Eisenman (1997, 38): "The logic or paradox of exoticism tends to set in motion a kind of insatiable regression: the more one is immersed in the exotic, the more one discovers sameness, and the more one seeks ever greater difference."

The Exotic Is (Over)full

The proliferation of the exotic resulting from the accumulation of superimposed meanings—itself a characteristic of the present chapter—can be documented in a number of ways. Despite the proverbial inscrutability of the Oriental, the Oriental idyll as a literary genre absorbed a vast quantity of new information and the insights of an Oriental scholarship gradually freed from the literalism both of inherited tradition and of rationalist historicizing. Hence, as Shaffer (1985) has stressed in her study of Coleridge's planned epic poem *The Fall of Jerusalem,* the new mythical landscape does not reflect ignorance about the Orient, but fairly bristles with the knowledge that had been acquired, not least through the mythological school in Biblical criticism. Similarly, the same poet's *Ancient Mariner* can be shown to betray a knowledge of the details of Captain Cook's second voyage (Smith 1956).

One response to the blankness of the uncharted wilderness is to attempt to order it in terms of a European grid. In Defoe's *Captain Singleton,* in which the pirate Bob Singleton and his men cross Africa from the East Coast to the Gulf of Guinea on foot,[17] the narrator comments: "It was very remarkable that we had now traveled a 1000 Miles without meeting any People, in the Heart of the whole Continent of *Africa,* where to be sure never Man set his Foot since the Sons of *Noah* spread themselves over the Face of the whole Earth" (Defoe 1990, 105). Convinced that he and his men have reached the heart of Africa, Singleton is surprised to find it so deserted. His amazement is forcefully expressed in the description of "an ugly, venomous, deformed kind of a Snake or Serpent" that he encounters there. Since his men "would not be perswaded but it was the Devil," he cannot understand "what Business Satan could have had there, where there were no People." This blankness is understandable in terms of the genesis of Defoe's text, for the absence of people in the heart of Africa reflects the knowledge contained in maps of the time, on which Defoe drew to a considerable extent.[18] However, his immediate response is to attempt to do away with this blankness by subsuming it under familiar parameters. One such parameter is the Biblical one, not only the evocation of the role of the serpent in the garden of Eden, but also the explicit reference to the myth of the population of the earth by the descendants of Noah. Another parameter, more prosaic this time, is contained in the continuation of the passage quoted above: "Here also our Gunner took an Observation with his Forestaff to determine our Latitude, and he found now, that having marched about 33 Days Northward, we were in 6 Degrees 22 Minutes South Latitude."

Two compensatory movements are at work here. The first is the attempt to reduce the alterity of the other by restating it in terms of the familiar—reinscribing the unknown continent within the terms of European systems of measurement (cf. Pregliasco 1992, 176–77). The second is the attempt to eliminate the elusiveness of the uncharted wilderness by pinning it down in figures—a number of days' march and a latitude.

Despite the apparently neutral tone of such precise figures, the motivation for filling in the blankness of the exotic lies in the narrator's own experience. In the case of Singleton, the absence of people is not just an ingenuous ethnographic observation, but a matter of life and death, for it is a warning that the barren expanses might not be capable of sustaining human life—including the narrator's—at all ("we began to be in great Suspense about Victuals"). We find another example of the response to blankness by filling it in with the superabundance of the narrator's own experience in *The Tempest* (I.ii.353–60). Having declared the linguistic blankness of Caliban:

> Abhorred slave,
> Which any print of goodness will not take,

Miranda proceeds to fill in the *tabula rasa:*

I pitied thee,
Took pains to make thee speak, taught thee each hour
One thing or other . . . I endow'd thy purposes
With words that made them known.[19]

Likewise, the sixteenth-century Protestant missionaries to Brazil were disturbed by the evidence for a genuine Tupi culture, for they would have preferred a blank culture waiting to be overwritten by their own Christian message (Whatley 1986, 326).[20] In this respect, the Reverend Sheldon Dibble, editor of *Mooolelo Hawaii,* found that the natives of Hawaii made his work easier for him because "the ignorant mass, except when operated by God's spirit, exhibit a vacant and unmeaning stare, which indicates the emptiness within" (Obeyesekere 1992, 159). Other commentators on the inscrutability of South Sea islanders were troubled by a diversity in the possible ways of inscribing that blankness: George Foster commented on the Tahitian brought to England in 1774 that "O-Mai has been considered either as remarkably stupid, or very intelligent, according to the different allowances which were made by those who judged of his abilities" (Guest 1992, 102). There is another strand in the early accounts of the New World, however, in which "the Nothingness of the written New World"—certain writers refuse to even admit its existence—might be said to generate a complementary (over)fullness. The force of the paradisal negatives which Columbus borrows from the rhetorics of pastoral and dream vision to describe the New World—the absence of winter, weapons, private property, and so forth—is intended precisely to invoke a picture of the very fullness of delight (Campbell 1988, 222ff.). The same function can be attributed to the negatives in the old courtier Gonzalo's construction of a (logically incoherent) imaginary commonwealth (*The Tempest* II.1.143–52):

I' th' commonwealth I would by contraries
Execute all things; for no kind of traffic
Would I admit; no name of magistrate;
Letters should not be known; riches, poverty,
And use of service, none; contract, succession,
Bourn, bound of land, tilth, vineyard, none;
No use of metal, corn, or wine, or oil;
No occupation; all men idle, all;
And women too, but innocent and pure;
No sovereignty[21]

Indeed, such negatives are a characteristic of utopian literature, such as the description of the Golden Age in book I of Ovid's *Metamorphoses* (lines

96ff.): they correspond to the metaphor of the photographic negative, whose "development" is to be sought in the author's own society (cf. Lund 1990, 30–31). At the political level, the claim that the Native Americans of New England lacked settled habitation, domestic animals, and fences was used to support the argument that they had only a natural right to that territory and thus a right which could be extinguished by the arrival of those whose civil right was made evident through the clearing of land, the erection of fences, and the construction of houses (Seed 1995, 39).

Metonymically related to this inscription on virgin territory is the assumption that the female body is a blank sheet awaiting the attribution of significance through an act of (male) inscription.[22] The acts of inscription themselves could vary considerably. While Bougainville's description of the island of Tahiti as *la nouvelle Cythère* inscribed it within the fullness of a long and rich mythological tradition going back to the lotus island of Greco-Roman mythology—a theme that recurs in the work of Gauguin (Kramer 1977, 97–100)—the sexual freedom of the islanders met with a different response on the part of those who saw it as an example of climatically determined degeneracy. Captain Cook wavers between the two views: shocked at the promiscuity of the Tahitian women on his first visit to the island, he modified his view during the second visit, this time arguing that the licentious women formed only a small minority, while the majority were modest by European standards (Porter 1989). We find the same modesty attributed to the peoples of the Pacific in the fact that Omai, the visitor from the South Seas who swept through London society in 1774 and 1775, did *not* behave like a savage (Browne 1996, 164). Johann Forster, the naturalist for Cook's second voyage, presents an account of the island women that is marked by similar hesitancies and inconsistencies, as he sees them as combining a "primitive simplicity of manners" with civilizing powers (Guest 1996). These diverse judgments have less to do with the Tahitian women themselves than with a complex of metropolitan desires and anxieties about private virtue and public order, with Tahiti serving as the backdrop for the obsessive narratization of these fantasies and fears (Orr 1994). At a time when the science of botany, under the influence of Linnaeus, offered one of the few discourses on sex that were available to polite society, satires on the activities of Joseph Banks among the flowers of Tahiti and London underscored the elision of the pursuit of botanical science with the pursuit of fair women (Bewell 1996). We might see this writing of the erotic on the exotic in the bodies of the Tahitian women as a sign of the emptiness of the exotic, its function as a blank screen onto which a profusion of often mutually contradictory representations could be projected, resulting in the overcrammed fullness of the exotic.

Another area in which this proliferation can be seen is in the paintings reflecting the bizarre contents of the European cabinets of curiosities which were discussed in chapter 4. Georg Hinz, a North German artist from the second half of the seventeenth century, specialized in depictions of curiosity cabinets, often employing trompe l'oeil effects, and similar paintings can be found earlier in the century by Frans Francken the Younger. Allegories of the five senses draw on *Kunstkammer* attributes too, such as the allegory of Sight by Jan Brueghel the Elder, dating from 1617–18 (now in the Prado Museum in Madrid). Moreover, the predominantly seventeenth-century genre that has come to be known as sumptuous still life (Segal 1988) included depictions of both luxury items (goblets, jewelry) and exotic curiosities—which were luxury items too, of course (shells, tulips and other precious flowers, parrots, birds of paradise, etc.). In particular, as we have seen, a genre which allowed plenty of scope for the illustration and proliferation of objects from a *Wunderkammer* was the allegory of the four continents. One of the most well-known examples of the genre is probably the series of paintings of the four continents by the Antwerp-born artist Jan van Kessel the Elder (1626–79). His *Americque,* now in Munich, contains two Brazilian figures based on the paintings of Brazilian 'Tapuya' Indians made by the Dutch painter Albert Eckhout in 1641–43,[23] a third Amerindian figure in the foreground, wearing a headdress and a skirt of red feathers,[24] and various fauna and flora taken from Piso and Markgraf's *Historiae rerum naturalium Brasiliae.* Yet the scene is not fully American either: it includes a set of Javanese gamelan gongs, Japanese armor and arms, and shells which are either Indo-Pacific or pantropical (Whitehead and Boeseman 1989, 92–93), and the painting of an Indian suttee and the dancing figures in the doorway have their origin in the East Indies (Exh. Cat. Paris 1976, no. 109).

There is a similar lack of precision in geographic provenance in the attributes shared by personifications of both America and Africa—the lizard, palm tree, lion, crocodile, and bow and arrow are found associated with both America and Africa in allegories of the four continents (Le Corbeiller 1961, 219). The same lack of specificity characterizes the portrayal of America and Asia: thus, we find the typically Asiatic censer linked with America in Conrad Huber's *The Four Continents Celebrate Maria* (1791); in disregard of Ripa's iconographic guidelines, Tiepolo brackets the elephant (as well as a South American parrot) with Asia and the camel with Africa in the famous Würzburg frescoes,[25] while the American fresco includes an Oriental turban and vase, as well as (meaningless) letters written in Armenian (Poeschel 1985, 136; Alpers and Baxandall 1994, 162).[26] The feathered skirt, as we have seen, displays a similar tendency to shift continents. Though it took a dose of opium to get him there, Thomas de Quincey bore witness to the same indifference to geographic specificity in his 1821 version of the exotic Orient: "Under the connecting feeling of tropical heat and vertical sun-lights, I brought together all creatures, birds, beast, reptiles, all trees and plants, usages and appearances, that are found in all tropical regions, and assembled them together in China or Indostan" (1986, 109).

The simple amassing of objects that de Quincey's visions or Van Kessel's painting of "America" display has its parallels in compositions in which all four continents figure on one canvas, such as Frans Francken's *Allegory on the Abdication of Charles V* (see ch. 5). On the one hand, such representations reveal the lavishing of a good deal of attention on the details of the artifacts, resembling still lifes in their "realism." This in no way detracts from their allegorical nature, for as Pomian notes (1987, 67), there can be no doubt that Van Kessel's *Americque* depicts savagery situated among the symbols of riches for allegorical ends. On the other hand, this "realism" is combined with a lack of interest in geographic specificity, as realia drawn from regions thousands of miles from one another are juxtaposed in strange company with one another. It is remoteness which is important, not specificity. The blankness of the exotic, which permits this proliferation of geographically imprecise or irreconcilable elements, is more evocative and flexible than the specificity of a precise location in space.

The Exotic Is Not Exotic

In exploring the logic of the exotic, we have not yet dealt with the question of its exoticism itself. If the mechanisms delineated above really are at issue, why is it necessary to articulate the exotic on the bizarre or the anomalous? Why the trickery of the lure?

A first approach to the exotic might try to relate it to the structures of alterity, though without confusing the two. As stressed elsewhere (Mason 1990), in coming to terms with the Other, the perceiving self, advertently or inadvertently, reduces the other to the same in the very act of reflection. Comprehending the other entails an element of violence which cannot but deprive the other of its very otherness, for otherwise it would resist the act of assimilation to self by which it is cognized.

Seen in this light, the exotic would be that which is refractory to the egocentric attempts of self to comprehend other. After all, one of the characteristics of the exotic singled out earlier was its opacity, its refusal to give itself fully to the penetrating gaze of the beholder. The exotic, then, would be the trace of alterity that remains after the act of comprehension has taken place. The main objection to such an explanation, however, is that "reality" cannot be treated as something which opposes a sort of brute force to the attempts of *logos* to comprehend it. The site of generation of the exotic is not some supposed extralinguistic reality, but a representational site. In other words, the exotic is not originally located somewhere else and then secondarily reflected in representations. Rather, it is the product of those very representations, produced through the process of exoticization. If we are to proceed any further, it is therefore necessary to examine the mode of production of the exotic in more detail. If the exotic is not encountered but produced, we are still obliged to say something more about the site and modality of its production.

As far as the modality is concerned, some idea of the way in which the exotic can be given relatively more or less emphasis—the process of exoticization and deexoticization—can be gained from the differing style of presentation of two Native Americans. An etching (fig. 27; see following p. 112) of a Mohawk, Sychnecta, displayed in the Blauw Jan inn in Amsterdam in 1764, depicts him in antiquarian fashion, with a bow and arrow at a time when the flintlock musket had been in use among the Iroquois for well over a century. This and the inclusion of a palm tree in the background point to the curiosity and thirst for exotica among the Dutch audience. As Hamell notes: "Like the tomahawk and the palm tree in the background, they [the bow and arrow] were rather long-standing European visual symbols or metaphors for Sychnecta's otherworldliness—his exotism, as *Een Wilde*—a curiosity sufficient to amuse the curious of Amsterdam" (1987, 188). These attributes, besides answering the urge to heighten exoticism, may also be assumed to connote degrees of superiority and inferiority; the quaint Amerindian weapons appear as inferior to the weaponry of Europe.

We can gain some idea of just how much exotic coloring has been heaped on this portrait of Sychnecta by contrasting it with the figure of a Native American in the memorial to John Graves Simcoe in Exeter Cathedral. This figure, signed by the sculptor John Flaxman and completed in 1815,[27] is probably intended to represent an Iroquois. In this case, however, the exotic quality of the work has been deliberately toned down by the reduction of specifically ethnographic traits, thereby giving the figure an equal position within the framework of the piece instead of an inferior one (Smiles 1992). In fact, thanks to the existence of a preliminary drawing in preparation for the Simcoe memorial, we can see how Flaxman himself whittled down the exotic elements in progressive stages of his conception.

But if the process of exoticization takes place in this way, where are we to locate its site of production? At this point it is worth referring to some of the theses on colonialist discourse put forward by Homi Bhabha,[28] for he stresses the element of splitting—the *différance*—which also seems to be a characteristic of the exotic. Take the following passage (Bhabha 1994, 111):

> The discriminatory effects of the discourse of cultural colonialism, for instance, do not simply or singly refer to a "person," or a dialectical power struggle between self and other, or to a discrimination between mother culture and alien cultures. Produced through the strategy of disavowal, the *reference* of discrimination is always to a process of splitting as the condition of subjection: a discrimination between the mother culture and its bastards, the self and its doubles, where the trace of what is disavowed is not repressed but repeated as something *different*—a mutation, a hybrid.

To paraphrase, the exotic is not produced through the collision between ego's culture and alien cultures. The exotic is not a problem of genealogy or identity between two different cultures. The exotic is not waiting there to be appropriated. It is not a source of conflict, but an effect of discriminatory practices. Like the colonial, it is "dependent for its representation upon some strategic limitation or prohibition *within* the authoritative discourse itself" (Bhabha 1994, 86)

We can illustrate the themes of hybridity and discriminatory practices in the life and work of Paul Gauguin. To quote Eisenman: "His Tahitian was written (and presumably spoken) with a heavy French accent, in the same manner that his painted and written renditions of Polynesian history, religion, and social and sexual life remained Francophone in intonation. This very inflection—which may be termed Gauguin's 'hybridity'—is what makes his art so historically salient" (1997, 20).

The artist's appearance itself was a paragon of hybridity: he practiced with a bow and arrow after seeing the North American Indians in Buffalo Bill's show in Paris in 1889, but arrived in Tahiti wearing a cowboy hat over his shoulder-length hair—to the great amusement of the native Tahitians. As far as the discriminatory practices are concerned, it is interesting to note that, despite the opportunities for exposure to Oceanic art, he tended to make use of archaic models. Thus, the Tahitian female prostitutes in *Ta matete (The Market)* (1892) follow the style of Egyptian tomb painting,[29] and other "Tahitian" poses derive from Javanese temple art (Varnedoe 1984a). Gauguin's adoption of the Buddha as one of his major idol types is a sign of a syncretism and lack of interest in actual native products.[30] During his first visit to Tahiti, the artist seems to have drawn as much on J.-A. Moerenhout's already outdated *Voyages aux Îles du Grand Océan* (Paris, 1837) as on the world around him. This tendency is even more accentuated during his last period of production, for Gauguin's work in the Marquesas displays an almost total lack of native art forms: "Finally face to face with the native culture on whose art he had based himself in Tahiti, Gauguin was not interested" (Amishai-Maisels 1978, 341). The production of these "exotic" canvases, at any rate, is based on a refusal to countenance the artistic products of a culture that Gauguin cultivated precisely because it represented the exotic for him.

In discussing the hybridization that is an effect of colonialist discourse, Bhabha also brings out the subversive character of native questions when put to the authorities, questions of authority that the Authorities cannot answer: "The display of hybridity—its peculiar 'replication'—terrorizes authority with the *ruse* of recognition, its mimicry, its mockery" (1994, 115).[31]

These theses find a measure of confirmation in their explanatory power vis-à-vis the blankness of the exotic. To quote Bhabha again (1994, 112):

> Those discriminated against may be instantly recognized, but they also force a re-cognition of the immediacy and articulacy of authority—a disturbing effect that is familiar in the repeated hesitancy afflicting the colonialist discourse when it contemplates its discriminated subjects: the *inscrutability* of the Chinese, the *unspeakable* rites of the Indians, the *indescribable* habits of the Hottentots. It is not that the voice of authority is at a loss for words. It is, rather, that the colonial discourse has reached that point when, faced with the hybridity of its objects, the *presence* of power is revealed as something other than what its rules of recognition assert.[32]

And this explains why the *différance* which produces the exotic implies an act of deferral—the exotic functions as an articulation of displacement and dislocation, thrown up in the process of its formation to refer immediately away from itself. As the term *disavowal* implies, the reference here is to Freud's concept of *Verleugnung* as a strategy by which to maintain the narcissistic demand in the acknowledgment of difference.[33]

The use of Freudian terminology here should not be taken to imply some kind of psychoanalytical or psychohistorical interpretation. It is borrowed as an interpretive morphology, allowing us to fall back on what is undoubtedly a powerful metaphoric as a means of providing insight into the processes under discussion. In the present case, we are faced with a striking morphological resemblance between the deferral effected by the exotic and the unconscious process. It is the act of splitting (Heidegger would call it *Riss;* for Derrida it is the double inscription) which defies the originality or identity of what is to be defined. The refractory nature of the exotic, enticing by its charms and repudiating any effort to grasp it, inevitably results in specularity. In this case, the gaze of the observer is deflected to a replica situated *elsewhere.*

This elsewhere is at the same time a nowhere. If we follow Derrida in replacing the metaphysical concept of the unconscious by such a term as "a certain alterity," we can read his account as if its target were the exotic (1972a, 21):

> A certain alterity . . . is definitively removed from every process of representation by which we might summon it to appear in person. In this context and under this name, the unconscious is not, as is known, a hidden, virtual, potential presence. It differentiates itself [*il se diffère*], i.e. it is woven of differences and it dispatches or delegates representatives or mandatories; but there is no way that the mandating agent can "exist," as present, or as "itself," *in any site* [my italics], let alone be admitted to consciousness. In this sense . . . the "unconscious" is no more a "thing" than anything else, no more a thing than a virtual or concealed consciousness. This radical alterity *vis-à-vis* every possible mode of presence is marked in irreducible effects after the event, *nachträglich*.

The lure of the exotic is thus to defer the gaze elsewhere, but to a site *which is not a site*. By assuming the form of a representation, it acts as such without revealing that for which it stands. In the case of the Lafitau frontispiece discussed in chapter 5, the frontispiece constitutes that very reality to which it refers. There is no reference to something else—there is only reference to that which is constituted in the very act of referral. The same mechanism has been traced at the root of the hybrid, in which the combination of clearly attributable features with different origins leads to a composite being which is itself incapable of attribution. It cannot be placed within any existing scheme. It refers only to itself (Mason 1991a).

Far from having its origin *outside* (the root meaning of the prefix *exo-*), then, the exotic is produced *inside* discourse. It assumes the form of a representation, but one whose relation to its referent is one of opacity or blankness. Far from being a transparent sign through which something else can be seen, the exotic functions as a sign that is itself dense and which detracts from its own referentiality. The exotic spuriously refers outside itself by deferring the gaze away from itself toward that unique referent whose only reply is—boum. "Mimicry *repeats* rather than *re-presents*" (Bhabha 1994, 88).

Grasping the workings of this specular structure enables us to understand what is wrong with the notion that the exotic is that which is refractory to the egocentric attempts of self to comprehend other. The process by which the exotic is produced creates a reality effect—but that of an *exotic* reality—by suggesting the persistence of something that is resistant to the discourse which is bent on incorporating and assimilating it. It presents the lure of an opaque other that is refractory to self's attempts to impose the order of a *logos* on its perceptions. But this opaque other does not *exist* outside of the discourse that brings it into being. It is a pseudo-other, just as the exotic is a pseudoexotic, spawned by the discourse of self, which then re-presents its product as the exotic, in the same way that colonialist discourse spawns the hybrid which then, *nachträglich,* confronts and disturbs that very colonialist discourse itself.

It is possible to talk about the voice of the other and even to try to demonstrate a degree of receptivity toward it. But we can now see why the voice of the exotic, like the echo in a Marabar cave, is entirely devoid of distinction.

NOTES

Chapter 1: Infelicities, or the Exotic Is Never at Home

1. On this Diderotian argument, by which the travel of a few has left us all ultimately the poorer, see Pagden 1993, 165.
2. For details, reproductions of the paintings, and further bibliographic references to Peale's mastodon, see Egmond and Mason 1997, 7–18.
3. For a related argument on the provisional nature of the *historical* context, see Egmond and Mason 1997.
4. Austin attempted to classify the different infelicities under categories like Misfires, Abuses, Misinvocations, Misexecutions, Insincerities, Misapplications, Flaws, and Hitches, though not all cases are clear-cut. Greenblatt finds a misfire, a misinvocation, a misapplication, and a misexecution in Columbus's spectacularly infelicitous founding speech act in the New World (1991, 65).
5. Derrida's article "Signature événement contexte" (1972a, 365–93) was vigorously attacked by J. R. Searle, the philosopher of speech acts. Derrida's response to Searle, "Limited Inc a b c," ran to 134 pages. It was later supplemented by an additional contribution to the debate, "Vers une éthique de la discussion." These three texts of Derrida (together with a summary of Searle's objections) can be found in the enlarged edition of *Limited Inc.* (Derrida 1990a). See, too, the remarks on Austin's paper "The Meaning of a Word" (Austin 1979, 55–75) in Derrida 1988, 113ff.
6. Doubts have been raised by Searle and others about the accuracy of Derrida's reading of Austin (for an example see Dews 1992); in fact, it has even been suggested that Austin and Derrida say more or less the same things about language (Fish 1982; Rorty 1991, 86 n. 3). Those critics who do not even bother to take the whole Derrida-Searle dossier into account (see previous note) can be ignored. However, it would exceed the boundaries of the present chapter to go into this controversy in more detail.
7. Perhaps it is necessary to add that this possibility is not a necessity, as Derrida points out (1990a, 96). Incidentally, this argument has implications not only for the distinction between oral and written, but also for that between human and animal. In replacing the framework of speech act theory with the concept of the iterability of the mark, beyond human speech acts (Derrida 1990a, 248; cf. 1993, 90), Derrida is also attacking the notions of an ontotheological humanism and the classical nature/law opposition. But this is not the place to go into this Heideggerian discussion (cf. Corbey and Mason 1994).
8. The reference is to a letter with nineteen signatories, published in the *Times* on 9 May 1992, in protest against the proposal by the University of Cambridge to award an honorary degree to Jacques Derrida. The honorary doctorate was conferred on 11 June 1992.

9. Citations and references are to the earlier of the two English versions (of an article originally published in 1932 in *Logos* as "Zum Problem der Beschreibung und Inhaltsdeutung von Werken der bildenden Kunst"). Reference to the later version is made only when the modifications and corrections introduced there are relevant to the present argument.
10. A further problem in Panofsky's dependence on the history of types is indicated by the word *unquestionable*: despite the rigor of his analyses, not all of Panofsky's identifications have been accepted as unquestionable by later generations of scholars.
11. See esp. "The Visual Image: Its Place in Communication" in Gombrich 1982, 137–61.
12. Though it should be noted that Panofsky later abandoned the iconological project and attached exclusive importance to the scientific character and foundation of iconographic and thematic analysis; on this shift in emphasis between Panofsky's work of the 1930s and of the 1950s, see particularly Marin's remarks on Panofsky's 1955 rewriting of his 1936 essay on Poussin's *The Arcadian Shepherds* (Marin 1995, 106–25).
13. Althusser's analysis of the Hegelian totality (in Althusser et al. 1968, 1:112–49), which he contrasts with the hierarchically structured totality of Marx, has lost none of its original force.
14. For parallels between Lavater's theories and Ginzburg's "conjectural paradigm," see Flavell 1994.
15. On the terminological shift from *iconography in a deeper sense* (1962, 8) to *iconology,* Panofsky explained that, in reviving the "good old word" iconology—which Emile Mâle had already used in the modern sense, drawing explicitly on the title of Cesare Ripa's handbook for the representation of personifications, *Iconologia*—the term is to be used "wherever iconography is taken out of its isolation and integrated with whichever other method, historical, psychological or critical, we may attempt to use in solving the riddle of the sphinx" (Panofsky 1970, 57).
16. The term *family resemblance* is taken from Wittgenstein (1958, sec. 66). For further discussion see Egmond and Mason (1997, 1–6, 199–205).
17. Rampley even goes so far as to suggest that Warburg's most sensitive follower may in fact be not Panofsky but Walter Benjamin (1997, 48).
18. On Father Time see the discussion of the frontispiece to Joseph François Lafitau's *Moeurs des sauvages amériquains comparées aux moeurs des premiers temps* in chapter 5.
19. Panofsky (1962, 47 n. 44) connects this giraffe with one recorded as part of a shipment of rare animals from the Sultan to Luca Landucci in 1487. The first giraffe to appear in medieval Europe was in Ravenna in 1231 (Haskins 1927, 255).
20. Warburg discussed the serpent ritual of the Hopi—which he did not actually witness during his 1896 journey to New Mexico—in a lecture delivered on 21 April 1923 and published posthumously (Warburg 1938–39).
21. G. J. Hoogewerff had drawn the same distinction between ethnography and ethnology and between iconography and iconology—as well as between geography and geology and between cosmography and cosmology—in a lecture

that he delivered in Oslo in 1928 on "L'iconologie et son importance pour l'étude systématique de l'art Chrétien."

Chapter 2: The Exotic Genre

1. Characteristically, Milton's only reference to Indians in *Paradise Lost* is to "feathered cincture."
2. The feathered skirt worn by the Hawaiian princess Năhi'ena'ena at the reception of her brother on his return from England in 1825 is the exception which proves the rule: "only one was ever made and that in a particular place for a particular person to be worn on a special occasion" (Charlot 1991, 123). As Charlot points out, the wearing of Hawaiian cloaks and helmets, on the other hand, was not confined to one occasion, though their use seems to have been confined to people of high status. In this connection also see the chapter tellingly entitled "Feathers, Divinity and Chiefly Power" in Thomas 1995, 151–64.
3. "America" is usually represented by Brazilian figures based on the publications of Hans Staden and André Thevet (Wendt 1989, 196ff). On the slow arrival of information on the New World, see Hirsch 1976 and Adams 1976. There are important modifications to this picture for the French-speaking world in Kemp 1994.
4. Sturtevant notes that four of the men depicted in Weiditz's *Trachtenbuch* "wear breechclouts with a skirt-like row of large feathers pendant from the belt (curiously similar to the Brazilian feather skirts)" (1976, 426). Massing writes that these feathers "seem to be a later addition" (1991b, 518). On the importance of Weiditz's *Trachtenbuch*, see Defert 1987, 533–34.
5. This woodcut has been widely reproduced. See, for example, Sturtevant 1976, 425; idem 1991, 338; Massing 1991b, 516.
6. In a more recent survey of European first visual impressions of Indian America, Sturtevant does not entirely rule out the possibility that the feathered skirt may be ethnographically authentic, too, in view of the fact that it appears in illustrations on sixteenth-century maps—particularly of a ritual dance—where other details seem, in his opinion, to be quite accurate reflections of ethnographic reality (1991, 338–39). Elsewhere Sturtevant expresses the opinion that the Tupinamba wore feathered skirts, though perhaps only on special occasions (1988, 294).
7. This enormous frieze, which was to have been some fifty meters long, displays a remarkable attention to detail. Of the woodcuts which were completed, 139 have survived. Impressions from the 1526 edition are very rare; most surviving impressions are taken from later editions (1777, 1796, and 1883–84) (Bartrum 1995, 141–43).
8. On the special iconography of the Plains Indian warbonnet, a feathered headdress in which the feathers are swept backward, see Sturtevant 1990.
9. Burgkmair's drawing of a feathered skirt (once in the collection of Hans Sloane) is in fact a composite of Brazilian and Mexican items shown on an African model (Feest 1990, 25; 1995a, 332). Here, as in the woodcut of the people of Calicut, Burgkmair seems to have been confused as to what might be the proper characteristics of the various peoples depicted in his prints (Rowlands 1994, 258; cf. Rowlands and Bartrum 1993, nos. 99, 100).

10. Though many of the details of the life and activities of Cornelis Bos are shrouded in mystery, the hypothetical biography by Schéle (1965, 20ff.) can now be corrected on a number of points by Van der Coelen's study (1995), which draws on archival sources. We know that Bos was in Antwerp in 1544, when he was deported for associating with the Loïst sect. He may have spent part of 1544–45 in Paris, where he would have come into contact with the School of Fontainebleau and the experiments of French book illustrators with strapwork and grotesques, but by 1546 he was in Nuremberg. After a couple of years in refuge in Germany, he moved to Groningen in the north of the Netherlands. The Groningen archives enable us to establish 1555 as the year of the artist's death.
11. A series of masks by Floris is taken from the decoration of the Vatican Logge and the Domus Aurea; the same source is indicated for a series of friezes by Cornelis Bos depicting various grotesques, strapwork, imaginary creatures, animals, and tendrils (De Jong and De Groot 1988, nos. 78 [Floris] and 17 [Bos]).
12. In a separate monograph on the seventeenth-century Antwerp cabinet, Fabri notes that exotic scenes are a feature of late-seventeenth-century pieces (1991, 100–102). European hunting scenes are replaced by exotic variants, typical foreign costume makes its appearance (often in connection with allegories of the four continents), and exotic buildings, animals, and practices are depicted.
13. See chapter 46 (Modus Piscandi Mirabilis) of his *Descriptio de Partibus Infidelium.* For other discussions of cormorant fishing, see Mason 1987b; MacGregor 1989b, 313–14; and Jackson 1997, who provides a survey of fishing using cormorants in China, Japan, Italy, France, and England.
14. For discussion of other examples (with illustrations), see Mason 1993a. It has been suggested that the works of Sebastiano del Piombo (1485–1547) from his Roman years reflect the discovery of the Americas (Donattini 1992, 116–17). While the platyrrhine monkey, probably a marmoset, in a portrait of Cardinal Antonio del Monte (National Gallery of Ireland, Dublin; cf. Hirst 1981, 101) from the middle years of the second decennium of the sixteenth century appears to be of a kind connected with the New World, the controversial nature of many of the identifications in del Piombo's paintings makes it impossible to go further than a verdict of *non liquet* at this stage.
15. In some cases this assimilation was facilitated by the treatment of ancient artifacts as exotica. For a case study of a particularly persistent example, that of the reception of ancient Near Eastern artifacts, see Bohrer 1989.
16. These events are the decision of Julius II in August 1511 to establish several bishoprics in the New World; the presentation of a petition to Leo X in 1513 urging him to send preachers to help convert the Indians; and an oration delivered by Tomasso Fedra Inghirami to Julius in 1510 on the role of the recent geographic discoveries in the divine plan (Colbert 1985, 186).
17. This headdress is absent from a drawing in Paris relating to the composition (Colbert 1985, 186 n. 10).
18. The parallel that Colbert draws with an early-seventeenth-century costume design by Giulio Parigi is irrelevant. Moreover, by that time at least one European had appeared in public in an item of headgear combining a helmet with exotic feathers: Archduke Ferdinand II included some feathers from one of the

pre-Columbian feather headdresses inherited from his father in the helmet that he wore on the occasion of his second marriage (Scheicher 1985, 34).

19. *Exempli gratia,* I refer to the remarkable plumes on the helmets in a wool and silk tapestry from the South Netherlands, dating from ca. 1520, depicting the installation of Philip the Fair in 1494 (Rijksmuseum Amsterdam, inv. no. BK-NM-8838).
20. Once again *exempli gratia,* I refer to Albrecht Dürer's *grisaille* drawing of Calvary (Galleria degli Uffizi, Florence, inv. no. 8406), dated to 1505, in which a soldier is identified as Oriental not only by his feathered headdress but also by his curved sword.
21. There are two rooms in the Vatican which bear similar names. The Loggetta, decorated by Giovanni da Udine under Raphael's instruction, drawing on the decorations of the Domus Aurea, was preceded by the so-called Loggia of Raphael, also in the Vatican, which was completed by 1519 (Dacos 1969b, 105ff.; cf. Bedini 1997, 163–69).
22. In his life of Raphael, Vasari refers to Giovanni as an unrivaled painter of animals, who depicted "all the animals owned by Pope Leo, namely the chameleon, the civet cats, the apes, the parrots, the lions, the elephants, and other even more exotic beasts" (1965, 310).
23. The original Dutch text runs: Daer is oock een Landtschap, wesende een West-Indien, met veel naeckt volck, met een bootsighe Clip, en vreemt ghebouw van huysen en hutten: doch is onvoldaen gelaten (Van Mander 1604, fol. 229).
24. Karel van Mander (1548–1606), a Flemish painter who spent most of his life in Haarlem, is best known for his *Schilderboeck* (1604), a Vasari-like compilation of biographic profiles of Dutch painters.
25. Van de Waal (1952, 1:91) suggested that the painting, which he referred to as "Columbus' Landing," drew on some dramatic enactment of the discovery of America like that staged for Henri II in Rouen in 1550 (on which see ch. 6).
26. This practice was not confined to the sixteenth century. In a letter of 20 June 1645 to Constantijn Huygens, J. Brosterhuisen refers to etchings of a few West Indian landscapes (*enighe West Indische landtschappen*) for Johan Maurits von Nassau-Siegen, though the latter had recently returned from the Dutch colony in Brazil (Worp 1915, 161). Indeed, the very name of the Dutch West Indian Company is an indication of the application of this specific geographic label to a much larger area than what are now called the West Indies. As for the eighteenth century, King has drawn attention to the confusion in Sir Hans Sloane's catalog of miscellanies, such as "A West Indian basket made of birch bark from Canada," resulting from the general use of the term *West Indies* for much of the Americas, including Canada and South America (1994, 234).
27. Pierron's brief reference to the *West Indian Landscape* (1912, 95) indicates that he had not seen the painting, which had been discovered only three years earlier.
28. The claims of noble descent made by Mostaert's grandson Niclaes Suycker were exaggerated boasts to enhance the social status of the sheriff (Thierry de Bye Dólleman 1963, 124).
29. There is only evidence that one painting by Mostaert entered Margaret's collection. This was a portrait of Philibert of Savoye, which the artist presented in person to her in Malines in January 1521 (Duverger 1979).

30. For a biographic sketch of Suycker, see Exh. Cat. Amsterdam 1993, 161.
31. The topicality of American themes was not just an aesthetic question, for the precious objects from the New World also had a highly political purpose, in that they symbolized the expansiveness of the Habsburg empire and the subjection of the new territories to Habsburg rule. A later example of this imperial propaganda can be found in a series of twelve prints illustrating the victories of Charles V (designed by Maarten van Heemskerck and executed by Dirck Volckertsz. Coornhert), which included a depiction of the victory of the imperial troops over the Amerindians in 1530 (Exh. Cat. Berlin 1982, no. 5/20, pl. 81; Exh. Cat. Utrecht/'s-Hertogenbosch 1993, no. 201f).
32. For Dürer's high estimation of Patinir as a landscape painter, see Panofsky 1971, 209.
33. Gibson relates Mostaert's landscape style to an older generation of Dutch artists, but he notes the similarity of Mostaert's Antwerp *St. Christopher* to Patinir's version of this subject in Madrid (1989, 43). A contemporary and fellow townsman of Haarlem, Frans Jansz, was also familiar with Patinir's landscapes in the 1520s (ibid.).
34. This would immediately exclude a reference either to Coronado or to the Portuguese in Brazil.
35. The presence of this figure rules out the possibility that the painting could be a representation of Columbus's landing on the island of Goanin in 1492–93, since the possession of such an unmistakably European attribute necessarily implies that there has already been previous contact with Europeans.
36. Typical features of the Wild Man are long hair, a hairy body, human and animal traits, dress of animal skins or nudity, and the use of a club as a weapon.
37. By contrast, the seventeenth-century Peruvian Indian Felipe Guaman Poma de Ayala portrayed Indian men as beardless; the only two exceptions in his work may be interpreted as deliberate deviations from the norm for a special purpose: see Adorno 1981, 97 n. 14.
38. For the persistence of the bow and arrow in the iconography of the Amerindian in later centuries, see chapter 8.
39. Compare the headgear in the watercolor drawing of a bearded "Tartar or Uzbek man" by the English artist John White, which is probably copied from an engraving (Hulton 1984, pl. 72).
40. For comprehensive discussions of the sources from the sixteenth and seventeenth centuries, see Huddleston 1967 and Gliozzi 1976, 371–443.
41. Portuguese sources, in particular, stressed the Chinese origins (Gliozzi 1976, 387 n. 57).
42. (Exotic) fauna and flora were neither geographically specific nor generically specific. As far as the question of genre is concerned, the presence of a unicorn on Herri Bles's *Sermon of St. John* (Dresden, Staatliche Kunstsammlungen, illustrated in Gibson 1989, pl. 2.50) in no way implies that this biblical scene should be treated mythologically.
43. Cuttler interprets a detail on the extreme left-hand margin of the painting as the erect fragment of a classical pier. After close observation of the painting in situ, I find this rather unconvincing. Even if this were the case, however, interpretation of the presence of a classical artifact in the painting would not necessarily conflict with an American reference.

44. Perhaps we should add the pose of the couple on the far left, where the scene of a woman restraining a man from going to war might be seen to have classical overtones.
45. For the persistence of this classicizing influence on later representations, including photographs, of the exotic, see chapter 6.
46. For knowledge about America in the Netherlands during the sixteenth century, see Schmidt 1994. Lechner 1992 examines the books on America that could be found in Dutch private libraries, but the period he covers, extending to 1655, does not throw much light on the formative early period.
47. This phenomenon is not confined to New World representations. For instance, Renaissance statues of Neptune display a similar iconographic fluidity because of the lack of classical models to imitate (Freedman 1995).
48. Panofsky 1962, ills. 22 and 23 are taken from editions of Vitruvius dating from 1521 and 1547, respectively.
49. In a study of scenes of tempest and shipwreck in Dutch painting, Goedde makes the same point that the locations of the desolate shores depicted in some paintings are uncertain. He suggests that a painting by Jan Peeters, *Ships in Distress off a Wild Coast* (Kunsthistorisches Museum, Vienna), represents the unlikely combination of a Dutch ship, a Turkish galley, and natives dressed in skins who "are almost surely American Indians" (1989, 107). Though dating from about 1650, this painting betrays the same lack of geographic precision that characterized Mostaert's composition from more than a hundred years before—a hallmark of the exotic genre.
50. See, for example, plates 1.7, 1.31, 2.21, 2.40, 2.43, 2.44, 2.45, 2.46, 2.65, and 3.19 in Gibson 1989.
51. Orley fell out of favor with his patron in 1527, but was reinstated by her successor, Maria of Hungary, five years later, serving as her major court painter until his death in 1541.
52. Viz. a head with a feather necklace and a seated figure made of gold, wearing an armor of feathers and holding an arrow the size of a spear in his right hand; see the reproduction and discussion in Vandenbroeck 1992, 109.
53. Van Mander (1604, fol. 229) refers to a painting of St. Hubert by Mostaert as evidence for the artist's close attention to nature and life.
54. Representations of Jerome as an ascetic in the wilderness were prevalent in the Middle Ages, were continued by Joachim Patinir in the early sixteenth century, and persisted right through the seventeenth century. The development of the Erasmian version of Jerome in his study as an exemplar of humanist Christian scholarship dates from the early sixteenth century (Gibson 1989, 13).
55. The Dutch text runs:

> Dan en weet ick niet/wat seldtsamer cluchten
> Van herdershutten en boeren ghehuchten
> In klip-kuylen/hol-boomen en op staken
> Wy stichten sullen/met wanden en daken.
> [Then we shall make I know not what kinds of bizarre sorts
> Of shepherds' huts and peasant hamlets,
> In rocky caves, hollow trees and on stakes
> With walls and roofs.]

56. See pl. 159 in Exh. Cat. Brussels 1963. This large panel (88 × 165 cm) by Cornelis van Dalem (d. Bavel 1573), by whom there are only six paintings extant, was acquired by the Boijmans Van Beuningen Museum in Rotterdam in 1996. It must have been executed at about the same time as a smaller composition to which it bears a strong resemblance, the same painter's lost *Landscape with the Flight into Egypt* (formerly in the Gemäldegalerie of the State Museums in Berlin), which dates from 1565. Comparison of Van Dalem's panel with the Mostaert painting is revealing above all of the enormous difference between the two works: *The Dawn of Civilization* does not contain any of the exotic elements which make Mostaert's panel so enigmatic. On Van Dalem see Allart 1993, esp. 117–21.
57. Cuttler denies any such resemblance (1989, 196).
58. There are plenty of literary sources glorifying such a Golden Age presentation of America, which have their roots in Columbus's belief that he had landed close to the earthly paradise (Colón 1984, 132, 215; cf. Flint 1992, 149–81; Kadir 1992, 144–45).
59. Misguided attempts to connect representations with historical events continue to dog studies of the early iconography of America. For example, Montrose (1993) has unconvincingly conjectured that the scene on the well-known allegory of America engraved by Theodor Galle after a drawing by Jan van der Straet (illustrated, e.g., in Mason 1990, 168) alludes to an incident reported to have taken place during the third of Vespucci's alleged four voyages. First, the attempt to interpret a generic, allegorical scene in historical terms is puzzling. Second, on the logic of Montrose's argument, the regularity with which such allegories feature in personifications of the four continents would oblige one to identify the historical events which underlie representations of the other three continents as well—a task as impossible as it is futile. Third, the engraving does not tally with Vespucci's account at all; for instance, it is clear that Vespucci and his men watched the unhappy fate of their companion from on board, while in the engraving Vespucci is on land. Fourth, it can be demonstrated that the scene of a severed leg being roasted on a spit in the Galle/Van der Straet engraving goes back to the earliest depictions of America on maps. In fact, this image can lay claim to being one of the earliest, if not the earliest, stereotypes of America. In a catalog of "extant illustrations prior to de Bry and having some claim to ethnographic accuracy" compiled by William Sturtevant in 1976, the first entry is a Portuguese manuscript map (Kunstmann II) of the coasts of the South Atlantic dated to 1502. The Brazilian coast bears a scene of a white man skewered on a spit being turned over a fire by a kneeling, naked, curly-haired, bearded, brown-skinned man (Sturtevant 1976, 420). There is thus no need or reason to connect this image with a specific episode in any one of Vespucci's voyages.
60. Linzeler lists the series of twelve prints as follows: (1) Bellona, (2) Triumphal procession, (3) Victory, (4) Grotesque combat, with peasants mounted on donkeys, (5) Triumph of Bacchus, (6) Battle of men and animals, including camel, horse, elephant, and dragon, (7) Combat of naked warriors, (8) Centauromachia, (9–12) Combat of horsemen and foot soldiers (1932, 272ff.).
61. Linzeler notes with reference to the seventh of the series: "Some of them wear bundles of feathers on their heads and around their waists" (1932, 274).

62. Note that Lestringant, too, refers to the Piero di Cosimo cycle and assumes that Delaune was familiar with the iconographic sources on human origins.
63. The name Becanus is an allusion to his birth in the village of Hilvarenbeek in Brabant in the southern Netherlands.
64. On Goropius's seventeenth-century successors (the Dutchman Marcus Zeurius Boxhornius and the Dane Ole Worm) and detractors (Athanasius Kircher and Brian Walton), see Cornelius 1965, 20–21.
65. Attributed to I. van der Block; dated between 1609 and 1616; now in the Pommersches Museum in Gdansk; illustrated in Exh. Cat. Berlin 1989, no. 94.

Chapter 3: Ethnographic Realism and the Exotic Portrait

1. For a facsimile edition of some of the sixteenth-century botanical illustrations in *Libri Picturati* A 18 to A 30, see *The Clutius Botanical Watercolors: Plants and Flowers of the Renaissance* (New York: Harry N. Abrams, 1998).
2. For biographic details on Eckhout, see esp. Thomsen 1938, Van Gelder 1960, and Whitehead and Boeseman 1989, 162–68.
3. There is a full discussion of the historical nomenclature of race in Dutch and Portuguese Brazil in Forbes 1988. According to Markgraf, the term *mameluco* (*mamaluco* is a Tupi term, according to Forbes 1988, 129) was applied in the seventeenth century to the offspring of a Brazilian mother and a European father; *mulato* was applied to the offspring of an Ethiopian (i.e., Negro) mother and a European (i.e., Dutch or Portuguese) father.
4. At the time of writing (June 1997), the paintings are arranged in pairs in a room of the Nationalmuseet: the side walls are occupied by the half-blood pair and by the Black African pair, respectively, while the long wall contains the horizontal painting of a dance (surmounted by three still lifes of Brazilian flora), flanked on either side by the pairs of Brazilian Indians. As we shall see, this admirable arrangement well conveys the internal relations of the paintings to one another.
5. See the letter from D. de Wilhelm to Constantijn Huygens of 27 August 1644 (Worp 1915, 52).
6. Lunsingh Scheurleer's suggestion that the Delft painter Leonaert Bramer (1596–1674) was the artist of these frescoes has much to commend it (1979, 145). First, we know from an inscription beneath a self-portrait of Bramer that he worked for "son Excellence Conte Maurice de Nasou." Second, Bramer was one of the few Dutch painters in the seventeenth century who had experience in the art of fresco painting, a technique that he probably learned during his stay in Italy. As none of his frescoes has survived, we have no direct means of telling what they looked like. At any rate, the prestigious commissions for interior decorations that he carried out in the palaces of Stadholder Frederik Hendrik, Prince of Orange, in the 1630s suggest that he had a reputation for large-scale decorative projects, which is borne out by his extant ceiling designs. Third, Bramer often chose to depict unconventional subject matter or to illustrate unusual episodes from conventional narratives. Fourth, his paintings include a number of Orientals, and he executed figure drawings of a Turk, a Negro, a man and woman in Persian dress, and an old man in Oriental attire, all of which suggests that he would have had little difficulty in handling the

exotic figures depicted on the walls of the Mauritshuis. On the life and works of Bramer, see Exh. Cat. Delft 1994.

7. Besides the eight ethnographic paintings, the 'Tapuya' dance scene, and the twelve still lifes of Brazilian produce now in Copenhagen, there were two portraits of Johan Maurits and three paintings of an envoy from the Congo and his traveling companions, who visited Brazil in 1643.
8. Where were the paintings between 1644 and 1654? Perhaps some of them at least were in the house of Jacob van Campen in Amersfoort. An entry in the diaries of Stadhouder Willem Frederik for 1647 records that he saw "the paintings that Count Maurits had made of all kinds of things in the West Indies to make tapestries from them" (Visser 1995, 436). In view of the connection between Albert Eckhout and Jacob van Campen, these paintings may have included some of Eckhout's work. I am grateful to Peter van der Ploeg for drawing this passage to my attention.
9. A watercolor copy of Eckhout's Negro woman and child in the British Museum shows the woman with a brand above her left breast (Whitehead and Boeseman 1989, 75, pl. 54).
10. The effects of the ethnographic label are considered in more detail in chapter 7 and in Mason 1997b.
11. The dance was a popular subject in depictions of the early contact between Europe and the non-European world. Besides Eckhout's 'Tapuya' dance, we can compare John White's 1585 watercolor of Indians dancing around a circle of posts. On the persistence of this interest in dance, see chapter 6.
12. In this respect, these drawings form a striking contrast to the twenty-seven drawings of Hottentots, datable by watermark to between 1688 and 1707, in the South Africa Library (Smith and Pheiffer 1993). The work of a Dutch artist, probably a competent amateur, who had also spent some time in Sumatra, these lively scenes of dancing, milking, and other everyday activities are very different from the stereotypical portraits discussed by Bassani and Tedeschi.
13. Little is known about the man himself. He may have accompanied Amadas and Barlowe on their reconnaissance of the North American coast in 1584 (Hulton 1978, 1984, 8). Most of the sixty or so drawings that have survived, however, were made during the following year, when he spent about twelve months in Raleigh's Virginia, based on the fort on Roanoke Island. Collaborating with Thomas Harriot, whose *A briefe and true Report of the new found Land of Virginia* was published in London in 1588, it was White's task to illustrate Harriot's observations of Indian life with sketch maps and ethnographic and natural historical portraits. The drawings that Sir Hans Sloane acquired from John White's descendants around 1706 were not originals, as he supposed, but copies of White's original drawings (Rowlands 1994, 249).
14. Webber also did a watercolor of the same scene, with slight modifications, but Bartolozzi's engraving is based on the version in oils (Joppien and Smith 1988, 127).
15. Kaeppler (1992, 466) records the similar case of the artist Titian Ramsay Peale, whose oil painting of the volcanic eruption on Hawaii represented natives watching the event in their feathered cloaks and helmets in 1840. Peale's images of Hawaiian featherwork were taken from the artifacts in the Peale museum in Philadelphia, which included "a magnificent Dress Cloak, made of the skins

of birds of elegant plumage . . . worn in the winter season by a chief, on the N.W. coast of America" (Peale 1991, 340). An earlier example of the use of artifacts from the Peale museums is the painting "Man in a Feathered Helmet" by Rembrandt Peale, one of Titian's brothers, dating from around 1815; the feathered helmet can be identified with the "elegant feathered Helmet Cap from the Sandwich Islands" which appears in an inventory of Rembrandt Peale's museum in Baltimore in 1815 (348, pl. 3). An earlier inventory (1804) already included "a Throne of curious workmanship, said to be executed by the King of the Pelew islands, out of a solid piece" (Peale 1988, 765). A number of exotic articles from the South Seas were accessioned by Charles Willson Peale's museum in 1808 (1084–85).

16. In a different genre—historical painting—nineteenth-century classicizing painters like Sir Lawrence Alma-Tadema made use of a similar aesthetic in which the precise depiction of archaeological artifacts was intended to enhance the sense of "being there" in the past.
17. For discussion of this tension between aesthetic and documentary considerations in criticism of Western American art, see Anderson 1992.
18. Broos applies the qualification "unmediated realism" to Eckhout's other depictions of the people, flora, and fauna of Brazil, as well as to the oil painting on paper of two tortoises that is now in the Mauritshuis in The Hague (1987, 126). This painting is of two life-sized tortoises of a South American type (*Testudo denticulata*) that was unknown in European art before Eckhout introduced it (Van Gelder 1960). The format of the painting (30.5 × 51 cm) suggests that it is related to the *Libri Picturati* in Cracow.
19. Joppien is here referring to the oil sketches in the Cracow *Libri Picturati*, including figure 9.
20. A similar case of the constitution of an alleged group through the act of anthropological nomenclature may be that of the so-called Ciboney, presumed to be the earliest inhabitants of the Caribbean islands. Like the Tupi word *Tapuya*, the word *Ciboney* may have been a disparaging term used by the dominant Arawakan-speaking culture on Hispaniola to refer to those who were not involved in the agricultural economy (Hulme 1986, 58). It should be noted, however, that Hulme's hypotheses on Carib and Arawak ethnicities have been called into question (Boucher 1992, 5–6).
21. The following analysis assumes that the paintings can be treated as a series (i.e., the systems of relations situated there are based on the existence of a relatively defined and delimited system). The paintings of Black Africans also deserve further study in terms of a different morphological chain: the iconography of Black Africans. Particularly on the European preoccupation with skin pigmentation, the fragments of Negro skins in the collections of European anatomists and naturalists, and the consequent reduction of the image of the Black to fragments of skin, see Mazzolini 1998.
22. For other examples of such differentiation in terms of degrees of wildness and for its absence in most accounts of the Hottentots, see Harbsmeier 1994a, 219 n. 35.
23. The emphasis on the rhetoric (or poetics) and politics of representations is evident in the titles to such works as Clifford and Marcus 1986, Stallybrass and White 1986, and Karp and Lavine 1991. For a pioneering study along similar

lines in the field of language—"the material word"—see Silverman and Torode 1980.

24. The question of whether the botany in the Copenhagen paintings is to be attributed to Eckhout or to Frans Post will not be discussed here. Frans Post, who is well known for his landscape paintings, seems to have had a division of labor with Albert Eckhout. While Post was to record the Brazilian scenery, Eckhout was to paint the flora and fauna, including human portraits. It has been suggested that this division of labor might have been carried out on a single canvas, a practice which was not uncommon at the time: Van Gelder (1960) detected the hand of Eckhout in the foreground vegetation and human and animal figures in landscapes painted by Post and the existence of landscape backgrounds by Post in paintings attributed to Eckhout. A similar division of labor was practiced by a brother of Frans Post, the architect Pieter Post: in a 1655 painting, *The Granting of the Charter by Count Willem II of Holland,* Pieter Post was responsible for the architectural background, whereas the figures were executed by Caesar van Everdingen (Terwen and Ottenheym 1993, 159).

    Eckhout may have collaborated with other artists, too. Certain motifs related to his Brazilian paintings appear in a set of trompe l'oeil paintings depicting baskets of fruit and leaves, executed in the Hoogerhuis, Amersfoort, by Jacob van Campen. It is uncertain whether Eckhout actually had a hand in these paintings or whether Van Campen slavishly drew on Eckhoutian motifs. Van Gelder (1960, 21), Joppien (1979a, 340), and Whitehead and Boeseman (1989, 98–99) favor the thesis of collaboration between the two artists, whereas Buvelot (1995, 76) favors an attribution to Van Campen alone. The same question arises in connection with the exotic artifacts on a canvas of a triumphal pageant of East and West in the memorial hall to Frederick Hendrik (the "Oranjezaal") in Huis ten Bosch, The Hague. The program for the paintings in this hall, as well as the execution of a number of them, are the work of Jacob van Campen, but collaboration with Eckhout has been suggested in this case as well.

25. The botanical details are taken from Whitehead and Boeseman 1989.
26. In the typical landscape, each element is supposed to harmonize with the others to produce a unified representation. The isolated elements are homogeneous, each symptomatic of the whole of which it is a part. Iconographically, one could speak of a certain level of redundancy, since each of the elements might be supposed to be communicating the same message.
27. Among the criticisms of Gilbert's thesis, see esp. Settis (1990, 7–10). One of the paintings which Gilbert claimed to lack a subject, Giorgione's *Tempest,* has been subjected to a rigorous iconological interpretation by Settis himself.
28. For recent discussions see, for example, De Jongh 1995 and Van Eck et al. 1996.
29. Though the present discussion relates the Eckhout paintings to seventeenth-century conventions, there are good candidates for the existence of an iconographic double function during the earlier period. For instance, in an important methodological excursus in his catalog of paintings in the Royal Fine Arts Museum in Antwerp, Vandenbroeck has argued that the Master of Frankfurt's *Schutterfeest,* perhaps dating from 1493, combines realistic and allegorical

elements (1985, 103a-b). The same writer also draws attention to the combination of hydraulic techniques and love allegory in the work of the Master of the Amsterdam Print Cabinet (cf. Filedt Kok 1985, 241).

30. Clubs similar but not identical to the one depicted in the painting are preserved in the Nationalmuseet in Copenhagen (Dam-Mikkelsen and Lundbæk 1980, 32; Exh. Cat. Schleswig 1997, 2:333).
31. I am grateful to Joanna Overing for this suggestion.
32. For other diabolical associations of American fauna, compare the inclusion of a sinister locustlike creature, drawing on the iconography of the devil, among the otherwise faithfully executed renderings of New World insects on a panel from an eighteenth-century cabinet after Jan van Kessel in the Smithsonian Institution (Ritterbush 1985, 149–53, with illustration on 150). For a similar painting of insects attributed to Van Kessel, see Fitton and Gilbert 1994, 120–21. Likewise, there is a satanic rendering of the American sloth in an engraving by Theodor de Bry (Ashworth 1985, 59). The diabolical associations of Amerindians themselves are further discussed in Mason 1987a and 1990, 52–63.
33. The story of Adam and Eve recurs in a Brazilian setting on a carved coconut shell in Copenhagen which depicts "a Tapuya Adam and Eve standing beside what may be a papaya" (Whitehead and Boeseman 1989, 68; cf. Dam-Mikkelsen and Lundbæk 1980, 22, and Gundestrup 1991, 2:54).
34. For a fuller discussion of this antiquarian background to the Eckhout paintings, see Egmond and Mason 1997, 184–94.
35. For examples of the assimilation of Irish, American Indians, women, the poor, and others to an animal state in early modern England, see Thomas 1983, 41–50. A late-seventeenth-century painting of a Negress and monkey by Jan Jebsen (Schloss Rosenborg, Copenhagen) belongs to the same complex.
36. In this connection we could point to the slang use of the Dutch word *vogelen* (birding) to mean copulate (Sutton 1984, xxv). A painting from the mid-1660s by Nicolaes Berchem combines exoticism and eroticism in the depiction of a Moor presenting a parrot to a lady.
37. In this painting, red seems to be used to highlight objects with a sexual connotation: the face of the bird, the sash into which the woman's pipe is tucked, the necklace hanging just above her breasts, and the decorative bands on the bowl she is carrying in her right hand—the roundedness of both the bowl and the fruit it contains echoes the full form of her exposed breasts. I am grateful to Adam Jones for drawing my attention to the use of the color red in this painting.
38. There is a mid-sixteenth-century representation of a South American guinea pig in the herbarium of Georg Öllinger (Öllinger and Quicchelberg 1553, fol. 641).
39. We might compare the figure of a Polynesian woman as depicted in an appendix to Spielbergen's *Nieuwe Oost ende West Indische Navigation,* published in 1618, and the version of the same woman which the de Brys introduced a year later in part 11 of the *Great Voyages*. The former is depicted with a child, but in the latter version the child has disappeared. "The changes are precisely those linking this figure to the paradigm of the savage woman: the disappear-

ance of the child removes all connotation of motherhood and nursing from the anatomical anomaly" (Bucher 1981, 135).

40. On the role of the figure of the Amazon in early modern discourse on gender, see Davis 1975, 124–51.
41. Compare Hulme's discussion of the "feminizing" of the Arawak and the "masculinizing" of the Caribs in the chivalrous interpretation of their significance for a European audience (1994, 170–71).
42. "Spiegel van ondankbaarheyt, vertoont in de mishandeling van de heeren gebroeders De Witten," in *'t Zwart toneel-gordyn, opgeschoven voor de Heeren Gebroederen Cornelis en Joan De Witt* (n.p., 1677).

Chapter 4: Presentations of the Exotic

1. For the contrast between metonymic and synecdochic museum presentations, see Bann (1984, 85–92).
2. Parshall sees the relationship between *artificia* and *naturalia* in the Renaissance collection of curiosities as a parallel rather than a hierarchical one (1993, 555). As he points out, this implies an independence of the former from a purely mimetic role.
3. On the relative freedom from a humanistic reverence for classical authority on the part of these travelers and writers, see Hoeniger 1985.
4. The work of "armchair scholars" is attacked from a different angle, but to the same end, by Du Haillan, for whom it was experience in courtly society which conferred authority on the writer (Simonin 1992, 211).
5. Thevet's rival Jean de Léry was less fortunate in bringing back curiosities from Brazil. During the famine which his crew suffered on the return journey, they ended up eating the monkeys and parrots that had been destined for collectors at home and had to make do with "putting them into the cabinet of their memory" (Léry 1990, 208).
6. Paré mentions a toucan presented to Charles V by a gentleman from Provence; the French surgeon unsuccessfully attempted to embalm it. He had more success with a bird of paradise, which he proudly displayed in his own collection (Paré 1971, 128–30). On the evidence of Paré's text, we know that his collection also included the skeletons of conjoined twins, an ostrich, and a chameleon, as well as needles, stones, and a flying fish from America (cf. Wilson 1993, 70). Both Paré and Thevet include the same engraving of a toucan; Pierre Belon had to be satisfied with an engraving of the beak, which, he states, could be found in several curiosity cabinets (1997, 184).
7. For a concise survey of the collections of the Austrian Habsburgs from the Middle Ages to the turn of the twentieth century, see DaCosta Kaufmann 1994.
8. See also the surveys of literature on collections by Pomian 1993 and Herklotz 1994.
9. The collection had previously been displayed in Veracruz and Valladolid. For this and other collections of Americana in the southern Netherlands between 1520 and 1530, see Vandenbroeck 1992.
10. Settis (1993) sees a parallel between the preservation of precious objects in churches and their later transfer to secular *Wunderkammern* (documented in Schlosser 1978), on the one hand, and the fate of sculptures from antiquity,

on the other, which were often preserved by being recycled within a Christian setting during the period before the Renaissance.

11. For example, Logan cites three cases of "North European style" collections in Italy (1979, 99 n. 44). For other criticisms of Schlosser's distinction, compare Schnapper (1988, 12) and Olmi (1992, 298).
12. In the context of a discussion of eighteenth-century collections, Stafford suggests a link between ruins and the figure of speech known as aposiopesis (1994, 240)—in both cases, there was a liberation from the constraints of syntax and punctuation, which encouraged the process of imaginative reading in and projection.
13. The head of an Atlantic walrus was cut off and sent to Pope Leo X in a barrel of salt in 1519. Dürer's well-known drawing of a walrus head is probably of the same specimen; the artist whose illustration of the same head was used in Conrad Gessner's *Historia Animalium* must have added the rest of the body from a verbal description (Seaver 1996, 9–12).
14. On Montaigne as a typical representative of the Mannerist combination of natural artifice and artificial nature, particularly his penchant for grottoes, see Ginzburg 1993. For a survey of ornamented bezoars, see Van Tassel 1973, 251–54. The same article contains a discussion of the reliability of the old labels (247–49).
15. The collection in Schloss Ambras, for instance, included small Calvaries and mountain landscapes sculpted in coral, as well as a saber with a coral hilt (Scheicher et al. 1977, 55–56, 137–38, 209).
16. One of the papers contributed by Hans Sloane to the *Philosophical Transactions* was a demonstration that "The Tartarian Lamb, *Agnus Scythicus,* or *Barmometz,* heretofore imposed on the credulous as a kind of Zoophyte, or vegetating Animal" was in fact the lower part of the root of a fern (De Beer 1953, 100; Cannon 1994, 146–47).
17. On the methods and difficulties of transporting plants in the sixteenth century, see Olmi 1991, 12.
18. On the difficulties of obtaining and preserving flamingos, see the correspondence of Peiresc to Cassiano dal Pozzo (Peiresc 1989, 44, 51, 55).
19. For examples see items 1.8 and 1.14 in Exh. Cat. Stuttgart 1987; for the scene of the dismembering of a whale painted on the shoulder blade of a Greenland whale, see Barthelmess 1994; it is not clear whether this example is taken from a collection of curiosities or from the office of a whaling company.
20. For other coconut beakers from Brazil, see Fritz (1983, ill. 110a ['Tapuya']), Whitehead and Boeseman (1989, 68–69), and Schütte and Walz (1997, no. 201). Fritz provides a list of references to coconut beakers and other coconut creations in collections right up to Goethe (1983, 72–80). A relatively large number of sixteenth-century examples of coconut beakers from the northern Netherlands have been preserved, with one of the earliest dating from before the middle of the century (see Kloek, Halsema-Kubbes, and Baarsen 1986, 161–62). Many coconut beakers have featured in exhibitions in northern Europe and the United States during the last couple of decennia: compare, for example, Exh. Cat. Berlin 1982, no. 7/43; Exh. Cat. Amsterdam 1986, nos. 333 and 341; Exh. Cat. Washington 1991, no. 11; Exh. Cat. Amsterdam 1992, nos. 328–29; Exh. Cat. Antwerp 1992, no. 82.

21. On the importance of astrology in the architecture and public life of the Medici and their contemporaries, see Rossi 1991, 155–62; the case for Ulisse Aldrovandi's relative immunity from such considerations has been argued by Olmi (1976, 67–94).
22. Cavallara's letter, one of the earliest written accounts of an Italian collection of curiosities, is published (with commentary) in Franchini et al. 1979, 48–51. For later discussions of alleged giants' bones, see Egmond and Mason 1997, 8.
23. On this tendency to specialization, see Olmi 1992, 178–84. On the other hand, Meijers (1993b) argues that, far from disappearing from the scene during the eighteenth century, the "encyclopaedic" collection of objects flourished then as never before. What did change, in her view, is not the desire to know and possess everything, but the content and form which this desire assumed.
24. On the relatively unknown figure of Carlo Antonio dal Pozzo (1606–89), see Sparti 1990.
25. Another proud sixteenth-century owner of a feathered cloak from Brazil was the physician Joannes Goropius Becanus, who claimed to have a feathered *palliolum* in his possession (1569, 1039). Goropius was the author of a history of the ancient world which argued that the Dutch were the remnant of the antediluvian peoples.
26. See Feest's detailed discussion of this item (cat. no. 12) in MacGregor 1983, 130–35.
27. The Codex Vindobonensis and the turquoise mosaic shield in Vienna.
28. Francisco Hernández (1514–87), the personal physician of Felipe II, was sent to Mexico in 1570 to investigate the natural resources of the viceroyalty. During his seven years in Mexico, he asked native artists to illustrate his work, which they are reported to have colored as realistically as possible. In this way some twelve hundred pictures were produced, but the work proved too expensive to publish, and the bound manuscripts were destroyed in the Escorial library fire of 1671. On the reception history of Hernández's work in northern Europe, see López Piñero and Pardo Tomás 1994 and 1996 and Varey and Chabrán 1995.
29. For instance, Monardes's illustration of an armadillo was based on the armadillo in the museum of Argote de Molina (Morán and Checa 1985, 129–38).
30. For a brief survey of French collections in the seventeenth century, in which Americana are conspicuous by their absence, see MacGregor 1983, 81–84.
31. For the documentary value of Thoresby's diary on the collections of his day, see Brears 1989.
32. For example, Leith-Ross draws attention to a plant, believed to be an antidote to the bite of the phalangium spider, which must have reached Bavaria in the sixteenth century, as the court artist Hoefnagel painted it along with a group of Mexican plants. As she notes, "It is unlikely to have been the only American plant to reach mainland Europe in the sixteenth century" (1984, 182).
33. It is estimated that the botanical garden of Oxford University at this time had around two dozen plants native to the Americas; a similar figure is given for the botanical garden in Leiden (Varey and Chabrán 1995, 350 nn. 56 and 58).
34. The catalog is reproduced in Allen 1964, 247–312.

35. See, in particular, the essays on the foundation of the Ashmolean Museum in MacGregor 1983.
36. The first volume was published in 1707; the second appeared in 1725.
37. A letter by Paludanus to Ortelius in 1595 suggesting an exchange of curiosities was accompanied by an American dart or arrowhead (Tracy 1980, 36).
38. The most famous collection in the southern Netherlands was that of the cartographer Abraham Ortelius in Antwerp. The exotic plants in the botanical garden of the Antwerp apothecary Peeter van Coudenberghe (1517–99) are discussed in Exh. Cat. Antwerp 1996. For the botanical garden and collection of curiosities of Charles de Saint Omer (1533–69), see Wille 1997. Van der Veen has suggested that collections of exotica were rarer in the southern Netherlands than in the North (1993, 163), but this statement requires further systematic research on the southern collections for its verification.
39. An early example of how these objects could find their way into representations may be provided by the drawings of armadillos (*Tolypeutes conurus, Is. Geoffr.* and *Dasypus novemcinctus (L.)*) included in an album in the Rijksmuseum Amsterdam assembled for Charles V from the work of different artists in the third quarter of the sixteenth century, if Boon is correct in assuming that the drawings in question are based on mounted specimens (1978, nos. 560 and 561; the illustrations are to be found in Schapelhouman 1987). This album, *LIBRO de diversos animales, aves, peces y reptiles, que el emperador Carlos V mandó dibujar a su pintor Lamberto Lombardo en Bruxelas ANO MDXLII,* contains the earliest naturalistic representations of animals in northern Europe after Dürer and Hofmann. See also Egmond and Mason 1994.
40. The Peruvian balsam (*Myroxylon peruiferum*), whose medicinal use was borrowed from the Mexicans by Cortés's troops, was introduced to Europe as a febrifuge almost immediately after the conquest of Mexico (Pardo Tomás and López Terrada 1993, 215). It should not be confused—though it often was—with true Peruvian bark or quinine (*Cinchona vera*) (De Beer 1953, 27–28).
41. Pyle 1996 identifies the artist of the natural history illustrations in Ms Urb. Lat. 276 (Pietro Decembrio Candido's *De animantium naturis*) with Ghisi.
42. For some Americana in the Museo Cartaceo of dal Pozzo, see Exh. Cat. London 1993, nos. 123 (tomato), 140 (dried fruit with markings of a human face, from Central or South America), and 148 (Codex Badianus with drawings of Mexican plants). On this codex see also Solinas 1989 and Mason 1997a.
43. Thus, the first catalog by Adam Olearius for the *Gottorfische Kunstkammer* included ten images taken directly from the catalog of the Danish collector Ole Worm (Drees 1997, 12 n. 16).
44. In 1743 one of Sloane's correspondents asked for his advice on the identification of what seemed to be "a Maremaid's Hand and Arm" from the coast of Brazil (MacGregor 1995, 84). Debate on the existence of tritons and sirens off the Brazilian coast went back to the sixteenth century; see Léry 1990, 97–98.
45. Defoe showed a lively interest in the collection of Sir James Balfour in the University of Edinburgh (MacGregor 1983, 90). He referred to the "great Chamber of the Duke's Rarities" in Munich in *Memoirs of a Cavalier* (Defoe 1991, 97). Defoe is here following William Watt's *The Swedish Intelligencer* (1632). For the plundering of the Munich collection by the Swedish army in 1632, *pace* Defoe, see Schlosser 1978, 149.

46. For the echoes of the decline of the feudal aristocracy and its eventual incorporation in the life of the court in Montaigne's work, see Kohl 1981, 28.
47. Visitors to the courtly masques designed by Inigo Jones, such as George Chapman's Memorable Masque of 1613, could see white ostrich feathers on the figure of an Indian torchbearer (Peacock 1990, 172).
48. Johan Maurits's interest in collections continued after his return. As Stadholder in Kleve from 1647, he may well have influenced the interest in collections and archaeology of Friedrich Wilhelm, Elector of Brandenburg (1620–88) (MacGregor 1993, 12 n. 24).
49. See the letter from A. Vorstius to Constantijn Huygens of 20 December 1644 (Worp 1915, 107).
50. One wonders how many of the sixty pieces of "Indian" hand weapons, arrows, shafts, javelins, and bows that Rembrandt owned came from the Americas (New Netherland?) and how many from Asia.
51. The persistence of the phenomenon of "Tupinambization" can be gauged from the following mid-seventeenth-century example. In a letter appended to his *Petits Traitez en forme de Lettres escrites à diverses personnes studieuses* (Paris, 1648), the Pyrrhonist François La Mothe Le Vayer records the case of a man called Lambel who could speak all manner of languages in his sleep. After the man had replied in Canadian to a question in Canadian and in English to a question in English, a certain Monsieur de Guitaut uttered the words "Paraousti Satouriona," which he had come across in André Thevet's portrait of a so-called King of Florida, published in 1584 in the French cosmographer's *Vrais Pourtraits*. When Lambel responded by babbling in his sleep, a sailor who happened to be among the twenty-five or so persons present declared that he was speaking the language of the Tupinamba. In his eyes, at least, there was no reason to suppose that the Indians of Florida were any different from the Tupinamba of Brazil (Lestringant 1991a, 318).
52. On geographic uncertainty about the location of "Brazil" in the sixteenth century, see Lestringant 1994, 84ff.
53. The evaluation of visual representations as against textual representations has changed over the years. Whitehead gives the example of the Latin descriptions of Tupinamba bows and arrows given by Marcgrave, which are perhaps based on actual handling of the objects in Brazil. Despite their usefulness, he claims, "they simply cannot rival the wealth of data to be extracted from the superb picture of a Tupinamba Indian holding perhaps even the same bow and arrows and painted by Marcgrave's colleague Albert Eckhout" (1987, 141).
54. The immediate impact of the publication of these scenes can be gauged from the evidence of the so-called Drake Manuscript, a set of almost two hundred watercolors depicting American fauna, flora, and ethnographica with accompanying captions (cf. Lestringant 1996, 265–90). A facsimile edition is available (*Histoire Naturelle des Indes* 1996).
55. The process of "aztequización" can also be found at work *inside* Mexico: Van Doesburg describes it in terms of an *interpretatio imperialis* (1996, 28), an attempt by the Mexican national state to reinterpret its precolonial past. He also provides striking examples of the "Aztec-centric" character of Mexican historiography vis-à-vis the cultural heritage of non-Nahua peoples from the Cuicatec region.

Chapter 5: Incorporations of the Exotic

1. Representations connected with the public displays of exotic peoples are discussed in chapter 6.
2. Vincent's catalog was published in Amsterdam by François Halma, the publisher of works by such other Amsterdam collectors as Nicolaes Witsen and Georg Rumphius.
3. There is also a drawing which has been supposed to represent the interior of Vincent's cabinet in Haarlem, executed by Gerrit Rademaker (Exh. Cat. Amsterdam 1992, no. 306), but it is unclear what relation it bears to De Hooghe's print.
4. For an extremely realistic illustration of the interior of a collection of curiosities, see Schepelern 1990 on the 1655 illustration to the *Museum Wormianum*.
5. Meijers 1996 has argued the case for the existence of a personification of America in the *Kunstkammer* of Czar Peter the Great in St. Petersburg; that personification has dark skin pigmentation, is naked except for a feathered skirt and collar, and is holding an arrow. Czar Peter visited Levinus Vincent's collection during his first stay in the Netherlands in 1697–98.
6. They include Maria Sybilla Merian (1647–1717), daughter of the Frankfurt bookseller and engraver Matthias Merian (who continued the publication of De Bry's volumes of voyages). Maria Sybilla Merian sailed to Surinam with her youngest daughter in 1699 and spent two years there collecting, drawing, and preparing objects of natural history. Her illustrated report on these natural historical investigations was published in 1705. Czar Peter the Great, an avid collector, bought two volumes of drawings by Merian during his stay in the Netherlands in 1717; on these and other drawings by Merian now in St. Petersburg, see Lebedeva 1996. There is a description of the *Pipa pipa* by John Gabriel Stedman (1988, 210–11). See further Exh. Cat. Amsterdam 1992, nos. 262f, 299, 305.
7. For some potential candidates who can be ruled out, see Van der Veen 1992, 58 n. 27.
8. At a later date, during his stay in Surinam in the 1770s, John Gabriel Stedman collected Amerindian and Bush Negro items, as well as making drawings, for Dutch collections of curiosities (Stedman 1988). Some of these items are now in the Rijksmuseum voor Volkenkunde, Leiden, the Netherlands (Price and Price 1979; Whitehead 1986).
9. There are two reasons for rejecting a psychologizing explanation here. First, the articulation of the (absent) figure of Vincent with the representation under discussion is a *structural* matter, not a psychological one. Second, any attempt to explain the representation in psychological terms would entail the laying down of that particular interpretive protocol, while the tenor of the present work is to argue in favor of contextual openness or open-mindedness.
10. See, in particular, the detailed discussion by De Certeau 1985; cf. Vidal-Naquet 1981, 177–81.
11. Cf. Clifford 1986b, 101, on Lafitau and the connection of ethnographic accounts to different allegorical referents.
12. Incidentally, evidence of the interest aroused by his work in the Netherlands can be seen from the publication of the first Dutch translation only seven years after the original French edition. A later Dutch edition of the work was pub-

lished by H. W. van Welbergen and P. H. Charlois in Amsterdam in 1751, and a German version appeared in the following year.

13. Since Lafitau himself did not design the frontispiece, there is the theoretical possibility of a discrepancy between the artist's intentions and those of the writer (for an example of such a discrepancy in an eighteenth-century frontispiece, see Broberg 1985, 94). Moreover, it may be the case that Lafitau was not in a position to check all the illustrations to his work (Sturtevant 1988, 298). Nevertheless, since questions of intention are left out of account in the present analysis, "Lafitau's frontispiece" and "Lafitau's text" will be treated as belonging to a single work.
14. As Panofsky points out, the wings, for instance, never appear in classical representations of Kronos.
15. Incidentally, it is interesting to note the attention paid by Clifford to the female gender of the writer because, in his discussion (1986a, 1) of another representation of an ethnographer engaged in "writing culture"—the photograph of Stephen Tyler on the cover of Clifford and Marcus 1986—he curiously ignores the presence of two female figures in the picture. The title of Clifford's essay "Partial Truths" hereby acquires an ironic ring.
16. The winged genii pose no iconographic problems. They regularly appear as the assistants of Father Time in Renaissance iconography (cf., e.g., Panofsky 1962, fig. 55); in the engraving of Tempus for Johann Georg Hertel's 1758–60 edition of Ripa's *Iconologia* (Ripa 1971, 11), two putti looking into a mirror represent past and future, while two other putti, bearing the emblems of night and day, record history in a book. (Hertel's edition, which differs appreciably from earlier editions of Ripa, is chosen because its publication date in the middle of the eighteenth century brings it close to the works under consideration.) For present purposes, there is no need to go into the details of the Christian iconography of the tableau to the rear of the print.
17. For these identifications, which can all be found in the texts accompanying the other plates in the two volumes, see De Certeau 1985, 70–71. Although coins, reliefs, and statues had been excavated by the thousands by Lafitau's time, he follows sixteenth-century mythographic practice (cf. Seznec 1953) in drawing on reproductions rather than on original models.
18. The Artemis illustrated by de Montfaucon was later acquired by the collector Sir John Soane; see Thornton and Dorey 1992, 71. The unfamiliar objects introduced in the foreground of the frontispiece thus presuppose a knowledge of the sources of the plates which appear later in the book.
19. For some seventeenth-century precursors of these trends, see Schnapper 1988, 165.
20. One can go back even earlier in the search for precursors: Lorenzo Pignoria's speculative theory that the religion of the Amerindians was derived from ancient Egypt went into print (as an appendix to Cartari's guide to the mythological figures of classical antiquity) in the early seventeenth century (Seznec 1931; cf. Mason 1997a).
21. This move toward natural curiosities might also be seen as a regression to medieval preoccupations—but times had changed (Schlosser 1978, 180–82).
22. The process of 'reading off' which he and others employed, both to establish a system of correspondences between the Americas and other cultures and to

fill in the gaps in the historical or ethnographic records, has been examined elsewhere (Mason 1990, 57).

23. For a survey of iconographic references to cannibalism in allegorical representations of America, see Wendt 1989, 156ff.
24. The present illustration is taken from the French translation published in The Hague by T. Johnson and J. van Duren in 1727.
25. For the personification of Wisdom as a beautiful woman dressed in robes of white and turquoise, with a sun symbol on her breast, accompanied by books, scrolls, and a lamp, see Ripa 1971, 136.
26. By A. Moetjens in The Hague. The 1732 frontispiece is of artistically inferior quality to that from the first edition; an example of the carelessness of the artist can be seen in the fact that the female scribe is writing upside down.
27. This does not mean that other considerations, such as the psychoanalytical aspects adduced by De Certeau (1985), may not play an important part as well.
28. Although the following discussion is confined to allegories of the four continents, there are important iconographic parallels in the personifications of individual nations or continents as well. For instance, in a portrait of the Habsburg emperor Charles V by Enea Vico, dating from 1550, the allegorical female figures include "Germania" and "Africa," alluding to imperial victories in Tunis (1535) and Mühlberg (1547); see Exh. Cat. Utrecht/'s-Hertogenbosch 1993, no. 200.
29. In New Spain itself, a female allegorical figure of America features in a description of the triumphal arch erected by the students of the Colegio de San Pedro y San Pablo to commemorate the arrival of the relics sent to Mexico by Pope Gregory XIII in 1575 (Grañén Porrúa 1994, 119).
30. Ortelius, in fact, depicted five continents: Asia, Europe, America, Africa, and Tierra del Fuego. The frontispieces to some early-seventeenth-century editions of Mercator likewise split America into "Peruana" and "Magellanica," the former accompanied by a lion and the latter by an elephant. The standardization and consolidation of the iconography of the four continents did not get under way until the seventeenth century. For a survey of frontispieces from the sixteenth to the nineteenth century, see Tooley 1975. Exh. Cat. Mexico City 1994 is a rich source for allegorical and emblematic illustration in New Spain, including frontispieces.
31. For Tiepolo's dependence on travel accounts, such as the publications on the Americas by De Bry and on the Levant by de Bruyn, for the iconography of the Würzburg frescoes, see Ashton 1978.
32. The earliest printed editions of costume books appeared in the 1560s, based on a slightly older series of etchings by Enea Vico.
33. The edition of Ripa's *Iconologia* published in Rome in 1593 was not illustrated.
34. For a reproduction see Exh. Cat. Berlin 1982, pl. 26.
35. On the norm of posing women to face more frontally than men, see Honig's remarks (1990) on a portrait of Lady Dacre by Hans Eworth. In female profiles, by contrast, the woman's eye and face are deflected, thereby rendering her "decorously chaste, the depersonalized and passionless object of passion" (Simons 1988, 21).

36. The proviso "in this context" is necessary because in other contexts America may be linked with, say, Asia or Africa by means of the "floating signifier" of the feathered skirt. In the case of the allegories of the four continents, however, the iconographic point is that they are distinguishable from one another within a single painting or print, irrespective of the possibility that their ordering may be different in other paintings, prints, or contexts of a different kind.
37. There is an unusual variant in which the four continents are represented by young children in a painting from 1688 by Gregor Brandmüller, now in the Musée du Nouveau Monde in La Rochelle (reproduced with a brief discussion in Lefrançois 1992).

Chapter 6: Exotic Spectacles

1. The earliest *three-dimensional* representation of Native Americans may be the Harman memorial in Burford, Oxfordshire (Mason 1988b).
2. The presence in the collection of Sir Hans Sloane of "the kidneys of a malefactor hang'd at Tyburn wherein appear two ureters & two basons in each kidney" (Day 1994, 70) illustrates the way in which interest in the victims of public executions could shade into interest in anatomic abnormality.
3. For instance, the writer of an essay in the catalog to the exhibition "Wunderkammer des Abendlandes," which was held in Bonn from November 1994 to February 1995, claimed: "Living people used to be put on show . . . It is not done any longer" (Sjørslev 1994, 177).
4. The performance is covered in the video *The Couple in the Cage: A Guatinaui Odyssey* (1993, 30 minutes). There is a striking reversal of the role between European and non-European in the case of the German physician and botanist Engelbert Kaempfer, whose movements in Japan were very restricted by the Japanese officials. On his arrival in Tokyo, after having been closely guarded by day and locked in at night, Kaempfer was obliged to dance, sing, jump, and mime European manners and customs for the edification of the emperor and the nobility (Coats 1969, 65).
5. The poster of "Prince Kari-Kari" is reproduced in Ex. Cat. Haarlem 1993, 67.
6. The commercial use for display purposes of those born with a handicap or abnormality, though obviously related to the display of exotic peoples, will be left out of the present account; for some examples see Wilson (1993, 56, 72) and Exh. Cat. Haarlem 1993.
7. The most influential version of this story is that in the *Divisiecronyke* of 1517 by Cornelius Aurelius, from which this citation is taken (f. 239). See Van de Waal 1952 and Tilmans 1992.
8. See the survey in Feest 1987, 613–20.
9. The present discussion is confined to those events in which there is evidence for participation by native peoples themselves. It therefore leaves out of account performances such as the pantomime *Omai, or a trip round the world,* staged in Covent Garden in 1785. Although the consultant to that production was John Webber, who had accompanied Cook on his last voyage as ship's artist, and the cast included a procession of people from fifteen countries visited by Cook, there is no evidence that the actors were not English. Similarly, although Japanese masquerades seem to have dressed up as Africans, Javanese, and Portuguese—Japan's conspicuously other Others in the second half of the

sixteenth century—there is nothing to suggest that non-Japanese themselves took part in these celebrations (Toby 1994).

10. Hamy 1907a drew attention long ago to a contemporary bas relief from the Hôtel du Brésil in Rouen, which represents Brazilian Indians engaged in tree felling; cf. Exh. Cat. Paris 1976, 15.
11. An official account of the festivities, *C'est la déduction du sumptueux ordre plaisantz spectacles et magnifiques théâtres dressés et exhibés par les citoiens de Rouen ville metropolitaine du pays de Normandie* . . . , ran into a second edition in Rouen in 1551. It included a woodcut (redone for the second edition) depicting the scene, "obviously one or two removes from observed reality" (Sturtevant 1991, 340). Though "too small and crudely done to be valuable ethnographically" (Sturtevant 1976, 428), it seems to have served as a model for Pierre Desceliers's world map of 1553. See also the preceding note.
12. The destruction of mock native villages was not confined to the sixteenth century; the British Royal Air Force bombed mock native villages into submission during the Hendon Air Pageants of the 1920s (Hansen 1996, 715).
13. It may well have been these same Tupinamba Indians who furnished Montaigne with some of the material for his essay "Des cannibales," though his claims to draw on oral rather than written sources should be taken *cum grano salis* (cf. Lestringant 1990, 137; Greenblatt 1991, 148).
14. Dance was one of the means of assimilating the rural classes of Europe, like the "natives" in the Bay of Spezia, to the exotic, non-European peoples. Thus Webber, one of the artists who accompanied Captain Cook in the Pacific, also provided an illustration of a European peasant dance for Laurence Sterne's *A Sentimental Journey through France and Italy* (Joppien and Smith 1988, 34).
15. This watercolor view of the spectacle (there is a color reproduction in Exh. Cat. Paris 1992, 117) includes more ethnographically accurate details than the better-known woodcut (Sturtevant 1976, 428), such as the Tupinamba practice of using *Bixa orellana* to color the skin red.
16. These cases of military theater in the Spanish colonies in the New World have their present-day counterparts in Mexico and Peru (Wachtel 1977). For their counterparts in Peru, see Cummins (1991, 223), who argues that colonial portraits of Inca nobles, far from being autonomous native expressions, were a part of the same colonial acculturation process.
17. The first Eskimos who can be securely documented in Europe were the woman and child who were brought to Zeeland (the Netherlands) in 1567 and displayed for an admission charge in an inn in The Hague (Sturtevant and Quinn 1987). They were also exhibited in Antwerp, where the spectacular objects on show included a massive wild boar. One of those who saw them in Antwerp was Goropius Becanus (1569, 1046).
18. For the alleged interest of the female spectators in the sexual prowess of exotic peoples on display, compare "Have we some Indian with the great tool come to court, the women so besiege us?" (*Henry VIII,* V.iv).
19. A small group of Eskimos were paddling about in their kayaks, as well as giving demonstrations of the use of whips, as late as the Chicago World Exhibition in 1893 (Hinsley 1991, 350).
20. Later, during the last quarter of the eighteenth century, Joseph Banks com-

missioned portraits of Inuit who had been brought from Labrador to England in 1769 and 1773 (Joppien 1994, 89–90).

21. The only surviving picture positively identified as a representation of this Eskimo is the watercolor drawing by Lucas de Heere (Sturtevant and Quinn 1987, 75).
22. On Pocahontas see esp. the subtle analysis by Hulme 1985.
23. Digard (1990, 31–36) draws attention to the coincidence between interest in exotic peoples and interest in exotic animals during the nineteenth century, and in particular to the role played by the Jardin d'Acclimatation in Paris.
24. There was considerable confusion between the Canaries and the Antilles at this time, so that Amerindians could be mistaken for natives of the Canaries and vice versa (Zapperi 1985, 312; cf. Hulme 1994, 172ff.).
25. The simultaneous display of humans and animals was not a European prerogative: besides its collection of birds and animals, the menagerie of Motecuhzoma contained human exhibits, including albinos, dwarfs, and hunchbacks (Cortés 1972, 110–11).
26. On the nineteenth-century portrayal of the London poor as improvident nomads, indifferent to marriage, repugnant to regular and continuous labor, resembling "many savage nations" in their permanent opposition to the forces of law and order, compare Stallybrass and White 1986, 128–29.
27. The production of an inner exotic through the anthropologization of peasant communities is a highly ambiguous process, since, as a symbol of the continuity of primitive beliefs, it is the exotic that becomes the repository of nationalist sentiment.
28. Harvey argues that the exaggeration of difference between metropolitan and colonial cultures implied in the nineteenth- and early-twentieth-century exhibitions has been replaced by "the proximity of simulated experience" of today's technologies, which generate effects apparently without regard for cultural or racial difference (1996, 125–26). Her discussion of the spectacle of Expo '92 ably brings out the fact that inequality is now situated in the ability to produce and consume images. Whether the "proximity of simulated experience" has replaced the exotic, however, as she states, remains a moot point.
29. The cast of John Gay's first play, the "Tragi-Comical Farce" *The Mohocks* (1712), included six Mohocks with the colorful names Abaddon, Moloch, Whisker, Mirmidon, Cannibal, and Gogmagog.
30. Of the group of nine Aborigines taken from Australia by the showman R. A. Cunningham in 1883, only three were still alive at the end of 1885 when Prince Roland Bonaparte photographed them in Paris (Poignant 1992, 51–54).
31. Thus, in the preface to his *Recherches Philosophiques sur les Américains,* Cornelius de Pauw cites the fact that a Patagonian girl taken to the Netherlands by Sebald de Weert in 1599 grew to a height of only four and a half feet as evidence that there were no giants in Patagonia (1774, xii–xiii).
32. On the history and subsequent fate of this blue whale, see Egmond and Mason 1997, 18–23.
33. On the connections between Africans and bestiality implied by the colonial exhibitions, see Corbey (1988, 1989) and Coombes (1994, 101–2).
34. One of the people who saw the Tierra del Fuegians on show in Paris was the artist Odilon Redon, who made sketches of them (Gott 1992, 52–53). While

his reaction to the Dahomeans on show in 1891 was to equate them with French peasants (Exh. Cat. Chicago-Amsterdam-London 1994, 173 n. 117), he later reused his sketches of the Tierra del Fuegians in *noirs* which suggested an equivalence between Amerindians and "primitive" human beings (139). Flaubert's reaction to a group of South Africans on display in Rouen in 1853 was similar; he compared them to the first human beings on earth, coeval with toads and crocodiles (Lestringant 1994, 25–26).

35. In this respect one could see these presentations as three-dimensional equivalents of the "galleries of nations" or "costume books" which popularized the figure of Captain Cook and the images of various peoples whom he visited for more than fifty years after his death. The influence of illustrations from Cook's voyages on this popular imagery is discussed by Joppien 1979b.
36. The same process is at work in the construction of representations of the world before humankind came to people it—the prehistoric world. Many of these representations combined and confused fauna and flora from widely disparate eras (Rudwick 1992).
37. For this reading of Soane's museum and the British Museum each against the grain of the other (John Soane's design for the British Museum was rejected), see Preziosi 1994, 147–50; for more details on Soane's museum, see Elsner 1994 and Thornton and Dorey 1992.
38. On the unusual history and nature of the museum at Hampton Institute, see Ruffins 1992, 519.
39. The Pitt Rivers Museum in Oxford has a photograph dating from around 1885, entitled "Naga Trophies," in which a collection of material culture is arranged around a Naga man sitting on the floor (Elizabeth Edwards, personal communication). On the use of human figures as the equivalent of big-game trophies, see Coombes 1994, 12 and esp. 197–98.
40. On the contents of the Leverian Museum, see King 1996.
41. This shift can be documented within the lifetime of A.H.L.F. Pitt Rivers. While the collection housed in the museum in Oxford bearing his name resembled the ethnological collection of the British Museum and was primarily intended for scholarly purposes, the restored medieval building, exotic zoo, and Sunday concerts on his estate in Farnham conformed to his ideal of a popular museum which could educate the lower classes and thereby make them less amenable to social revolution (Chapman 1985, 38–39).
42. Instructive in this respect are the changes effected in the display of Herbert Ward's collection of African objects after it had been acquired by the Smithsonian Institution (Arnoldi 1992, 447–48).
43. For an early diorama-type display of Canadian Indian artifacts mounted by the Marquis de Sérent in Versailles for educational purposes, see Feest 1984, 89.
44. A pioneer in the use of dramatic natural historical presentations was Charles Willson Peale. A visitor to his museum in Philadelphia in 1787 remarked on the "most romantic and amusing manner" in which the natural curiosities were displayed, amid a mound of soil, trees, and rocks, reminding him of Noah's Ark (Peale 1983, 461 n. 3, 482–85).
45. Ellenius uses the term *ecological vision* in connection with wildlife paintings by the late-nineteenth-century Swedish artist Bruno Liljefors to indicate "the

intimate interplay between living organisms and the contact with their particular environments" (1985, 148). Liljefors also worked on dioramas in the 1890s (159).

46. This was not Church's first one-picture exhibition, for he had already exhibited *Niagara* (1857) at a commercial gallery in New York (Kelly 1989, 50). On the draperies, see the anonymous photograph of *Heart of the Andes* in its original frame (56). There is some question as to whether dried tropical plants were actually present; see Kelly 1989, 73 n. 114.
47. There was often a clear division of labor between the activities of the photographer, who recorded what were by definition unique portraits, and the greater scope accorded ethnographic artists to bring their portrayals in line with "racial" types (cf. Theye 1995, 10). In this sense, the photographer by no means replaced the artist because their concerns were different.
48. On the obligatory nature of photographic captions, see the remarks by Benjamin (1968, 226).
49. Indeed, if one is prepared to follow the Derridan argument advanced by Pinney, there is much to be gained from viewing photography as a kind of "archipeinture," which stands to painting as speech does to writing. Both speech and photography have a privileged proximity to the communicating presence, while in writing and painting the meaning is constantly deferred (Pinney 1992a, 93 n. 20).
50. This fascination was shared by artists, too. One might compare the air of mystery surrounding an Indian rite in *Hopi Niman Kachina Dance at Walpi,* a canvas painted by the modernist artist Frank Applegate around 1926 (Lamar 1992, 179, with reproduction).
51. From the 1890s, the Hopi snake dance was the most frequently described and photographed Indian ceremony of the Southwest (Truettner 1986, 89). The presence of photographers soon led to changes in the dance itself, later followed by a ban on photography (Dilworth 1996, 71–72).
52. Smith (1992, 80) traces the ethnographic convention to roots in the Hellenistic period and singles out the Dying Gaul (a Roman copy after a bronze original dating from approximately 230–220 B.C.) as an example of an ethnic type whose ethnicity is marked by costume and adornment—in this case, his wild hair, moustache, and the torque around his neck.
53. The book in question is *Anatomia per uso et intelligenza del disegno* (Rome, 1691) by Bernardino Genga and Giovanni Maria Lancisi. The plates, which present famous antique statues "considered anatomically," were owned and used by a number of artists; see Kornell 1996 and Exh. Cat. Ottawa 1996, no. 104. On the Borghese Gladiator see Haskell and Penny 1981, no. 77.
54. Stedman referred to the classical figures of Tritons and mermaids to describe groups of naked boys and girls playing in the Suriname river and to refer to his fellow sailors (Price and Price 1985).
55. In his *Visions of the Daughters of Albion,* Blake combined Europe, Africa, and America in a single "soul," Oothoon (Erdman 1954, 221).
56. Guest (1989, 48ff.) suggests that the same kind of opposition is at work in the tattooed female figure in William Hodges's canvas *A View Taken in the Bay of Otaheite Peha* (1776). Although her pose may recall paintings by Titian,

Tintoretto, and Poussin, the detailed representation of the tattoos alludes to the tradition of ethnographic portraiture.

57. These photographs were commissioned for the International Exhibition in Melbourne in 1866 and were clearly intended to function as a visual spectacle.
58. This is another area in which there is continuity between the prephotographic and the photographic image. For instance, in the corpus of Menominee portraits spanning the years 1825–60, Kasprycki (1990, 119) was able to find only one representation of an economic activity: "Fishing by torch light," the theme of an oil painting by Paul Kane (who had met Catlin in 1843), painted around the middle of the nineteenth century. In this case, it is the particular charm and picturesque appearance of the scene which are emphasized.
59. Compare F. W. Barton's photographic portrayals of young girls from South-East Papua New Guinea, combining Edwardian high-art genre with the odalisques of orientalizing fantasy (Macintyre and MacKenzie 1992, 162). The combination of classical poses with erotic fantasy is a dominant characteristic of Barton's entire photographic corpus.
60. In fact, this postcard combines three continents. As Corbey points out, the Gabonese postage stamp on this postcard also refers to European conceptions of Africa rather than to the ethnographic "reality" of Gabon: the headdress of the figure portrayed is reminiscent of that attributed to South American Indians rather than Africans.

Chapter 7: Displaying the Exotic

1. According to Flam (1984, 238 nn. 58 and 60), the two sculptures, assumed to be the work of Derain himself, are no longer traceable.
2. The fact that Ward had been in Africa gave the attention that he paid to detail an aura of naturalism; on the other hand, the predominance of aesthetic considerations in his portrayal of African subjects gave them a timeless quality, which Marles (1996) has brought into connection with the denial of coevality implied by the ethnographic present.
3. Many of these categories are embraced in the work of the Ostend artist James Ensor (1860–1942), who exerted an influence on Emil Nolde. In particular, Ensor's fascination with carnival masks should be related to the discovery of the primitive mask by other artists of his time, as well as his deployment of them as a form of social satire.
4. Slightly earlier than the Stieglitz exhibition was Robert Coady's exhibition of modern European art, the work of American Negro children, and South Seas sculpture in Washington Square Gallery (Levin 1984, 464).
5. For de Zayas's views on art from Africa and the Pacific, see the extracts from his unpublished manuscript on Stieglitz in Norman (1973, 100).
6. On displays in the 1930s and 1940s, see Varnedoe (1984b, 654 n. 20). A shift from strict ethnological contextualism to abstract symbolism can be seen in René d'Harnoncourt's exhibition of objects from the South Seas in the Museum of Modern Art in 1946. On similar trends in museum displays in the Netherlands, see the brief survey in Konijn (1993).
7. There was a Peruvian mummy on show in the Musée d'Ethnologie du Trocadéro from 1879, which was reproduced in *L'Illustration* in April 1882 (cf. Eisenman 1992, 225 n. 104). The influence of this mummy and its illustrations

is a subject which requires further investigation before we can determine whether the influence exerted in each case was direct or indirect. For example, it is possible that it influenced Odilon Redon's charcoal *L'Accusé;* if so, we do not know whether Gauguin was influenced by the mummy, by its reproduction, or by Redon's version of it.

8. It should be clear that I do not share the essentialism implied here and in other passages of Rushing's study.
9. Sensitivity to these issues also characterizes the tape-slide "Expeditions" on race and colonial iconography by Black Audio/Film Collective (1991), in which archival reading of colonial discourse isolates the zoological/Cuvierial moment, the eugenic/Darwinist moment, the evangelical/expeditionary moment, and the millenarian/redemptionist moment.
10. The following examples are taken from Exh. Cat. New York 1988: 53, 169, and 125, respectively; the whimsical commentaries are by Susan Vogel.
11. An amusing reversal of this process is exemplified by a basket now in the collection in Vienna of material from Cook's third voyage. Though it featured in an 1806 auction catalog as "A curious cap; Nootka Sound," it does not come from the Northwest coast of America (it may have come from South Africa), and it is not a cap (Feest 1995b, 174–75).
12. For a reconstruction of the itinerary of the Oporto collection, see Bouquet and Freitas Branco 1988, 46ff.
13. For the ways in which native weapons could be taken to evoke either of these possibilities, compare Thomas (1991, 161). In the case of two staves from Benin, labeled first as "ivory idols carried by the executioner" and later, under the influence of the exhibition of over three hundred bronze plaques from Benin in 1897, as "two carved ivory maces or staves of office from Benin" (Coombes 1994, 27), we can detect the same transition from imputed savagery to recognition of cultural skill.
14. Gombrich's article (1991, 162–87), a discussion of the titles given to twentieth-century works of art, is relevant to the present considerations in a number of ways.
15. Another artifact and label from the same Portuguese collection—no. 101, an "engraved bone dagger, Dallmann's Bay, Sepik (?), 26.5 cm (l), 4.5 cm (w)"—bears the "original" label "Baia de Dalmann, Arq. Palmer, O. Antarctico" (Bouquet and Freitas 1988, 136). Once again, a discourse—featuring the Antarctic this time, perhaps through an unconscious association with Eskimos—introduces exotic-sounding names to convey a general sense of the faraway at the expense of geographic or ethnographic precision.
16. For present purposes, I am treating a catalog entry as a label, too, irrespective of whether it corresponds to a printed text on show in the vicinity of the object on display or not. For this extended use of the term *label*, see Baxandall 1991, 37. Because I did not see the exhibition in Portugal, I have to telescope the relation between the exhibition itself and its "trace" in the catalog (for the distinction see Bouquet 1991 and 1992).
17. Cf. Bouquet 1992, 202, on the aestheticizing tendency of photography.
18. On the problems involved in the two-dimensional reproduction of skulls to provide "measurable" scientific data, see Spencer 1992.
19. Egypt did not have a monopoly on mummification, but the word *mummy* had

(and still has) a primarily Egyptian reference for a European audience. On Egyptian mummia see esp. Dannenfeldt 1985.

20. In a survey of Sepik art, Thomas notes that "the Sepik region of northern New Guinea has long been renowned for the richness and diversity of its artistic traditions" (1995, 37).
21. There is a twin detachment at work here, since detachment "refers not only to the physical act of producing fragments, but also to the detached attitude that makes that fragmentation and its appreciation possible" (Kirshenblatt-Gimblett 1991, 388).
22. The fact that exotic artifacts have a context not only in the cultures from which they are taken, but also within the colonial and postcolonial relations of the cultures which appropriate them, is stressed by Jones (1992, 235) in her discussion of the presentation of ethnographic artifacts in Gallery 33, Birmingham.
23. Some of the political ramifications of this have begun to emerge with the change in policy, in such bodies as the Smithsonian Institution, in response to Native American demands for the removal of the bones of their ancestors from display and for their repatriation. For a recent case of the (forced) "repatriation" of bones from the Treblinka death camp in Poland to Israel, see Kugelmass 1992, 393. The public display of live humans is discussed in chapter 6.
24. For example, the two chameleons which Peiresc received in 1633 from Thomas d'Arcos in Tunisia died within a few weeks, before a painter could record their colors; Peiresc then proceeded to dissect them (Peiresc 1989, 127). An example from the late eighteenth century is provided by the close links between the menagerie and the zoological cabinet of Prince William V in the Netherlands (Pieters 1980).
25. As Bouquet has demonstrated in publications subsequent to the 1988 catalog (Bouquet 1991, 1992), in which she convincingly runs rings around her detractors, she is well aware of the framing and reframing effects of labels.
26. Of course, a label is an artifact, too—but who is interested in the dimensions, watermark, or provenance of a museum label?

Chapter 8: The Elementary Structures of the Exotic

1. See the discussion of modern, modernist, postmodernist, and contemporary in Osborne 1992.
2. For "learning to curse" as the only voice open to suppressed populations, see esp. Quint 1993.
3. It is not certain that this is the work of Léry himself, for Thevet accused Léry of having plagiarized it from Villegagnon. There are similar disputes on the lists of native words recorded by Cartier.
4. Compare the English lesson given to an Indian by John Brereton, which consisted of his being able to repeat the words: "How now, sirrha, are you so sawcy with my Tobacco?" (Greenblatt 1991, 105).
5. As we have already seen, Thevet introduced into his accounts not only exotic words but also exotic images. For a study of exotic words and images in the work of a contemporary, Pierre Belon, where the lists of exotic words sometimes take on Rabelaisian dimensions, see Bertrand 1993 and Glardon 1997, xxvii–xxxv.

6. Including Setebos "for their big Devil" (*al diavolo grande*)—another link with *The Tempest* (I.ii.375 and V.1.261; cf. Kermode 1958, xxxii). Boon has suggested that Pigafetta intended to contrast the kings of Indonesia with the diabolical, antipodal Patagonians, thereby inscribing Indonesia and Patagonia as ethnological antitheses or rhetorically perfect extremes (1990, 12).
7. Leerssen arrives independently at the same conclusion in his discussion of the use of footnotes in early-nineteenth-century Anglo-Irish fiction to explain Gaelic terms to the foreign readers: the Gaelic terms "are all glossed in footnotes and thus almost *rendered exotic* (because deemed incomprehensible) *by the very act of explanation*" [my italics] (1991a, 280; cf. idem 1996, 200–201).
8. The passage occurs in three different versions of this chapter of *Candide,* with the geographic location fluctuating among Arabia, China, and Persia.
9. Théodat's *Grand Voyage au pays des Hurons [. .] avec un dictionnaire de la langue huronne* (Paris, 1632).
10. Nevertheless, Voltaire tends to create an exotic flavor in his plays and stories through the creation of an exotic milieu rather than by the use of linguistic props (Netton 1989, 36).
11. For exotic words in Latin literature, see Syme 1991, 269–86.
12. Jones discusses early word lists for West Africa (1990a, 91–92). For an analysis of the contents of such lists by Pigafetta, Cartier, Lescarbot, and others, see Launay-Demonet 1987. Florike Egmond also draws my attention to the fragmentary compilations of underworld jargon in archival documents relating to the trials of criminals.
13. Léry's sparring partner André Thevet characteristically mocked Léry's resemblance to an oyster: if it were so, it was because he resembled an oyster in being locked up, not between his two natural shells, but in the fort of Coligny.
14. As Leerssen acutely points out (1991b, 137 n. 11), Forster is here ironically toying with the topoi of penetration, which were part and parcel of the colonial adventure tale à la Rudyard Kipling and Rider Haggard.
15. On the uncanny way in which this silence repeats others (*Heart of Darkness, Nostromo*), see Bhabha 1994, 124.
16. For iteration in the naming activities of André Thevet (two Brazilian voyages, two crossings of Sinai, two Thevet Islands), see Lestringant 1991c, 49.
17. The plot of this novel, which was long regarded as a work of nonfiction, is best summarized by the author himself: "The Life, Adventures, and Pyracies of the famous Captain Singleton, Containing an Account of his being set on Shore in the Island of *Madagascar,* his Settlement there, with a Description of the Place and Inhabitants: Of his Passage from thence, in a Paraguay, to the main Land of *Africa,* with an Account of the Customs and Manners of the People: His great Deliverances from the barbarous Natives and wild Beasts: Of his meeting with an *Englishman,* a Citizen of *London,* among the *Indians,* the great Riches he acquired, and his Voyage Home to *England:* As also Captain *Singleton's* Return to Sea, with an Account of his many Adventures and Pyracies with the famous Captain *Avery* and others."
18. On Defoe's sources for *Robinson Crusoe* (1719), *Captain Singleton* (1720), and *A New Voyage Round the World* (1724), see Baker 1963, 158–72, who comments: "In some cases he used geography for his own ends, but for essentials he relied on the best authorities available, and his writings thus faithfully

reflect the geographic knowledge of a well-educated Englishman at the beginning of the eighteenth century" (172). One of the main sources for *Captain Singleton* was Olfert Dapper's monumental book on Africa, available in the English translation by John Ogilby (1670); on Dapper's sources see the tentative reconstruction by Jones 1990b.

19. For an analysis of this interchange on learning to curse, see Greenblatt 1990, 25.
20. Elsewhere I have drawn attention to this aspect of the naming activity of Columbus, which is not the inscription of European names on virgin soil, but the reinscription over an object which has already received the trace of a name from its earlier discoverers, like a palimpsest (Mason 1987b, 164). On toponymy as a symbolic performance, see also Obeyesekere 1992, 12–13.
21. Shakespeare is here drawing on Montaigne's "Des cannibales" (1962, 204): "C'est une nation . . . en laquelle il n'y a aucune espece de trafique; nul cognoissance de lettres; nulle science de nombres; nul nom de magistrat, ny de superiorité politique; nul usage de service, de richesse ou de pauvreté; nuls contrats; nulles successions; nuls partages; nulles occupations qu' oysives; nul respect de parenté que commun; nuls vestemens; nulle agriculture; nul metal; nul usage de vin ou de bled." However, as Hamlin suggests (1994, 441), the parallels between *The Tempest* and Renaissance (inchoate) ethnographic literature are not just intertextual; they are interconceptual.
22. On the "shared discursive stream" of amatory and imperialist writings, see particularly Greene 1995.
23. See chapter 3.
24. There is an even greater riot of color in the multicolored feathered skirts painted by van Kessel in a scene of cannibalism (acquired in 1989 by the Musée du Nouveau Monde in La Rochelle) which draws heavily on various prints by De Bry (for a reproduction see Lefrançois 1992).
25. The placing of the camel in Africa implies a focus on the Levant; Tiepolo's sources must have included de Bruyn's account of his travels in the Levant (Ashton 1978). The elephant in the continent of Asia implies a similar narrowing down of the focus to the subcontinent of India.
26. An intricately worked seventeenth-century cabinet from Augsburg includes allegories of the senses, mythological scenes, allegories of Night and Day and of Time and Vanity, and a representation of the four continents (Bruijntjes 1992). The most striking feature of the latter is the presence of an elephant, bearing a quiver with arrows in its trunk, to accompany the figure of America.
27. John Flaxman (1755–1826) already had some experience in depicting exotic peoples and carried out careful preliminary studies to ensure ethnographic accuracy. The busts of Laurence Sterne designs that he supplied to the house of Wedgwood for their pottery in 1781 were not always as authentic (Cash 1986, 299).
28. As Young has pointed out (1990, 146), each of Bhabha's articles can be seen to illuminate specific moments in the ambivalent and cumulative apparatus of colonial discourse, and it is the ambivalence of the latter which makes it impossible to come up with a consistent meta-language or a consistent illuminating concept. For a different reading of Bhabha, see Thomas 1994a, along with the comments in Mason 1995.

29. The status of the women in *The Market* is indicated not only by the fact that one of them is smoking a cigarette, but also by the health inspection certificates that two of them are holding like the painted fans of French society women (Eisenman 1997, 155).
30. This is not to suggest that Gauguin's response to the world of Tahiti was *primarily* conditioned by a response to archaic art, but it would require a full study of his Tahitian work to arrive at a verdict on the relative importance of the various stimuli to which he was exposed. On Gauguin's ten-day firsthand encounter with Maori art in Auckland during his second voyage to Tahiti in 1895, see Nicholson et al. 1995.
31. In his reading of a late-nineteenth-century photograph of two Chamars, from what is now Uttar Pradesh, standing beneath a banyan tree, Pinney suggests that this image might be saying completely opposite things at the same time: it both bears witness to the power of Orientalist discourse, placing the Chamars as a caste in a tangled web of Otherness, and conjures up a vision of a people hidden in the dark vegetation of the jungle, "free from the deathly illumination and scrutiny of Western science" (1992b, 172).
32. The inability of British administrators in India to distinguish one Bengalese from another led to the adoption of fingerprinting; it was a report on the success of fingerprinting in the Hooghly district which led Francis Galton to make a decisive contribution to fingerprint analysis (Ginzburg 1990, 121–23). Since Galton's methods place him firmly among the founding fathers of morphological analysis (Egmond and Mason 1997, 4), on which each of the chapters in this book draws, it is fitting that he should put in a fleeting appearance at this point as the inventor of an attempt to identify and control the exotic.
33. One of Freud's most succinct statements of the theme of disavowal (though he does not use this technical term *Verleugnung* there) can be found in his posthumously published short paper entitled "Medusa's Head" (Freud 1955, 273). He argues that the head of Medusa, surrounded by hair, represents the genitals of an adult female, the decapitation of Medusa stands for castration, and hence the stare of Medusa causes castration anxiety. On the other hand, Freud explains the effect of the gaze of Medusa, which transforms the onlooker into stone, as provoking an erection. The assurance that the onlooker still has a penis is a disavowal of what he has just seen: the representation of the female genitals whose "castration" renders her terrifying. On Freud's "Medusa's Head" see further Mason 1984, 68–69, and Derrida 1972b, 46 n. 24.

BIBLIOGRAPHY

Exh. Cat. refers to exhibition catalogs, alphabetized by city and ordered by year in this bibliography.

Achilles, K.

1982 "Indianer auf der Jagd: Der neue Kontinent in den *Venationes* des Johannes Stradanus." In Exh. Cat. Berlin: 161–72.

Ackerman, J. S.

1991 *Distance Points: Essays in Theory and Renaissance Art and Architecture.* Cambridge: MIT Press.

Adams, T. R.

1976 "Some Bibliographical Observations on and Questions about the Relationship between the Discovery of America and the Invention of Printing." In *First Images of America,* 2: 529–36. Edited by F. Chiappelli. Berkeley and Los Angeles: University of California Press.

Adorno, R.

1981 "On Pictorial Language and the Typology of Culture in a New World Chronicle." *Semiotica* 36, no. 1/2: 51–106.

Aimi, A., de Michele, V., and Morandotti, A.

1985 "Towards a History of Collecting in Milan in the Late Renaissance and Baroque Periods." In *The Origins of Museums,* 24–28. Edited by O. Impey and A. MacGregor. Oxford: Clarendon Press.

Allart, D.

1993 "Un paysagiste à redécouvrir: Cornelis van Dalem (Anvers, avant 1543?–Bavel, 1573)." *Revue belge d'archéologie et d'histoire de l'art* 62: 95–120.

Allen, M.

1964 *The Tradescants: Their Plants, Gardens and Museum 1570–1662.* London: Michael Joseph.

Alpers, S., and Baxandall, M.

1994 *Tiepolo and the Pictorial Intelligence.* New Haven: Yale University Press.

Althusser, L., Balibar, E., Macherey, P., and Rancière, J.

1968 *Lire le capital,* 4 vols. Paris: Maspero.

Amishai-Maisels, Z.

1978 "Gauguin's Early Tahitian Idols." *Art Bulletin* 60, no. 2: 331–41.

Anderson, N. K.

1990 "'Wondrously Full of Invention': The Western Landscapes of Albert Bierstadt." In Exh. Cat. New York: 69–107.

1992 "'Curious Historical Artistic Data': Art History and Western American Art." In *Discovered Lands, Invented Pasts: Transforming Visions of the American West*, 1–35. By J. D. Prown, N. K. Anderson, W. Cronon, B. W. Dippie, M. A. Sandweiss, S. Prendergast Schoelwer, and H. R. Lamar. New Haven: Yale University Press.

Andresen-Tetel, J.
1985 "Images des langues américaines au XVIIIe siècle." In *L'homme des lumières et la découverte de l'autre,* 135–45. Edited by D. Droixhe and Pol-P. Gossiaux. Brussels: Editions de l'Université de Bruxelles.

Arnoldi, M. J.
1992 "A Distorted Mirror: The Exhibition of the Herbert Ward Collection of Africana." In *Museums and Communities: The Politics of Public Culture,* 428–57. Edited by I. Karp, C. M. Kreamer, and S. D. Lavine. Washington, D.C.: Smithsonian Institution Press.

Ashton, M.
1978 "Allegory, Fact, and Meaning in Giambattista Tiepolo's Four Continents in Würzburg." *Art Bulletin* 60, no. 1: 109–25.

Ashworth, W. B., Jr.
1985 "The Persistent Beast: Recurring Images in Early Zoological Illustration." In *The Natural Sciences and the Arts: Aspects of Interaction from the Renaissance to the Twentieth Century*, 46–66. Edited by A. Ellenius. Acta Universitatis Upsaliensis, Figura Nova Series 22. Stockholm: Almqvist & Wiksell International.
1990 "Natural History and the Emblematic World View." In *Reappraisals of the Scientific Revolution,* 303–32. Edited by D. C. Lindberg and R. S. Westman. Cambridge: Cambridge University Press.
1991 "Remarkable Humans and Singular Beasts." In *The Age of the Marvelous,* 113–44. Edited by J. Kenseth. Hanover: Hood Museum of Art.

Austin, J. L.
1962 *How to Do Things with Words.* Oxford: Oxford University Press.
1979 *Philosophical Papers*, 3d ed. Edited by J. O. Urmson and G. J. Warnock. Oxford: Oxford University Press.

Baker, J. N. L.
1963 *The History of Geography.* Oxford: Blackwell.

Bann, S.
1984 *The Clothing of Clio: A Study of the Representations of History in Nineteenth-Century Britain and France.* Cambridge: Cambridge University Press.

Barker, F.
1984 *The Tremulous Human Body*. London: Methuen.

Barthelmess, K.
1989 "Walkinnladen in Wanten: Maritime Motivkunde als historische Datierungshilfe." *Deutschen Schiffahrtsarchiv* 12: 243–64.
1994 "Neun bemalte Walschulterblätter und ein beschnitzter Wal-Humerus (Oberarmknochen)." *Deutschen Schiffahrtsarchiv* 17: 253–72.

Barthelmess, K., and Münzing, J.
1991 *Monstrum Horrendum: Wale und Waldarstellungen in der Druckgraphik des 16. Jahrhunderts und ihr motivkundlicher Einfluss.* Hamburg: Schriften des Deutschen Schiffahrtsmuseums 29.

Bartholinus, T.
1654 *Historiarum anatomicarum rariorum, Centuria I et II.* Amsterdam.

Bartrum, G.
1995 *German Renaissance Prints 1490–1550.* London: British Museum Press.

Bassani, E., and Tedeschi, L.
1990 "The Image of the Hottentot in the Seventeenth and Eighteenth Centuries: An Iconographic Investigation." *Journal of the History of Collections* 2, no. 2: 157–86.

Bätschmann, O.
1990 *Nicolas Poussin: Dialectics of Painting.* Translated by Marko Daniel. London: Reaktion.

Baudrillard, J., and Guillaume, M.
1994 *Figures de l'altérité.* Paris: Descartes & Cie.

Baumunk, B.-D.
1982 "'Von Brasilischen fremden Völkern': Die Eingeborenen-Darstellungen Albert Eckhouts." In Exh. Cat. Berlin: 188–99.

Baxandall, M.
1991 "Exhibiting Intention: Some Preconditions of the Visual Display of Culturally Purposeful Objects." In *Exhibiting Cultures: The Poetics and Politics of Museum Display*, 33–41. Edited by I. Karp and S. D. Lavine. Washington, D.C.: Smithsonian Institution Press.

Bedini, S. A.
1997 *The Pope's Elephant.* Manchester, England: Carcanet Press.

Beer, G. R. de
1953 *Sir Hans Sloane and the British Museum.* London: Oxford University Press.

Belon, P.
1997 *L'histoire de la nature des oyseaux.* Edited by P. Glardon. Geneva: Droz [1555].

Benedictis, C. de
1991 *Per la storia del collezionismo italiano.* Florence: Ponte alle Grazie.

Benjamin, W.
1968 *Illuminations: Essays and Reflections.* Edited and with an introduction by H. Arendt, translated by H. Zohn. New York: Schocken Books.

Bergvelt, E., and Kistemaker, R. (eds.)
1992 *De wereld binnen handbereik: Nederlandse kunst- en rariteitenverzamelingen, 1585–1735.* Zwolle, Netherlands: Waanders.

Bertrand, D.
1993 "Les stratégies de Belon pour une représentation exotique." *Nouvelle revue du seizième siècle* 11: 5–17.

Bewell, A.

1994 "Constructed Places, Constructed Peoples: Charting the Improvement of the Female Body in the Pacific." *Eighteenth-Century Life* 18, no. 3: 37–54.

1996 "'On the Banks of the South Sea': Botany and Sexual Controversy in the Late Eighteenth Century." In *Visions of Empire: Voyages, Botany, and Representations of Nature,* 173–93. Edited by D. P. Miller and P. H. Reill. Cambridge: Cambridge University Press.

Bhabha, H. K.

1994 *The Location of Culture*. London: Routledge.

Black Audio / Film Collective

1991 "Expeditions: On Race and Nation." In *The Myth of Primitivism: Perspectives on Art,* 72–83. Edited by S. Hiller. London: Routledge.

Blühm, A.

1996 "In Living Colour: A Short History of Colour in Sculpture in the Nineteenth Century." In *The Colour of Sculpture 1840–1910,* 11–60. Edited by A. Blühm and P. Curtis. Zwolle, Netherlands: Van Gogh Museum Amsterdam, Waanders Uitgeverij.

Bohrer, F. N.

1989 "Assyria as Art: A Perspective on the Early Reception of Ancient Near Eastern Artifacts." *Culture and History* 4: 7–33.

Bolens-Duvernay, J.

1991 "Mammouths et patagons: De l'espèce à la race dans l'Amérique de Buffon." *L'homme* 31, no. 119: 7–21.

1995 *Les géants patagons*. Paris: Michalon.

Boogaart, E. van den

1979 "Infernal Allies: The Dutch West India Company and the Tarairiu 1631–1654." In *Johan Maurits van Nassau-Siegen 1604–1679: A Humanist Prince in Europe and Brazil,* 519–38. Edited by E. van den Boogaart. The Hague: Johan Maurits van Nassau Stichting.

Boon, J. A.

1990 *Affinities and Extremes: Crisscrossing the Bittersweet Ethnology of East Indies History, Hindu-Balinese Culture, and Indo-European Allure*. Chicago: University of Chicago Press.

Boon, K. G.

1978 *Netherlandish Drawings of the Fifteenth and Sixteenth Centuries in the Rijksmuseum,* 2 vols. The Hague: Staatsuitgeverij.

Boucher, P. P.

1992 *Cannibal Encounters: Europeans and Island Caribs, 1492–1763*. Baltimore: Johns Hopkins University Press.

Bouquet, M. R.

1991 "Images of Artefacts: Photographic Essay." *Critique of Anthropology* 11, no. 4: 333–56.

1992 "Framing Knowledge: The Photographic 'Blind Spot' between Words and Things." *Critique of Anthropology* 12, no. 2: 193–207.

Bouquet, M. R., and Branco, J. Freitas
1988 *Artefactos Melanésios: Reflexões pós-modernistas / Melanesian Artefacts: Postmodernist Reflections.* Lisbon: Museu de Etnologia, Instituto de Investigação Científica Tropical.

Brandão, A. F.
1986 *Dialogues of the Great Things of Brazil.* Translated and annotated by F. A. H. Hall, W. F. Harrison, and D. W. Welker. Albuquerque: University of New Mexico Press.

Brasil-Holandês
1995 *Brasil-Holandês / Dutch Brazil,* 5 vols. Rio de Janeiro: Editora Index.

Braun, B.
1993 *Pre-Columbian Art and the Post-Columbian World: Ancient American Sources of Modern Art.* New York: Harry N. Abrams.

Brears, P. C. D.
1989 "Ralph Thoresby: A Museum Visitor in Stuart England." *Journal of the History of Collections* 1, no. 1: 213–24.

Breckenridge, C. A.
1989 "The Aesthetics and Politics of Colonial Collecting: India at World Fairs." *Comparative Studies in Society and History* 31, no. 2: 195–216.

Brett, G.
1991 "Unofficial Versions." In *The Myth of Primitivism: Perspectives on Art,* 113–36. Edited by S. Hiller. London: Routledge.

Broberg, G.
1985 "Natural History Frontispieces and Ecology." In *The Natural Sciences and the Arts: Aspects of Interaction from the Renaissance to the Twentieth Century,* 84–97. Edited by A. Ellenius. Acta Universitatis Upsaliensis, Figura Nova Series 22. Stockholm: Almqvist & Wiksell International.

Broos, B.
1987 *Meesterwerken in het Mauritshuis.* The Hague: Staatsuitgeverij.

Brown, P. F.
1996 *Venice and Antiquity: The Venetian Sense of the Past.* New Haven: Yale University Press.

Browne, J.
1996 "Botany in the Boudoir and Garden: The Banksian Context." In *Visions of Empire: Voyages, Botany, and Representations of Nature,* 153–72. Edited by D. P. Miller and P. H. Reill. Cambridge: Cambridge University Press.

Bruijn, A. de
1581 *Omnium pene Europae, Asiae, Aphricae atque Americae gentium habitus.* Antwerp.

Bruintjes, J.
1992 "'Een met stroo ingelegd schryvtafeltje': Een 17de-eeuws Augsburgs kunstkastje in de collectie Bisschop." *Antiek* 27, no. 2: 60–70.

Bruyn, J.

1987 "Toward a Scriptural Reading of Seventeenth-Century Dutch Landscape Painting." In Exh. Cat. Amsterdam/Boston: 84–103.

1996 "Dutch Cheese: A Problem of Interpretation." In *Ten Essays for a Friend: E. de Jongh 65*, 99–106. Edited by X. van Eck, P. Hecht, G. Luijten, L. van Tilborgh, and I. Veldman. Zwolle, Netherlands: Waanders.

Bucher, B.

1981 *Icon and Conquest: A Structural Analysis of the Illustrations of de Bry's Great Voyages*. Translated by Basia Miller Gulati. Chicago: University of Chicago Press [Fr. ed. 1977].

Burns, S.

1993 "The Price of Beauty: Art, Commerce, and the Late Nineteenth-Century American Studio Interior." In *American Iconology*, 209–38. Edited by D. C. Miller. New Haven: Yale University Press.

Buvelot, Q.

1995 "Jacob van Campen als schilder en tekenaar." In *Jacob van Campen: Het klassieke ideaal in de Gouden Eeuw*, 53–119. Edited by J. E. Huisken, K. A. Ottenheym, and G. Schwartz. Amsterdam: Royal Palace Amsterdam Foundation and Architectura & Natura Press.

Cámara, E.

1995 "The Lightning of Ubiquity: Cross-sights, Crossroads." In *Strategies for Survival—Now!* 163–73. Edited by C. Chambert. Lund: Swedish Art Critics Association Press.

Campbell, M. B.

1988 *The Witness and the Other World: Exotic European Travel Writing, 400–1600*. Ithaca: Cornell University Press.

Campen, J. van

1995 "De verzameling van de amateur-sinoloog J.Th. Royer in het Rijksmuseum." *Bulletin van het Rijksmuseum* 43, no. 1: 3–35 [Eng. summary on 78–81].

Cannon, J. F. M.

1994 "Botanical Collections." In *Sir Hans Sloane: Collector, Scientist, Antiquary*, 136–49. Edited by A. MacGregor. London: British Museum Press.

Cartari, V.

1581 *Les images des dieux des anciens*. Lyon.

Cash, A. H.

1986 *Laurence Sterne: The Early and Middle Years*. London: Methuen.

Cazort, M.

1996 "The Theatre of the Body." In Exh. Cat. Ottawa: 11–42.

Céard, J.

1977 *La nature et les prodiges: L'insolite au XVIe siècle, en France*. Geneva: Droz.

Certeau, M. de

1982 *La fable mystique XVIe—XVIIe siècle*. Paris: Gallimard.

1985 "Histoire et anthropologie chez Lafitau." In *Naissance de l'ethnologie?* 62–89. Edited by C. Blanckaert. Paris: Cerf.

Chapman, W. R.
1985 "Arranging Ethnology: A.H.L.F. Pitt Rivers and the Typological Tradition." In *Objects and Others: Essays on Museums and Material Culture,* 15–48. Edited by G. W. Stocking, Jr. Madison: University of Wisconsin Press.

Charlot, J.
1991 "The Feather Skirt of Nāhi'ena'ena: An Innovation in Postcontact Hawaiian Art." *Journal of the Polynesian Society* 100, no. 2: 119–65.

Cheles, L.
1991 *Lo studiolo di Urbino: Iconografia di un microcosmo principesco.* Modena: Franco Cosimo Panini.

Chinard, G.
1911 *L'exotisme américain dans la littérature française au XVIe siécle.* Paris: Hachette.

Chirelstein, E.
1990 "Lady Elizabeth Pope: The Heraldic Body." In *Renaissance Bodies: The Human Figure in English Culture c. 1540–1660,* 36–59. Edited by L. Gent and N. Llewellyn. London: Reaktion.

Clifford, J.
1986a "Introduction: Partial Truths." In *Writing Culture: The Poetics and Politics of Ethnography,* 1–26. Edited by J. Clifford and G. E. Marcus. Berkeley and Los Angeles: University of California Press.
1986b "On Ethnographic Allegory." In *Writing Culture: The Poetics and Politics of Ethnography,* 98–121. Edited by J. Clifford and G. E. Marcus. Berkeley and Los Angeles: University of California Press.
1988 *The Predicament of Culture.* Cambridge: Harvard University Press.
1991 "Four Northwest Coast Museums: Travel Reflections." In *Exhibiting Cultures: The Poetics and Politics of Museum Display,* 212–54. Edited by I. Karp and S. D. Lavine. Washington, D.C.: Smithsonian Institution Press.

Clifford, J., and Marcus, G. E. (eds.)
1986 *Writing Culture: The Poetics and Politics of Ethnography.* Berkeley and Los Angeles: University of California Press.

Cluverius, P.
1616 *De Germania Antiqua.* Leiden.

Coats, A. M.
1969 *The Quest for Plants: A History of the Horticultural Explorers.* London: Studio Vista.

Coelen, P. van der
1995 "Cornelis Bos—Where Did He Go? Some New Discoveries and Hypotheses about a Sixteenth-Century Engraver and Publisher. *Simiolus* 23, no. 2–3: 119–46.

Colbert, C.
1985 "'They Are Our Brothers': Raphael and the American Indian." *Sixteenth Century Journal* 16, no. 2: 181–90.

Colin, S.
1987 "The Wild Man and the Indian in Early Sixteenth Century Book Illustration." In *Indians and Europe: An Interdisciplinary Collection of Essays,* 5–36. Edited by C. F. Feest. Göttingen/Aachen: Herodot/Rader Verlag.

Colón, C.
1984 *Textos y documentos completos,* 2d ed. Prólogo y notas de Consuelo Varela. Madrid: Alianza Editorial.

Conrad, R.
1987 "Mutual Fascination: Indians in Dresden and Leipzig." In *Indians and Europe: An Interdisciplinary Collection of Essays*, 455–73. Edited by C. F. Feest. Göttingen/Aachen: Herodot/Rader Verlag.

Coombes, A. E.
1991 "Ethnography and the Formation of National and Cultural Identities." In *The Myth of Primitivism: Perspectives on Art,* 189–214. Edited by S. Hiller. London: Routledge.
1994 *Reinventing Africa: Museums, Material Culture and Popular Imagination.* New Haven: Yale University Press.

Copenhaver, B. P.
1991 "A Tale of Two Fishes: Magical Objects in Natural History from Antiquity through the Scientific Revolution." *Journal of the History of Ideas* 52, no. 3: 373–98.

Corbey, R.
1988 "Alterity: The Colonial Nude." *Critique of Anthropology* 8, no. 3: 75–92.
1989 *Wildheid en Beschaving: De Europese Verbeelding van Afrika*. Baarn, Netherlands: Ambo.

Corbey, R., and Mason, P.
1994 "Limited Company." *Anthrozoös* 7, no. 2: 90–102.

Cornelius, P.
1965 *Languages in Seventeenth- and Early Eighteenth-Century Imaginary Voyages*. Geneva: Droz.

Cortés, H.
1972 *Letters from Mexico.* Translated and edited by A. R. Pagden. London: Oxford University Press.

Cummins, T. B. F.
1991 "We Are the Other: Peruvian Portraits of Colonial *Kurakakuna.*" In *Transatlantic Encounters: Europeans and Andeans in the Sixteenth Century,* 203–31. Edited by K. J. Andrien and R. Adorno. Berkeley and Los Angeles: University of California Press.

Cuttler, C. D.
1989 "Errata in Netherlandish Art: Jan Mostaert's 'New World' Landscape." *Simiolus* 19, no. 3: 191–97.

Dacos, N.
1969a "Présents Américains à la Renaissance: L'assimilation de l'exotisme." *Gazette des Beaux-Arts* 73: 57–64.

1969b *La découverte de la Domus Aurea et la formation des grotesques à la Renaissance.* Studies of the Warburg Institute, vol. 31. London: Warburg Institute.

DaCosta Kaufmann, T.
1994 "From Treasury to Museum: The Collections of the Austrian Habsburgs." In *The Cultures of Collecting,* 137–54. Edited by J. Elsner and R. Cardinal. London: Reaktion.

Dam-Mikkelsen, B., and Lundbæk, T.
1980 *Etnografiske genstande i Det kongelige danske Kunstkammer 1650–1800.* Nationalmuseets Skrifter, Etnografisk raekke 17. Copenhagen: Nationalmuseet.

Dannenfeldt, K.
1985 "Egyptian Mumia: The Sixteenth Century Experience and Debate." *Sixteenth Century Journal* 16, no. 2: 163–80.

Davis, N. Z.
1975 *Society and Culture in Early Modern France.* Stanford: Stanford University Press.

Day, M.
1994 "Humana: Anatomical, Pathological and Curious Human Specimens in Sloane's Museum." In *Sir Hans Sloane: Collector, Scientist, Antiquary,* 69–76. Edited by A. MacGregor. London: British Museum Press.

Defert, D.
1987 "Les collections iconographiques du XVIe siècle." In *Voyager à la Renaissance: Actes du colloque de Tours 1983,* 531–43. Edited by J. Céard and J.-Cl. Margolin. Paris: Maisonneuve & Larose.

Defoe, D.
1989 *Moll Flanders.* London: Penguin [1722].
1990 *Captain Singleton.* Oxford: Oxford University Press [1720].
1991 *Memoirs of a Cavalier.* Oxford: Oxford University Press [1720].

Derrida, J.
1972a *Marges.* Paris: Minuit.
1972b *La Dissémination.* Paris: Seuil.
1980 *La Carte Postale de Socrate à Freud et au-delà.* Paris: Flammarion.
1986 *Parages.* Paris: Galilée.
1987 *Ulysse gramophone: Deux mots pour Joyce.* Paris: Galilée.
1988 *Mémoires pour Paul de Man.* Paris: Galilée.
1990a *Limited Inc.* Paris: Galilée.
1990b *Memoires d'aveugle.* Paris: Réunion des Musées Nationaux.
1993 *Passions.* Paris: Galilée.
1995 *Points . . . Interviews, 1974–1994.* Edited by E. Weber. Stanford: Stanford University Press.

Dews, P.
1992 "Writing in the Lifeworld: Deconstruction as a Paradigm of a Transition to Modernity." In *Postmodernism and the Re-reading of Modernity,* 274–300. Edited by F. Barker, P. Hulme, and M. Iversen. Manchester, England: Manchester University Press.

Digard, J.-P.
1990 *L'homme et les animaux domestiques: Anthropologie d'une passion.* Paris: Fayard.

Dilworth, L.
1996 *Imagining Indians in the Southwest: Persistent Visions of a Primitive Past.* Washington, D.C.: Smithsonian Institution Press.

Dippie, B. W.
1992 "Representing the Other: The North American Indian." In *Anthropology and Photography 1860–1920,* 132–36. Edited by E. Edwards. New Haven: Yale University Press.

Doesburg, G. B. van
1996 "La Herencia del Señor Tico: La fundación y desintegración de una casa real cuicateca. Un estudio introductorio de la historiografía cuicateca y explicación de los llamados Códices Porfirio Díaz y Fernández Leal," 2 vols. Ph.D. diss., Leiden University.

Donattini, M.
1992 "Orizzonti geografici dell'editoria italiana (1493–1560)." In *Il Nuovo Mondo nella coscienza italiana e tedesca del Cinquecento,* 79–154. Edited by A. Prosperi and W. Reinhard. Bologna: Mulino.

Drees, J.
1997 "Die 'Gottorfische Kunst-Kammer': Anmerkungen zu ihrer Geschichte nach historischen Textzeugnissen." In Exh. Cat. Schleswig, 2: 11–28.

Durand, J.-Y.
1991 "'Où la terre s'achève et la mer commence': Une anthropologie du bout de l'Europe." *Terrain* 17: 120–34.

Durrans, B.
1988 "The Future of the Other: Changing Cultures on Display in Ethnographic Museums." In *The Museum Time-Machine: Putting Cultures on Display,* 144–69. Edited by R. Lumley. London: Routledge.

Duverger, J.
1979 "Jan Mostaert, Ereschilder van Margareta van Oostenrijk." In *Festschrift für Wolfgang Krönig,* 41: 113–17. Edited by P. Ludwig. Aachen: Aachener Kunstblätter.
1980 "Margareta van Oostenrijk (1480–1530) en de Italiaanse Renaissance." In *Relations artistiques entre les Pays-Bas et l'Italie à la Renaissance: Études dédiées à Suzanne Sulzberger,* 127–42. Edited by N. Dacos. Études d'Histoire de l'Art, vol. 4. Brussels: Institut Historique Belge de Rome.

Eatough, G.
1984 *Fracastoro's Syphilis.* Introduction, text, translation, and notes by Geofrrey Eatough. Liverpool: Francis Cairns.

Eck, X. van, Hecht, P., Luijten, G., Tilborgh, L. van, and Veldman, I. (eds.)
1996 *Ten Essays for a Friend: E. de Jongh 65.* Zwolle, Netherlands: Waanders.

Edwards, E.
1992a "Introduction." In *Anthropology and Photography 1860–1920,* 3–17. Edited by E. Edwards. New Haven: Yale University Press.

1992b "Science Visualized: E. H. Man in the Andaman Islands." In *Anthropology and Photography 1860–1920,* 108–21. Edited by E. Edwards. New Haven: Yale University Press.

1995a "Visuality and History: A Contemplation on Two Photographs of Samoa by Capt. W. Acland, Royal Navy." In *Picturing Paradise: Colonial Photography of Samoa, 1875 to 1925,* 49–58. Edited by C. Blanton. Daytona Beach, Fla.: Southeast Museum of Photography.

1995b "Jorma Puranen—Imaginary Homecoming." *Social Identities* 1, no. 2: 317–22.

Egmond, F.

1997 *Een bekende Scheveninger: Adriaen Coenen en zijn Visboeck van 1578.* The Hague: Centre for the Genealogy of Scheveningen [incl. Eng. summary].

Egmond, F., and Mason, P.

1994 "Armadillos in Unlikely Places: Some Unpublished Sixteenth-Century Sources for New World *Rezeptionsgeschichte* in Northern Europe." *Ibero-Amerikanisches Archiv* 20, no. 1–2: 3–52.

1995 "Report on a Wild Goose Chase." *Journal of the History of Collections* 7, no. 1: 25–43.

1996 "Skeletons on Show: Learned Entertainment and Popular Knowledge." *History Workshop Journal* 41, no. 1: 92–116.

1997 *The Mammoth and the Mouse: Microhistory and Morphology.* Baltimore: Johns Hopkins University Press.

Ehrenreich, P.

1894 "Über einige ältere Bildnisse südamerikanischer Indianer." *Globus: Illustrierte Zeitschrift für Länder- und Völkerkunde* 66, no. 6: 81–90.

Eisenman, S. F.

1992 *The Temptation of Saint Redon: Biography, Ideology and Style in the Noirs of Odilon Redon.* Chicago: University of Chicago Press.

1997 *Gauguin's Skirt.* London: Thames & Hudson.

Ellenius, A.

1985 "Ecological Vision and Wildlife Painting towards the End of the Nineteenth Century." In *The Natural Sciences and the Arts: Aspects of Interaction from the Renaissance to the Twentieth Century,* 147–65. Edited by A. Ellenius. Acta Universitatis Upsaliensis, Figura Nova Series 22. Stockholm: Almqvist & Wiksell International.

Elsner, J.

1994 "A Collector's Model of Desire: The House and Museum of Sir John Soane." In *The Cultures of Collecting,* 155–76. Edited by J. Elsner and R. Cardinal. London: Reaktion.

Erdman, D. V.

1954 *Blake: Prophet against Empire.* Princeton: Princeton University Press.

Exh. Cat. Amsterdam

1986 *Kunst voor de beeldenstorm.* Edited by J. P. Filedt Kok, W. Halsema-Kubes, and W. Th. Kloek. The Hague: Staatsuitgeverij.

1992 *De wereld binnen handbereik: Nederlandse kunst- en rariteitenverzamelin-*

gen, 1585–1735. Amsterdams Historisch Museum. Edited by E. Bergvelt and R. Kistemaker. Zwolle, Netherlands: Waanders.

1993 *Dawn of the Golden Age: Northern Netherlandish Art 1580–1620*. Rijksmuseum Amsterdam. Zwolle, Netherlands: Waanders.

1996 *Peter de Grote en Holland: Culturele en wetenschappelijke betrekkingen tussen Rusland en Nederland ten tijde van tsaar Peter de Grote*. Amsterdams Historisch Museum. Edited by R. Kistemaker, N. Kopaneva, and A. Overbeek. Bussum: Thoth.

1997 *Mirror of Everyday Life: Genreprints in the Netherlands 1550–1700*. Edited by E. de Jongh and G. Luijten, Rijksmuseum Amsterdam. Ghent: Snoeck-Ducaju & Zoon.

Exh. Cat. Amsterdam/Boston

1987 *Masters of Seventeenth-Century Dutch Landscape Painting*. Edited by P. Sutton. Boston: Rijksmuseum Amsterdam/Museum of Fine Arts; Philadelphia: Philadelphia Museum of Art.

Exh. Cat. Antwerp

1992 *America, Bride of the Sun: 500 Years Latin America and the Low Countries*. Edited by P. Vandenbroeck. Antwerp: Royal Museum of Fine Arts.

1993 *The Panoramic Dream: Antwerp and the World Exhibitions 1885–1894–1930*. Edited by M. Nauwelaerts. Antwerp: Bouwcentrum.

1996 *Peeter van Coudenberghe: Apotheker-Botanicus (1517–1599) en Tijdgenoten*. Edited by G. De Munck and H. Wille. Antwerp: Antwerp Royal Association of Apothecaries (KAVA).

Exh. Cat. Bamberg

1988 *Die Neuen Welten in alten Büchern: Entdeckung und Eroberung in frühen deutschen Schrift- und Bildzeugnissen*. Edited by U. Knefelkamp and H.-J. König. Bamberg: Staatsbibliothek.

Exh. Cat. Berlin

1982 *Mythen der Neuen Welt: Zur Entdeckungsgeschichte Lateinamerikas*. Edited by K.-H. Kohl. Berlin: Frölich and Kaufmann.

1989 *Europa und der Orient 800–1900*. Edited by G. Sievernich and H. Budde. Berliner Festspiele. Berlin: Bertelsmann Lexikon.

Exh. Cat. Bologna

1992 *Bologna e il Mondo Nuovo*. Edited by L. Laurencich Minelli. Museo Civico Medievale. Bologna: Grafis.

Exh. Cat. Bonn

1994 *Wunderkammer des Abendlandes: Museum und Sammlung im Spiegel der Zeit*. Coordinated by A. Kulenkampff and D. von Drachenfels. Bonn: Kunst- und Ausstellungshalle der Bundesrepublik Deutschland.

Exh. Cat. Brussels

1963 *De Eeuw van Brueghel: De schilderkunst in België in de 16de eeuw*. Brussels: Royal Museum of Fine Arts.

Exh. Cat. Chicago/Amsterdam/London

1994 *Odilon Redon: Prince of Dreams 1840–1916*. Organized by D. W. Druick, F. Leeman, and M. Stevens. New York: Harry N. Abrams.

Exh. Cat. Delft

1994 *Leonaert Bramer, 1596–1674: Ingenious Painter and Draughtsman in Rome and Delft.* By M. Plomp, J. ten Brink Goldsmith, A. Quarles von Ufford, and M. Kersten. Zwolle, Netherlands: Waanders.

Exh. Cat. Dordrecht/Leeuwarden

1988 *Meesterlijk Vee: Nederlandse Veeschilders 1600–1900.* Edited by G. Jansen. Dordrecht: Dordrechts Museum; Zwolle, Netherlands: Fries Museum, Leeuwarden.

Exh. Cat. Haarlem

1993 *De tentoongestelde mens: Reuzen, dwergen en andere wonderen der natuur.* Edited by B. C. Sliggers and A. A. Wertheim. Teylers Museum Haarlem. Zutphen, Netherlands: Walburg Press.

Exh. Cat. Leipzig

1995 *Afrika in Leipzig: Erforschung und Vermittlung eines Kontinents 1730–1950.* Edited by A. Jones. Leipzig: Instituten für Afrikanistik und Ethnologie/Museum für Völkerkunde.

Exh. Cat. London

1990 *Fake? The Art of Deception.* Edited by M. Jones. London: British Museum Press.

1993 *The Paper Museum of Cassiano dal Pozzo.* British Museum, Quaderni Puteani 4. Milan: Olivetti.

Exh. Cat. Mexico City

1994 *Juegos de Ingenio y Agudeza: La pintura emblemática de la Nueva España.* Museo Nacional de Arte. Mexico City: Ediciones del Equilibrista and Turner Libros.

Exh. Cat. New York

1984 *"Primitivism" in Modern Art: Affinity of the Tribal and the Modern*, 2 vols. Edited by W. Rubin. New York: Museum of Modern Art.

1988 *ART/Artifact: African Art in Anthropology Collections.* New York: Center for African Art.

1990 *Albert Bierstadt: Art and Enterprise.* Edited by N. K. Anderson and L. S. Ferber. New York: Brooklyn Museum.

1991 *Africa Explores: Twentieth Century African Art.* Edited by S. Vogel. New York: Center for African Art.

Exh. Cat. Ottawa

1996 *The Ingenious Machine of Nature: Four Centuries of Art and Anatomy.* Edited by M. Cazort, M. Kornell, and K. B. Roberts. Ottawa: National Gallery of Canada.

Exh. Cat. Paris

1976 *L'Amérique vue par l'Europe.* Edited by H. Honour. Paris: Grand Palais, Éditions des Musées Nationaux.

1992 *Americas Lost 1492–1713: The First Encounter.* Edited by D. Lévine. Paris: Musée de l'Homme, Bordas.

Exh. Cat. Prague

1997 *Rudolf II and Prague.* Organized by E. Fučíková. Prague: Prague Castle; London: Thames & Hudson; Milan: Skira Editore.

Exh. Cat. Schleswig

1997 *Gottorf im Glanz des Barock: Kunst und Kultur am Schleswiger Hof 1544–1713,* 4 vols. Edited by U. Kuhl. Schleswig: Schleswig-Holsteinisches Landesmuseum.

Exh. Cat. Stuttgart

1987 *Exotische Welten, Europäische Phantasien.* Edited by T. Osterwold and H. Pollig. Stuttgart: Institut für Auslandsbeziehungen, Edition Cantz.

Exh. Cat. The Hague

1979 *Zo wijd de wereld strekt.* Edited by E. van den Boogaart and F. J. Duparc. The Hague: Johan Maurits van Nassau Stichting.

Exh. Cat. Utrecht/'s Hertogenbosch

1993 *Maria van Hongarije: Koningin tussen keizers en kunstenaars, 1508–1558.* Edited by B. van den Boogert and J. Kerkhoff. Rijksmuseum Het Catharijneconvent Utrecht and Noordbrabants Museum 's-Hertogenbosch. Zwolle, Netherlands: Waanders.

Exh. Cat. Vienna

1994 *La prima donna del mondo: Isabella d'Este.* Edited by S. Ferino-Pagden. Vienna: Kunsthistorisches Museum Vienna.

Exh. Cat. Washington

1986 *Art in New Mexico, 1900–1945: Paths to Taos and Santa Fe.* Edited by C. C. Eldredge, J. Schimmel, and W. H. Truettner. National Museum of American Art, Smithsonian Institution. New York: Abbeville Press.

1991 *Circa 1492: Art in the Age of Exploration.* Edited by J. A. Levenson. Washington, D.C.: National Gallery of Art and Yale University Press.

Fabian, J.

1983 *Time and the Other: How Anthropology Makes Its Object.* New York: Columbia University Press.

Fabri, R.

1991 *De 17de-eeuwse Antwerpse kunstkast: Typologische en historische aspecten.* Verhandelingen van de Koninklijke Academie der Wetenschappen, Letteren en Schone Kunsten van België 53. Brussels: Palais der Academieën.

1992 "Luxury Furniture from Antwerp in Latin America." In Exh. Cat. Antwerp: 49–56.

Falk, T.

1987 "Frühe Rezeption der Neuen Welt in der graphische Kunst." In *Humanismus und Neue Welt,* 37–64. Edited by W. Reinhard. Acta Humaniora, Mitteilung XV der Kommission für Humanismusforschung. Bonn: Deutsche Forschungsgemeinschaft.

Feest, C. F.

1984 "From North America." In Exh. Cat. New York: 85–98.

1985 "Mexico and South America in the European Wunderkammer." In *The Origins of Museums,* 237–44. Edited by O. Impey and A. MacGregor. Oxford: Clarendon Press.

1986 "Zemes Idolum Diabolicum: Surprise and Success in Ethnographic Kunstkammer Research." *Archiv für Völkerkunde* 40: 181–98.

1987 "Indians and Europe? Editor's Postscript." In *Indians and Europe: An Interdisciplinary Collection of Essays*, 609–28. Edited by C. F. Feest. Göttingen/Aachen: Herodot/Rader Verlag.

1988 "Jacques Le Moyne minus four." *European Review of Native American Studies* 1, no. 1: 33–38.

1990 "Vienna's Mexican Treasures: Aztec, Mixtec, and Tarascan Works from the Sixteenth Century Austrian Collections." *Archiv für Völkerkunde* 44: 1–64.

1992 "North America in the European *Wunderkammer*." *Archiv für Völkerkunde* 46: 61–109.

1993 "European Collecting of American Indian Artefacts and Art." *Journal of the History of Collections* 5, no. 1: 1–11.

1995a "The Collecting of American Indian Artifacts in Europe, 1493–1750." In *America in European Consciousness, 1493–1750*, 324–60. Edited by K. Ordahl Kupperman. Chapel Hill: University of North Carolina Press.

1995b "Cook Voyage Material from North America: The Vienna Collection." *Archiv für Völkerkunde* 49: 111–86.

Fermor, S.

1993 *Piero di Cosimo: Fiction, Invention and Fantasia*. London: Reaktion.

Ferrari, G.

1987 "Public Anatomy Lessons and the Carnival: The Anatomy Theatre of Bologna." *Past and Present* 117: 50–106.

Filedt Kok, J. P.

1985 *Livelier than Life: The Master of the Amsterdam Cabinet or the Housebook Master, ca. 1470–1500*. Amsterdam: Rijksmuseum.

Findlen, P.

1994 *Possessing Nature: Museums, Collecting, and Scientific Culture in Early Modern Italy*. Berkeley and Los Angeles: University of California Press.

Firlet, E. M.

1996 *Smocza Jama na Wawelu*. Cracow: Universitas.

Fish, S.

1982 "With the Compliments of the Author: Reflections on Austin and Derrida." *Critical Inquiry* 8: 693–721.

Fitton, M., and Gilbert, P.

1994 "Insect Collections." In *Sir Hans Sloane: Collector, Scientist, Antiquary*, 112–22. Edited by A. MacGregor. London: British Museum Press.

Flacke, M.

1993 "De herinrichting van Duitse musea in de Weimar-republiek." In *Verzamelen. Van Rariteitenkabinet tot Kunstmuseum*, 409–30. Edited by E. Bergvelt, D. Meijers, and M. Rijnders. Gaade Uitgevers, Netherlands: Open Universiteit Heerlen.

Flam, J. D.

1984 "Matisse and the Fauves." In Exh. Cat. New York: 211–39.

Flaubert, G.

1881 *Bouvard et Pécuchet*. Paris.

Flavell, K.
1994 "Mapping Faces: National Physiognomies as Cultural Prediction." *Eighteenth-Century Life* 18, no. 3: 8–22.

Flint, R. W.
1996 "American Showmen and European Dealers: Commerce in Wild Animals in Nineteenth-Century America." In *New Worlds, New Animals: From Menagerie to Zoological Park in the Nineteenth Century,* 97–108. Edited by R. J. Hoage and W. A. Deiss. Baltimore: Johns Hopkins University Press.

Flint, V. I. J.
1992 *The Imaginative Landscape of Christopher Columbus.* Princeton: Princeton University Press.

Forbes, J. D.
1988 *Black Africans and Native Americans: Color, Race and Caste in the Evolution of Red-Black Peoples.* Oxford: Blackwell.

Forster, E. M.
1985 *A Passage to India* [1924]. Harmondsworth, England: Penguin.

Fothergill, A.
1992 "Of Conrad, Cannibals, and Kin." In *Representing Others: White Views of Indigenous Peoples.* Edited by M. Gidley. Exeter Studies in American and Commonwealth Arts 4: 37–59. Exeter: University of Exeter Press.

Franchini, D., Margonari, R., Olmi, G., Signorini, R., Zanca, A., and Tellini-Perina, C. (a cura di).
1979 *La Scienza a Corte: Collezionismo eclettico, natura e immagine a Mantova fra Rinascimento e Manierismo.* Rome: Bulzoni.

Freedberg, D.
1993 "Cassiano and the Art of Natural History." In Exh. Cat. London: 141–53.

Freedman, L.
1995 "Neptune in Classical and Renaissance Visual Art." *International Journal of the Classical Tradition* 2, no. 2: 219–37.

Freud, S.
1955 *The Standard Edition of the Complete Psychological Works of Sigmund Freud,* vol. 18. London: Hogarth Press and Institute of Psycho-Analysis.

Fritz, R.
1983 *Gefässe aus Kokosnuss in Mitteleuropa: 1250–1800.* Mainz am Rhein, Germany: Philipp von Zabern.

Froning, S.
1996 "'A la rencontre des Amériques' at the Musée de l'Homme in Paris: Artifacts or Societies on Display in the French Ethnographic Museum?" *European Review of Native American Studies* 10, no. 1: 25–36.

Fuchs, [R.], and Breen, J.
1916 "Aus dem 'Itinerarium' des Christian Knorr von Rosenroth." *Jaarboek Amstelodanum* 14: 201–56.

Fučíková, E.

1985 "The Collection of Rudolf II at Prague: Cabinet of Curiosities or Scientific Museum?" In *The Origins of Museums: The Cabinet of Curiosities in Sixteenth- and Seventeenth-Century Europe,* 47–53. Edited by O. Impey and A. MacGregor. Oxford: Clarendon Press.

Fuller, J.

1983 "Introduction." In *John Gay: Dramatic Works,* 1: 1–76. Edited by John Fuller. Oxford: Clarendon Press.

Gamwell, L., and Wells, R. (eds.)

1989 *Sigmund Freud and Art: His Personal Collection of Antiquities.* London: Thames & Hudson.

García, G.

1607 *Origen de los indios de el nuevo mundo: E Indias occidentales.* Valencia.

Gelder, H. E. van

1960 "Twee Braziliaanse schildpadden door Albert Eckhout." *Oud Holland* 75: 5–30 [Eng. summary on 29–30].

Gelder, R. van

1993 "Noordnederlandse verzamelingen in de zeventiende eeuw." In *Verzamelen: Van Rariteitenkabinet tot Kunstmuseum,* 123–44. Edited by E. Bergvelt, D. Meijers, and M. Rijnders. Gaade Uitgevers, Netherlands: Open Universiteit Heerlen.

George, W.

1969 *Animals and Maps.* London: Secker and Warburg.

Gibson, W. S.

1989 *Mirror of the Earth: The World Landscape in Sixteenth-Century Flemish Painting.* Princeton: Princeton University Press.

Gidley, M.

1987 "R. B. Townshend's 1903 Snake Dance Photographs in Focus." *European Review of Native American Studies* 1, no. 2: 9–14.

1992a "Photographic Images of North American Indians." In *Beeld en Verbeelding van Amerika,* 2: 55–72. Edited by E. van Erven and J. Weerdenburg. Utrecht: Studium Generale, Utrecht University.

1992b "Edward S. Curtis' Indian Photographs: A National Enterprise." In *Representing Others: White Views of Indigenous Peoples.* Edited by M. Gidley. Exeter Studies in American and Commonwealth Arts 4: 103–19. Exeter: University of Exeter Press.

Gilbert, C.

1952 "On Subject and Non-Subject in Renaissance Pictures." *Art Bulletin* 34: 202–16.

Ginzburg, C.

1990 *Myths, Emblems, Clues.* Translated by John and Anne Tedeschi. London: Hutchinson Radius [1986].

1993 "Montaigne, Cannibals and Grottoes." *History and Anthropology* 6, no. 2–3: 125–55.

Glardon, P.

1997 "Introduction." In *Pierre Belon du Mans: L'histoire de la nature des oyseaux*, xiii–lxxi. Facsimile edition of the 1555 edition with introduction and notes by Philippe Glardon. Geneva: Droz.

Gliozzi, G.

1976 *Adamo e il nuovo mondo*. Florence: Nuova Italia Editrice.

Goedde, L. O.

1989 *Tempest and Shipwreck in Dutch and Flemish Art: Convention, Rhetoric, and Interpretation*. University Park: Pennsylvania State University Press.

Goethe, J. W. von

1971 *Elective Affinities*. Translated and with an introduction by R. J. Hollingdale. London: Penguin Books [*Die Wahlverwandtschaften*, 1809].

Goldmann, S.

1987 "Zur Rezeption der Völkerausstellungen um 1900." In Exh. Cat. Stuttgart: 88–93.

Goldwater, R.

1986 *Primitivism in Modern Art*, rev. and enlarged ed. Cambridge: Belknap Press of Harvard University Press [1938].

Golson, L. M.

1969 "Landscape Prints and Landscapists of the School of Fontainebleau c. 1543–c. 1570." *Gazette des Beaux-Arts* 73: 95–110.

Gombrich, E.

1982 *The Image and the Eye: Further Studies in the Psychology of Pictorial Representation*. Oxford: Phaidon Press.

1991 *Topics of Our Time: Twentieth-Century Issues in Learning and Art*. London: Phaidon Press.

Gordon, D. E.

1984 "German Expressionism." In Exh. Cat. New York: 369–403.

Goropius Becanus, J.

1569 *Origines Antwerpianae*. Antwerp: Plantijn.

Gott, T.

1992 "La genèse du symbolisme d'Odilon Redon: Un nouveau regard sur le Carnet de Chicago." *Revue de l'Art* 96: 51–62.

Grañén Porrúa, M. I.

1994 "El grabado libresco en la Nueva España, sus emblemas y alegorías." In Exh. Cat. Mexico City: 117–31.

Green, D.

1985 "Veins of Resemblance: Photography and Eugenics." *Oxford Art Journal* 7, no. 2: 3–16.

Greenberg, K.

1990 "The Nose, the Lie, and the Duel in the Antebellum South." *American Historical Review* 95, no. 1: 57–74.

Greenblatt, S. J.
1980 *Renaissance Self-fashioning*. Chicago: University of Chicago Press.
1990 *Learning to Curse: Essays in Early Modern Culture*. London: Routledge.
1991 *Marvelous Possessions: The Wonder of the New World*. Oxford: Clarendon Press.

Greene, R.
1995 "Petrarchism among the Discourses of Imperialism." In *America in European Consciousness, 1493–1750*, 130–65. Edited by K. Ordahl Kupperman. Chapel Hill: University of North Carolina Press.

Greenhalgh, P.
1989 "Education, Entertainment and Politics: Lessons from the Great International Exhibitions." In *The New Museology*, 74–98. Edited by P. Vergo. London: Reaktion.

Guest, H.
1989 "The Great Distinction: Figures of the Exotic in the Work of William Hodges." *Oxford Art Journal* 12, no. 2: 36–58.
1992 "Curiously Marked: Tattooing, Masculinity, and Nationality in Eighteenth-Century British Perceptions of the South Pacific." In *Painting and the Politics of Culture: New Essays on British Art 1700–1850*, 101–34. Edited by J. Barrell. Oxford: Oxford University Press.
1996 "Looking at Women: Forster's Observations in the South Pacific." In *Johann Reinhold Forster: Observations Made during a Voyage round the World*, xli–liv. Edited by N. Thomas, H. Guest, and M. Dettelbach. Honolulu: University of Hawaii Press.

Gundestrup, B.
1985 "From the Royal Kunstkammer to the Modern Museums of Copenhagen." In *The Origins of Museums*, 128–35. Edited by O. Impey and A. MacGregor. Oxford: Clarendon Press.
1991 *Det kongelige danske Kunstkammer 1737*, 2 vols. Copenhagen: Nationalmuseet and Nyt Nordisk Forlag Arnold Busck.

Gutiérrez Estévez, M.
1993 "Mayas, españoles, moros y judíos en baile de máscaras: Morfología y retórica de la alteridad." In *De Palabra y Obra en el Nuevo Mundo*, Edited by G. H. Gossen, J. J. Klor de Alva, M. Gutiérrez Estévez, and M. León-Portilla. Vol. 3: *La formación del otro*, 323–76. Madrid: Siglo XXI de España.

Haberland, W.
1988a "'Diese Indianer sind falsch': Neun Bella Coola im Deutschen Reich 1885/86." *Archiv für Völkerkunde* 42: 3–67.
1988b "Adrian Jacobsen on Pine Ridge Reservation, 1910." *European Review of Native American Studies* 1, no. 1: 11–15.

Hall, E.
1989 *Inventing the Barbarian: Greek Self-definition through Tragedy*. Oxford: Clarendon Press.

Hamell, G. R.
1987 "Mohawks Abroad: The 1764 Amsterdam Etching of Sychnecta." In *Indians*

and Europe: An Interdisciplinary Collection of Essays, 175–93. Edited by C. F. Feest. Göttingen/Aachen: Herodot/Rader Verlag.

Hamlin, W. H.

1994 "Attributions of Divinity in Renaissance Ethnography and Romance; or, Making Religion of Wonder." *Journal of Medieval and Renaissance Studies* 24, no. 3: 415–47.

Hamy, E.-T.

1907a "Le bas-relief de l'Hotel du Brésil au Musée Départemental d'Antiquités de Rouen." *Journal de la Société des Américanistes de Paris,* nouv. sér., 4, no. 1: 1–6.

1907b "L'*Album des habitants du Nouveau Monde* d'Antoine Jacquard, graveur poetivin du commencement du XVIIe siècle." *Journal de la Société des Américanistes de Paris,* nouv. sér., 4, no. 2: 225–36.

1908 "Les Indiens de Rasilly peints par Du Viert et gravés par Firens et Gaultier (1613): Étude iconographique et ethnographique." *Journal de la Société des Américanistes de Paris,* nouv. sér., 5: 21–52.

Hansen, P. H.

1996 "The Dancing Lamas of Everest: Cinema, Orientalism, and Anglo-Tibetan Relations in the 1920s." *American Historical Review* 101, no. 3: 712–47.

Harbsmeier, M.

1994a *Wilde Völkerkunde: Andere Welten in deutschen Reiseberichten der Frühen Neuzeit.* Frankfurt: Campus.

1994b "Schauspiel Europa: Die außereuropäische Entdeckung Europas im 19. Jahrhundert am Beispiel afrikanischer Texte." *Historische Anthropologie: Kultur, Gesellschaft, Alltag* 2, no. 3: 331–50.

1995 "Die Exotik des Fortschritts: Das Europa des 19. Jahrhunderts in Reiseberichten aussereuropäischer Reisender." In *Fortschritt ohne Ende—Ende des Fortschritts?* 36: 24–45. Edited by S. A. Jørgensen. Text and Kontext, Sonderreihe. Copenhagen: Wilhelm Fink Verlag.

1997 "Bodies and Voices from Ultima Thule: Inuit Explorations of the Kablunat from Christian IV to Knud Rasmussen." International Network on the History of Polar Science, Working Paper 11, Department of History of Science and Ideas, Umeå University.

Harms, W.

1985 "On Natural History and Emblematics in the Sixteenth Century." In *The Natural Sciences and the Arts: Aspects of Interaction from the Renaissance to the Twentieth Century,* 67–83. Edited by A. Ellenius. Acta Universitatis Upsaliensis, Figura Nova Series 22. Stockholm: Almqvist & Wiksell International.

Harvey, P.

1996 *Hybrids of Modernity: Anthropology, the Nation State and the Universal Exhibition.* London: Routledge.

Haskell, F., and Penny, N.

1981 *Taste and the Antique: The Lure of Classical Sculpture, 1500–1900.* New Haven: Yale University Press.

Haskins, C. H.
1927 *Studies in the History of Mediaeval Science,* 2d ed. New York: Ungar [1924].

Heikamp, D.
1976 "American Objects in Italian Collections of the Renaissance and Baroque: A Survey." In *First Images of America,* 1: 455–82. Edited by F. Chiappelli. Berkeley and Los Angeles: University of California Press.

Heikamp, D., and Anders, F.
1970 "Mexikanische Altertümer aus süddeutschen Kunstkammern." *Pantheon* 28: 205–20.

Hemming, J.
1984 "The Indians of Brazil in 1500." In *The Cambridge History of Latin America,* 1: 119–43. Edited by L. Bethell. Cambridge: Cambridge University Press.

Hendrix, L.
1997 "Natural History Illustration at the Court of Rudolf II." In Exh. Cat. Prague: 157–71.

Hennin, J. de
1681 *De zinrijke gedachten, toegepast op de vijf sinnen van 's menschen verstand.* Amsterdam.

Hentsch, T.
1988 *L'orient imaginaire.* Paris: Editions de Minuit.

Herklotz, I.
1994 "Forschungsberichte: Neue Literatur zur Sammlungsgeschichte." *Kunstchronik* 47, no. 3: 117–35.

Heron-Allen, E.
1928 *Barnacles in Nature and in Myth.* London: Oxford University Press.

Hinsley, C. M.
1989 "Zunis and Brahmins: Cultural Ambivalence in the Gilded Age." In *Romantic Motives: Essays on Anthropological Sensibility,* 169–207. Edited by G. W. Stocking, Jr. History of Anthropology, vol. 6. Wisconsin: University of Wisconsin Press.
1991 "The World as Marketplace: Commodification of the Exotic at the World's Columbian Exposition, Chicago, 1893." In *Exhibiting Cultures: The Poetics and Politics of Museum Display,* 344–65. Edited by I. Karp and S. D. Lavine. Washington, D.C.: Smithsonian Institution Press.

Hirsch, R.
1976 "Printed Reports on the Early Discoveries and Their Reception." In *First Images of America,* 2: 537–52. Edited by F. Chiappelli. Berkeley and Los Angeles: University of California Press.

Hirst, M.
1981 *Sebastiano del Piombo.* Oxford: Clarendon Press.

Histoire Naturelle des Indes
1996 *Histoire Naturelle des Indes: The Drake Manuscript in the Pierpont Morgan Library.* London: Norton.

Hockings, P.

1992 "The Yellow Bough: Rivers's Use of Photography in *The Todas.*" In *Anthropology and Photography 1860–1920,* 179–86. Edited by E. Edwards. New Haven: Yale University Press.

Hoeniger, F. D.

1985 "How Plants and Animals Were Studied in the Mid–Sixteenth Century." In *Science and the Arts in the Renaissance*, 130–48. Edited by J. W. Shirley and F. D. Hoeniger. New Jersey-London-Ontario: Associated University Presses.

Holberton, P.

1995 "Giorgione's *Tempest* or 'little landscape with the storm with the gypsy': More on the Gypsy, and a Reassessment." *Art History* 18, no. 3: 383–404.

Honig, E. A.

1990 "In Memory: Lady Dacre and Pairing by Hans Eworth." In *Renaissance Bodies: The Human Figure in English Culture c. 1540–1660,* 60–85. Edited by L. Gent and N. Llewellyn. London: Reaktion.

Honour, H.

1975 *The New Golden Land: European Images of America from the Discoveries to the Present Time.* London: Allen Lane.

1979 "Science and Exoticism: The European Artist and the Non-European World before Johan Maurits." In *Johan Maurits van Nassau-Siegen 1604–1679: A Humanist Prince in Europe and Brazil,* 269–96. Edited by E. van den Boogaart. The Hague: Johan Maurits van Nassau Stichting.

Howe, K.

1995 "The Death of Cook: Exercises in Explanation." *Eighteenth-Century Life* 18, no. 3: 198–211.

Huddleston, L. E.

1967 *Origins of the American Indians: European Concepts, 1492–1729.* Latin American Monographs, no. 11, Institute of Latin American Studies. Austin: University of Texas Press.

Hulme, P.

1978 "Columbus and the Cannibals: A Study of the Reports of Anthropophagy in the Journal of Christopher Columbus." *Ibero-Amerikanisches Archiv* (Neue Folge) 4: 115–39.

1985 "Polytropic Man: Tropes of Sexuality and Mobility in Early Colonial Discourse." In *Europe and Its Others,* 2: 17–32. Edited by F. Barker, P. Hulme, M. Iversen, and D. Loxley. Colchester: University of Essex.

1986 *Colonial Encounters: Europe and the Native Caribbean 1492–1979.* London: Methuen.

1994 "Tales of Distinction: European Ethnography and the Caribbean." In *Implicit Understandings*, 157–97. Edited by S. B. Schwartz. Cambridge: Cambridge University Press.

Hulton, P.

1978 "Images of the New World: Jacques Le Moyne de Morgues and John White." In *The Westward Enterprise: English Activities in Ireland, the Atlantic, and*

America 1480–1650, 195–214. Edited by K. R. Andrews, N. P. Canny, and P. E. H. Hair. Liverpool: Liverpool University Press.

1984 *America 1585: The Complete Drawings of John White.* Chapel Hill: University of North Carolina Press and British Museum Press.

Idiens, D.

1987 "Eskimos in Scotland, c. 1682–1924." In *Indians and Europe: An Interdisciplinary Collection of Essays,* 161–74. Edited by C. F. Feest. Göttingen/Aachen: Herodot/Rader Verlag.

Inden, R.

1990 *Imagining India.* Oxford: Blackwell.

Iversen, M.

1993 "Retrieving Warburg's Tradition." *Art History* 16, no. 4: 541–53.

Jackson, C. E.

1997 "Fishing with Cormorants." *Archives of Natural History* 24, no. 2: 189–211.

Jacobs, M.

1995 *The Painted Voyage: Art, Travel and Exploration 1564–1875.* London: British Museum Press.

Jaffé, D.

1989 "The Barberini Circle: Some Exchanges between Peiresc, Rubens, and Their Contemporaries." *Journal of the History of Collections* 1, no. 2: 119–47.

Janson, H. W.

1961 "The 'Image Made by Chance' in Renaissance Thought." In *De artibus opuscula XL: Essays in honor of Erwin Panofsky,* 2 vols., 254–66. Edited by M. Meiss. New York: New York University Press.

Jones, A.

1990a *Zur Quellenproblematik der Geschichte Westafrikas 1450–1900.* Studien zur Kulturkunde 99. Stuttgart: Franz Steiner Verlag.

1990b "Decompiling Dapper: A Preliminary Search for Evidence." *History in Africa* 17: 171–209.

Jones, J. P.

1992 "The Colonial Legacy and the Community: The Gallery 33 Project." In *Museums and Communities: The Politics of Public Culture,* 221–41. Edited by I. Karp, C. M. Kreamer, and S. D. Lavine. Washington, D.C.: Smithsonian Institution Press.

Jong, M. de, and Groot, I. de

1988 *Ornamentprenten I: 15de & 16de eeuw.* Amsterdam: Rijksprentenkabinet; The Hague: Staatsuitgeverij.

Jongh, E. de

1995 *Kwesties van betekenis: Thema en motief in de Nederlandse schilderkunst van de zeventiende eeuw.* Leiden: Primavera.

Joppien, R.

1979a "The Dutch Vision of Brazil: Johan Maurits and His Artists." In *Johan Maurits van Nassau-Siegen 1604–1679: A Humanist Prince in Europe and Brazil,*

297–376. Edited by E. van den Boogaart. The Hague: Johan Maurits van Nassau Stichting.

1979b "The Artistic Bequest of Captain Cook's Voyages—Popular Imagery in European Costume Books of the Late Eighteenth and Early Nineteenth Centuries." In *Captain James Cook and His Times,* 187–210. Edited by R. Fisher and H. Johnston. London: Croom Helm.

1994 "Sir Joseph Banks and the World of Art in Great Britain." In *Sir Joseph Banks: A Global Perspective,* 87–103. Edited by R. E. R. Banks, B. Elliott, J. G. Hawkes, D. King-Hele, and G. L. Lucas. Kew: Royal Botanic Gardens.

Joppien, R., and Smith, B.

1988 *The Art of Captain Cook's Voyages.* Volume 3: *The Voyage of the Resolution and Discovery 1776–1786.* New Haven: Yale University Press.

Kadir, D.

1992 *Columbus and the Ends of the Earth: Europe's Prophetic Rhetoric as Conquering Ideology.* Berkeley and Los Angeles: University of California Press.

Kaeppler, A. L.

1992 "*Ali'i* and *Maka'āinana:* The Representation of Hawaiians in Museums at Home and Abroad." In *Museums and Communities: The Politics of Public Culture,* 458–75. Edited by I. Karp, C. M. Kreamer, and S. D. Lavine. Washington, D.C.: Smithsonian Institution Press.

Karp, I., and Lavine, S. D. (eds.)

1991 *Exhibiting Cultures: The Poetics and Politics of Museum Display.* Washington, D.C.: Smithsonian Institution Press.

Kasprycki, S. S.

1990 "Menominee Portraits, 1825–1860." *Archiv für Völkerkunde* 44: 65–31.

Kaufmann, L. F.

1984 *The Noble Savage: Satyrs and Satyr Families in Renaissance Art.* Studies in Renaissance Art History, no. 2. Ann Arbor, Mich.: UMI Research Press.

Kelly, F.

1989 "A Passion for Landscape: The Paintings of Frederic Edwin Church." In *Frederic Edwin Church,* 32–75. Edited by F. Kelly, S. J. Gould, J. A. Ryan, and D. Rindge. Washington, D.C.: National Gallery of Art.

Kemp, M.

1995 "'Wrought by No Artist's Hand': The Natural, the Artificial, the Exotic, and the Scientific in Some Artifacts from the Renaissance." In *Reframing the Renaissance: Visual Culture in Europe and Latin America 1450–1650,* 176–96. Edited by C. Farago. New Haven: Yale University Press.

1996 "'Implanted in Our Natures': Humans, Plants, and the Stories of Art." In *Visions of Empire: Voyages, Botany, and Representations of Nature,* 197–229. Edited by D. P. Miller and P. H. Reill. Cambridge: Cambridge University Press.

1998 "The *Temple of Flora:* Robert Thornton, Plant Sexuality and Romantic Science." In *L'interpretazione del mondo fisico nei testi e nelle immagini.* Edited by L. Tongiorgi Tomasi, G. Olmi, and A. Zanca. Florence: Leo Olschki.

Kemp, W.

1994 "Les éditions du *Nouveau Monde et navigations de Vespuce* (1517–v.1534):

Diffusion du premier récit de voyage 'américain' imprimé en français." *Bulletin du Bibliophile*, no. 2: 273–301.

Kermode, F.
1958 *The Tempest*. Edited by Frank Kermode. London: Methuen.

Keyser, M.
1993 "Wat van ver komt . . . De exotische mens tentoongesteld." In Exh. Cat. Haarlem: 57–68.

Kiernan, V.
1989 "Noble and Ignoble Savages." In *Exoticism in the Enlightenment*, 86–116. Edited by G. S. Rousseau and R. Porter. Manchester, England: Manchester University Press.

King, J. C. H.
1985 "North American Ethnography in the Collection of Sir Hans Sloane." In *The Origins of Museums*, 232–36. Edited by O. Impey and A. MacGregor. Oxford: Clarendon Press.
1994 "Ethnographic Collections: Collecting in the Context of Sloane's Catalogue of 'Miscellanies'." In *Sir Hans Sloane: Collector, Scientist, Antiquary*, 228–44. Edited by A. MacGregor. London: British Museum Press.
1996 "New Evidence for the Contents of the Leverian Museum." *Journal of the History of Collections* 8, no. 2: 167–86.

Kirshenblatt-Gimblett, B.
1991 "Objects of Ethnography." In *Exhibiting Cultures: The Poetics and Politics of Museum Display*, 386–443. Edited by I. Karp and S. D. Lavine. Washington, D.C.: Smithsonian Institution Press.

Kloek, W. T., Halsema-Kubbes, W., and Baarsen, R. J.
1986 *Art before the Iconoclasm: Northern Netherlandish Art 1525–1580*. The Hague: Staatsuitgeverij.

Kohl, K.-H.
1981 *Entzauberter Blick: Das Bild vom Guten Wilden und die Erfahrung der Zivilisation*. Berlin: Medusa.

König, H.-J.
1988 "Amerika." In Exh. Cat. Bamberg: 74–91.

Konijn, F.
1993 "A Universal Language of Art: Two Exhibitions of Non-Western Art in Dutch Museums of Modern Art." In *Art, Anthropology and the Modes of Re-presentation*, 23–30. Edited by H. Leyten and B. Damen. Amsterdam: Royal Tropical Institute.

Kopplin, M.
1987 "'Amoenitates exoticae': Exotische Köstlichkeiten im Zeitalter des Barock." In Exh. Cat. Stuttgart: 318–29.

Kornell, M.
1996 "The Study of the Human Machine: Books of Anatomy for Artists." In Exh. Cat. Ottawa: 43–70.

Kramer, F.

1977 *Verkehrte Welten: Zur imaginären Ethnographie des 19. Jahrhunderts*. Frankfurt am Main: Syndikat.

Krauss, R.

1984 "Giacometti." In Exh. Cat. New York: 503–33.

Kügelgen Kropfinger, H. von

1983 "El frontispicio de François Gerard para la obra de viaje de Humboldt y Bonpland." *Jahrbuch für Geschichte von Staat, Wirtschaft und Gesellschaft Lateinamerikas* 20: 575–616.

Kugelmass, J.

1992 "The Rites of the Tribe: American Jewish Tourism in Poland." In *Museums and Communities: The Politics of Public Culture,* 382–427. Edited by I. Karp, C. M. Kreamer, and S. D. Lavine. Washington, D.C.: Smithsonian Institution Press.

Lafitau, J.-F.

1724 *Moeurs des sauvages amériquains comparées aux moeurs des premiers temps*, 2 vols. Paris: Saugrain & Hochereau.

Lamar, H. R.

1992 "Looking Backward, Looking Forward: Selected Themes in Western Art since 1900." In *Discovered Lands, Invented Pasts: Transforming Visions of the American West,* 167–92. By J. D. Prown, N. K. Anderson, W. Cronon, B. W. Dippie, M. A. Sandweiss, S. Prendergast Schoelwer, and H. R. Lamar. New Haven: Yale University Press.

Landau, D., and Parshall, P.

1994 *The Renaissance Print 1470–1550*. New Haven: Yale University Press.

Launay-Demonet, M.-L.

1987 "Les mots sauvages: Étude des listes utiles à ceux qui veulent naviguer." In *Voyager à la Renaissance: Actes du colloque de Tours 1983,* 497–508. Edited by J. Céard and J.-C. Margolin. Paris: Maisonneuve & Larose.

Laurencich-Minelli, L.

1982 "Bologna und Amerika vom 16. bis zum 18. Jh." In Exh. Cat. Berlin 1982: 147–54.

1985 "Museography and Ethnographical Collections in Bologna during the Sixteenth and Seventeenth Centuries." In *The Origins of Museums,* 17–23. Edited by O. Impey and A. MacGregor. Oxford: Clarendon Press.

1992 "Bologna e il Mondo Nuovo." In Exh. Cat. Bologna: 9–23.

Lazzaro, C.

1995 "Animals as Cultural Signs: A Medici Menagerie in the Grotto at Castello." In *Reframing the Renaissance: Visual Culture in Europe and Latin America 1450–1650,* 197–227. Edited by C. Farago. New Haven: Yale University Press.

Lazzerini, L.

1994 "Le radici folkloriche dell'anatomia: Scienza e rituale all'inizio dell'età moderna." *Quaderni Storici* 85, no. 1: 193–233.

Lebedeva, I. N.

1996 "De nalatenschap van Maria Sibylla Merian in Sint-Petersburg." In Exh. Cat. Amsterdam: 60–66.

Lechner, J.

1992 "Dutch Humanists' Knowledge of America." *Itinerario* 16, no. 2: 101–13.

Le Corbeiller, C.

1961 "Miss America and Her Sisters: Personifications of the Four Parts of the World." *Metropolitan Museum of Art Bulletin* 19 (April): 209–23.

Leerssen, J.

1991a "Fiction Poetics and Cultural Stereotype: Local Colour in Scott, Morgan, and Maturin." *Modern Language Review* 86, no. 2: 273–84.

1991b "Echoes and Images: Reflections upon Foreign Space." In *Alterity, Identity, Image,* 123–38. Edited by R. Corbey and J. Leerssen. Amsterdam: Rodopi.

1996 *Remembrance and Imagination: Patterns in the Historical and Literary Representation of Ireland in the Nineteenth Century.* Cork: Cork University Press.

Lefrançois, T.

1992 "L'allégorie de l'Amérique à travers les collections du Musée du Nouveau Monde à La Rochelle." *Révue du Louvre* 42, no. 5/6: 53–62.

Leith-Ross, P.

1984 *The John Tradescants: Gardeners to the Rose and Lily Queen.* London: Peter Owen.

Le Roy Ladurie, E.

1995 *Le Siècle des Platter 1499–1628.* Paris: Fayard.

Léry, J. de

1990 *History of a Voyage to the Land of Brazil, Otherwise Called America.* Translated and introduced by Janet Whatley. Berkeley and Los Angeles: University of California Press [1580].

Lestringant, F.

1987a "The Myth of the Indian Monarchy: An Aspect of the Controversy between Thevet and Léry (1575–1585)." In *Indians and Europe: An Interdisciplinary Collection of Essays,* 37–60. Edited by C. F. Feest. Göttingen/Aachen: Herodot/Rader Verlag.

1987b "La flèche du Patagon ou la preuve des lointains: Sur un chapitre d'André Thevet." In *Voyager à la Renaissance: Actes du colloque de Tours 1983,* 467–96. Edited by J. Céard and J.-C. Margolin. Paris: Maisonneuve & Larose.

1990 *Le Huguenot et le Sauvage: L'Amérique et la controverse coloniale, en France, au temps des Guerres de Religion (1555–1589).* Paris: Aux Amateurs de Livres.

1991a *André Thevet: Cosmographe des derniers Valois.* Travaux d'Humanisme et Renaissance, no. 251. Geneva: Droz.

1991b "Le déclin d'un savoir: La crise de la cosmographie à la fin de la renaissance." *Annales ESC* 46, no. 2: 239–60 [reprinted in F. Lestringant, *Écrire le monde à la Renaissance: Quinze études sur Rabelais, Postel, Bodin et la littérature géographique,* 319–40. Caen, France: Paradigme, 1993].

1991c *L'atelier du cosmographe ou l'image du monde à la Renaissance.* Paris: Bibliothèque de Synthèse, Albin Michel.

1994 *Le cannibale: Grandeur et décadence.* Paris: Perrin.

1996 *L'expérience huguenote au nouveau monde (XVIe siècle).* Geneva: Droz.

Levin, G.

1984 "American Art." In Exh. Cat. New York: 453–74.

Levine, J. M.

1977 *Dr. Woodward's Shield: History, Science, and Satire in Augustan England.* Berkeley and Los Angeles: University of California Press.

Levine, L.

1994 *Men in Women's Clothing: Anti-theatricality and Effeminization, 1579–1642.* Cambridge: Cambridge University Press.

Leyten, H., and Damen, B. (eds.)

1993 *Art, Anthropology and the Modes of Re-presentation.* Amsterdam: Royal Tropical Institute.

Linzeler, A.

1932 *Inventaire du Fonds Français: Graveurs du seizième siècle,* vol. 1. Paris: Maurice Le Garrec.

Lloyd, J.

1991a "Emil Nolde's 'Ethnographic' Still Lifes: Primitivism, Tradition, and Modernity." In *The Myth of Primitivism: Perspectives on Art,* 90–112. Edited by S. Hiller. London: Routledge.

1991b *German Expressionism: Primitivism and Modernity.* New Haven: Yale University Press.

Logan, A.-M.

1979 *The "Cabinet" of the Brothers Gerard and Jan Reynst.* Royal Dutch Academy of Arts and Sciences, Arts Monographs, New Series 99. Amsterdam: North Holland Publishing Company.

López, S.

1993 "The 'Other' in the Land of the Globetrotters." In *Art, Anthropology and the Modes of Re-presentation,* 45–57. Edited by H. Leyten and B. Damen. Amsterdam: Royal Tropical Institute.

López Piñero, J. M., and Tomás, J. Pardo

1994 *Nuevos materiales y noticias sobre la historia de las plantas de Nueva España, de Francisco Hernández.* Valencia: Instituto de Estudios Documentales e Históricos sobre la Ciencia, Universitat de València-C.S.I.C.

1996 *La influencia de Francisco Hernández (1515–1587) en la constitución de la botánica y la Matera Médica Modernas.* Valencia: Instituto de Estudios Documentales e Históricos sobre la Ciencia, Universitat de València-C.S.I.C.

Lowie, R. H.

1963a "The 'Tapuya'." In *Handbook of South American Indians.* Vol. 1: *The Marginal Tribes,* 553–56. Edited by J. H. Steward. New York: Cooper Square.

1963b "The Tarairiu." In *Handbook of South American Indians.* Vol. 1: *The Marginal Tribes,* 563–66. Edited by J. H. Steward. New York: Cooper Square.

Lugli, A.

1983 *Naturalia et Mirabilia: Il collezionismo enciclopedico nelle Wunderkammern d'Europa.* Milan: Gabriele Mazzotta.

Lund, A. A.
1990 *Zum Germanenbild der Römer: Eine Einführung in die antike Ethnographie.* Heidelberg: Carl Winter Universitätsverlag.

Lunsingh Scheurleer, T. H.
1975 "Un amphithéâtre d'anatomie moralisé." In *Leiden University in the Seventeenth Century: An Exchange of Learning,* 217–77. Edited by T. H. Lunsingh Scheurleer and G. Posthumus Meyjes. Leiden: Brill.
1979 "The Mauritshuis as Domus Cosmographica." In *Johan Maurits van Nassau-Siegen: A Humanist Prince in Europe and Brazil,* 143–89. Edited by E. van den Boogaart. The Hague: Johan Maurits van Nassau Stichting.
1985 "Early Dutch Cabinets of Curiosities." In *The Origins of Museums,* 115–20. Edited by O. Impey and A. MacGregor. Oxford: Clarendon Press.

Luttervelt, R. van
1948–49 "Jan Mostaert's West-Indisch landschap." *Nederlandsch Kunsthistorisch Jaarboek* 2: 105–17.

MacCormack, S.
1995 "Limits of Understanding: Perceptions of Greco-Roman and Amerindian Paganism in Early Modern Europe." In *America in European Consciousness, 1493–1750,* 79–129. Edited by K. Ordahl Kupperman. Chapel Hill: University of North Carolina Press.

MacDonald, G. F.
1992 "Change and Challenge: Museums in the Information Society." In *Museums and Communities: The Politics of Public Culture,* 158–81. Edited by I. Karp, C. M. Kreamer, and S. D. Lavine. Washington, D.C.: Smithsonian Institution Press.

MacGregor, A.
1983 "Collectors and Collections of Rarities in the Sixteenth and Seventeenth Centuries." In *Tradescant's Rarities: Essays on the Foundation of the Ashmolean Museum 1683, with a Catalogue of the Surviving Early Collections,* 70–97. Edited by A. MacGregor. Oxford: Clarendon Press.
1989a "The King's Disport: Sports, Games and Pastimes of the Early Stuarts." In *The Late King's Goods: Collections, Possessions and Patronage of Charles I in the Light of the Commonwealth Sale Inventories,* 403–21. Edited by A. MacGregor. Oxford: Oxford University Press.
1989b "Animals and the Early Stuarts: Hunting and Hawking at the Court of James I and Charles I." *Archives of Natural History* 16, no. 3: 305–18.
1993 "Antiquarian Attitudes: Changing Responses to the Past in the Museum Environment." *Nordisk Museologi* 1993, no. 2: 7–18.
1994 "The Life, Character and Career of Sir Hans Sloane." In *Sir Hans Sloane: Collector, Scientist, Antiquary, Founding Father of the British Museum,* 11–44. Edited by A. MacGregor. London: British Museum Press.
1995 "The Natural History Correspondence of Sir Hans Sloane." *Archives of Natural History* 22, no. 1: 79–90.
1996 "King Charles I: A Renaissance Collector?" *Seventeenth Century* 11, no. 2: 141–60.

MacGregor, A. (ed.)

1983 *Tradescant's Rarities: Essays on the Foundation of the Ashmolean Museum 1683, with a Catalogue of the Surviving Early Collections.* Oxford: Clarendon Press.

1994 *Sir Hans Sloane: Collector, Scientist, Antiquary, Founding Father of the British Museum.* London: British Museum Press.

Macintyre, M., and MacKenzie, M.

1992 "Focal Length as an Analogue of Cultural Distance." In *Anthropology and Photography 1860–1920,* 158–64. Edited by E. Edwards. New Haven: Yale University Press.

Mack, J.

1990 *Emil Torday and the Art of the Congo 1900–1909.* London: British Museum Press.

Man, P. de

1981 "Pascal's Allegory of Persuasion." In *Allegory and Representation: Selected Papers from the English Institute, 1979–80,* New Series, no. 5, 1–25. Edited by S. J. Greenblatt. Baltimore: Johns Hopkins University Press.

Mander, K. van

1604 *Het schilder-boeck.* Haarlem.

Marin, L.

1995 *Sublime Poussin.* Paris: Seuil.

Marles, H.

1996 "Arrested Development: Race and Evolution in the Sculpture of Henry Ward." *Oxford Art Journal* 19, no. 1: 16–28.

Mason, P.

1984 *The City of Men: Ideology, Sexual Politics and the Social Formation.* Göttingen: Edition Herodot.

1987a "Seduction from Afar: Europe's Inner Indians." *Anthropos* 82: 581–601.

1987b "Notes on Cormorant Fishing: Europe and Its Others." *Ibero-Amerikanisches Archiv* Neue Folge, 13, no. 2: 147–74.

1990 *Deconstructing America: Representations of the Other.* London: Routledge.

1991a "Half a Cow." *Semiotica* 85, no. 1/2: 1–39.

1991b "Continental Incontinence, *Horror vacui* and the Colonial Supplement." In *Alterity, Identity, Image,* 151–90. Edited by R. Corbey and J. Leerssen. Amsterdam: Rodopi.

1992 "La lección anatómica: Violencia colonial y complicidad textual." *Foro Hispánico* 4: 131–55.

1993a "Escritura fragmentaria: Aproximaciones al otro." In *De Palabra y Obra en el Nuevo Mundo.* Vol. 3: *La formación del otro,* 395–430. Edited by G. H. Gossen, J. J. Klor de Alva, M. Gutiérrez Estévez, and M. León-Portilla. Madrid: Siglo XXI de España.

1993b "Carib against All Odds: On Colonial and Textual Violence." *European Review of Latin American and Caribbean Studies* 55: 95–107.

1994 "Classical Ethnography and Its Influence on the European Perception of the Peoples of the New World." In *The Classical Tradition and the Americas,* 1:

135–72. Edited by W. Haase and M. Reinhold. Berlin: Walter de Gruyter and Co.

1995 "The Limits of Colonial Culture." *Anthropos* 90: 576–81.

1996 "Figures of America." *Eighteenth-Century Life* 20, no. 3: 107–16.

1997a "The Purloined Codex." *Journal of the History of Collections* 9, no. 1: 1–30.

1997b "Contextos de un cráneo: Espacio histórico e inscripciones históricas." *Portugaliae Historica* Nova Série 2.

1997c "Moving Mountains and Raising the Dead." In *Códices, Caciques y Comunidades: Cuadernos de la AHILA* 5: 247–64. Edited by M.E.R.G. Jansen and L. Reyes García.

1998a "Lecciones superficiales: Transparencia y opacidad en las Américas, siglo XVI." *Aisthesis: Revista Chilena de Investigaciones Estéticas* 32.

1998b "Of Turkeys and Men: Towards a Historical Iconography of New World Ethnographic and Natural Historical Representation." In *Natura-Cultura: L'interpretazione del mondo fisico nei testi e nelle immagini.* Edited by L. Tongiorgi Tomasi, G. Olmi, and A. Zanca. Florence: Leo Olschki.

Massing, J. M.

1991a "The Quest for the Exotic: Albrecht Dürer in the Netherlands." In Exh. Cat. Washington: 115–19.

1991b "Early European Images of America: The Ethnographic Approach." In Exh. Cat. Washington: 515–20.

Maus, K. E.

1991 "Proof and Consequences: Inwardness and Its Exposure in the English Renaissance." *Representations* 34: 29–52.

Maybury-Lewis, D.

1965 "Some Crucial Distinctions in Central Brazilian Ethnology." In *Anthropos* 60: 340–58.

Mazzolini, R. G.

1998 "Frammenti di pelle e immagini di uomini." In *Natura-Cultura: L'interpretazione del mondo fisico nei testi e nelle immagini.* Edited by L. Tongiorgi Tomasi, G. Olmi, and A. Zanca. Florence: Leo Olschki.

McKay, C.

1994 "Kandinsky's Ethnography: Scientific Field Work and Aesthetic Reflection." *Art History* 17, no. 2: 182–208.

1996 "'Fearful Dunderheads': Kandinsky and the Cultural Referents of Criminal Anthropology." *Oxford Art Journal* 19, no. 1: 29–41.

Meijers, D.

1993a "The Museum and the 'Ahistorical' Exhibition: The Latest Gimmick by the Arbiters of Taste, or an Important Cultural Phenomenon?" In *Place—Position—Presentation—Public,* Symposium at the Jan van Eyck Academy, Maastricht, April 1992, 28–39. Edited by I. Gevers. Amsterdam: De Balie.

1993b "Het 'encyclopedische' museum van de achtiende eeuw." In *Verzamelen: Van Rariteitenkabinet tot Kunstmuseum,* 205–24. Edited by E. Bergvelt, D. Meijers, and M. Rijnders. Gaade Uitgevers: Open Universiteit Heerlen.

1995 *Kunst als Natur: Die Habsburger Gemäldegalerie in Wien um 1780.* Translated by R. Wiegmann. Schriften des Kunsthistorischen Museums 2. Milan: Skira Editore [1991].

1996 "De Kunstkamera van Peter de Grote: De Nederlandse bijdrage aan een nieuw type museum." In Exh. Cat. Amsterdam: 22–36.

Menninger, A.

1995 *Die Macht der Augenzeugen: Neue Welt und Kannibalen-Mythos, 1492–1600.* Stuttgart: Franz Steiner Verlag.

1996 "Die Kannibalen Amerikas und die Phantasien der Eroberer: Zum Problem der Wirklichkeitswahrnehmung aussereuropäischer Kulturen durch europäische Reisende in der frühen Neuzeit." In *Kannibalismus und europäische Kultur,* 115–41. Edited by H. Röckelein. Tübingen: Edition Diskord.

Métraux, A.

1932 "A propos de deux objets tupinamba conservés au Musée du Trocadéro." *Bulletin du Musée d'Ethnographie du Trocadéro* 3: 3–18.

Miedema, H.

1973 *Karel van Mander: Den grondt der edel vrij schilder-const*, 2 vols. Translated and with commentary by Hessel Miedema. Utrecht: Haentjens Dekker and Gumbert.

Mitchell, T.

1989 "The World as Exhibition." *Comparative Studies in Society and History* 31, no. 2: 217–36.

Montaigne, M. de

1962 *Oeuvres complètes.* Edited by A. Thibaudet and M. Rat, introduction and notes by M. Rat. Paris: Bibliothèque de la Pléiade, Gallimard.

Montrose, L.

1993 "The Work of Gender in the Discourse of Discovery." In *New World Encounters,* 177–217. Edited by S. Greenblatt. Berkeley and Los Angeles: University of California Press [1991].

Morán, J. M., and Checa, F.

1985 *El coleccionismo en España: De la cámara de maravillas a la galería de pinturas.* Madrid: Ediciones Cátedra.

Mortier, B. M. du

1991 ". . . Hiier sietmen Vrouwen van alderley Natien . . . ; Kostuumboeken bron voor de schilderkunst?" *Bulletin of the Rijksmuseum* 39, no. 4: 401–13.

Mowat, L.

1993 "Four Paintings by Edward A. Goodall at the Pitt Rivers Museum, Oxford." *Journal of the History of Collections* 5, no. 2: 223–29.

Mullaney, S.

1983 "Strange Things, Gross Terms, Curious Customs: The Rehearsal of Cultures in the Late Renaissance." *Representations* 3: 40–67.

Mulvey, C.

1987 "Among the Sag-a-noshes: Ojibwa and Iowa Indians with George Catlin in Europe, 1843–1848." In *Indians and Europe: An Interdisciplinary Collection of Essays*, 253–75. Edited by C. F. Feest. Göttingen/Aachen: Herodot/Rader Verlag.

Myers, K. J.
1993 "On the Cultural Construction of Landscape Experience: Contact to 1830." In *American Iconology*, 58–79. Edited by D. C. Miller. New Haven: Yale University Press.

Napier, R. G.
1987 "Across the Big Water: American Indians' Perceptions of Europe and Europeans, 1887–1906." In *Indians and Europe: An Interdisciplinary Collection of Essays*, 383–401. Edited by C. F. Feest. Göttingen/Aachen: Herodot/Rader Verlag.

Negro, A.
1996 *Il giardino dipinto del Cardinal Borghese: Paolo Bril e Guido Reni nel Palazzo Rospigliosi Pallavicini a Roma*. Rome: Àrgos.

Netton, I.
1989 "The Mysteries of Islam." In *Exoticism in the Enlightenment*, 23–34. Edited by G. S. Rousseau and R. Porter. Manchester, England: Manchester University Press.

Neverov, O.
1985 "'His Majesty's Cabinet' and Peter I's Kunstkammer." In *The Origins of Museums*, 54–61. Edited by O. Impey and A. MacGregor. Oxford: Clarendon Press.

Nicholson, B. et al.
1995 *Gauguin and Maori Art*. Auckland: Godwit Publishing and Auckland City Art Gallery.

Norman, D.
1973 *Alfred Stieglitz: An American Seer*. New York: Aperture Foundation.

Obeyesekere, G.
1992 *The Apotheosis of Captain Cook: European Mythmaking in the Pacific*. Princeton: Princeton University Press.

O'Hanlon, M.
1992 "Unstable Images and Second Skins: Artefacts, Exegesis and Assessments in the New Guinea Highlands." *Man* 27, no. 3: 587–608.

Öllinger, G., and Quicchelberg, S.
1553 "Magnarum medicine partium herbariae et zoographie imagines," MS 2362, Erlangen-Nürnberg University Library [facsimile published by Helga Lengenfelder, Munich, 1996].

Olmi, G.
1976 *Scienza e natura del secondo cinquecento*. Trento, Italy: Libera Università degli Studi di Trento.
1985 "Science-Honour-Metaphor: Italian Cabinets of the Sixteenth and Seventeenth Centuries." In *The Origins of Museums*, 5–16. Edited by O. Impey and A. MacGregor. Oxford: Clarendon Press.

1991 "'Molti amici in varij luoghi': Studio della natura e rapporti epistolari nel secolo XVI." *Nuncius Annali di Storia della Scienza* 6, no. 1: 3–31.

1992 *L'inventario del mondo: Catalogazione della natura e luoghi del sapere nella prima età moderna.* Annali dell'Instituto Storico Italo-Germanico, monografia 17. Bologna: Mulino.

1993 "From the Marvellous to the Commonplace: Notes on Natural History Museums (16th–18th Centuries)." In *Non-verbal Communication in Science prior to 1900,* 235–78. Edited by R. G. Mazzolini. Florence: Olschki.

Orr, B.

1994 "'Southern Passions Mix with Northern Art': Miscegenation and the *Endeavour* Voyage." *Eighteenth-Century Life* 18, no. 3: 212–31.

Osborne, P.

1992 "Modernity Is a Qualitative, Not a Chronological, Category: Notes on the Dialectics of Differential Historical Time." In *Postmodernism and the Rereading of Modernity,* 23–45. Edited by F. Barker, P. Hulme, and M. Iversen. Manchester, England: Manchester University Press.

Pagden, A. R.

1993 *European Encounters and the New World: From Renaissance to Romanticism.* New Haven: Yale University Press.

Panofsky, E.

1962 *Studies in Iconology: Humanistic Themes in the Art of the Renaissance.* New York: Harper.

1970 *Meaning in the Visual Arts.* Middlesex, England: Penguin.

1971 *The Life and Art of Albrecht Dürer,* 4th ed. Princeton: Princeton University Press [1943].

Pardo Tomás, J.

1998 "Le immagini delle piante americane nell' opera di Gonzalo Fernández de Oviedo (1478–1557)." In *Natura-Cultura: L'interpretazione del mondo fisico nei testi e nelle immagini.* Edited by L. Tongiorgi Tomasi, G. Olmi, and A. Zanca. Florence: Olschki.

Pardo Tomás, J., and López Terrada, M. L.

1993 *Las primeras noticias sobre plantas americanas en las relaciones de viajes y crónicas de Indias (1493–1553).* Valencia, Spain: Instituto de Estudios Documentales e Históricos sobre la Ciencia, Universitat de València-C.S.I.C.

Paré, A.

1971 *Des Monstres et Prodiges.* Edited by J. Céard. Geneva: Droz [1585].

Parkin, D.

1993 "Nemi in the Modern World: Return of the Exotic?" *Man* 28: 79–99.

Parshall, P.

1993 "Imago Contrafacta: Images and Facts in the Northern Renaissance." *Art History* 16, no. 4: 554–79.

Paudrat, J.-L.

1984 "From Africa." In Exh. Cat. New York: 125–75.

Pauw, C. de

1774 *Recherches philosophiques sur les Américains,* 3 vols. Berlin.

Peacock, J.
1990 "Inigo Jones as a Figurative Artist." In *Renaissance Bodies: The Human Figure in English Culture c. 1540–1660*, 154–79. Edited by L. Gent and N. Llewellyn. London: Reaktion.

Peale, C. W.
1983 *The Selected Papers of Charles Willson Peale and His Family.* Vol. 1: *Charles Willson Peale: Artist in Revolutionary America, 1735–1791.* Edited by L. B. Miller. New Haven: Yale University Press.
1988 *The Selected Papers of Charles Willson Peale and His Family.* Vol. 2: *Charles Willson Peale: The Artist as Museum Keeper, 1791–1810.* Edited by L. B. Miller. New Haven: Yale University Press.
1991 *The Selected Papers of Charles Willson Peale and His Family.* Vol. 3: *The Belfield Farm Years, 1810–1820.* Edited by L. B. Miller. New Haven: Yale University Press.

Peiresc, N.
1989 *Lettres à Cassiano dal Pozzo (1626–1637).* Edited and with commentary by J. F. Lhote and D. Joyal. Clermont-Ferrand, France: Adosa.

Pellegrin, N.
1987 "Vêtements de peau(x) et de plumes: La nudité des indiens et la diversité du monde au XVIe siècle." In *Voyager à la Renaissance: Actes du colloque de Tours 1983*, 509–30. Edited by J. Céard and J.-C. Margolin. Paris: Maisonneuve & Larose.

Pembroke, S.
1965 "Last of the Matriarchs: A Study in the Inscriptions of Lycia." *Journal for Economic and Social History of the Orient* 8: 117–47.

Pennington, L. E.
1978 "The Amerindian in English Promotional Literature 1575–1625." In *The Westward Enterprise: English Activities in Ireland, the Atlantic and America 1480–1650*, 175–94. Edited by K. R. Andrews, N. P. Canny, and P. E. H. Hair. Liverpool: Liverpool University Press.

Pierron, S.
1912 *Les Mostaert: Jean Mostaert, dit le Maitre d'Oultremont; Gilles et François Mostaert; Michel Mostaert.* Collection des Grands Artistes des Pays-Bas, Librairie Nationale d'Art et d'Histoire. Brussels-Paris: G. van Oest and Cie.

Pieters, F. F. J. M.
1980 "Notes on the Menagerie and Zoological Cabinet of Stadholder William V of Holland, Directed by Aernout Vosmaer." *Journal of the Society for the Bibliography of Natural History* 9, no. 4: 539–63.

Pieters, F. F. J. M., and Mörzer Bruyns, M. F.
1988 "Menagerieën in Holland in de 17e en 18e eeuw." *Holland* 20, no. 4–5: 195–209.

Pinney, C.
1990 "Colonial Anthropology in the 'Laboratory of Mankind.'" In *The Raj: India and the British 1600–1947*, 252–63. Edited by C. Bayley. London: National Portrait Gallery.

1992a "The Parallel Histories of Anthropology and Photography." In *Anthropology and Photography 1860–1920,* 74–95. Edited by E. Edwards. New Haven: Yale University Press.

1992b "Underneath the Banyan Tree: William Crooke and Photographic Depictions of Caste." In *Anthropology and Photography 1860–1920,* 165–73. Edited by E. Edwards. New Haven: Yale University Press.

Piwocka, M.

1996 "Arrases with Grotesques." In *The Flemish Arrases of the Royal Castle in Cracow,* 271–348. By J. Szablowski, A. Misiag-Bocheńska, M. Hennel-Bernasikowa, and M. Piwocka. Warsaw: Arkady.

Poeschel, S.

1985 *Studien zur Ikonographie der Erdteile in der Kunst des 16.-18. Jahrhunderts.* Munich: Scaneg.

Poignant, R.

1992 "Surveying the Field of View: The Making of the RAI Photographic Collection." In *Anthropology and Photography 1860–1920,* 42–73. Edited by E. Edwards. New Haven: Yale University Press.

Pomian, K.

1987 *Collectionneurs, amateurs et curieux. Paris, Venise: XVIe–XVIIIe siècle.* Paris: Gallimard.

1993 "Collections et musées (note critique)." *Annales ESC* 48, no. 6: 1381–1401.

Porter, R.

1989 "The Exotic as Erotic: Captain Cook at Tahiti." In *Exoticism and the Enlightenment,* 117–44. Edited by G. S. Rousseau and R. Porter. Manchester, England: Manchester University Press.

Pratt, M. L.

1992 *Imperial Eyes: Travel Writing and Transculturation.* London: Routledge.

Pregliasco, M.

1992 *Antilia: Il Viaggio e il Mondo Nuovo (XV-XVII secolo).* Turin: Einaudi.

Preziosi, D.

1994 "Modernity Again: The Museum as Trompe l'Oeil." In *Deconstruction and the Visual Arts: Art, Media, Architecture,* 141–50. Edited by P. Brunette and D. Wills. Cambridge: Cambridge University Press.

Price, D.

1989 "John Woodward and a Surviving British Geological Collection from the Early Eighteenth Century." *Journal of the History of Collections* 1, no. 1: 79–95.

Price, R., and Price, S.

1979 "John Gabriel Stedman's Collection of Eighteenth-Century Artifacts from Suriname." *Nieuwe West-Indische Gids* 53, no. 3–4: 121–40.

1985 "John Gabriel Stedman's 'Journal of a Voyage to the West Indies in ye Year 1772: In a Poetical Epistle to a Friend.'" *Nieuwe West-Indische Gids* 59, no. 3–4: 185–96.

1994 *On the Mall: Presenting Maroon Tradition-Bearers at the 1992 Festival of American Folklife.* Special Publications of the Folklore Institute, no. 4. Bloomington: Indiana University Press.

Pucci, S. R.
1989 "The Discrete Charms of the Exotic: Fictions of the Harem in Eighteenth-Century France." In *Exoticism and the Enlightenment,* 145–74. Edited by G. S. Rousseau and R. Porter. Manchester, England: Manchester University Press.

Pyle, C. M.
1996 "The Art and Science of Renaissance Natural History: Thomas of Cantimpré, Pier Candido Decembrio, Conrad Gessner, and Teodoro Ghisi in Vatican Library MS Urb. Lat. 276." *Viator* 27: 265–321.

Quartermaine, P.
1992 "Johannes Lindt: Photographer of Australia and New Guinea." In *Representing Others: White Views of Indigenous Peoples,* 84–102. Edited by M. Gidley. Exeter Studies in American and Commonwealth Arts, no. 4. Exeter: University of Exeter Press.

Quincey, T. de
1986 *Confessions of an English Opium Eater.* London: Penguin [1821].

Quint, D.
1993 "Voices of Resistance: The Epic Curse and Camões's Adamastor." In *New World Encounters,* 241–71. Edited by S. Greenblatt. Berkeley and Los Angeles: University of California Press.

Rabasa, J.
1994 "Pre-Columbian Pasts and Indian Presents in Mexican History." *Dispositio/n* 19, no. 46: 245–70.

Rae-Ellis, V.
1992 "The Representation of Trucanini." In *Anthropology and Photography 1860–1920,* 230–33. Edited by E. Edwards. New Haven: Yale University Press.

Rampley, M.
1997 "From Symbol to Allegory: Aby Warburg's Theory of Art." *Art Bulletin* 79, no. 1: 41–55.

Rawson, C.
1994 "Savages Noble and Ignoble: Natives, Cannibals, Third Parties, and Others in South Pacific Narratives by Gulliver, Bougainville, and Diderot, with Notes on the *Encyclopédie* and on Voltaire." *Eighteenth-Century Life* 18, no. 3: 168–97.

Reichenbach, H.
1996 "A Tale of Two Zoos: The Hamburg Zoological Garden and Carl Hagenbeck's Tierpark." In *New Worlds, New Animals: From Menagerie to Zoological Park in the Nineteenth Century,* 51–62. Edited by R. J. Hoage and W. A. Deiss. Baltimore: Johns Hopkins University Press.

Remak, H. H. H.
1978 "Exoticism in Romanticism." *Comparative Literature Studies* 15, no. 1: 53–65.

Rhodes, C.
1994 *Primitivism and Modern Art.* London: Thames & Hudson.

Ripa, C. da

1971 *Cesare Ripa: Baroque and Rococo Pictorial Imagery. The 1758–60 Hertel Edition of Ripa's "Iconologia" with 200 Engraved Illustrations*. Introduction, translation, and 200 commentaries by E. A. Maser. New York: Dover Publications.

Ritterbush, P. C.

1985 "The Organism as Symbol: An Innovation in Art." In *Science and the Arts in the Renaissance,* 149–67. Edited by J. W. Shirley and F. D. Hoeniger. New Jersey-London-Ontario: Associated University Presses.

Rorty, R.

1991 *Essays on Heidegger and Others: Philosophical Papers,* Vol. 2. Cambridge: Cambridge University Press.

Rossi, P. L.

1991 "Society, Culture and the Dissemination of Learning." In *Science, Culture and Popular Belief in Renaissance Europe,* 143–75. Edited by S. Pumfrey, P. L. Rossi, and M. Slawinski. Manchester, England: Manchester University Press.

Rostkowski, J.

1987 "The Redman's Appeal for Justice: Deskaheh and the League of Nations." In *Indians and Europe: An Interdisciplinary Collection of Essays,* 435–53. Edited by C. F. Feest. Göttingen/Aachen: Herodot/Rader Verlag.

Rowlands, J.

1994 "Prints and Drawings." In *Sir Hans Sloane: Collector, Scientist, Antiquary, Founding Father of the British Museum,* 245–62. Edited by A. MacGregor. London: British Museum Press.

Rowlands, J., and Bartrum, G.

1993 *Drawings by German Artists and Artists from German-speaking Regions of Europe in the Department of Prints and Drawings in the British Museum: The Fifteenth Century, and the Sixteenth Century by Artists born before 1530,* 2 vols. London: British Museum Press.

Rubin, W.

1984a "Modernist Primitivism: An Introduction." In Exh. Cat. New York: 1–81.

1984b "Picasso." In Exh. Cat. New York: 241–343.

Rudwick, M. J. S.

1992 *Scenes from Deep Time: Early Pictorial Representations of the Prehistoric World.* Chicago: University of Chicago Press.

Ruffins, F. D.

1992 "Mythos, Memory, and History: African American Preservation Efforts, 1820–1990." In *Museums and Communities: The Politics of Public Culture,* 506–611. Edited by I. Karp, C. M. Kreamer, and S. D. Lavine. Washington, D.C.: Smithsonian Institution Press.

Rushing, W. J.

1995 *Native American Art and the New York Avant-Garde.* Austin: University of Texas Press.

Ryan, M. T.
1981 "Assimilating New Worlds in the Sixteenth and Seventeenth Centuries." *Comparative Studies in Society and History* 23: 519–38.

Sahlins, M.
1985 *Islands of History*. Chicago: University of Chicago Press.

Said, E.
1978 *Orientalism*. New York: Random House.

Sandweiss, M. A.
1992 "The Public Life of Western Art." In *Discovered Lands, Invented Pasts: Transforming Visions of the American West,* 117–33. By J. D. Prown, N. K. Anderson, W. Cronon, B. W. Dippie, M. A. Sandweiss, S. Prendergast Schoelwer, and H. R. Lamar. New Haven: Yale University Press.

Sauer, C. O.
1971 *Sixteenth Century North America*. Berkeley and Los Angeles: University of California Press.

Sawday, J.
1995 *The Body Emblazoned: Dissection and the Human Body in Renaissance Culture*. London: Routledge.

Schama, S.
1987 *The Embarrassment of Riches: An Interpretation of Dutch Culture in the Golden Age*. London: Collins.

Schapelhouman, M.
1987 *Nederlandse tekeningen omstreeks 1600 in het Rijksmuseum*. The Hague: Staatsuitgeverij.

Scheicher, E.
1985 "The Collection of Archduke Ferdinand II at Schloss Ambras: Its Purpose, Composition and Evolution." In *The Origins of Museums,* 29–38. Edited by O. Impey and A. MacGregor. Oxford: Clarendon Press.

Scheicher, E., Gamber, O., Wegerer, K., and Auer, A.
1977 *Die Kunstkammer*. Kunsthistorisches Museum Wien. Innsbruck: Sammlungen Schloß Ambras.

Schéle, S.
1965 *Cornelis Bos: A Study of the Origins of the Netherland Grotesque*. Stockholm: Almqvist & Wiksell International.

Scheller, R. W.
1969 "Rembrandt en de encyclopedische kunstkamer." *Oud Holland* 84, no. 2–3: 81–145.

Schepelern, H.
1985 "Natural Philosophers and Princely Collectors: Worm, Paludanus and the Gottorp and Copenhagen Collections." In *The Origins of Museums,* 121–27. Edited by O. Impey and A. MacGregor. Oxford: Clarendon Press.
1990 "The Museum Wormianum Reconstructed: A Note on the Illustration of 1655." *Journal of the History of Collections* 2, no. 1: 81–85.

Schepelern, H. D., and Houkjær, U.
1988 *The Kronborg Series: King Christian IV and His Pictures of Early Danish History.* Kobberstiksamlingens Billedhefter 6. Copenhagen: Royal Museum of Fine Arts.

Scherer, J. C.
1992 "The Photographic Document: Photographs as Primary Data in Anthropological Enquiry." In *Anthropology and Photography 1860–1920,* 32–41. Edited by E. Edwards. New Haven: Yale University Press.

Schildkrout, E.
1988 "Art as Evidence: A Brief History of the American Museum of Natural History African Collection." In Exh. Cat. New York: 153–60.

Schlosser, J. von
1978 *Die Kunst- und Wunderkammern der Spätrenaissance,* 2d ed. (rev. and enlarged). Braunschweig: Klinkhardt and Biermann [1908].

Schmidt, B.
1994 "Innocence Abroad: The Dutch Imagination and the Representation of the New World, c. 1570–1670." Ph.D. diss., Harvard University.

Schnapper, A.
1986 "Persistance des géants." *Annales ESC* 41, no. 1: 177–200.
1988 *Le géant, la licorne, la tulipe: Collections françaises au XVIIe siècle.* Paris: Flammarion.
1994 *Curieux du grand siècle: Collections et collectionneurs dans la France du XVIIe siècle.* Paris: Flammarion.

Schneider, W. H.
1982 *An Empire for the Masses: The French Popular Image of Africa, 1870–1900.* Westport, Conn.: Greenwood Press.

Schöffer, I.
1975 "The Batavian Myth during the Sixteenth and Seventeenth Centuries." In *Britain and the Netherlands.* Vol. 5: *Some Political Mythologies: Papers Delivered to the Fifth Anglo-Dutch Historical Conference,* 78–101. Edited by J. S. Bromley and E. H. Kossmann. The Hague: Martinus Nijhoff.

Schupbach, W.
1985 "Some Cabinets of Curiosities in European Academic Institutions." In *The Origins of Museums,* 169–78. Edited by O. Impey and A. MacGregor. Oxford: Clarendon Press.

Schütte, R.-A., and Walz, A.
1997 *Bestandskatalog der Kostbarkeiten.* Braunschweig: Herzog Anton Ulrich-Museum.

Seaver, K. A.
1996 "'A Very Common and Usuall Trade': The Relationship between Cartographic Perceptions and 'Fishing' in the Davis Strait *circa* 1500–1550." In *Images and Icons of the New World: Essays on American Cartography,* 1–26. Edited by K. S. Cook. London: British Library.

Seed, P.
1995 *Ceremonies of Possession in Europe's Conquest of the New World, 1492–1640*. Cambridge: Cambridge University Press.

Seelig, L.
1985 "The Munich *Kunstkammer*, 1565–1807." In *The Origins of Museums*, 76–89. Edited by O. Impey and A. MacGregor. Oxford: Clarendon Press.

Segal, S.
1988 *A Prosperous Past*. The Hague: SDU.

Settis, S.
1990 *Giorgione's Tempest: Interpreting the Hidden Subject*. Translated by E. Bianchini. Cambridge: Polity Press [1978].
1993 "Des ruines au musée: La destinée de la sculpture classique." *Annales ESC* 48, no. 6: 1347–80.

Seznec, J.
1931 "Un essai de mythologie comparée au début du XVIIe siècle." *Mélanges d'Archéologie et d'Histoire* 48: 268–281.
1953 *The Survival of the Pagan Gods*. Translated by Barbara Sessions. Princeton: Princeton University Press [1940].

Shaffer, E.
1985 *"Kubla Khan" and the Fall of Jerusalem: The Mythological School in Biblical Criticism and Secular Literature 1770–1880*. Cambridge: Cambridge University Press.

Shelton, A. A.
1994 "Cabinets of Transgression: Renaissance Collections and the Incorporation of the New World." In *The Cultures of Collecting*, 177–203. Edited by J. Elsner and R. Cardinal. London: Reaktion.

Silva, R. K. de, and Beumer, W. G. M.
1988 *Illustrations and Views of Dutch Ceylon 1602–1796*. London: Serendib.

Silverman, D., and Torode, B.
1980 *The Material Word*. London: Routledge & Kegan Paul.

Simonin, M.
1992 *Vivre de sa plume au XVIe siècle, ou la carrière de François de Belleforest*. Geneva: Droz.

Simons, P.
1988 "Women in Frames: The Gaze, the Eye, the Profile in Renaissance Portraiture." *History Workshop Journal* 25: 4–30.
1995 "Portraiture, Portrayal, and Idealization: Ambiguous Individualism in Representations of Renaissance Women." In *Language and Images of Renaissance Italy*, 263–311. Edited by A. Brown. Oxford: Oxford University Press.

Sjørslev, I.
1994 "Drei Thesen über die Welt im ethnographischen Museum." In Exh. Cat. Bonn: 177–84.

Smiles, S.
1992 "A Native American in Stone: The Simcoe Memorial in Exeter Cathedral." In

Representing Others: White Views of Indigenous Peoples, 14–24. Edited by M. Gidley. Exeter Studies in American and Commonwealth Arts, no. 4. Exeter: University of Exeter Press.

Smith, A. B., and Pheiffer, R. H.
1993 *The Khoikhoi at the Cape of Good Hope: Seventeenth-Century Drawings in the South African Library.* Cape Town: South African Library.

Smith, B.
1956 "Coleridge's 'Ancient Mariner' and Cook's Second Voyage." *Journal of the Courtauld and Warburg Institutes* 19: 117–54 [reprinted in Smith 1992: 135–71].
1979 "Cook's Posthumous Reputation." In *Captain James Cook and His Times,* 159–85. Edited by R. Fisher and H. Johnston. London: Croom Helm.
1988 *European Vision and the South Pacific,* 2d ed. New Haven: Yale University Press.
1992 *Imagining the Pacific: In the Wake of the Cook Voyages.* New Haven: Yale University Press.

Snyder, J.
1976 "Jan Mostaert's West Indies Landscape." In *First Images of America,* 1: 495–502. Edited by F. Chiappelli. Berkeley and Los Angeles: University of California Press.

Solinas, F.
1989 "Il primo erbario azteco e la copia romana di Cassiano dal Pozzo." In *Il Museo Cartaceo di Cassiano dal Pozzo. Cassiano naturalista. Quaderni Puteani,* 1: 77–83. Edited by F. Haskell, H. McBurney, D. Freedberg, F. Solinas, and C. Napoleone. Milan: Olivetti.

Sparti, D. L.
1989 "Criteri museografici nella collezione dal Pozzo alla luce di documentazione inedita." In *Cassiano dal Pozzo: Atti del Seminario Internazionale di Studi,* 221–40. Edited by F. Solinas. Rome: De Luca.
1990 "Carlo Antonio dal Pozzo (1606–1689): An Unknown Collector." *Journal of the History of Collections* 2, no. 1: 7–19.
1992 *Le collezioni dal Pozzo: Storia di una famiglia e del suo museo nella Roma seicentesca.* Modena: Franco Cosimo Panini.

Spence, J. D.
1985 *The Memory Palace of Matteo Ricci.* London: Fontana.

Spencer, F.
1992 "Some Notes on the Attempt to Apply Photography to Anthropometry during the Second Half of the Nineteenth Century." In *Anthropology and Photography 1860–1920,* 99–107. Edited by E. Edwards. New Haven: Yale University Press.

Spicer, J.
1997 "Roelandt Savery and the 'Discovery' of the Alpine Waterfall." In Exh. Cat. Prague: 146–71.

Spierenburg, P.
1984 *The Spectacle of Suffering. Executions and the Evolution of Repression: From*

a Preindustrial Metropolis to the European Experience. Cambridge: Cambridge University Press.

Stafford, B. M.
1994 *Artful Science.* Cambridge: MIT Press.

Stallybrass, P., and White, A.
1986 *The Politics and Poetics of Transgression.* Ithaca: Cornell University Press.

Stedman, J. G.
1988 *Narrative of a Five Years Expedition against the Revolted Negroes of Surinam.* Edited with an introduction and notes by R. and S. Price. Baltimore: Johns Hopkins University Press.

Stewart, S.
1984 *On Longing.* Baltimore: Johns Hopkins University Press.

Street, B.
1992 "British Popular Anthropology: Exhibiting and Photographing the Other." In *Anthropology and Photography 1860–1920,* 122–31. Edited by E. Edwards. New Haven: Yale University Press.

Sturtevant, W. C.
1976 "First Visual Images of Native America." In *First Images of America,* 1: 417–54. Edited by F. Chiappelli. Berkeley and Los Angeles: University of California Press.
1988 "La Tupinambisation des Indiens d'Amérique du Nord." In *Les figures de l'Indien,* 293–303. Edited by G. Thérien. Cahiers du Département d'Études Littéraires 9. Ontario: Université du Québec à Montréal.
1990 "What Does the Plains Indian War Bonnet Communicate?" In *Art as a Means of Communication in Pre-Literate Societies,* 355–374. Proceedings of the 1985 Wright International Symposium on Primitive and Precolumbian Art, The Israel Museum, Jerusalem. Edited by D. Eban, E. Cohen, and B. Danet.
1991 "Indian America: First Visual Impressions in Europe." In *The Christopher Columbus Encyclopedia,* 1: 337–45. Edited by S. A. Bedini. New York: Simon & Schuster.

Sturtevant, W. C., and Quinn, D. B.
1987 "This New Prey: Eskimos in Europe 1567, 1576, and 1577." *Indians and Europe: An Interdisciplinary Collection of Essays,* 61–140. Edited by C. F. Feest. Göttingen/Aachen: Herodot/Rader Verlag.

Sutton, P. C.
1984 "Masters of Dutch Genre Painting." In *Masters of Seventeenth-Century Dutch Genre Painting,* xiii–lxvi. Edited by P. C. Sutton. London: Weidenfeld & Nicolson.

Swan, C.
1995 "*Ad vivum, naer het leven.* From the Life: Defining a Mode of Representation." *Word & Image* 11, no. 4: 353–72.

Sweetman, J.
1988 *The Oriental Obsession: Islamic Inspiration in British and American Art and Architecture 1500–1920.* Cambridge: Cambridge University Press.

Sylvester, D.

1994 *Looking at Giacometti.* London: Pimlico.

Syme, R.

1991 *Roman Papers*, vol. 6. Oxford: Oxford University Press.

Syndram, D.

1989 "Das Erbe der Pharaonen: Zur Ikonographie Ägyptens in Europa." In Exh. Cat. Berlin 1989: 18–57.

Tamplin, R.

1992 "Noblemen and Noble Savages." In *Representing Others: White Views of Indigenous Peoples,* 60–83. Edited by M. Gidley. Exeter Studies in American and Commonwealth Arts, no. 4. Exeter: University of Exeter Press.

Tassel, R. van

1973 "Bezoars." *Janus* 60: 241–59.

Terdiman, R.

1985 "Ideological Voyages: Concerning a Flaubertian Dis-Orient-ation." In *Europe and Its Others,* 1: 28–40. Edited by F. Barker, P. Hulme, M. Iversen, and D. Loxley. Colchester: University of Essex.

Terwen, J. J., and Ottenheym, K. A.

1993 *Pieter Post (1608–1669).* Zutphen, Netherlands: Walburg Press.

Thackray, J.

1994 "Mineral and Fossil Collections." In *Sir Hans Sloane: Collector, Scientist, Antiquary, Founding Father of the British Museum,* 123–35. Edited by A. MacGregor. London: British Museum Press.

Thevet, A.

1985 *Cosmographie de Levant.* Edited by Frank Lestringant. Geneva: Droz [1554].

1997 *Les singularités de la France antarctique.* Edited, introduced, and with notes by Frank Lestringant. Paris: Chandeigne [1557].

Theye, T.

1995 "'Licht- und Schattenbilder aus den Binnenlanden von Java': Franz Wilhelm Junghuhn, Karl Ritter von Scherzer und die Erdumsegelung der K. K. Fregatte 'Novara' in den Jahren 1857 bis 1859." *Fotogeschichte* 15, no. 56: 3–22.

Thierry de Bye Dólleman, M.

1963 "Jan Jansz: Mostaert, schilder, een beroemd Haarlemmer (ca. 1473–ca. 1555)." *Jaarboek van het Centraal Bureau voor Genealogie* 17: 123–36.

Thomas, K.

1983 *Man and the Natural World: Changing Attitudes in England 1500–1800.* Harmondsworth, England: Penguin.

Thomas, N.

1991 *Entangled Objects: Exchange, Material Culture, and Colonialism in the Pacific.* Cambridge: Harvard University Press.

1994a *Colonialism's Culture: Anthropology, Travel and Government.* Cambridge: Polity.

1994b "Licensed Curiosity: Cook's Pacific Voyages." In *The Cultures of Collecting,* 116–36. Edited by J. Elsner and R. Cardinal. London: Reaktion.

1995 *Oceanic Art*. London: Thames & Hudson.
1996 "Cold Fusion." *American Anthropologist* 98, no. 1: 9–16.

Thomsen, T.
1938 *Albert Eckhout ein niederländischer Maler und sein Gönner Johan Maurits der Brasilianer: Ein Kulturbild aus dem 17. Jahrhundert*. Copenhagen: Ejnar Munksgaard.

Thornton, P., and Dorey, H.
1992 *A Miscellany of Objects from Sir John Soane's Museum*. London: Lawrence King.

Tilmans, K.
1992 *Historiography and Humanism in Holland in the Age of Erasmus: Aurelius and the Divisiekroniek of 1517*. Bibliotheca Humanistica et Reformatica 51. Nieuwkoop, Netherlands: De Graaf [1988].

Toby, R. P.
1994 "The 'Indianness' of Iberia and Changing Japanese Iconographies of Other." In *Implicit Understandings,* 323–51. Edited by S. B. Schwartz. Cambridge: Cambridge University Press.

Tooley, R. E.
1975 *Title Pages from the Sixteenth to Nineteenth Centuries*. London: Map Collectors' Circle.

Tracy, J. D.
1980 *True Ocean Found: Paludanus' Letters on Dutch Voyages to the Kara Sea, 1595–1596*. Minneapolis: University of Minnesota Press.

Trexler, R. C.
1984 "We Think, They Act: Clerical Readings of Missionary Theatre in Sixteenth Century New Spain." In *Understanding Popular Culture: Europe from the Middle Ages to the Nineteenth Century,* 189–227. Edited by S. L. Kaplan. Berlin: Mouton.

Truettner, W. H.
1986 "The Art of Pueblo Life." In Exh. Cat. Washington: 59–99.

Vanbergen, J.
1990 "Nieuwe tendensen in de kunsthistorische interpretatie." *Tijdschrift voor Filosofie* 52, no. 1: 17–40.

Vandenbroeck, P.
1985 *Catalogus schilderijen 14e en 15e eeuw*. Antwerp: Koninklijk Museum voor Schone Kunsten.
1987 *Beeld van de Andere, Vertoog over het Zelf*. Antwerp: Koninklijk Museum voor Schone Kunsten.
1992 "Amerindian Art and Ornamental Objects in Royal Collections: Brussels, Mechelen, Duurstede, 1520–1530." In Exh. Cat. Antwerp: 99–119.

Vansina, J.
1992 "Photographs of the Sankuru and Kasai River Basin Expedition Undertaken by Emil Torday (1876–1931) and M. W. Hilton Simpson (1881–1936)." In

Anthropology and Photography 1860–1920, 193–205. Edited by E. Edwards. New Haven: Yale University Press.

Varey, S., and Chabrán, R.
1995 "Mexican Medicine Comes to England." *Viator* 26: 333–53.

Varnedoe, K.
1984a "Gauguin." In Exh. Cat. New York: 179–209.
1984b "Abstract Expressionism." In Exh. Cat. New York: 615–59.

Vasari, G.
1965 *Lives of the Artists.* Translated by G. Bull. Harmondsworth, England: Penguin [1568].

Vassalo e Silva, N.
1992 "Du marché de Goa au trésor des princes, le commerce des pierres précieuses orientales au XVIe siècle." *Les Ateliers des Interprètes,* no. 4: 111–18. Actes du Congrès "Le Portugal et l'Europe—le problème du centre et de la périphérie." Coimbra, Portugal.

Veen, J. van der
1992 "Liefhebbers, handelaren en kunstenaars: Het verzamelen van schilderijen en papierkunst." In *De wereld binnen handbereik: Nederlandse kunst- en rariteitenverzamelingen, 1585–1735,* 117–34. Edited by E. Bergvelt and R. Kistemaker. Zwolle, Netherlands: Waanders.
1993 "Galerij en kabinet, vorst en burger: Schilderijencollecties in de Nederlanden." In *Verzamelen: Van Rariteitenkabinet tot Kunstmuseum,* 145–64. Edited by E. Bergvelt, D. Meijers, and M. Rijnders. Gaade Uitgevers, Netherlands: Open Universiteit Heerlen.

Vespucci, A,
1984 *Il Mondo Nuovo di Amerigo Vespucci: Vespucci autentico e apocrifo.* Edited by M. Pozzi. Milan: Serra e Riva.

Vidal-Naquet, P.
1981 *Le chasseur noir: Formes de pensée et formes de société dans le monde grec.* Paris: Maspero.

Vincent, L.
1706 *Wondertooneel der Nature.* Amsterdam.

Visser, J. (ed.)
1995 *Gloria Parendi: Dagboeken van Willem Frederik, stadhouder van Friesland, Groningen en Drenthe 1643–1649, 1651–1654.* The Hague: Netherlands Historical Association.

Vitart, A.
1992 "American Curiosities." In Exh. Cat. Paris: 115–25.

Vogel, S.
1988 "Introduction." In Exh. Cat. New York: 11–17.
1991a "Extinct Art: Inspiration and Burden." In Exh. Cat. New York: 230–39.
1991b "Always True to the Object, in Our Fashion." In *Exhibiting Cultures: The Poetics and Politics of Museum Display,* 191–204. Edited by I. Karp and S. D. Lavine. Washington, D.C.: Smithsonian Institution Press.

Voltaire, F.-M.
1979 *Romans et Contes*. Edited by F. Deloffre and J. van den Heuvel. Paris: Bibliothèque de la Pléiade, Gallimard.

Waal, H. van de
1952 *Drie Eeuwen Vaderlandsche Geschied-Uitbeelding 1500–1800: Een iconologische Studie,* 2 vols. The Hague: Martinus Nijhoff.

Wachtel, N.
1977 *The Vision of the Vanquished: The Spanish Conquest of Peru through Indian Eyes, 1530–70*. New York: Harper & Row.

Warburg, A.
1938–39 "A Lecture on Serpent Ritual." *Journal of the Warburg Institute* 2: 277–92.

Weiss, P.
1995 *Kandinsky and Old Russia: The Artist as Ethnographer and Shaman*. New Haven: Yale University Press.

Wendt, A.
1989 *Kannibalismus in Brasilien: Eine Analyse europäischer Reiseberichte und Amerika-Darstellungen für die Zeit zwischen 1500 und 1654*. Europäische Hochschulschriften, Reihe XIX, Band 15. Frankfurt am Main: Peter Lang.

West, A.
1992 "The History of the Ethnography Collections of W. H. Lever." *Journal of the History of Collections* 4, no. 2: 273–83.

Whatley, J.
1986 "Savage Hierarchies: French Catholic Observers of the New World." *Sixteenth Century Journal* 17: 319–30.
1990 "Introduction." In *Jean de Léry: History of a Voyage to the Land of Brazil, Otherwise called America,* xv-xxxviii. Berkeley and Los Angeles: University of California Press.

Whitehead, N. L.
1986 "John Gabriel Stedman's Collection of Amerindian Artefacts." *Nieuwe West-Indische Gids* 60, no. 3–4: 203–8.

Whitehead, P. J. P.
1979 "George Markgraf and Brazilian Zoology." In *Johan Maurits van Nassau-Siegen: A Humanist Prince in Europe and Brazil,* 424–71. Edited by E. van den Boogaard. The Hague: Johan Maurits van Nassau Stichting.
1985 "Faces of the New World." *FMR America* 9: 125–40.
1987 "Earliest Extant Painting of Greenlanders." In *Indians and Europe: An Interdisciplinary Collection of Essays,* 141–59. Edited by C. F. Feest. Göttingen/Aachen: Herodot/Rader Verlag.

Whitehead, P. J. P., and Boeseman, M.
1989 *A Portrait of Dutch Seventeenth Century Brazil: Animals, Plants and People by the Artists of Johan Maurits of Nassau*. Royal Dutch Academy of Sciences, Natural History Monographs, series 2, part 87. Amsterdam: North-Holland.

Wille, H.
1997 "The Albums of Karel van Sint Omaars (1533–1569) (Libri Picturati A 16–31, in the Jagiellon Library in Krakow)." *Archives of Natural History* 24, no. 3: 423–37.

Williams, E. A.
1985 "Art and Artifact at the Trocadero: *Ars Americana* and the Primitivist Revolution." In *Objects and Others: Essays on Museums and Material Culture,* 146–66. Vol. 3 of the History of Anthropology. Edited by G. W. Stocking, Jr. Madison: University of Wisconsin Press.

Wills, D.
1995 *Prosthesis.* Stanford: Stanford University Press.

Wilson, D.
1993 *Signs and Portents: Monstrous Births from the Middle Ages to the Enlightenment.* London: Routledge.

Wittgenstein, L.
1958 *Philosophical Investigations,* 2d ed. Oxford: Blackwell.
1993 *Philosophical Occasions 1912–1951.* Edited by J. Klagge and A. Nordmann. Indianapolis: Hackett.

Worp, J. A.
1915 *Briefwisseling van C. Huygens, 1608–1687,* vol. 4. The Hague.

Wright, R. K.
1987 "The Traveling Exhibition of Captain Samuel Hadlock, Jr.: Eskimos in Europe, 1822–1826." In *Indians and Europe: An Interdisciplinary Collection of Essays,* 215–33. Edited by C. F. Feest. Göttingen/Aachen: Herodot/Rader Verlag.

Young, R.
1990 *White Mythologies: Writing History and the West.* London: Routledge.

Zapperi, R.
1985 "Arrigo le velu, Pietro le fou, Amon le nain et autres bêtes: Autour d'un tableau d'Agostino Carrache." *Annales ESC* 39, no. 2: 307–27.

Zeidler, J., and Hultgren, M. L.
1988 "'Things African Prove to be the Favorite Theme': The African Collection at Hampton University." In Exh. Cat. New York: 97–111.

Zinser, H.
1982 "Cuzco und Rom." In Exh. Cat. Berlin: 183–85.

INDEX

Numbers in italic typeface denote illustrations.

Library of Congress Cataloging-in-Publication Data

Mason, Peter, 1952–
Infelicities : representations of the exotic / Peter Mason.
p. cm.
Includes bibliographical references and index.
ISBN 0-8018-5880-1 (acid-free paper)
1. Europe—Civilization—Foreign influences. 2. Art, European—Foreign influences. 3. Exoticism in art—Europe. 4. Acculturation—Europe—History. 5. Indigenous peoples—Social life and customs—Foreign public opinion, European. 6. Europeans—Foreign countries—Attitudes—History. I. Title.
CB203.M37 1998
940—dc21 98-3490
CIP

JOHNS HOPKINS

The Johns Hopkins University Press
2715 N. Charles Street
Baltimore, Maryland 21218-4319

INFELICITIES
Representations of the Exotic

Peter Mason

0-8018-5880-1 £33.00 hardcover

Publication Date: March 19, 1999

This book is sent to you for review. Two copies of your review will be appreciated.